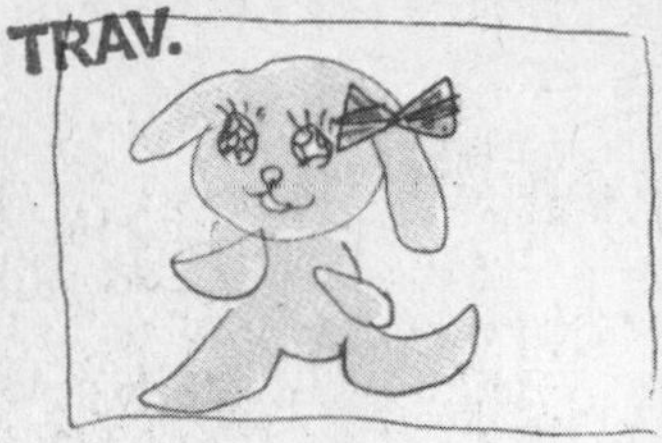
TRAV.

- A little girly
- Fancy
- Has a ribbon
- Doesn't taste good
- Twisting body

久保帯人

I'm gaining weight.
Not good. Very not good.
I don't know what to do.
Any suggestions?
Let me know if there's a good diet out there.
Preferably something fast and easy... without a lot of dietary restrictions... and that will make me popular with the ladies.
Tite Kubo

BLEACH is author Tite Kubo's second title. Kubo made his debut with *ZOMBIE POWDER*, a four-volume series for *WEEKLY SHONEN JUMP*. To date, *BLEACH* has been translated into numerous languages and has also inspired an animated TV series that began airing in Japan in 2004. Beginning its serialization in 2001, *BLEACH* is still a mainstay in the pages of *WEEKLY SHONEN JUMP*. In 2005, *BLEACH* was awarded the prestigious Shogakukan Manga Award in the *shonen* (boys') category.

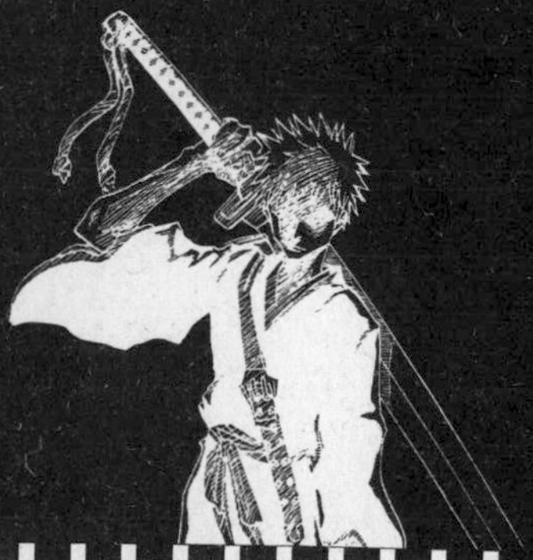

BLEACH
Vol. 2: GOODBYE PARAKEET, GOOD NIGHT MY SISTER
The SHONEN JUMP Graphic Novel Edition

STORY AND ART BY TITE KUBO

English Adaptation/Lance Caselman
Translation/Joe Yamazaki
Touch-up & Lettering/Andy Ristaino
Cover, Graphics & Design/Sean Lee
Editor/Kit Fox

Managing Editor/Frances E. Wall
Editorial Director/Elizabeth Kawasaki
VP & Editor in Chief/Yumi Hoashi
Sr. Director of Acquisitions/Rika Inouye
Sr. VP of Marketing/Liza Coppola
Exec. VP of Sales & Marketing/John Easum
Publisher/Hyoe Narita

Printed in the U.S.A.

Published by VIZ Media, LLC
P.O. Box 77010
San Francisco, CA 94107

SHONEN JUMP Graphic Novel Edition
10 9 8 7 6 5
First printing, July 2004
Second printing, April 2005
Third printing, June 2005
Fourth printing, December 2005
Fifth printing, April 2006

THE WORLD'S
MOST POPULAR MANGA

www.shonenjump.com

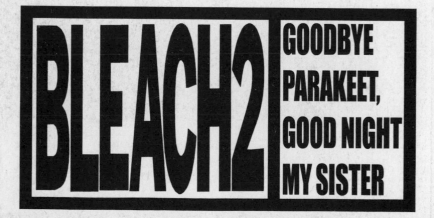

People have hope
Because they cannot see Death standing behind them

BLEACH 2

GOODBYE PARAKEET, GOOD NIGHT MY SISTER

Shonen Jump Graphic Novel

STARS AND

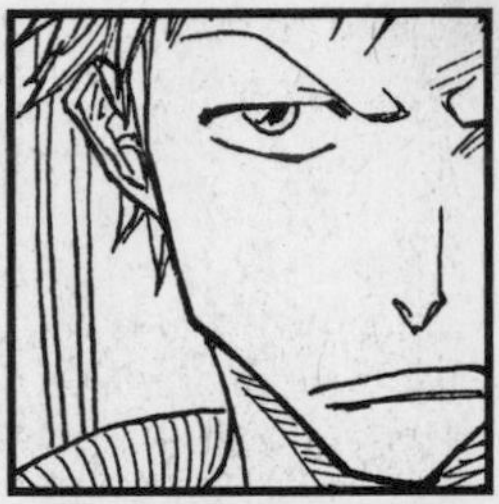

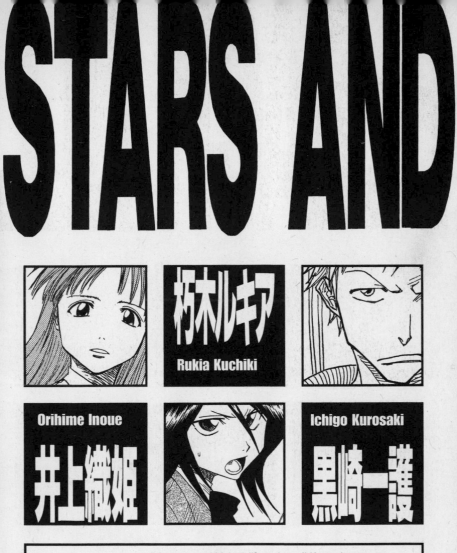

Ichigo Kurosaki

黒崎一護

朽木ルキア

Rukia Kuchiki

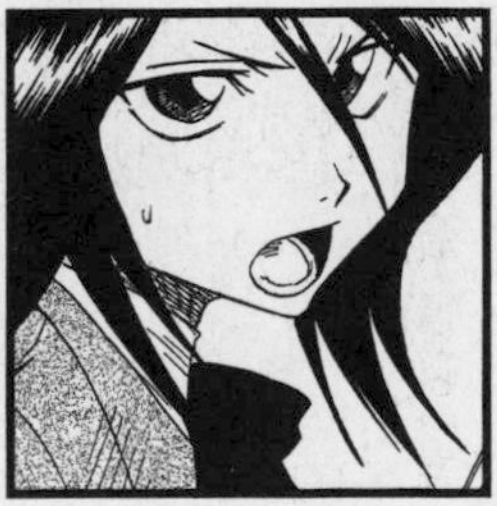

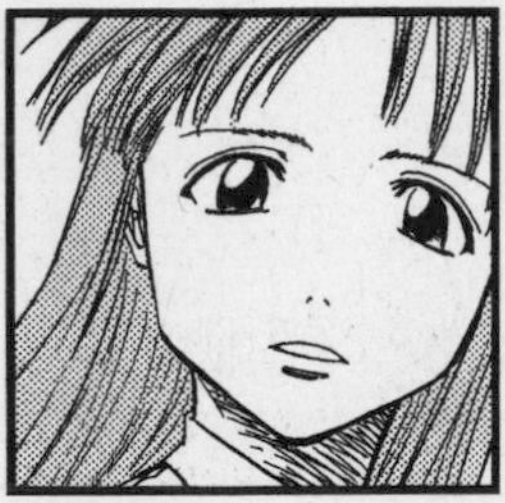

Orihime Inoue

井上織姫

plot

Fifteen-year-old Ichigo "Strawberry" Kurosaki can see ghosts. Otherwise, he was a typical (?) high school student until the day a Hollow—a malevolent lost soul—came to eat him, and the Soul Reaper Rukia Kuchiki stepped into his life. To defeat the Hollow and save his family, Ichigo let Rukia transfer some of her Soul Reaper powers to him. But when Rukia was left powerless, she recruited Ichigo for her war against the murderous, soul-gobbling Hollows. Now, Ichigo's near-invincible classmate Chad has turned up at the family clinic with strange wounds—and a mysterious parakeet!?

BLEACH ALL

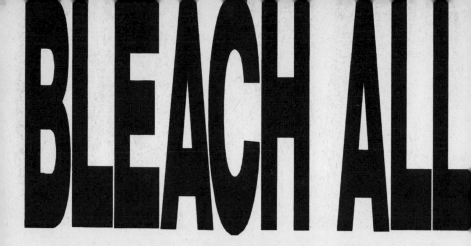

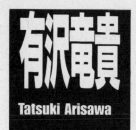

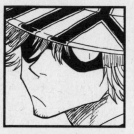

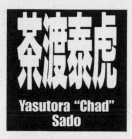

茶渡泰虎
Yasutora "Chad" Sado

有沢竜貴
Tatsuki Arisawa

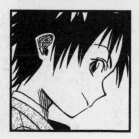

Kisuke Urahara
浦原喜助

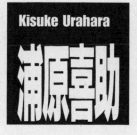

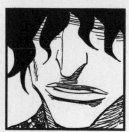

STORIES

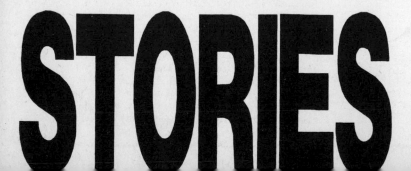

BLEACH2

GOODBYE PARAKEET, GOOD NIGHT MY SISTER

Contents

8. Chasing Chad		7
9. Monster Vs. New Girl (Smack Down)		27
10. Monster Vs. New Girl, Part 2 (The Substitute)		47
11. LEECH-BOMBS AND MOM		67
12. The Gate of the End		87
13. BAD STANDARD		107
14. School Daze!!!		127
15. Jumpin' Jack, Jolted		147
16. Wasted but Wanted		167

8. Chasing Chad

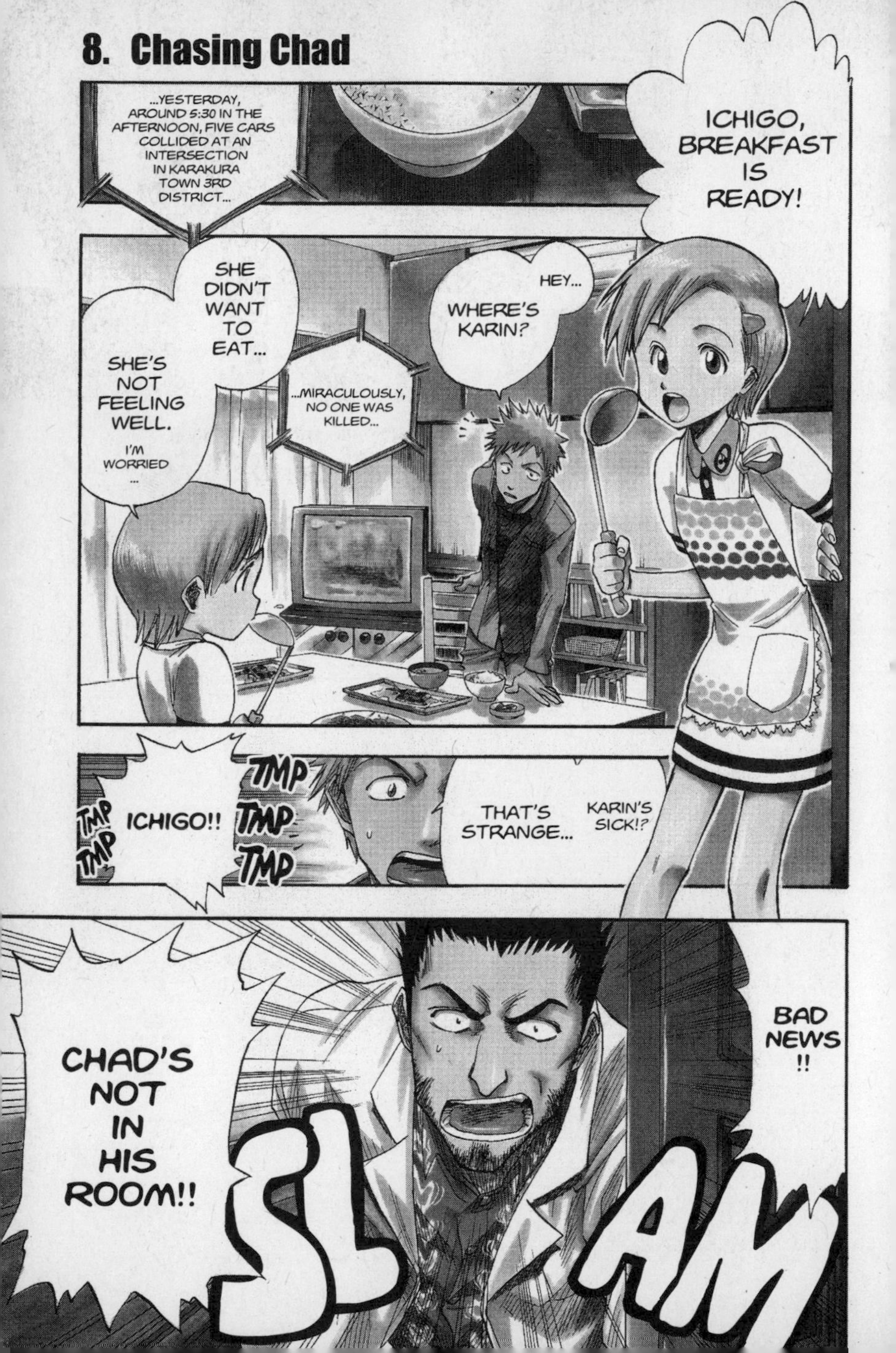
ICHIGO, BREAKFAST IS READY!
...YESTERDAY, AROUND 5:30 IN THE AFTERNOON, FIVE CARS COLLIDED AT AN INTERSECTION IN KARAKURA TOWN 3RD DISTRICT...
HEY...
WHERE'S KARIN?
...MIRACULOUSLY, NO ONE WAS KILLED...
SHE DIDN'T WANT TO EAT...
SHE'S NOT FEELING WELL.
I'M WORRIED ...
KARIN'S SICK!?
THAT'S STRANGE...
TMP TMP TMP
ICHIGO!!
TMP TMP
BAD NEWS !!
CHAD'S NOT IN HIS ROOM!!
SLAM

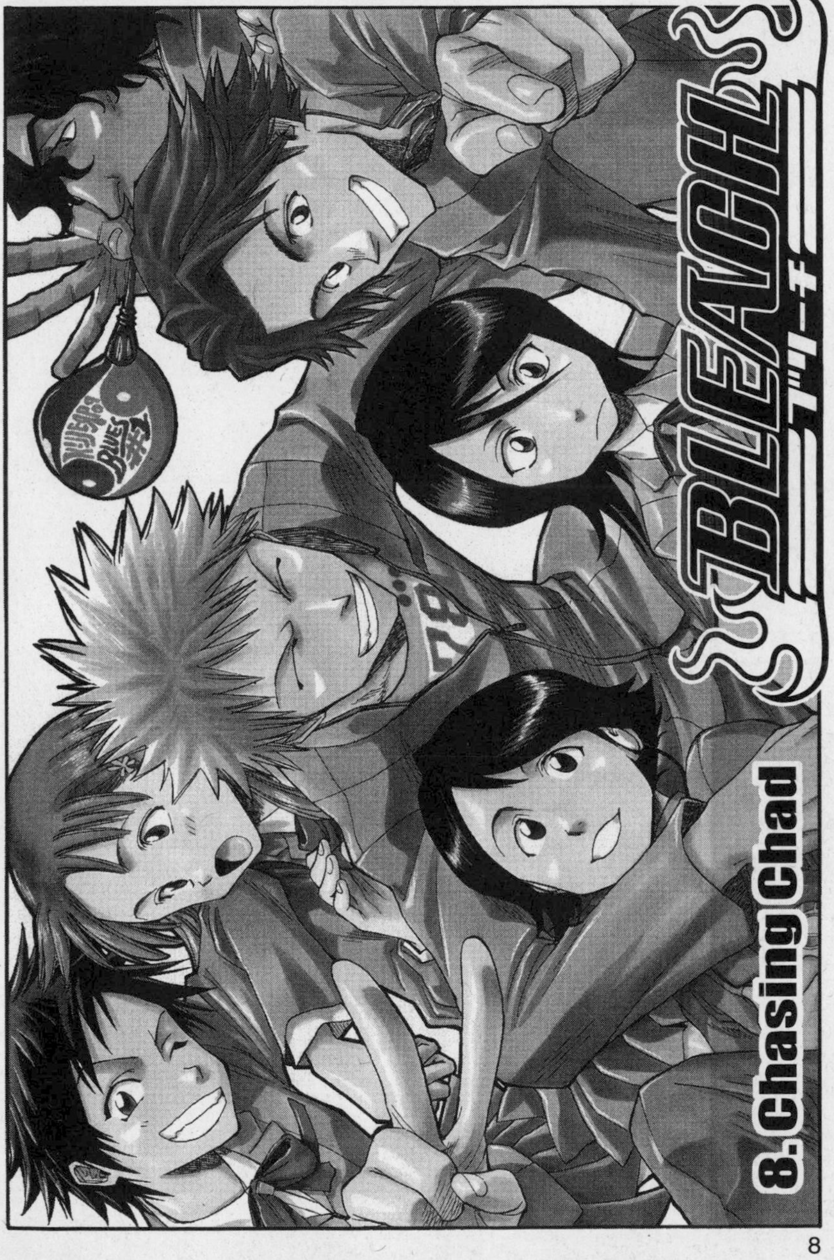
BLEACH
ブリーチ
8. Chasing Chad

READ THIS WAY

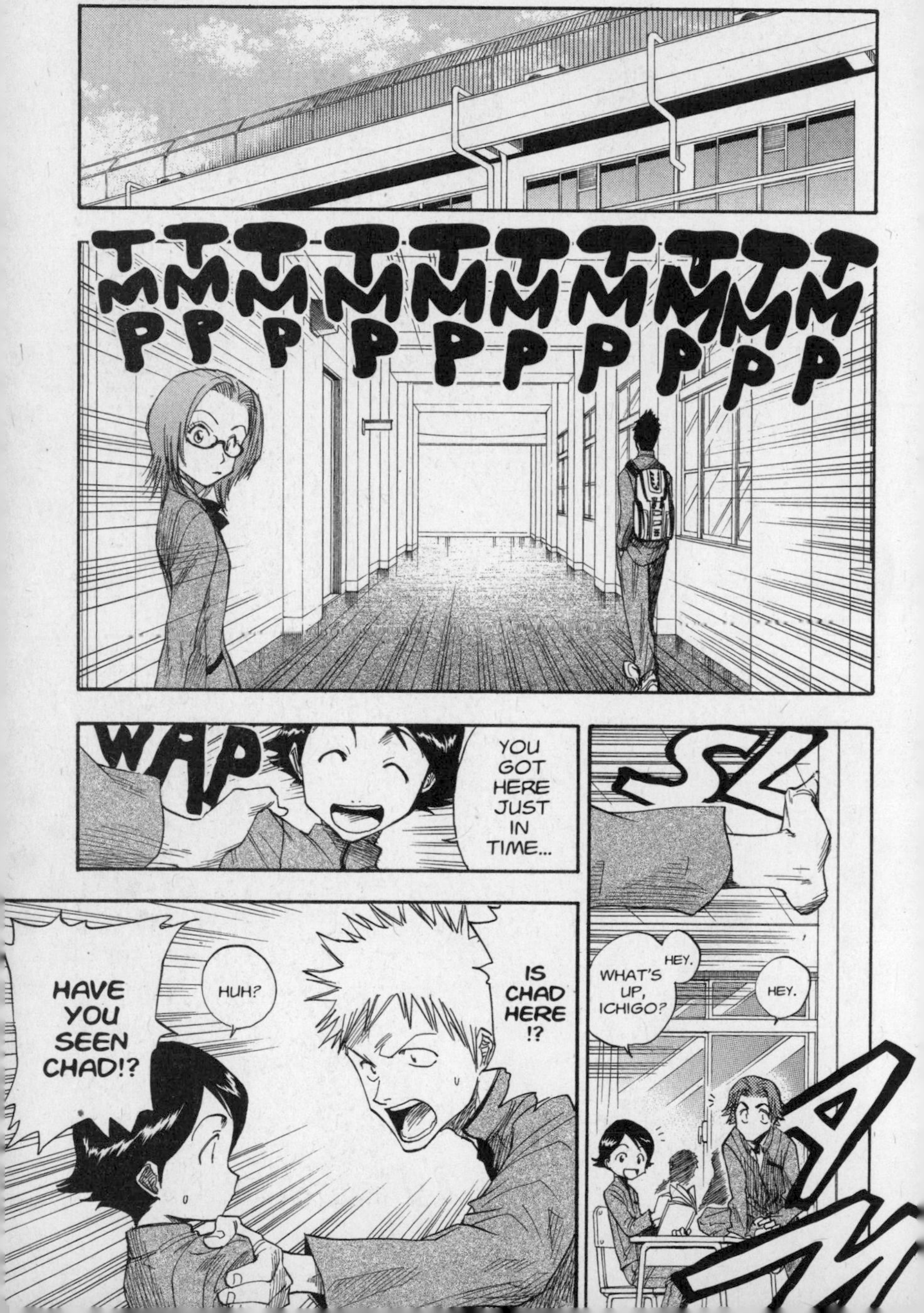

TMP TMP TMP TMP TMP TMP TMP TMP TMP TMP
SL
AM
HEY. WHAT'S UP, ICHIGO?
HEY.
WAP
YOU GOT HERE JUST IN TIME...
IS CHAD HERE!?
HUH?
HAVE YOU SEEN CHAD!?

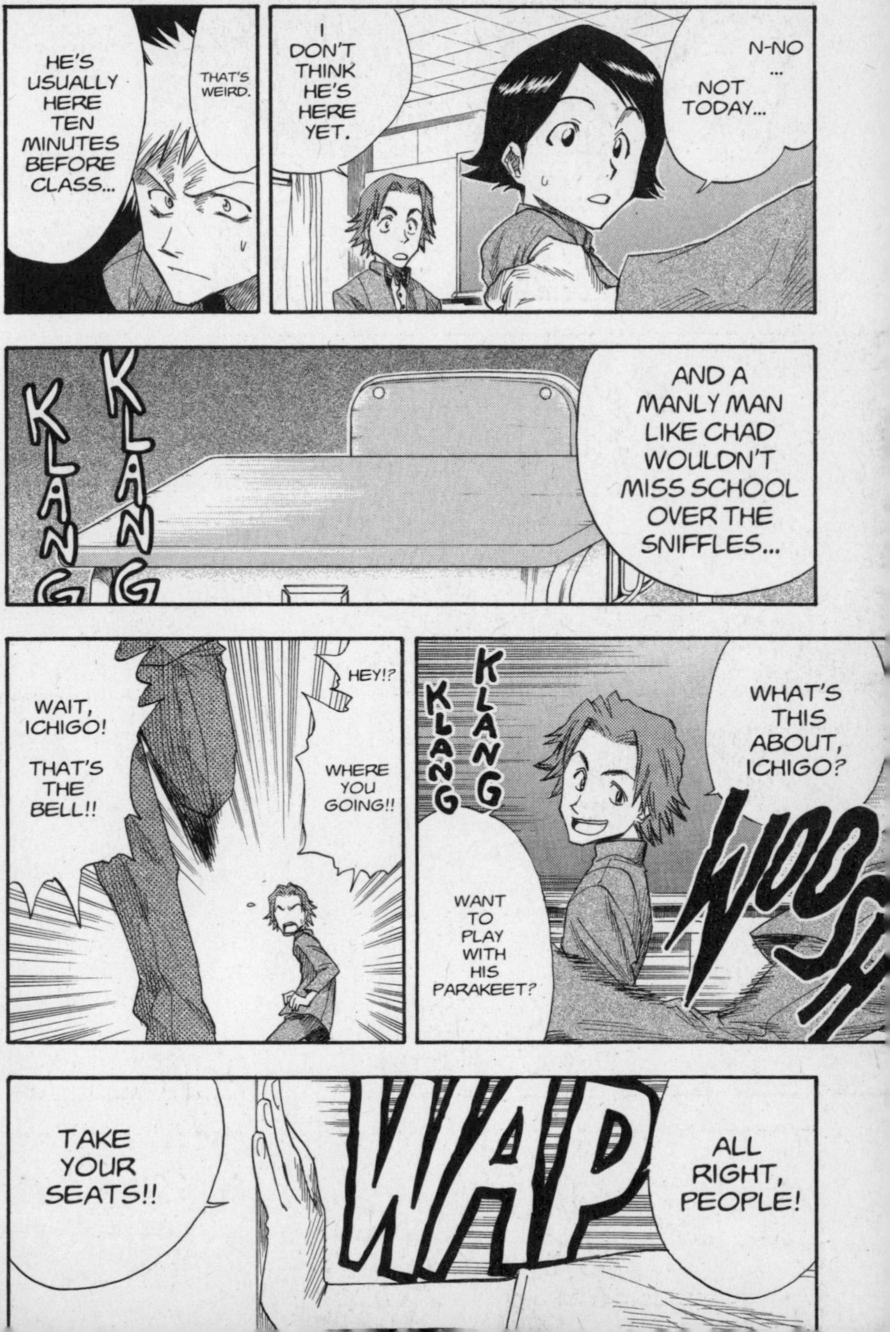
N-NO ... NOT TODAY...
I DON'T THINK HE'S HERE YET.
THAT'S WEIRD.
HE'S USUALLY HERE TEN MINUTES BEFORE CLASS...
AND A MANLY MAN LIKE CHAD WOULDN'T MISS SCHOOL OVER THE SNIFFLES...
KLANG
KLANG
WHAT'S THIS ABOUT, ICHIGO?
WOOSH
KLANG
KLANG
WANT TO PLAY WITH HIS PARAKEET?
HEY!?
WHERE YOU GOING!!
WAIT, ICHIGO! THAT'S THE BELL!!
ALL RIGHT, PEOPLE!
WAP
TAKE YOUR SEATS!!

READ THIS WAY

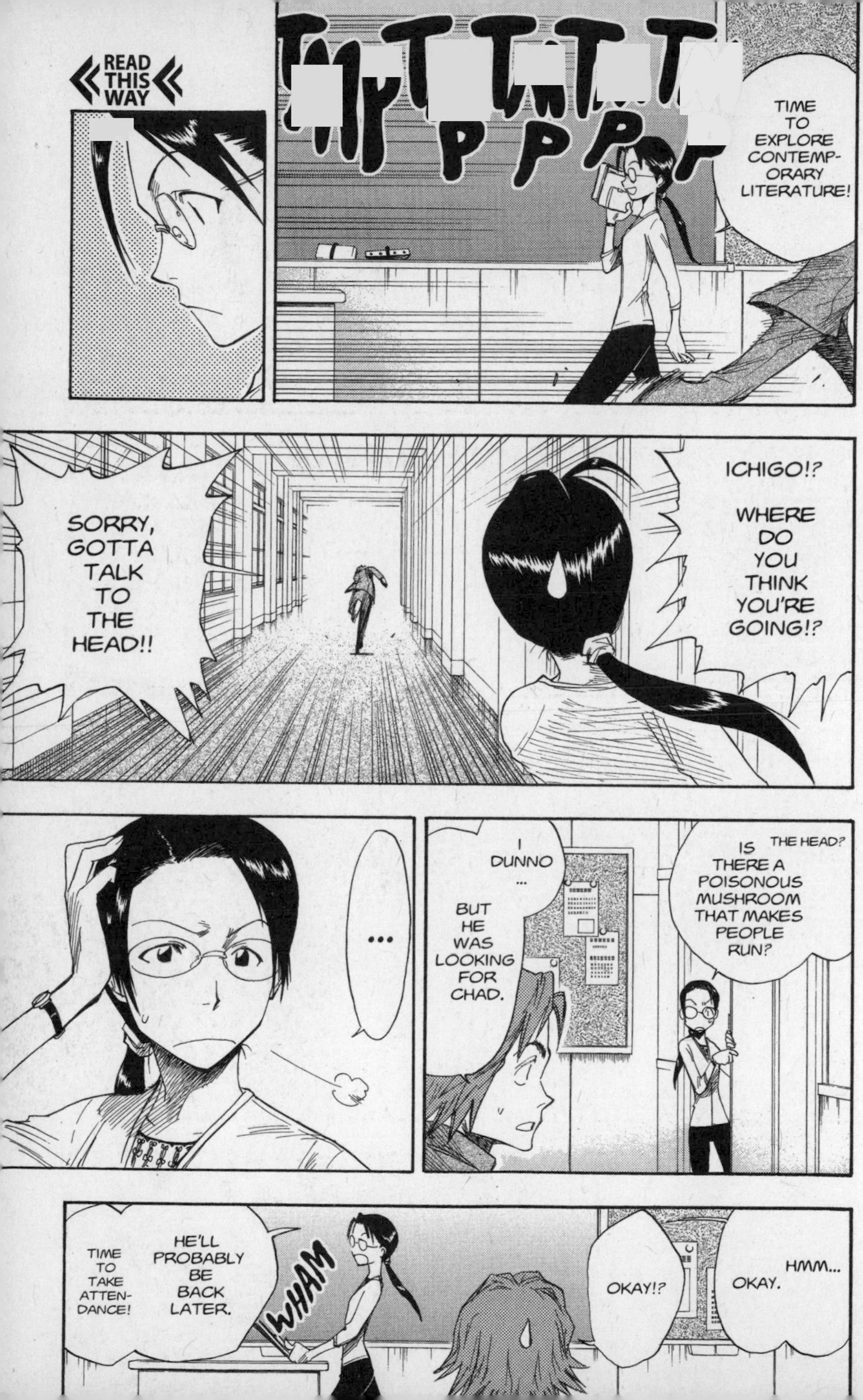

TIME TO EXPLORE CONTEMPORARY LITERATURE!
ICHIGO!? WHERE DO YOU THINK YOU'RE GOING!?
SORRY, GOTTA TALK TO THE HEAD!!
THE HEAD?
IS THERE A POISONOUS MUSHROOM THAT MAKES PEOPLE RUN?
I DUNNO... BUT HE WAS LOOKING FOR CHAD.
...
HMM... OKAY.
OKAY!?
HE'LL PROBABLY BE BACK LATER.
TIME TO TAKE ATTENDANCE!
WHAM

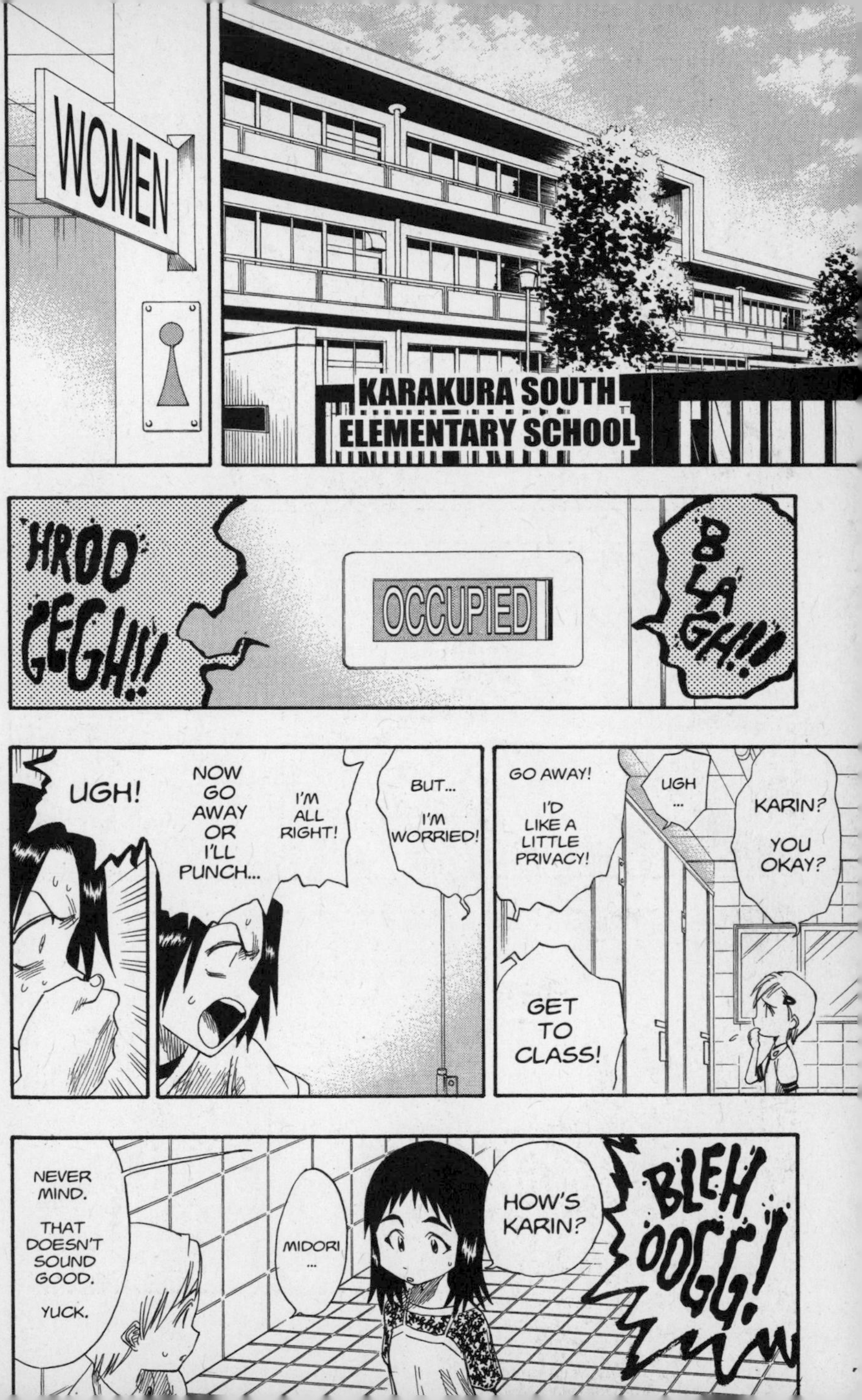
KARAKURA SOUTH ELEMENTARY SCHOOL
WOMEN
BLAGH!!
OCCUPIED
HROO GEGH!!
KARIN? YOU OKAY?
UGH ...
GO AWAY! I'D LIKE A LITTLE PRIVACY!
GET TO CLASS!
BUT... I'M WORRIED!
I'M ALL RIGHT!
NOW GO AWAY OR I'LL PUNCH...
UGH!
BLEH OOGG!
HOW'S KARIN?
MIDORI ...
NEVER MIND. THAT DOESN'T SOUND GOOD. YUCK.

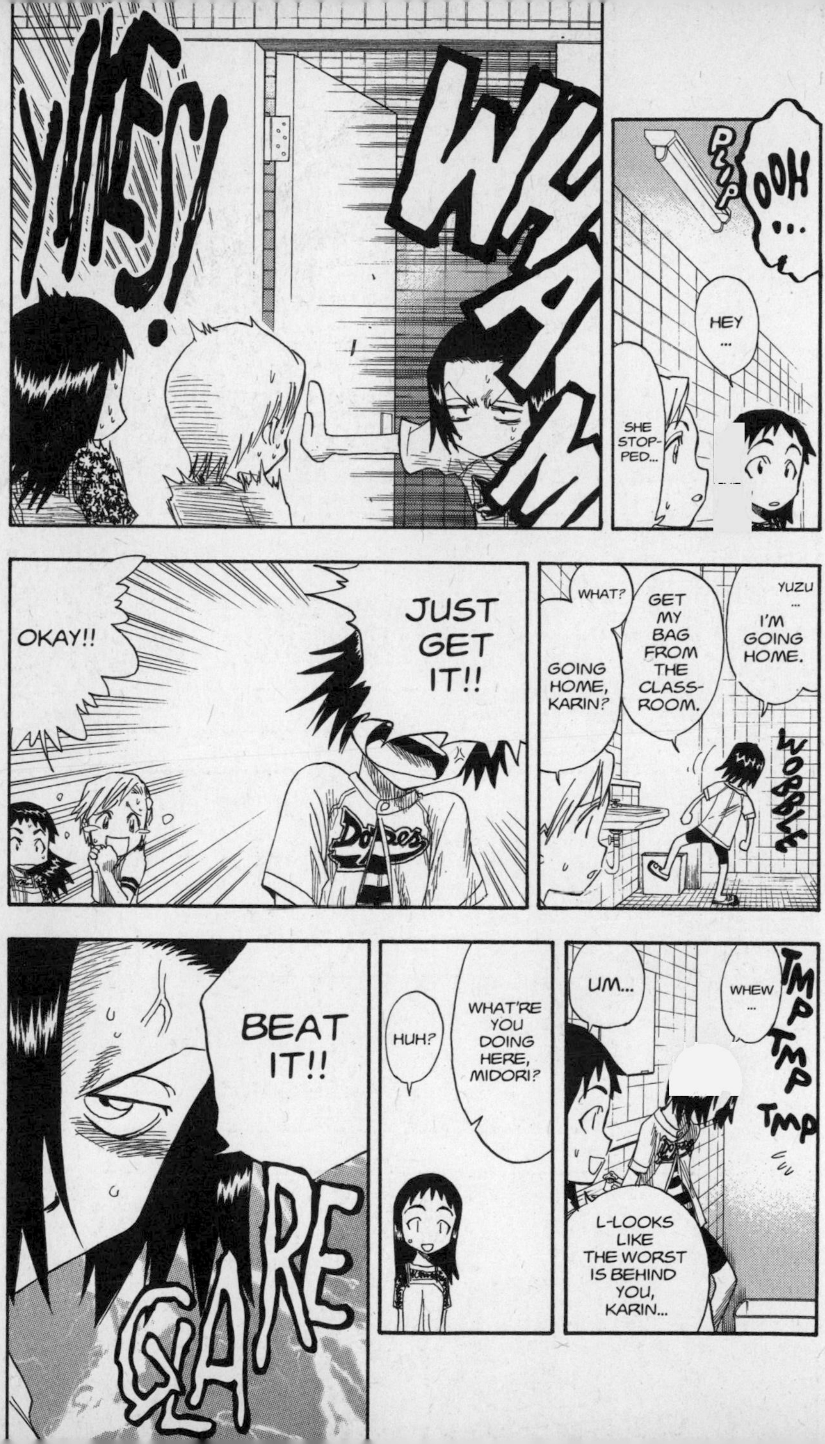
PIP
OOH ...
HEY ...
SHE STOP-PED...
WHAM
YIKES!
YUZU ... I'M GOING HOME.
WOBBLE
GET MY BAG FROM THE CLASS-ROOM.
WHAT?
GOING HOME, KARIN?
JUST GET IT!!
OKAY!!
TMP TMP TMP TMP
WHEW ...
UM...
L-LOOKS LIKE THE WORST IS BEHIND YOU, KARIN...
WHAT'RE YOU DOING HERE, MIDORI?
HUH?
BEAT IT!!
GARE

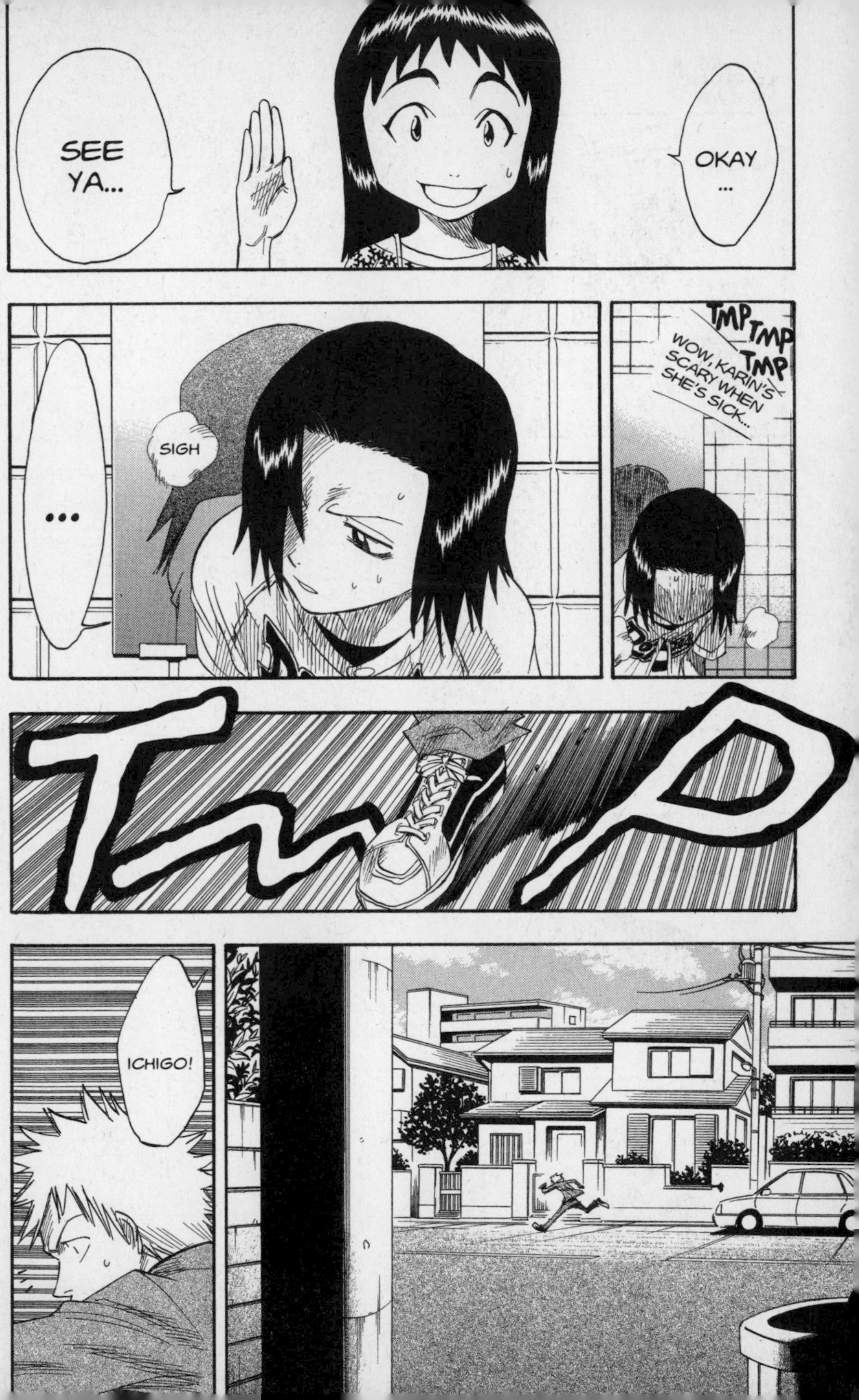
OKAY ...
SEE YA...
TMP TMP TMP
WOW, KARIN'S SCARY WHEN SHE'S SICK...
SIGH
...
TMP
ICHIGO!

READ THIS WAY

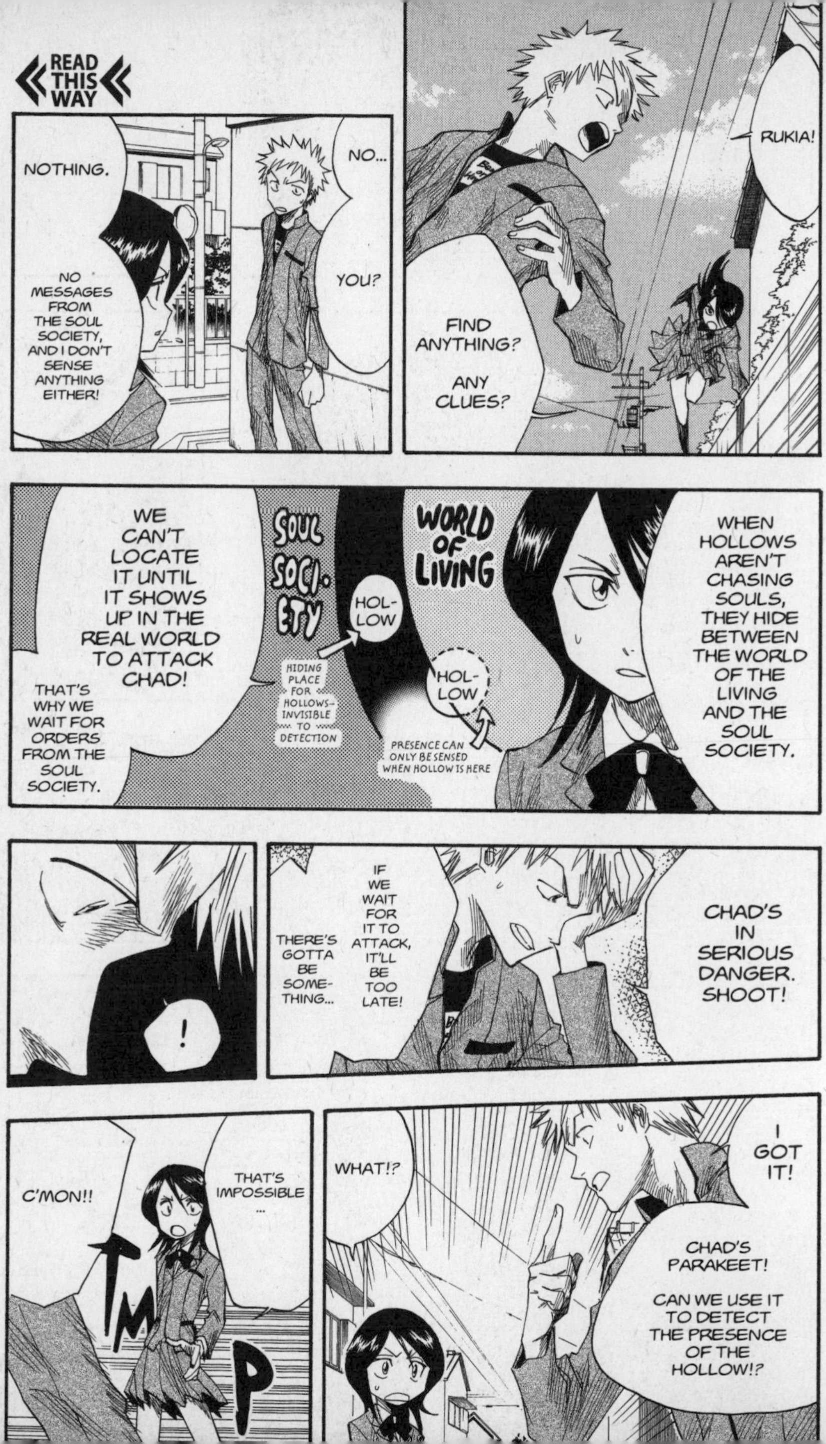
RUKIA!
FIND ANYTHING?
ANY CLUES?
NO...
YOU?
NOTHING.
NO MESSAGES FROM THE SOUL SOCIETY, AND I DON'T SENSE ANYTHING EITHER!
WHEN HOLLOWS AREN'T CHASING SOULS, THEY HIDE BETWEEN THE WORLD OF THE LIVING AND THE SOUL SOCIETY.
WORLD OF LIVING
HOL-LOW
PRESENCE CAN ONLY BE SENSED WHEN HOLLOW IS HERE
SOUL SOCI-ETY
HOL-LOW
HIDING PLACE FOR HOLLOWS—INVISIBLE TO DETECTION
WE CAN'T LOCATE IT UNTIL IT SHOWS UP IN THE REAL WORLD TO ATTACK CHAD!
THAT'S WHY WE WAIT FOR ORDERS FROM THE SOUL SOCIETY.
CHAD'S IN SERIOUS DANGER. SHOOT!
IF WE WAIT FOR IT TO ATTACK, IT'LL BE TOO LATE!
THERE'S GOTTA BE SOME-THING...
!
I GOT IT!
CHAD'S PARAKEET!
CAN WE USE IT TO DETECT THE PRESENCE OF THE HOLLOW!?
WHAT!?
THAT'S IMPOSSIBLE ...
C'MON!!
TMP

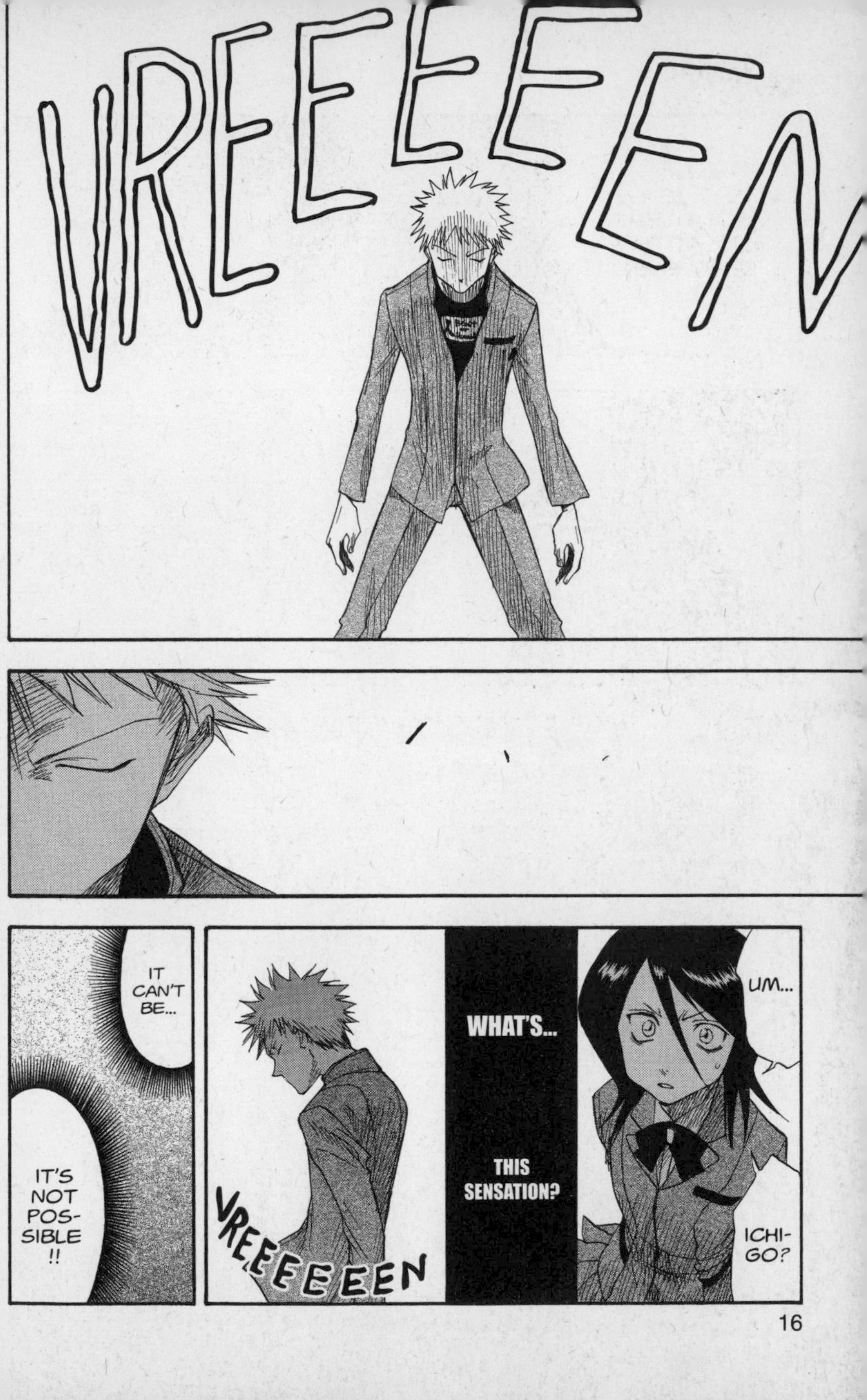
VREEEEEN
UM...
ICHI-GO?
WHAT'S...
THIS SENSATION?
VREEEEEEN
IT CAN'T BE...
IT'S NOT POS-SIBLE!!

READ THIS WAY

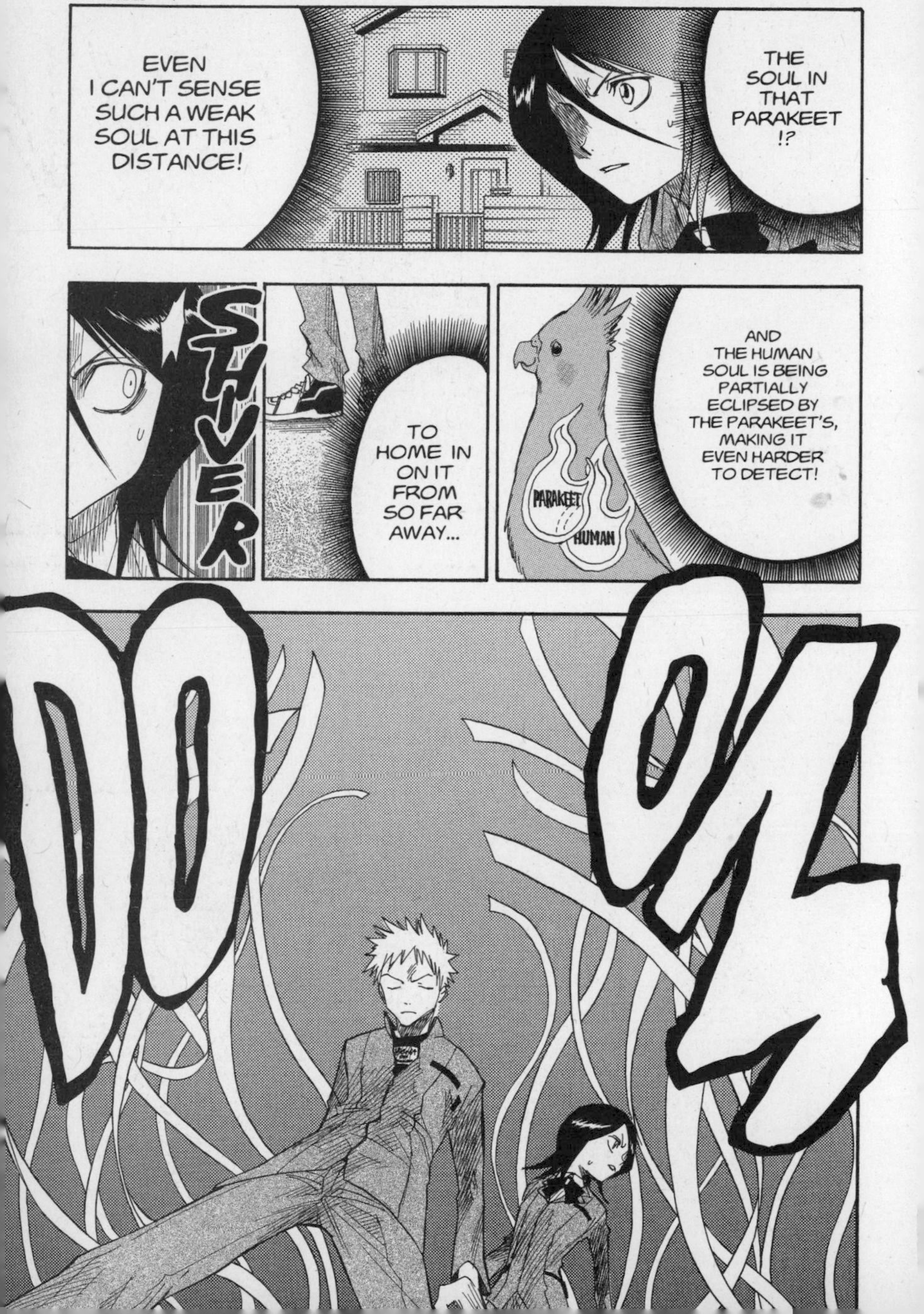
THE SOUL IN THAT PARAKEET !?
EVEN I CAN'T SENSE SUCH A WEAK SOUL AT THIS DISTANCE!
AND THE HUMAN SOUL IS BEING PARTIALLY ECLIPSED BY THE PARAKEET'S, MAKING IT EVEN HARDER TO DETECT!
PARAKEET
HUMAN
TO HOME IN ON IT FROM SO FAR AWAY...
SHIVER
DOOM

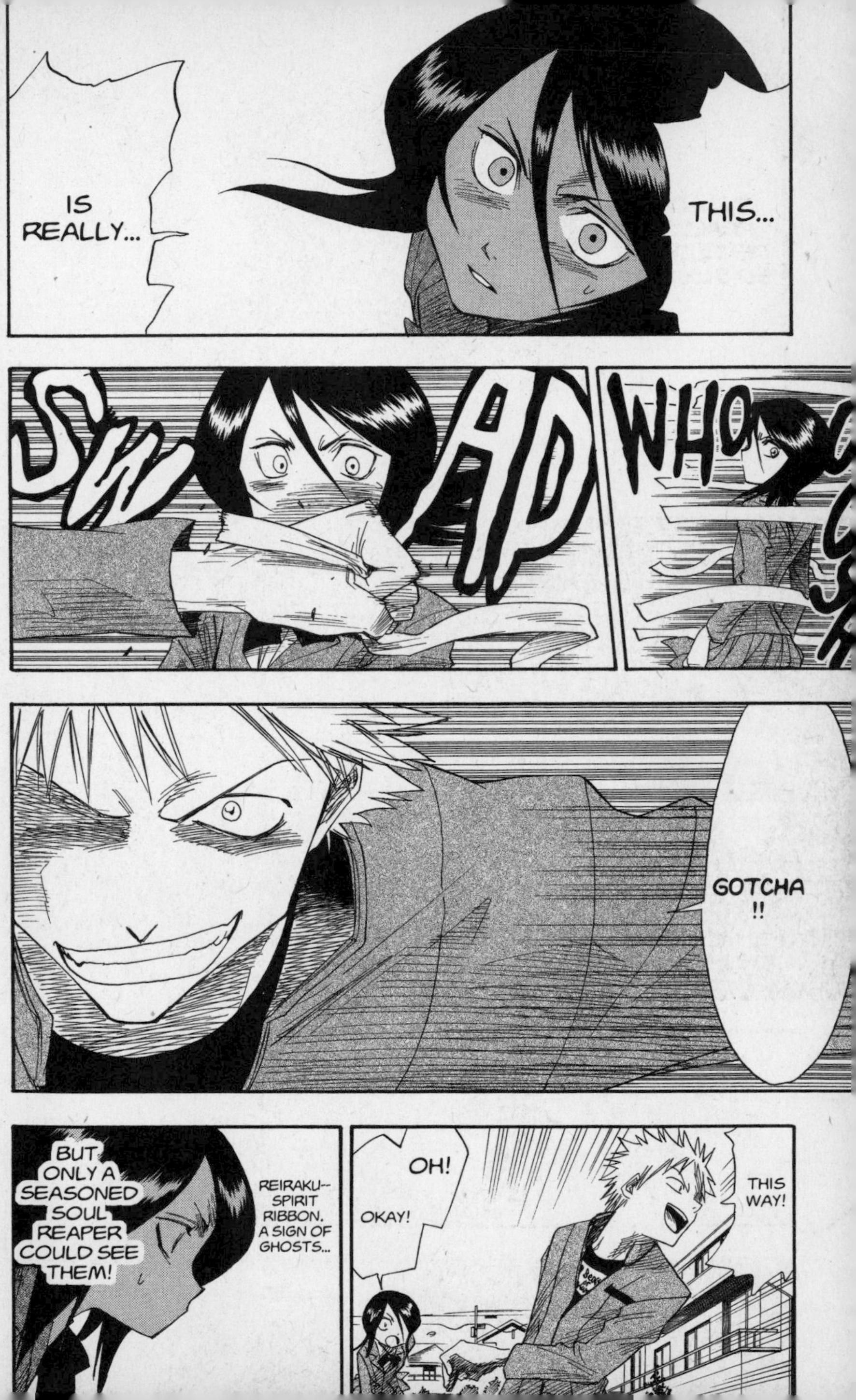
THIS...
IS REALLY...
WHOOSH
SWAD
GOTCHA !!
THIS WAY!
OH!
OKAY!
REIRAKU-- SPIRIT RIBBON. A SIGN OF GHOSTS...
BUT ONLY A SEASONED SOUL REAPER COULD SEE THEM!

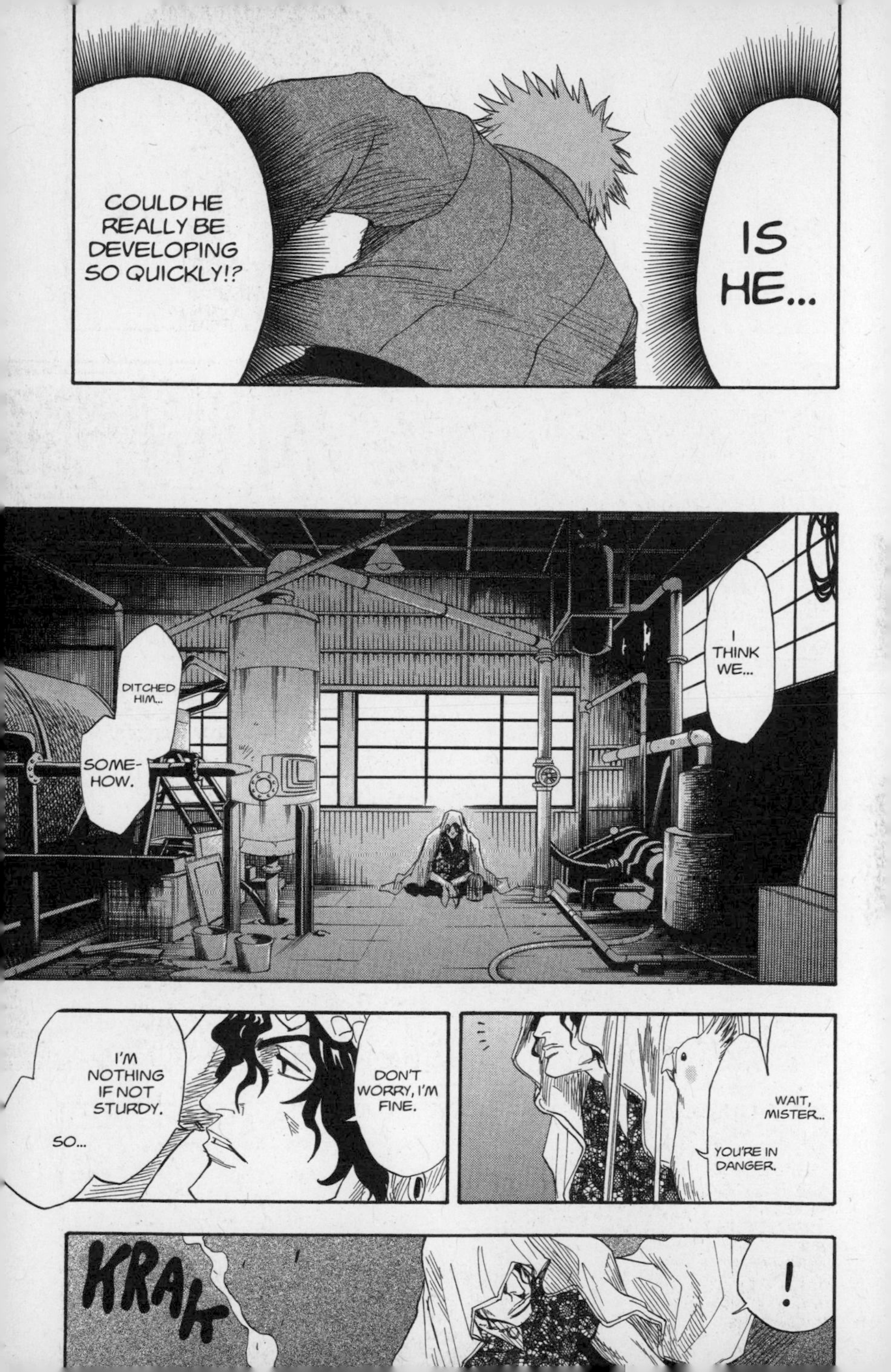
IS HE...
COULD HE REALLY BE DEVELOPING SO QUICKLY!?
I THINK WE...
DITCHED HIM...
SOME-HOW.
WAIT, MISTER..
YOU'RE IN DANGER.
DON'T WORRY, I'M FINE.
I'M NOTHING IF NOT STURDY.
SO...
!
KRAK

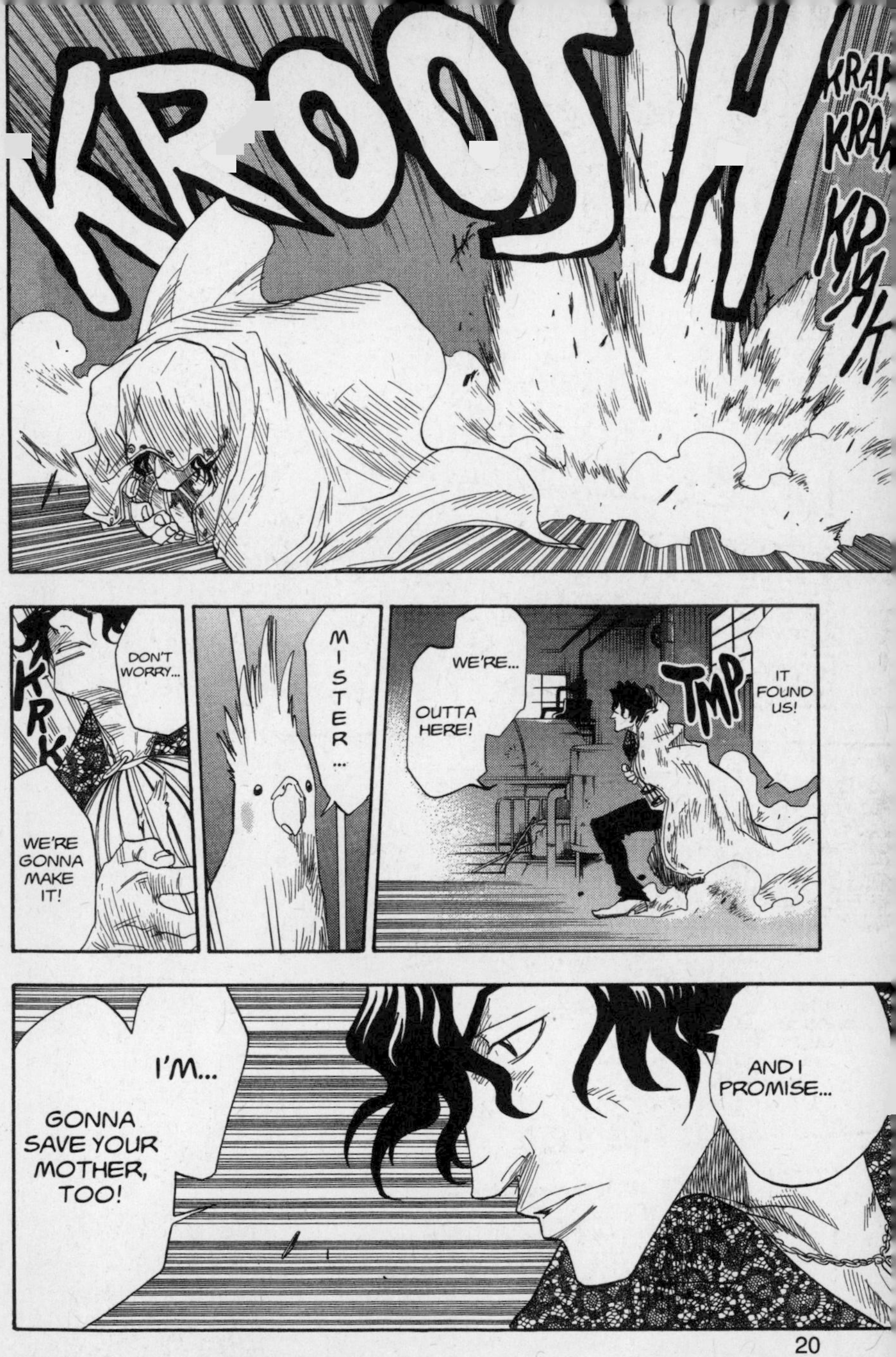
KROOSH!
KRAK
IT FOUND US!
TMP
WE'RE...
OUTTA HERE!
MISTER...
DON'T WORRY...
KRK
WE'RE GONNA MAKE IT!
AND I PROMISE...
I'M...
GONNA SAVE YOUR MOTHER, TOO!

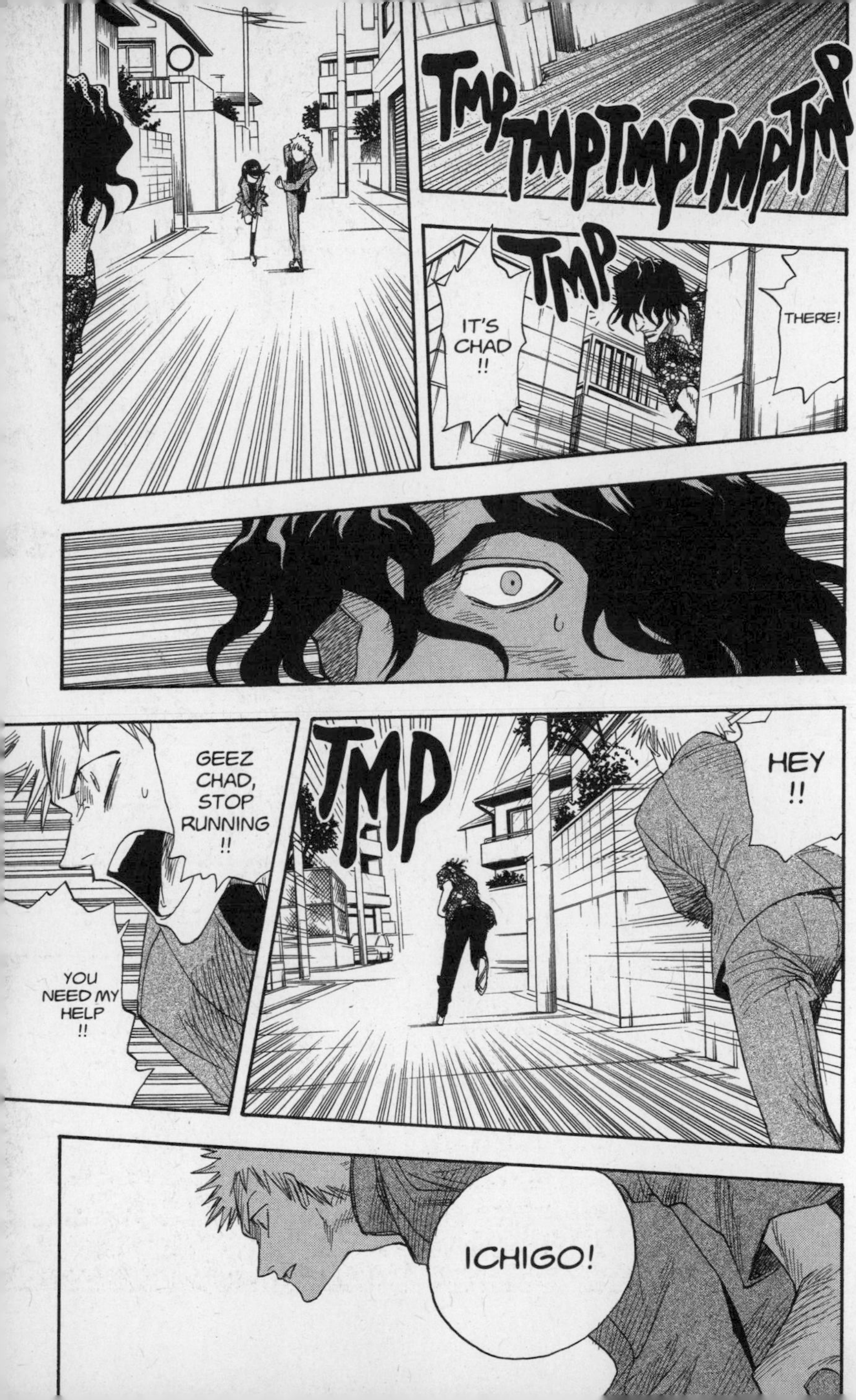
TMP TMPTMPTMPTMP
TMP
THERE!
IT'S CHAD !!
HEY !!
TMP
GEEZ CHAD, STOP RUNNING !!
YOU NEED MY HELP !!
ICHIGO!

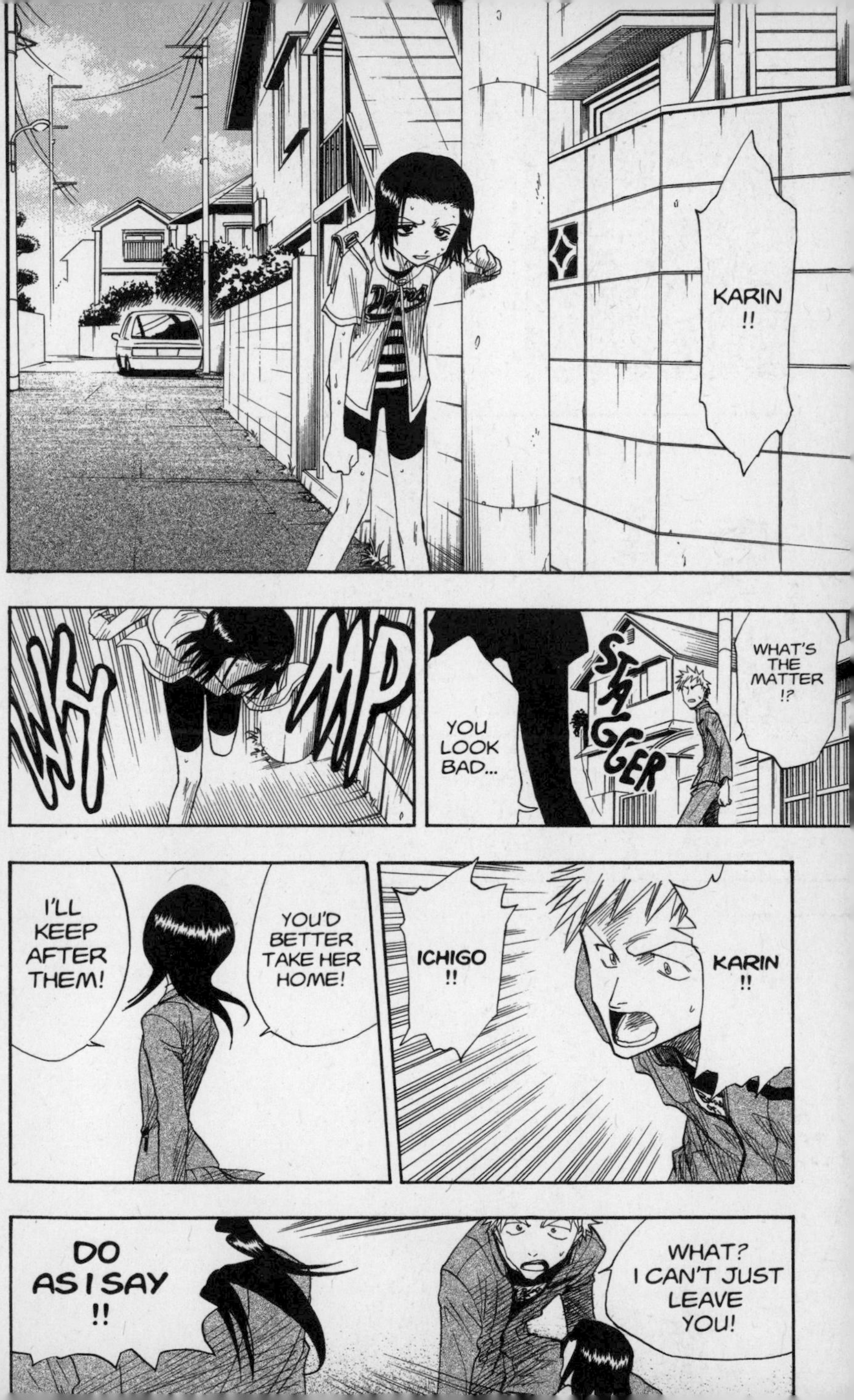
KARIN !!
WHAT'S THE MATTER !?
STAGGER
YOU LOOK BAD...
WH
MP
KARIN !!
ICHIGO !!
YOU'D BETTER TAKE HER HOME!
I'LL KEEP AFTER THEM!
WHAT? I CAN'T JUST LEAVE YOU!
DO AS I SAY !!

READ THIS WAY

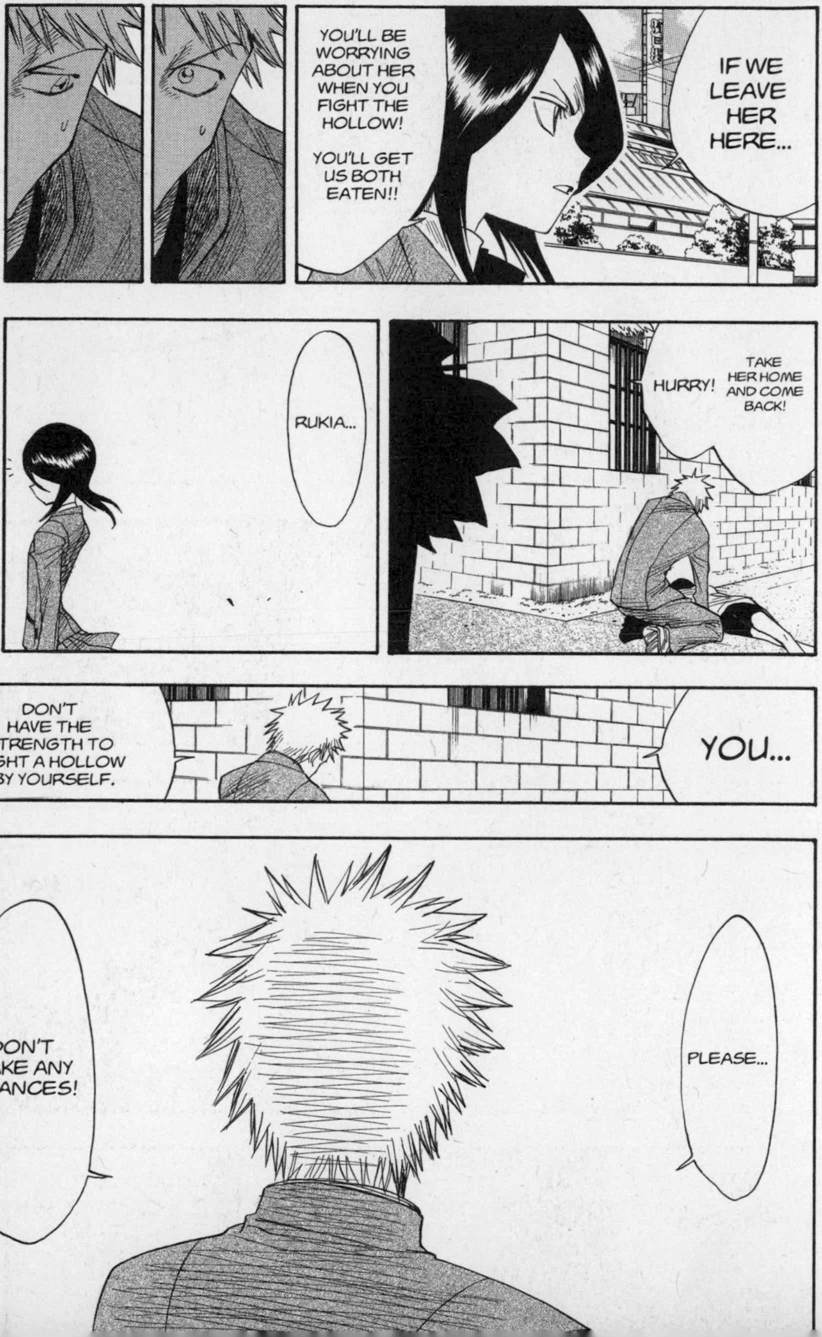
IF WE LEAVE HER HERE...
YOU'LL BE WORRYING ABOUT HER WHEN YOU FIGHT THE HOLLOW!
YOU'LL GET US BOTH EATEN!!
TAKE HER HOME AND COME BACK!
HURRY!
RUKIA...
YOU...
DON'T HAVE THE STRENGTH TO FIGHT A HOLLOW BY YOURSELF.
PLEASE...
DON'T TAKE ANY CHANCES!

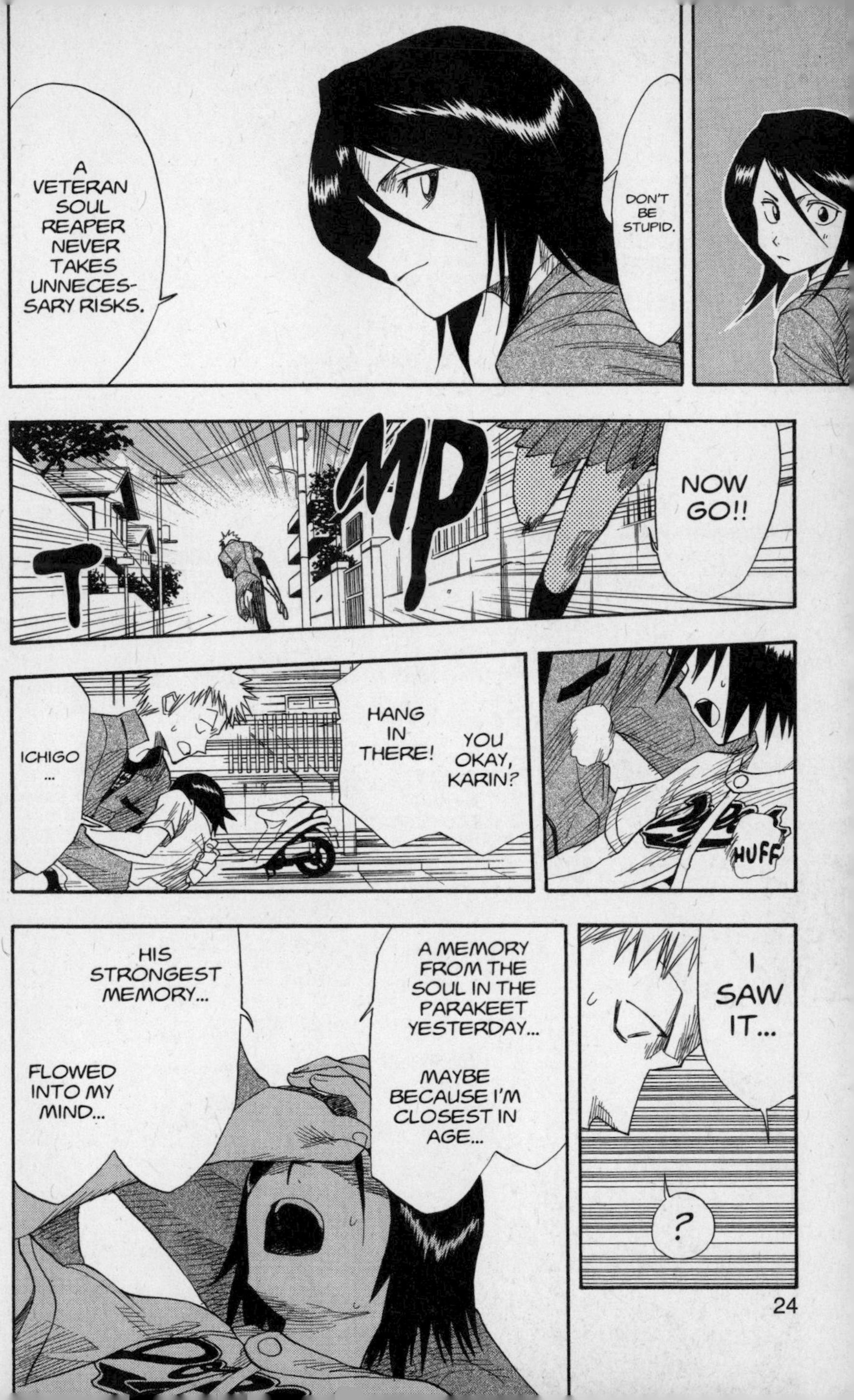
DON'T BE STUPID.
A VETERAN SOUL REAPER NEVER TAKES UNNECESSARY RISKS.
NOW GO!!
TMP
HUFF
YOU OKAY, KARIN?
HANG IN THERE!
ICHIGO...
I SAW IT...
?
A MEMORY FROM THE SOUL IN THE PARAKEET YESTERDAY...
MAYBE BECAUSE I'M CLOSEST IN AGE...
HIS STRONGEST MEMORY...
FLOWED INTO MY MIND...

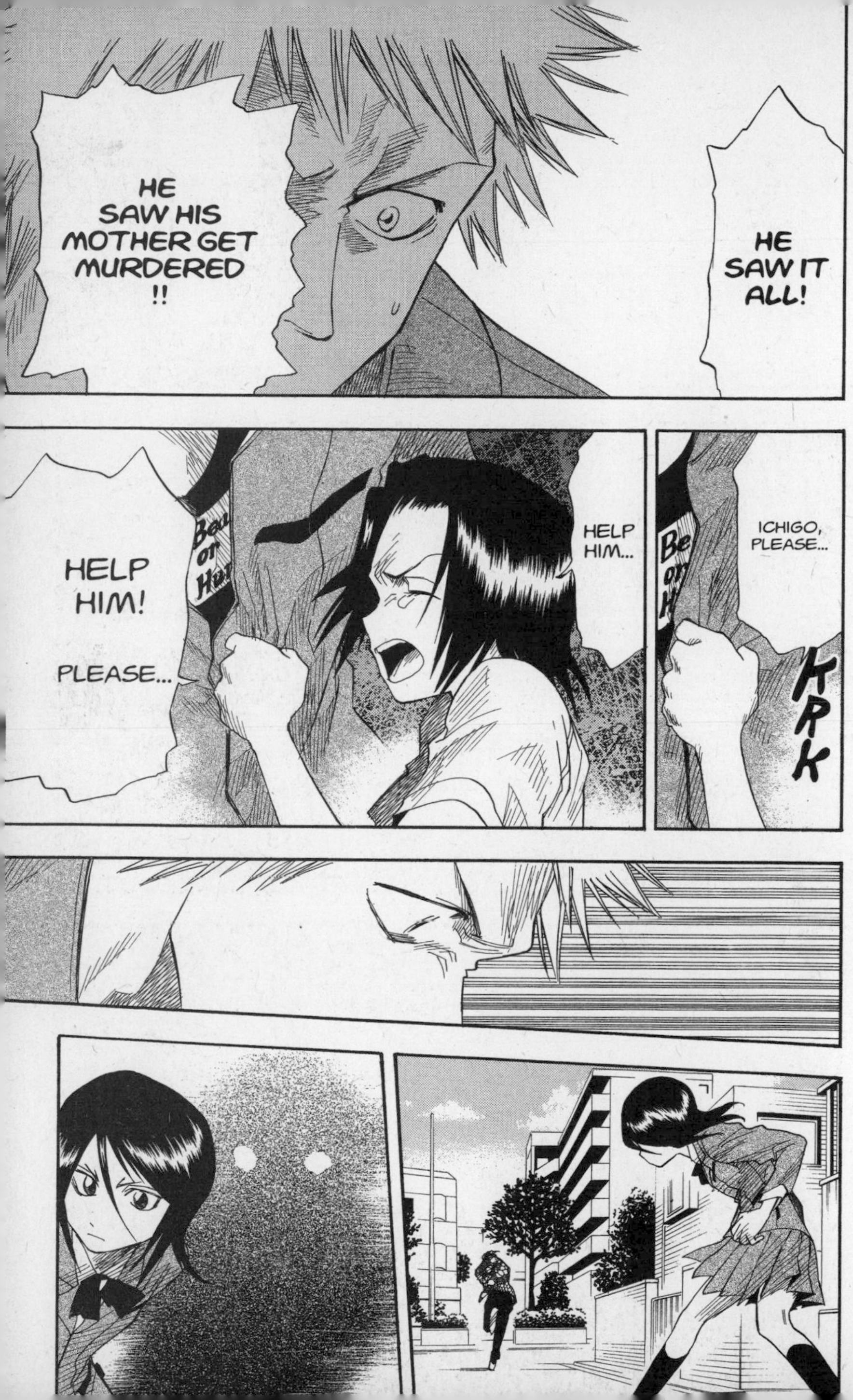
HE SAW IT ALL!
HE SAW HIS MOTHER GET MURDERED !!
ICHIGO, PLEASE...
KRK
HELP HIM...
HELP HIM!
PLEASE...

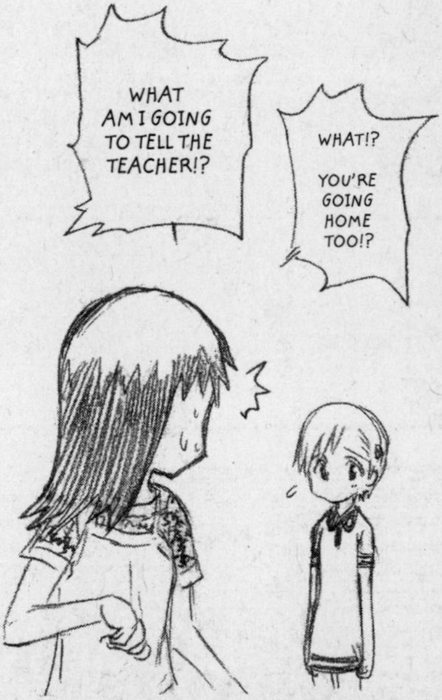
WHAT!? YOU'RE GOING HOME TOO!?
WHAT AM I GOING TO TELL THE TEACHER!?

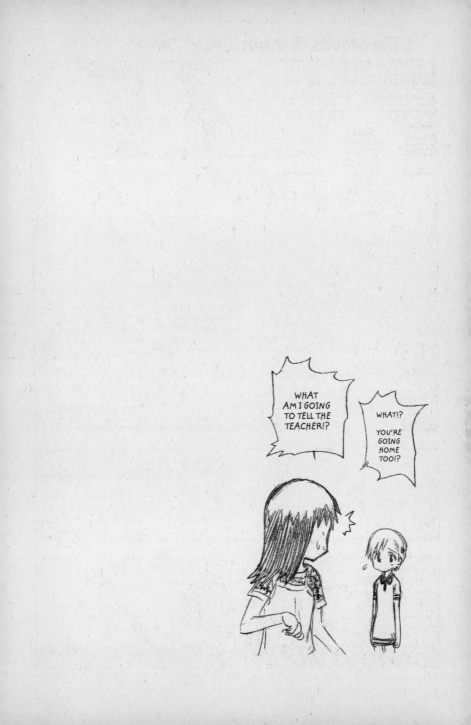

9. Monster Vs. New Girl (Smack Down)

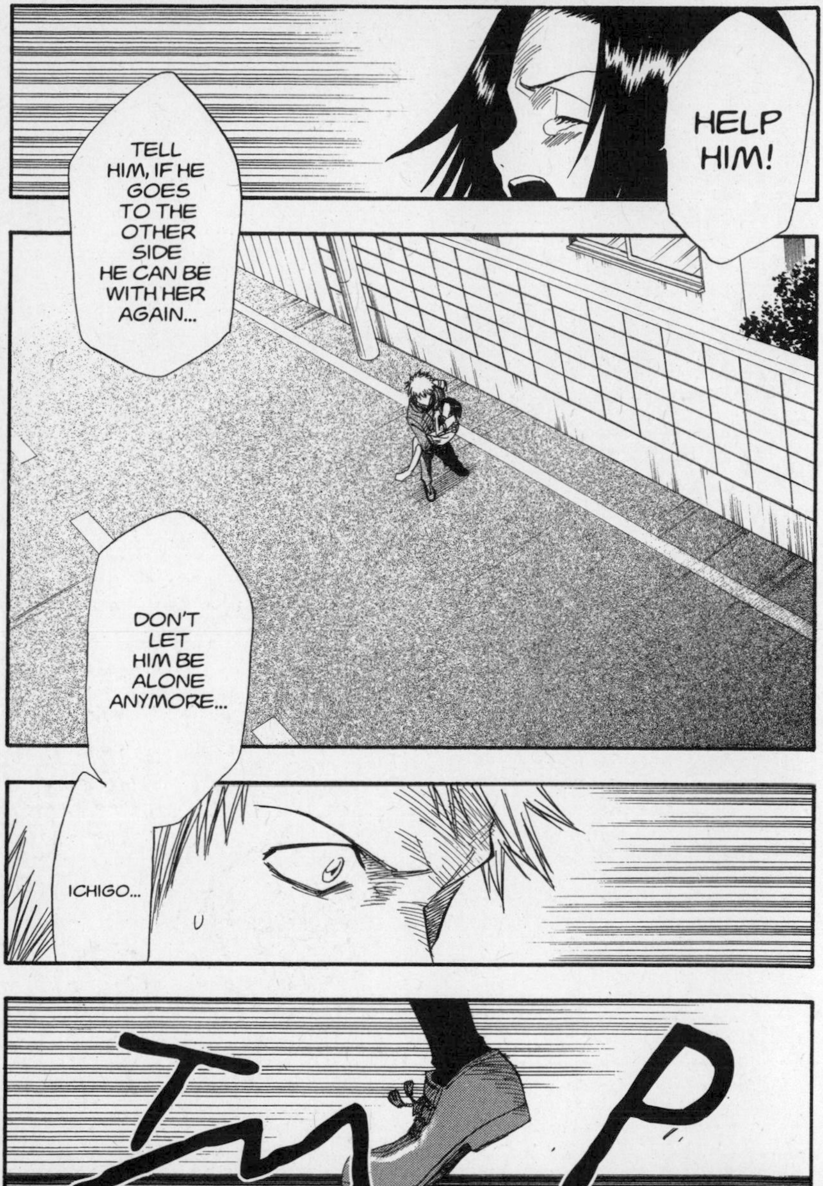
HELP HIM!
TELL HIM, IF HE GOES TO THE OTHER SIDE HE CAN BE WITH HER AGAIN...
DON'T LET HIM BE ALONE ANYMORE...
ICHIGO...
TMP

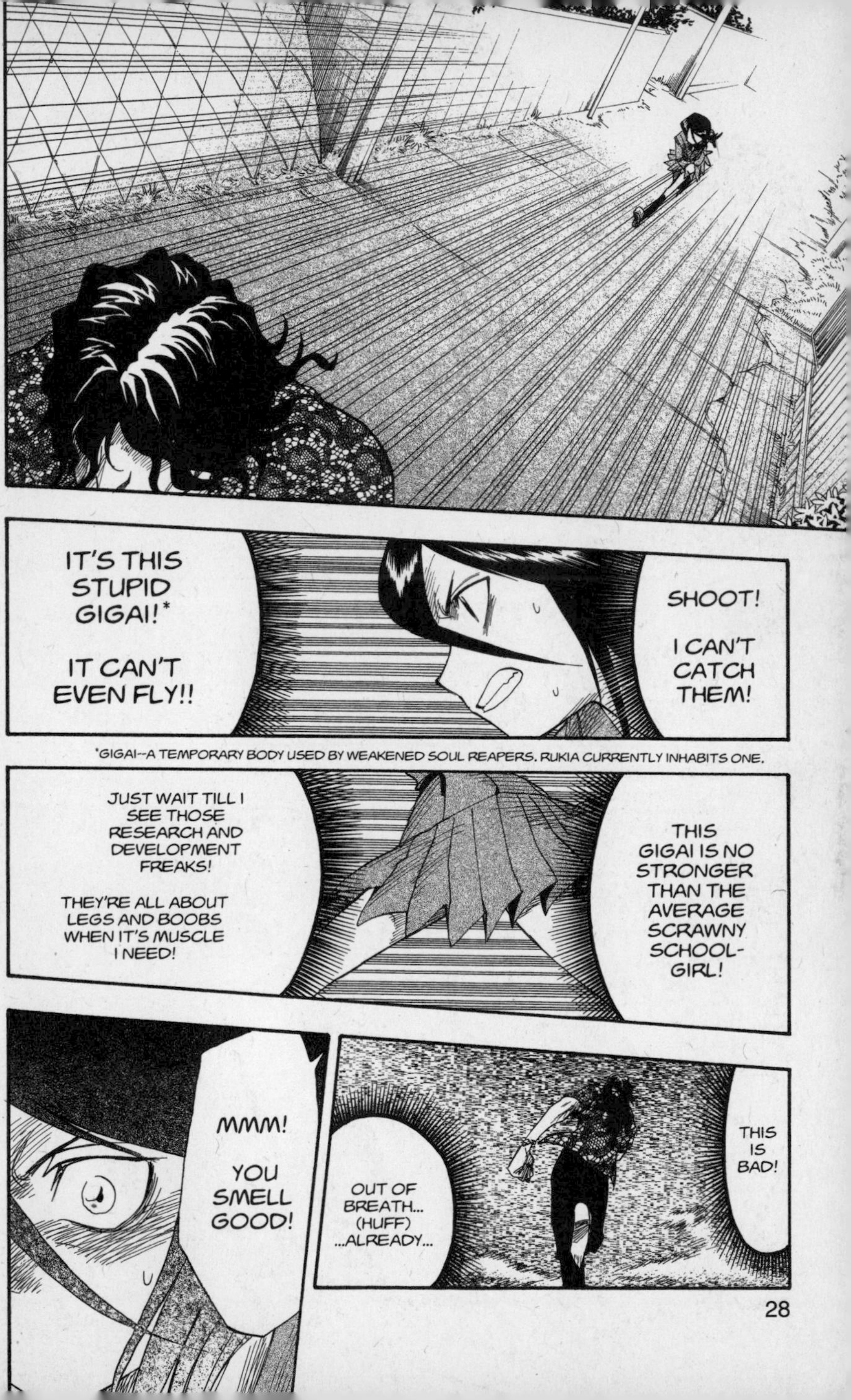
SHOOT!
I CAN'T CATCH THEM!
IT'S THIS STUPID GIGAI!*
IT CAN'T EVEN FLY!!
*GIGAI--A TEMPORARY BODY USED BY WEAKENED SOUL REAPERS. RUKIA CURRENTLY INHABITS ONE.
THIS GIGAI IS NO STRONGER THAN THE AVERAGE SCRAWNY SCHOOL-GIRL!
JUST WAIT TILL I SEE THOSE RESEARCH AND DEVELOPMENT FREAKS!
THEY'RE ALL ABOUT LEGS AND BOOBS WHEN IT'S MUSCLE I NEED!
THIS IS BAD!
OUT OF BREATH... (HUFF) ...ALREADY...
MMM!
YOU SMELL GOOD!

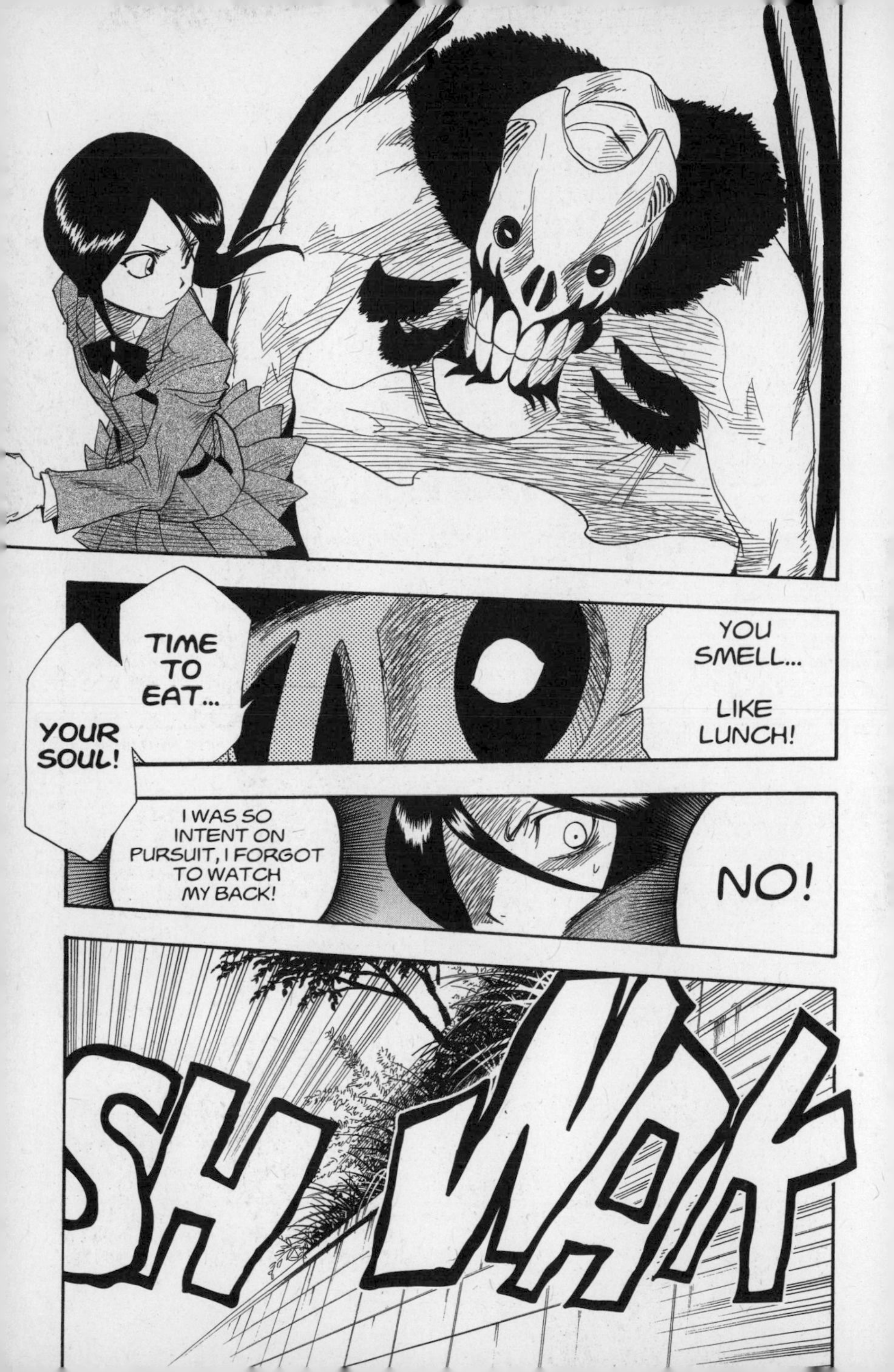
YOU SMELL... LIKE LUNCH!
TIME TO EAT...
YOUR SOUL!
NO!
I WAS SO INTENT ON PURSUIT, I FORGOT TO WATCH MY BACK!
SHWAK

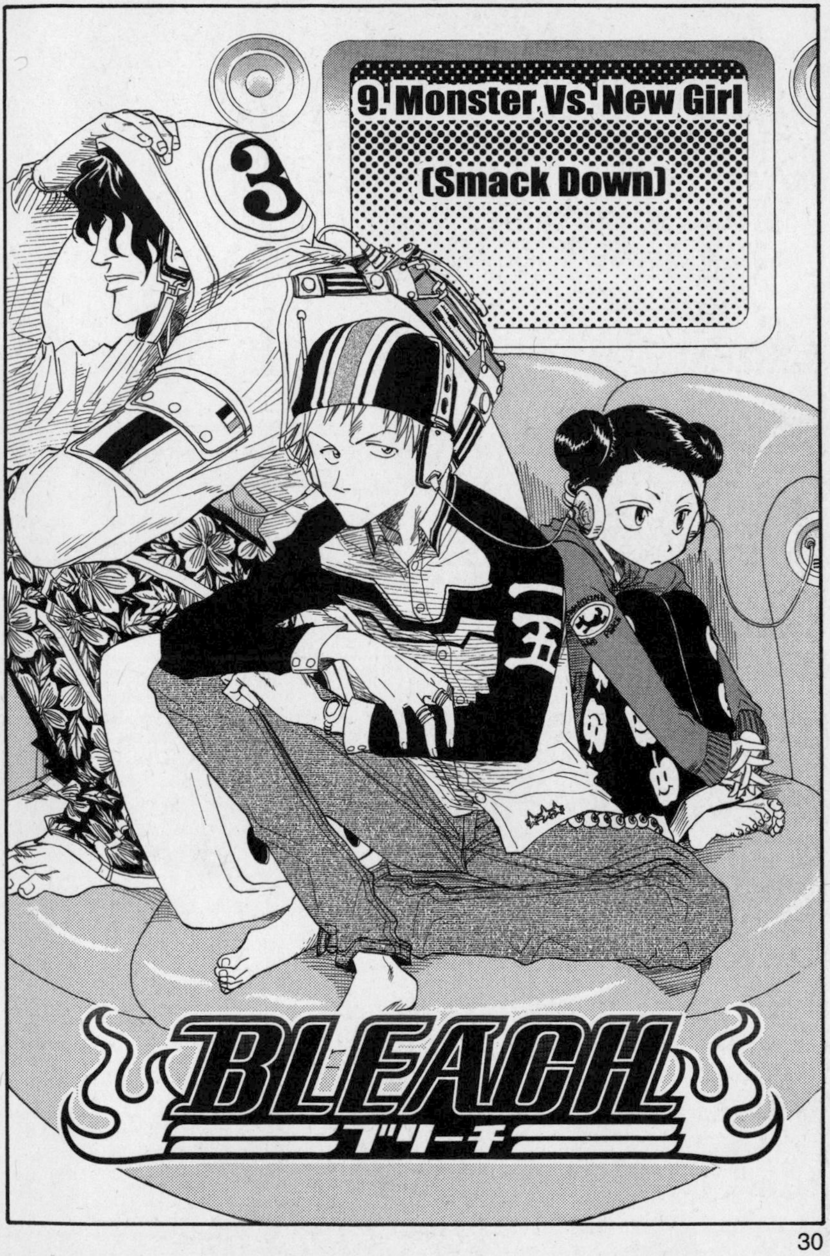
9. Monster Vs. New Girl
〔Smack Down〕
BLEACH
ブリーチ

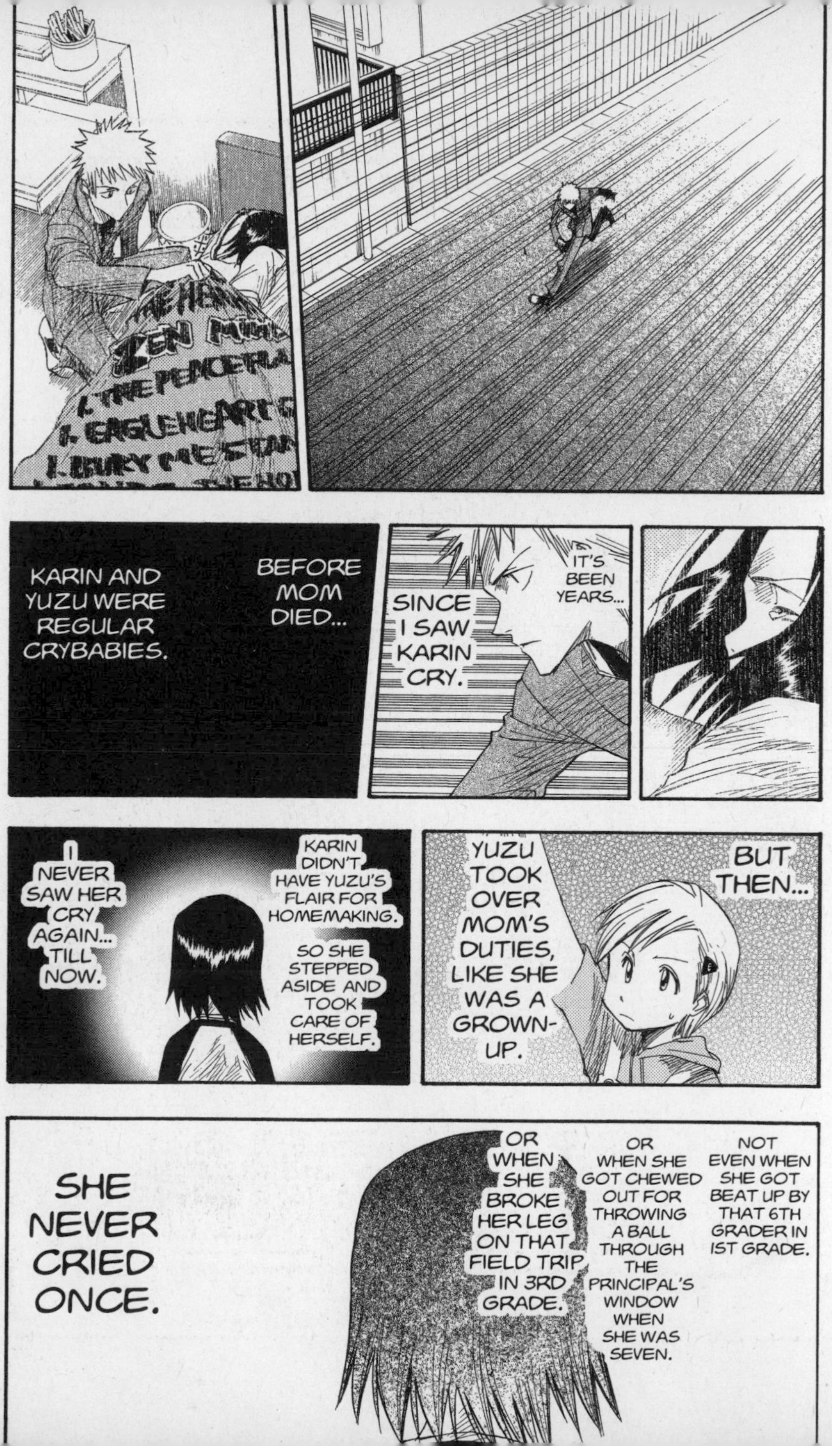
IT'S BEEN YEARS...
SINCE I SAW KARIN CRY.
BEFORE MOM DIED...
KARIN AND YUZU WERE REGULAR CRYBABIES.
BUT THEN...
YUZU TOOK OVER MOM'S DUTIES, LIKE SHE WAS A GROWN-UP.
KARIN DIDN'T HAVE YUZU'S FLAIR FOR HOMEMAKING.
SO SHE STEPPED ASIDE AND TOOK CARE OF HERSELF.
I NEVER SAW HER CRY AGAIN... TILL NOW.
NOT EVEN WHEN SHE GOT BEAT UP BY THAT 6TH GRADER IN 1ST GRADE.
OR WHEN SHE GOT CHEWED OUT FOR THROWING A BALL THROUGH THE PRINCIPAL'S WINDOW WHEN SHE WAS SEVEN.
OR WHEN SHE BROKE HER LEG ON THAT FIELD TRIP IN 3RD GRADE.
SHE NEVER CRIED ONCE.

READ THIS WAY

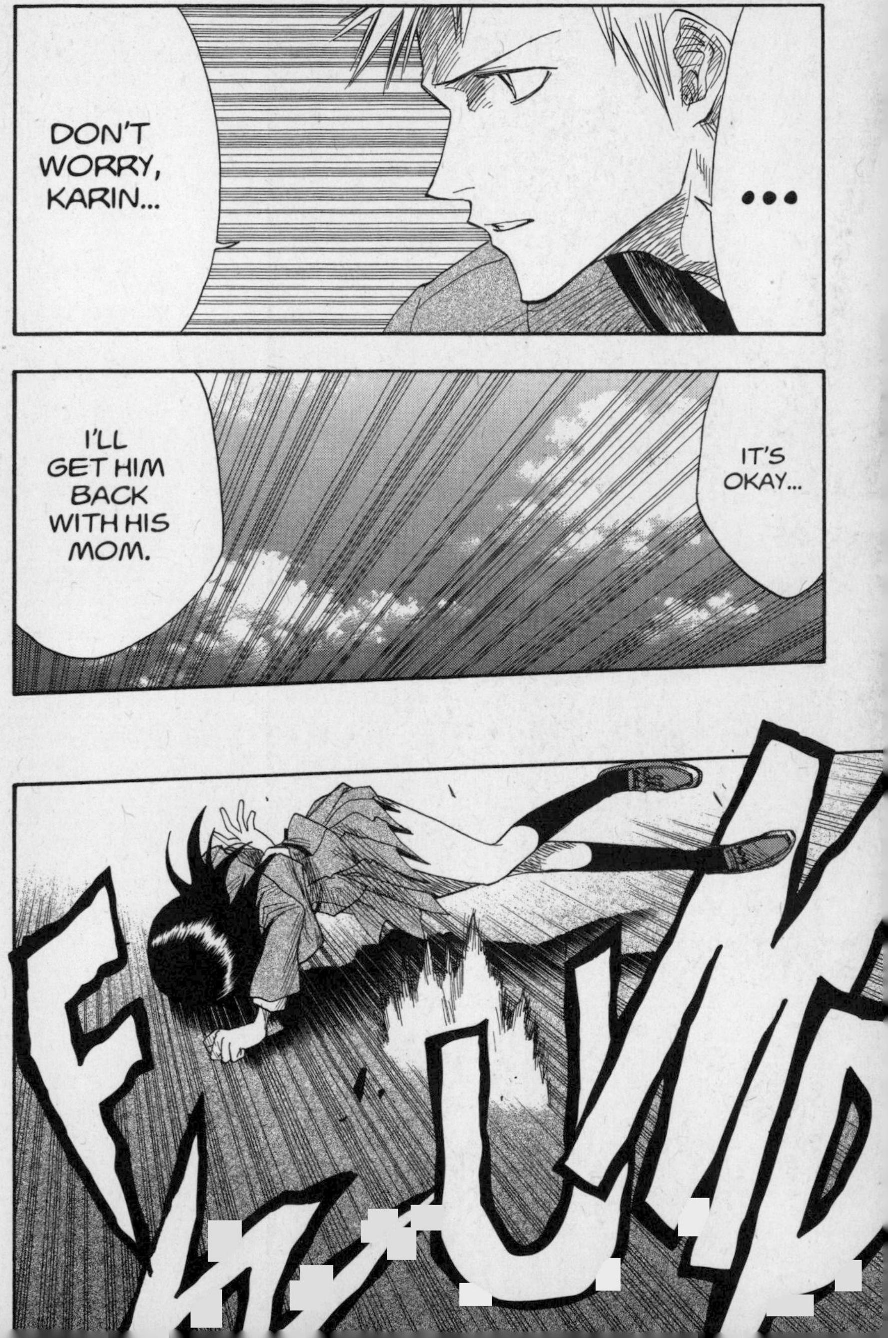
•••
DON'T WORRY, KARIN...
IT'S OKAY...
I'LL GET HIM BACK WITH HIS MOM.

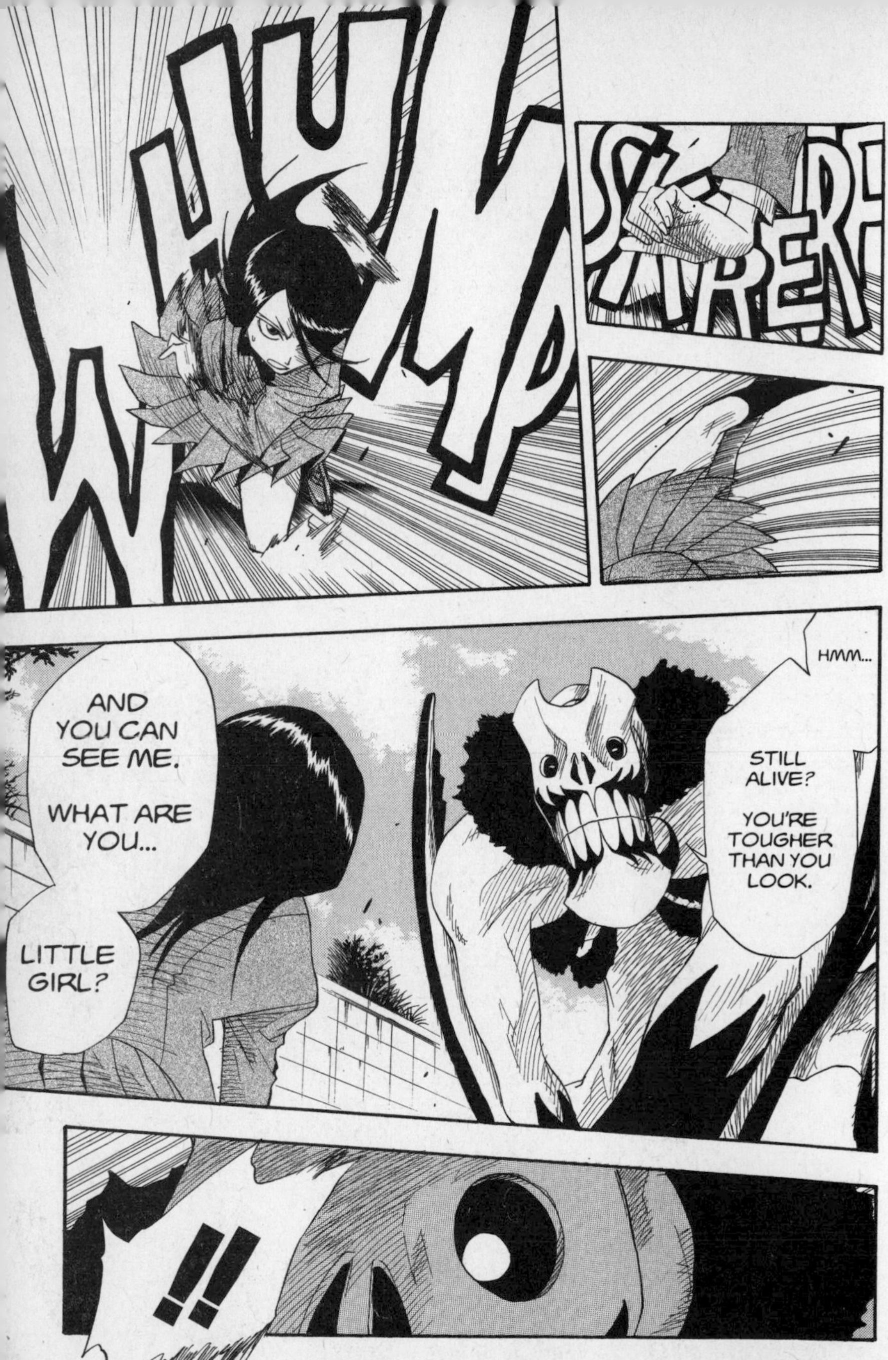
WHUMP
HMM...
STILL ALIVE?
YOU'RE TOUGHER THAN YOU LOOK.
AND YOU CAN SEE ME.
WHAT ARE YOU...
LITTLE GIRL?
!!

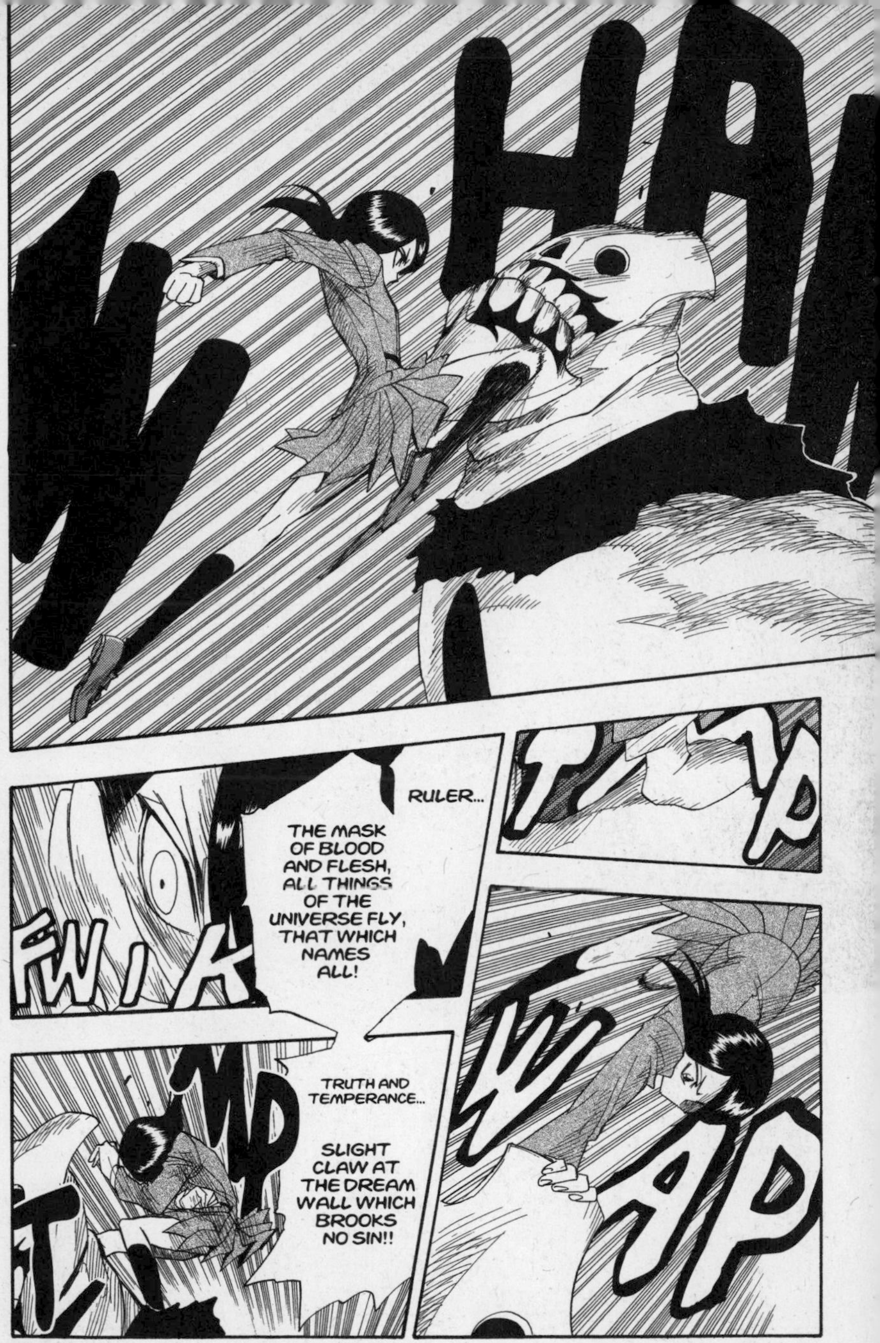
TAP
RULER...
THE MASK OF BLOOD AND FLESH, ALL THINGS OF THE UNIVERSE FLY, THAT WHICH NAMES ALL!
FWIK
WHAP
TRUTH AND TEMPERANCE...
SLIGHT CLAW AT THE DREAM WALL WHICH BROOKS NO SIN!!

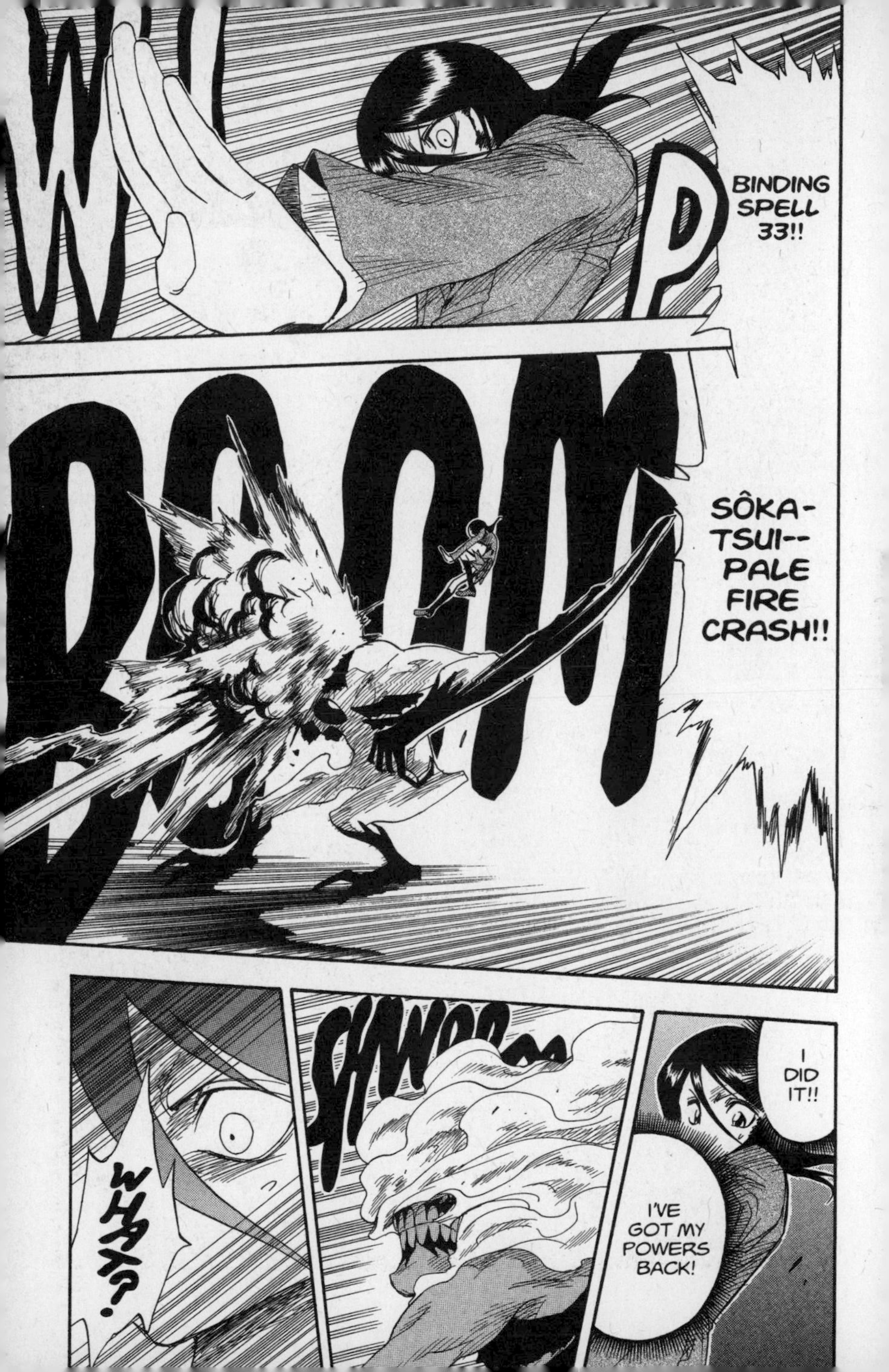
BINDING SPELL 33!!
BOOM
SÔKA-TSUI-- PALE FIRE CRASH!!
I DID IT!!
I'VE GOT MY POWERS BACK!
WHAT?!

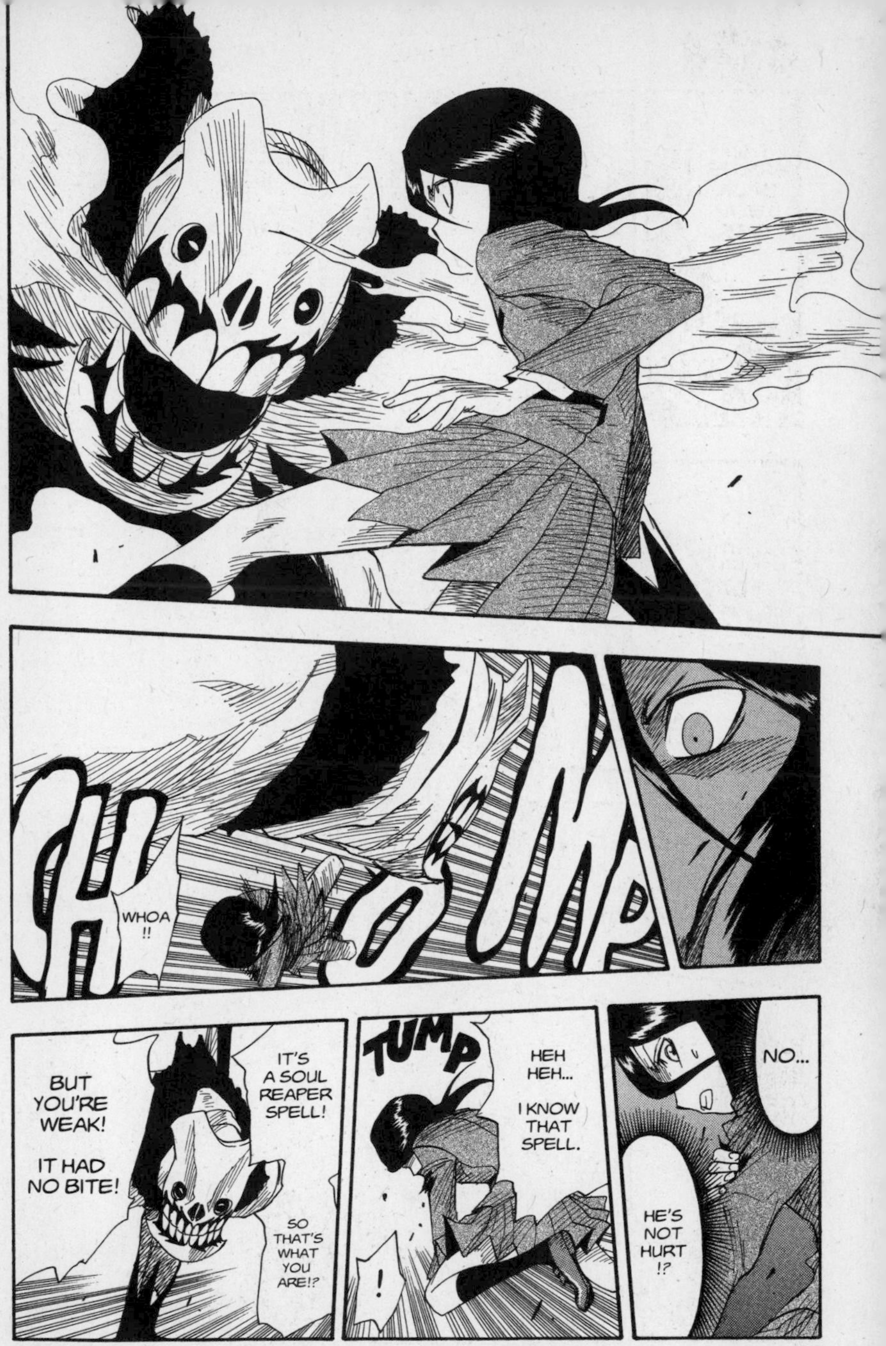
CHOMP
WHOA !!
NO...
HE'S NOT HURT !?
TUMP
HEH HEH...
I KNOW THAT SPELL.
!
IT'S A SOUL REAPER SPELL!
SO THAT'S WHAT YOU ARE!?
BUT YOU'RE WEAK!
IT HAD NO BITE!

READ THIS WAY

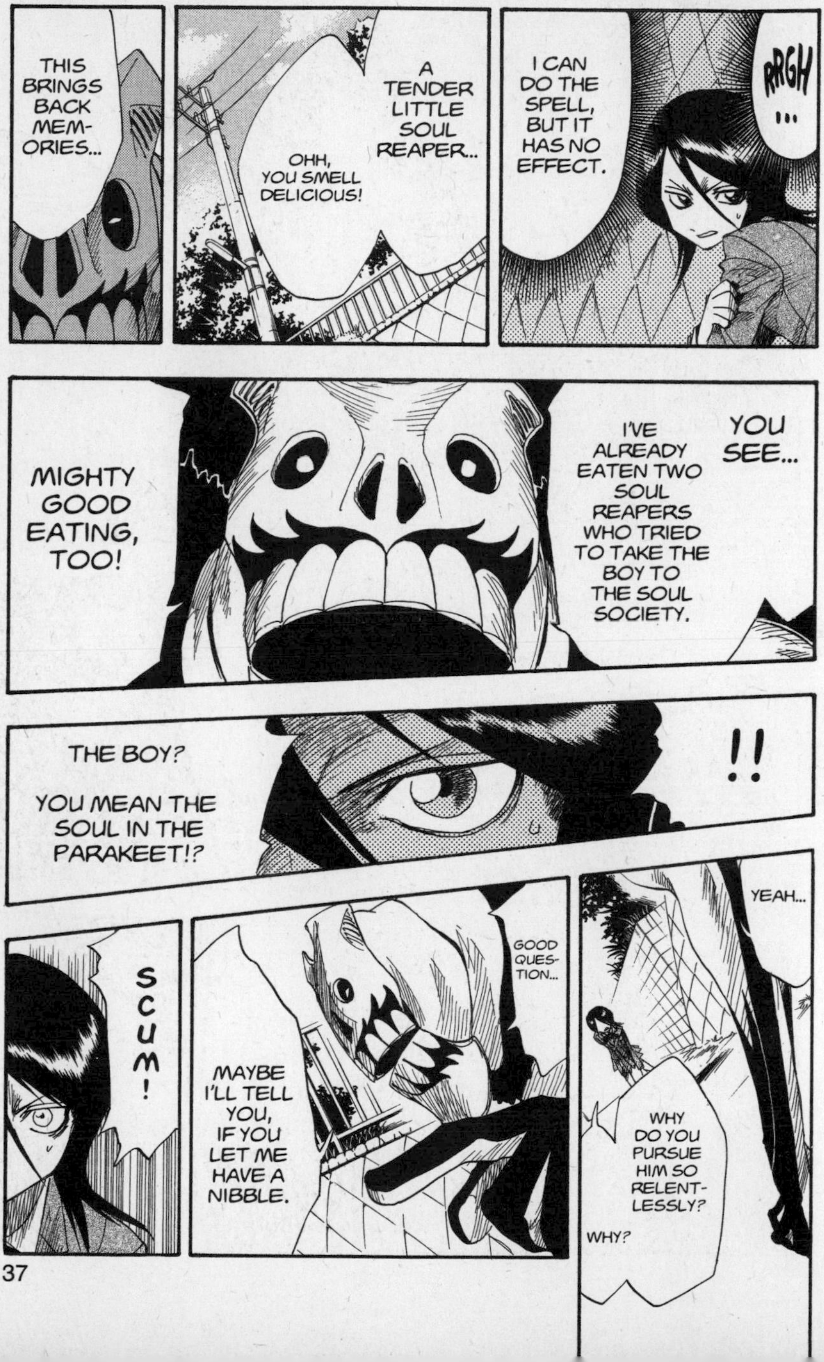
RRGH ...
I CAN DO THE SPELL, BUT IT HAS NO EFFECT.
A TENDER LITTLE SOUL REAPER...
OHH, YOU SMELL DELICIOUS!
THIS BRINGS BACK MEMORIES...
YOU SEE...
I'VE ALREADY EATEN TWO SOUL REAPERS WHO TRIED TO TAKE THE BOY TO THE SOUL SOCIETY.
MIGHTY GOOD EATING, TOO!
!!
THE BOY?
YOU MEAN THE SOUL IN THE PARAKEET!?
YEAH...
WHY DO YOU PURSUE HIM SO RELENTLESSLY?
WHY?
GOOD QUESTION...
MAYBE I'LL TELL YOU, IF YOU LET ME HAVE A NIBBLE.
SCUM!

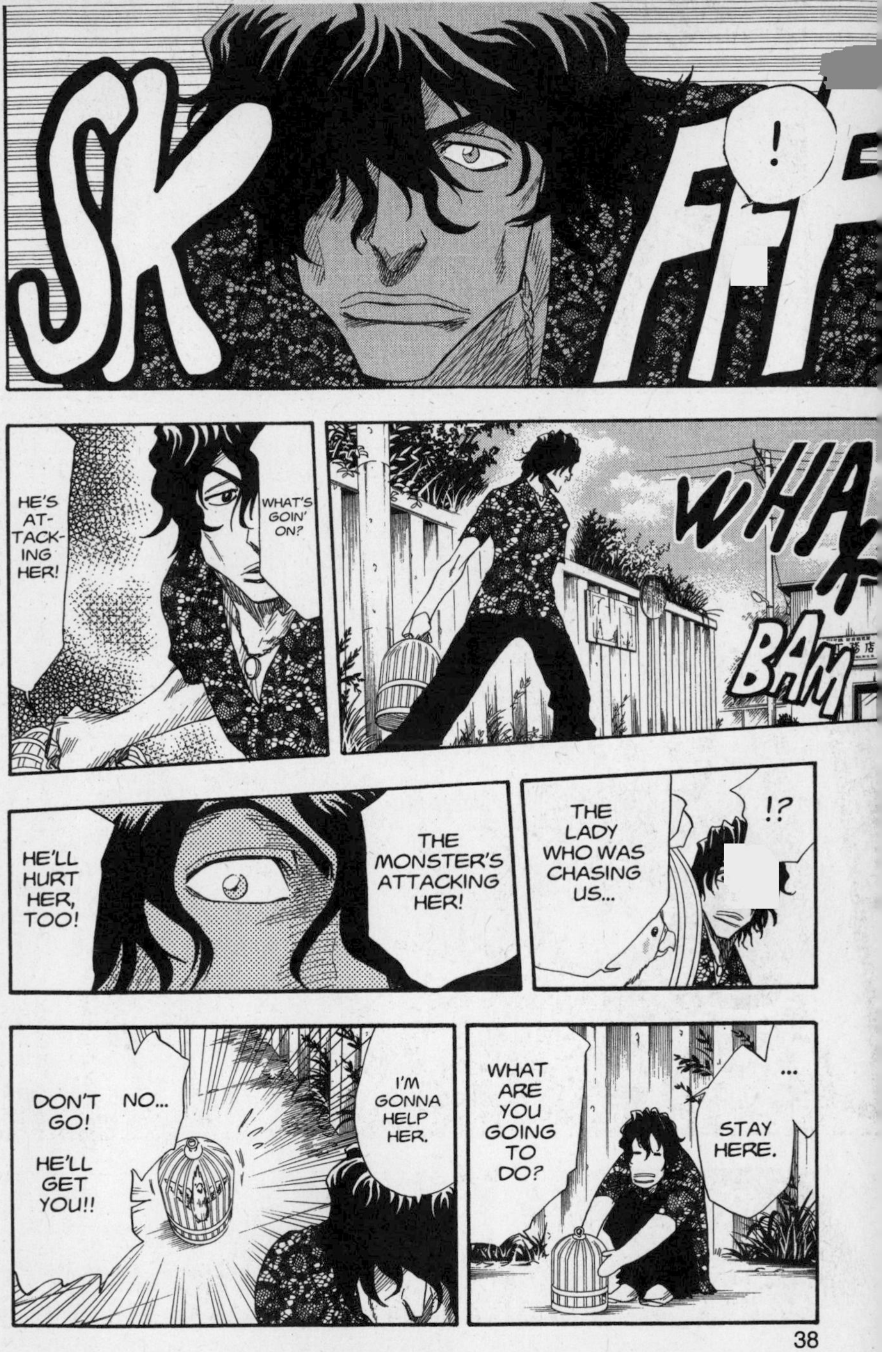
!
SK
FF
WHA
BAM
WHAT'S GOIN' ON?
HE'S AT-TACK-ING HER!
!?
THE LADY WHO WAS CHASING US...
THE MONSTER'S ATTACKING HER!
HE'LL HURT HER, TOO!
...
STAY HERE.
WHAT ARE YOU GOING TO DO?
I'M GONNA HELP HER.
NO...
DON'T GO!
HE'LL GET YOU!!

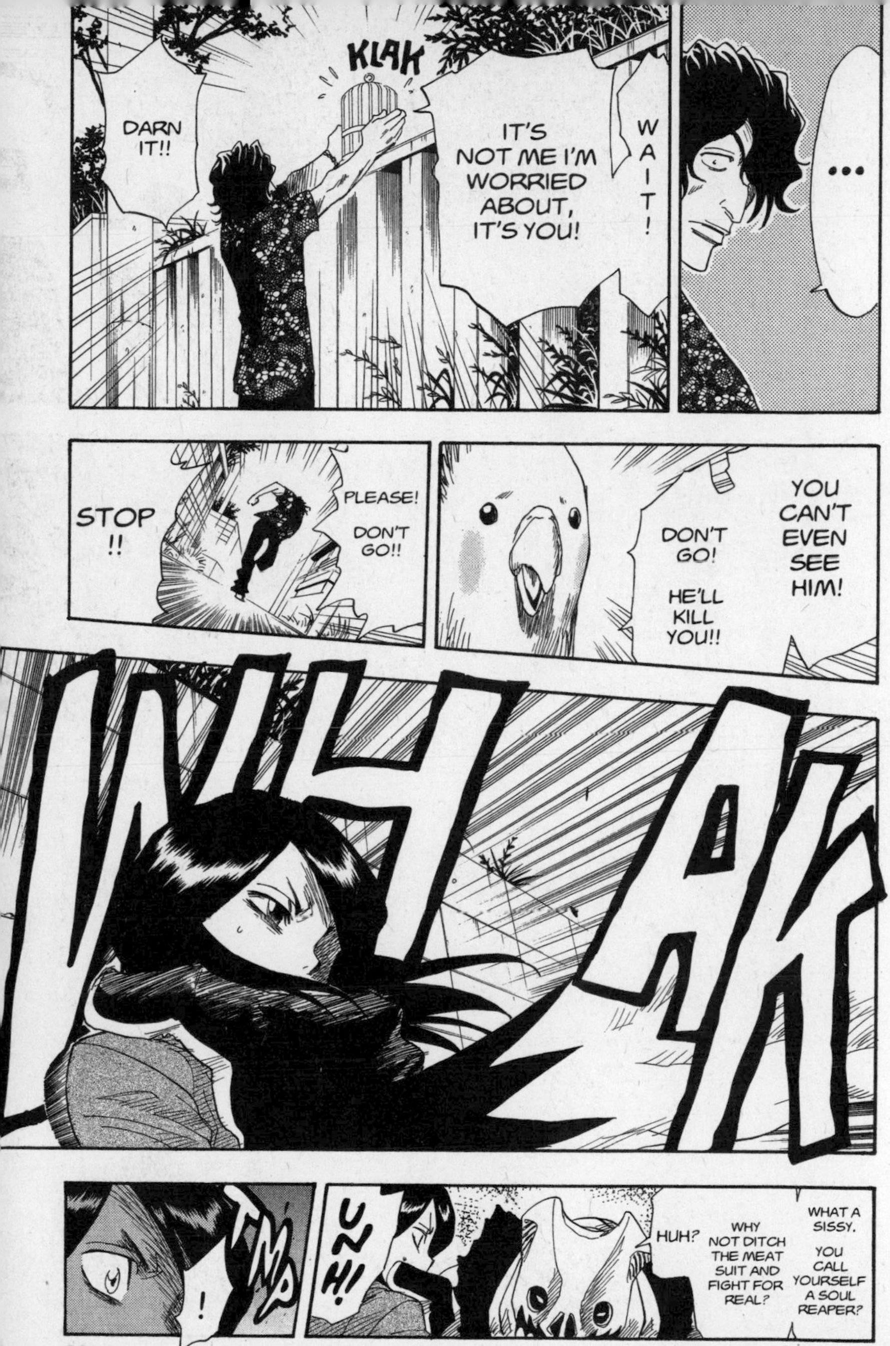
...
WAIT!
KLAK
IT'S NOT ME I'M WORRIED ABOUT, IT'S YOU!
DARN IT!!
YOU CAN'T EVEN SEE HIM!
DON'T GO! HE'LL KILL YOU!!
PLEASE! DON'T GO!!
STOP!!
WHAK
WHAT A SISSY. YOU CALL YOURSELF A SOUL REAPER?
WHY NOT DITCH THE MEAT SUIT AND FIGHT FOR REAL?
HUH?
UNH!
TMP
!

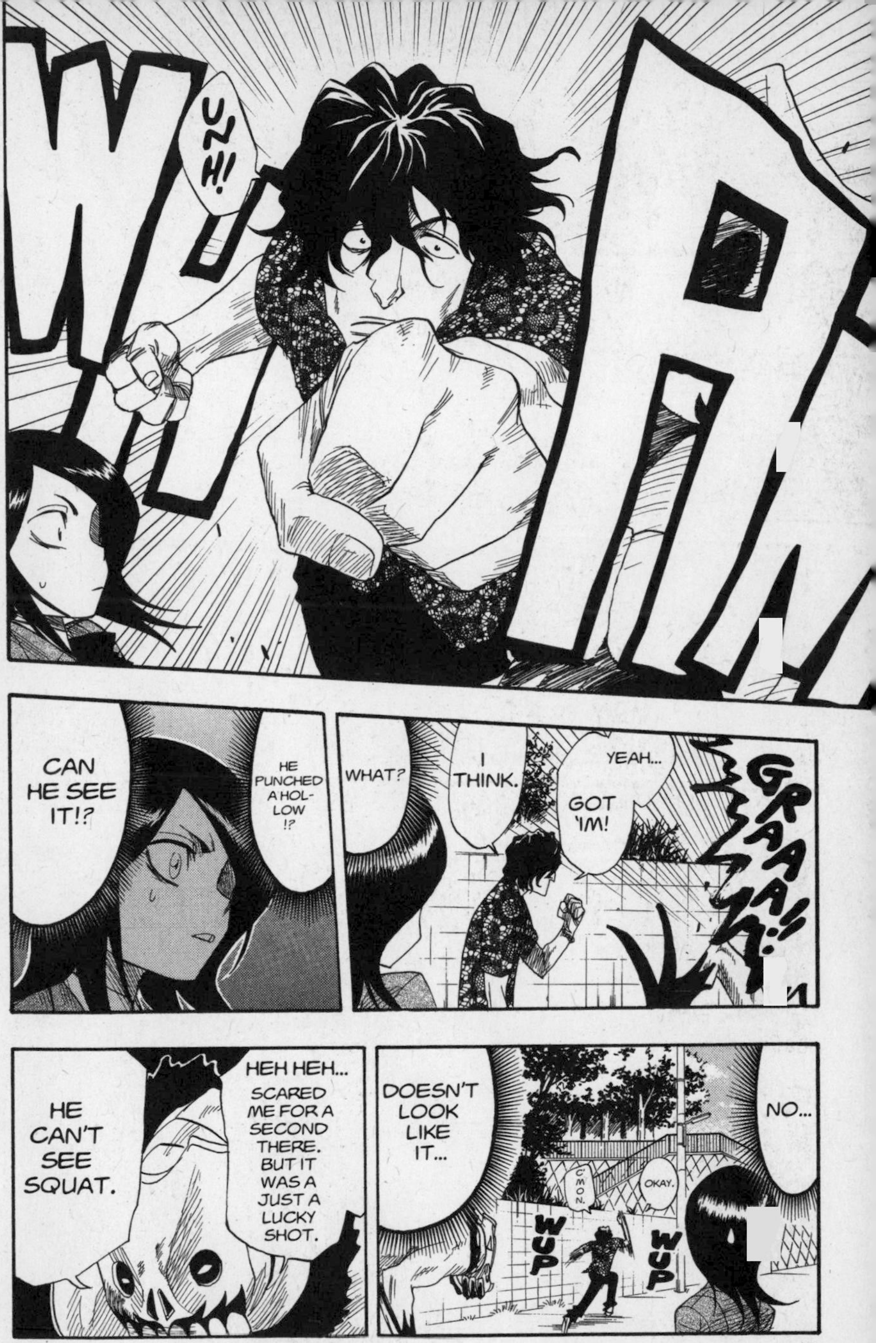
UNH!
YEAH...
GOT 'IM!
GRAAAAH!!
I THINK.
WHAT?
HE PUNCHED A HOL- LOW !?
CAN HE SEE IT!?
NO...
OKAY.
C'MON.
WUP
WUP
DOESN'T LOOK LIKE IT...
HEH HEH... SCARED ME FOR A SECOND THERE. BUT IT WAS A JUST A LUCKY SHOT.
HE CAN'T SEE SQUAT.

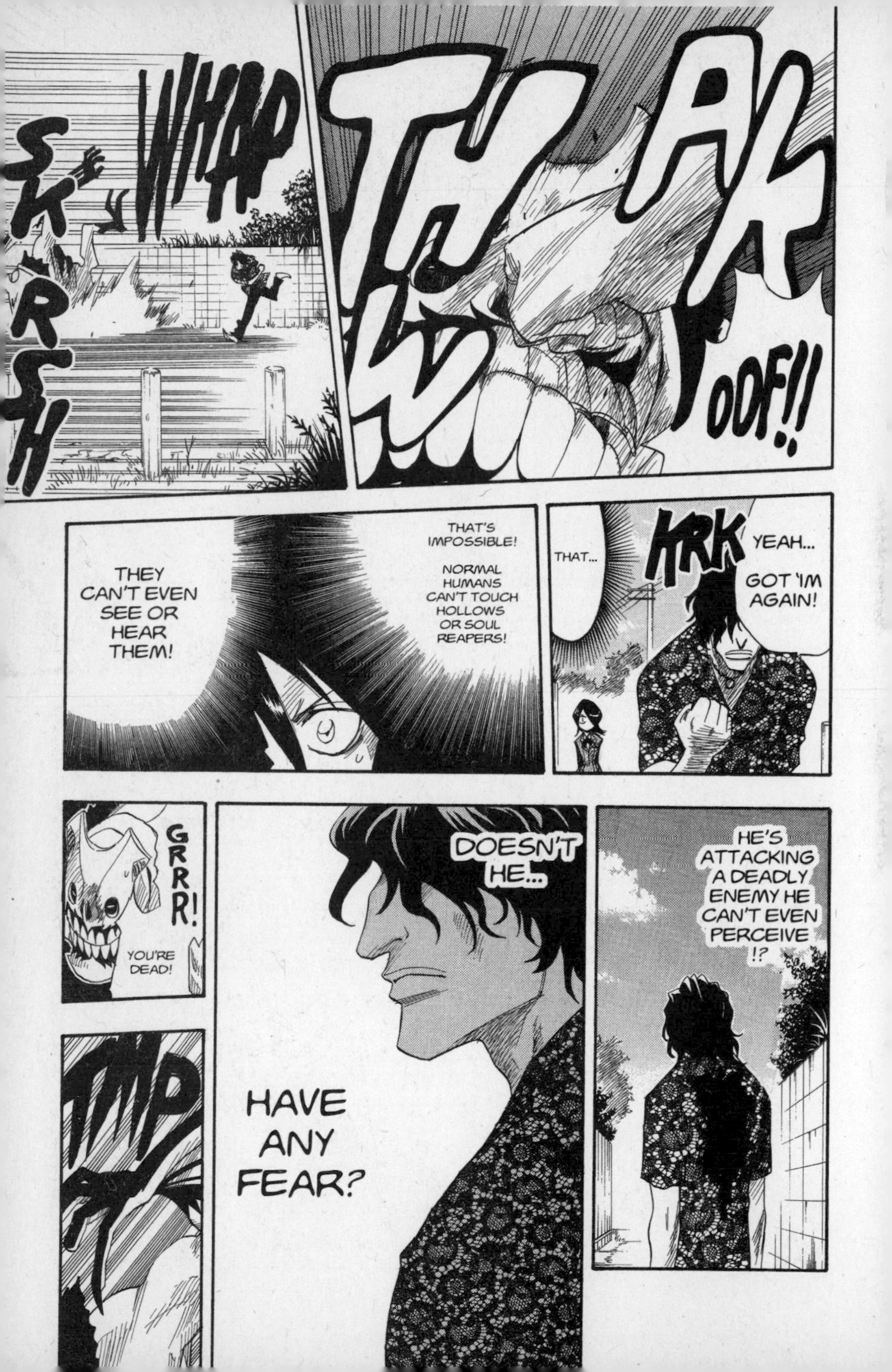
OOF!!
SKRSH
WHAP
THAT...
KRK
YEAH...
GOT 'IM AGAIN!
THAT'S IMPOSSIBLE!
NORMAL HUMANS CAN'T TOUCH HOLLOWS OR SOUL REAPERS!
THEY CAN'T EVEN SEE OR HEAR THEM!
HE'S ATTACKING A DEADLY ENEMY HE CAN'T EVEN PERCEIVE !?
DOESN'T HE...
HAVE ANY FEAR?
GRRR!
YOU'RE DEAD!
THP

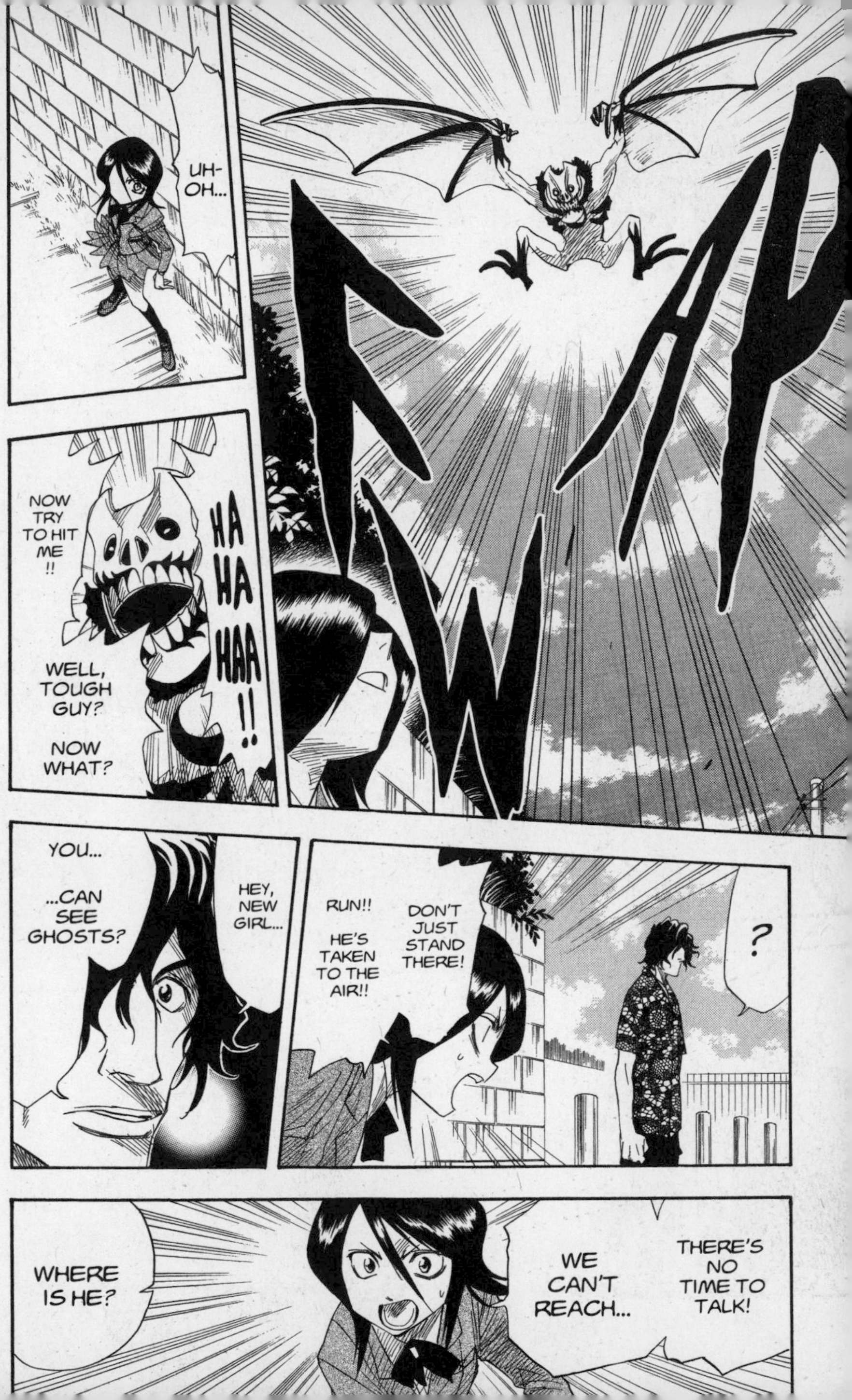
FWAP
UH-OH...
HA HA HAA!!
NOW TRY TO HIT ME!!
WELL, TOUGH GUY?
NOW WHAT?
?
DON'T JUST STAND THERE!
RUN!! HE'S TAKEN TO THE AIR!!
HEY, NEW GIRL...
YOU...
...CAN SEE GHOSTS?
THERE'S NO TIME TO TALK!
WE CAN'T REACH...
WHERE IS HE?

READ THIS WAY

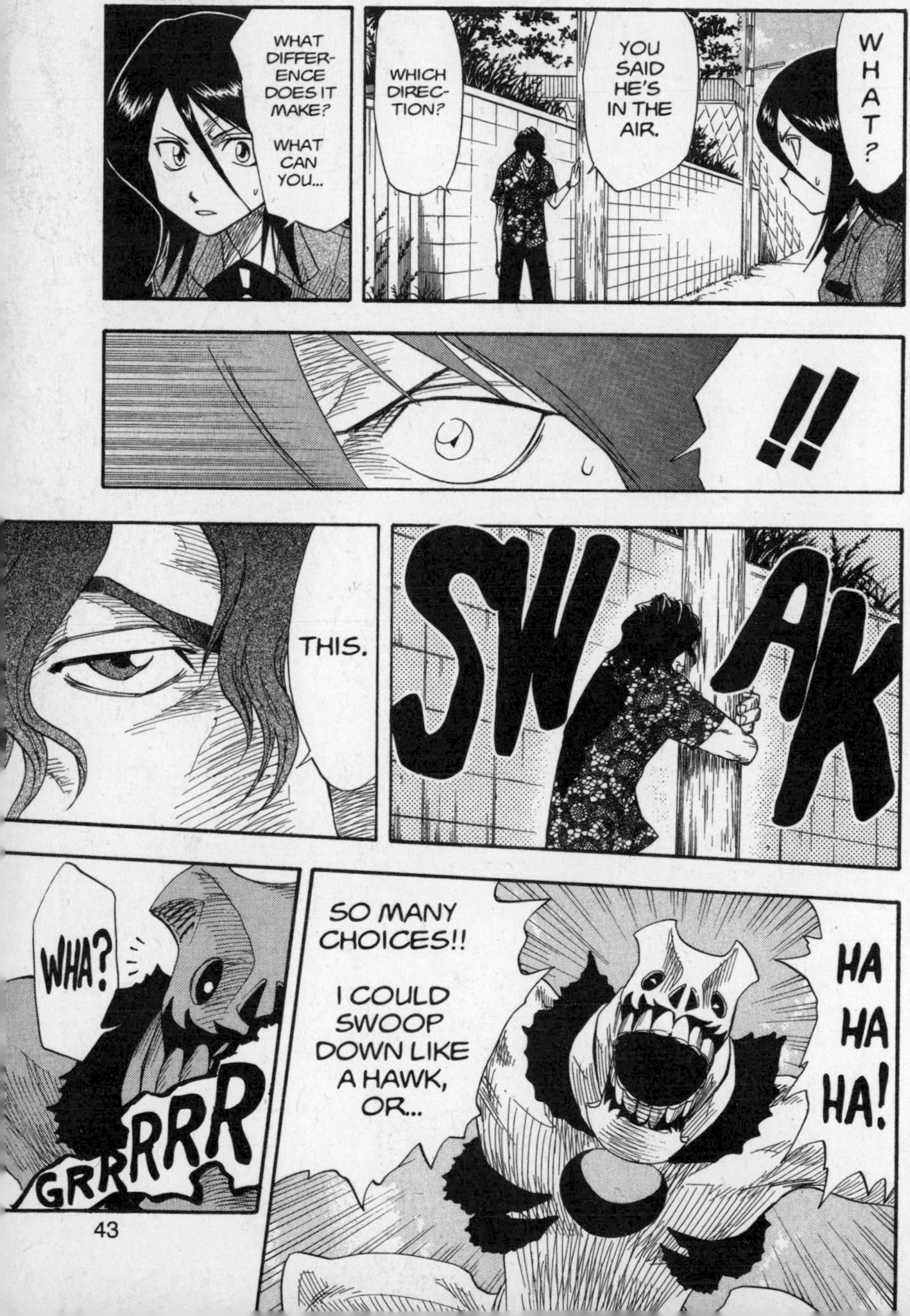

WHAT?
YOU SAID HE'S IN THE AIR.
WHICH DIRECTION?
WHAT DIFFERENCE DOES IT MAKE?
WHAT CAN YOU...
!!
SWAK
THIS.
HA HA HA!
SO MANY CHOICES!!
I COULD SWOOP DOWN LIKE A HAWK, OR...
WHA?
GRRRRRR

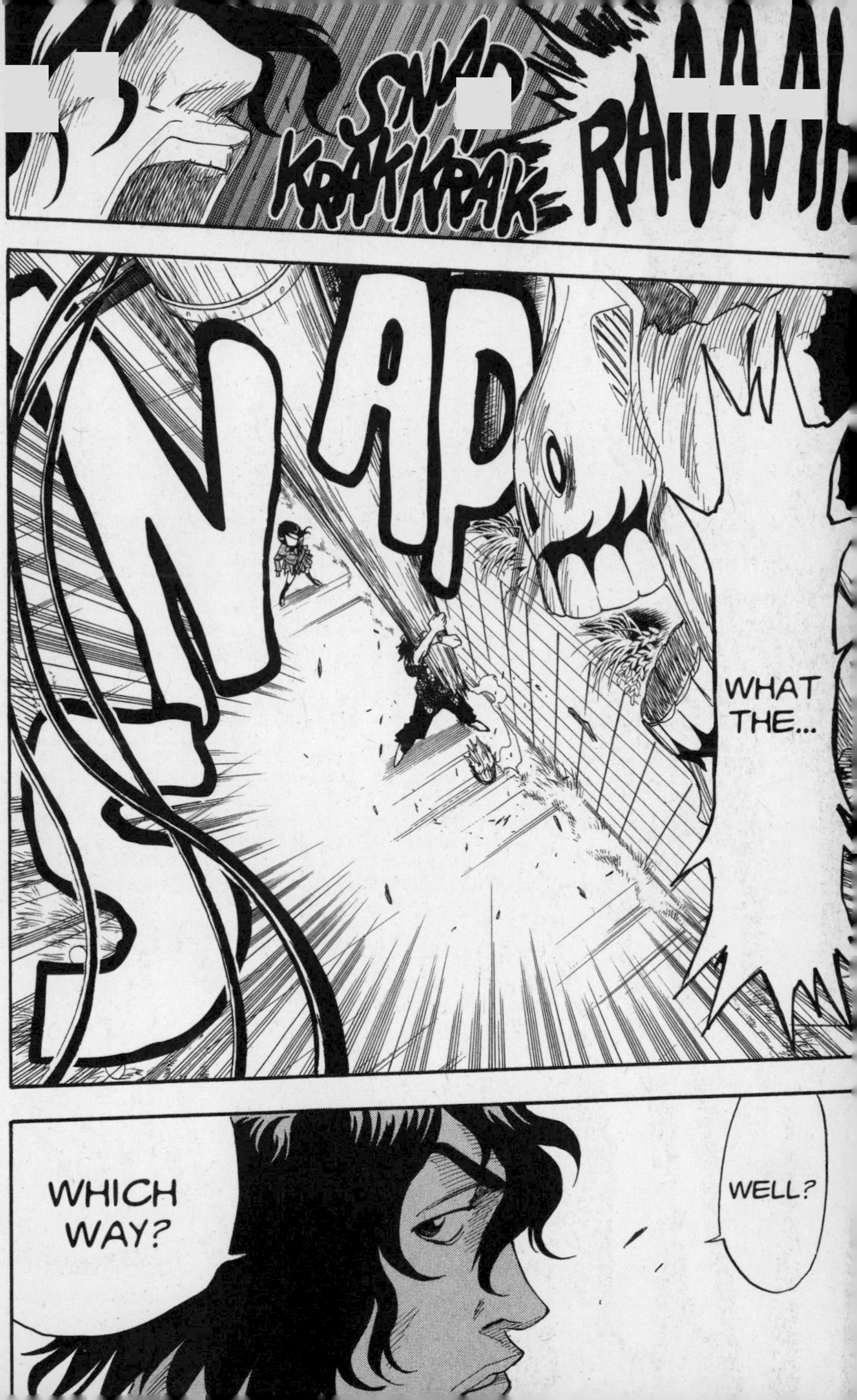
SNAP
KRAKKRAK
SNAP
WHAT THE...
WELL?
WHICH WAY?

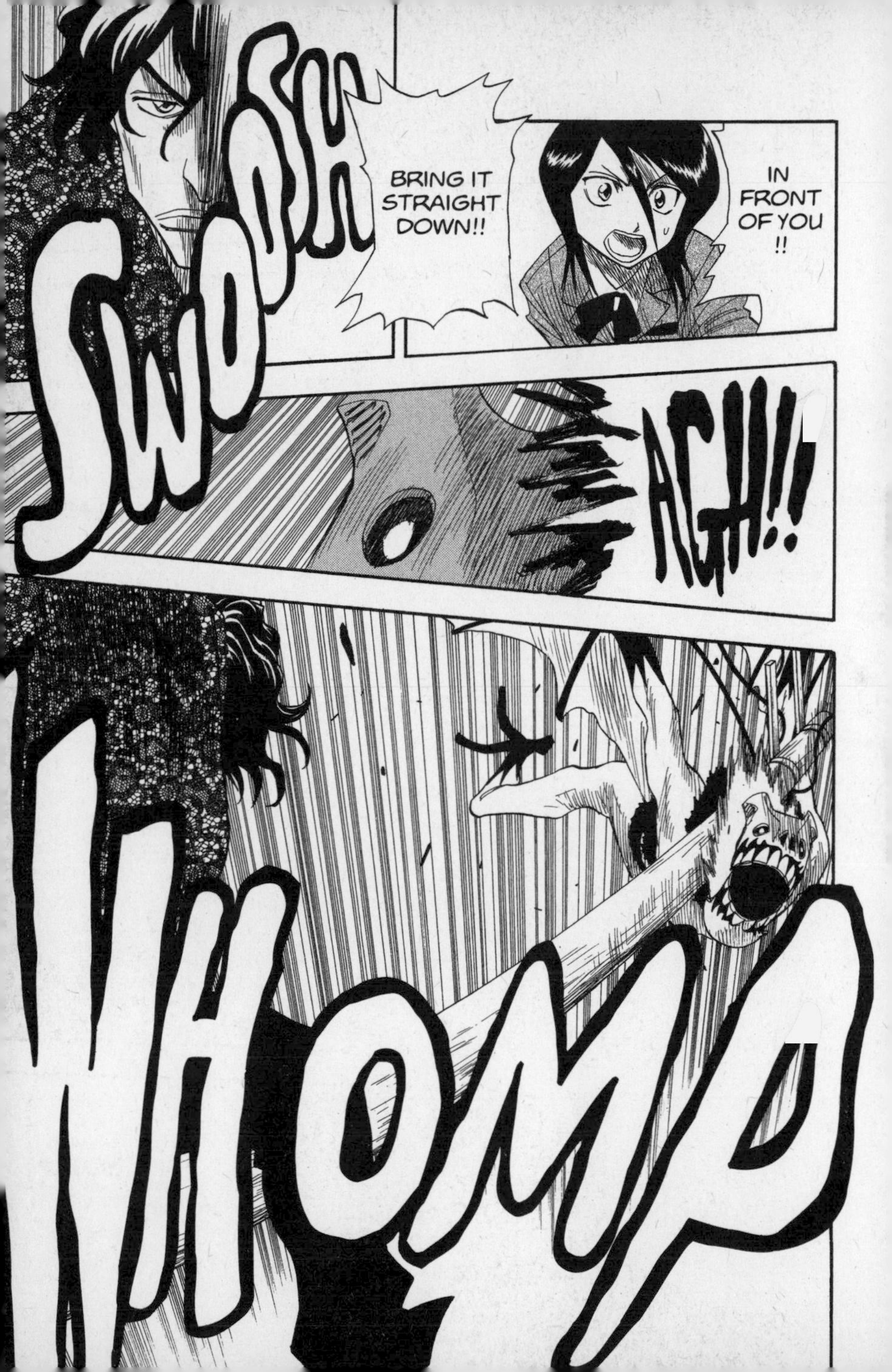
IN FRONT OF YOU !!
BRING IT STRAIGHT DOWN!!
SWOOSH
ACH!!

POWER OUTAGE

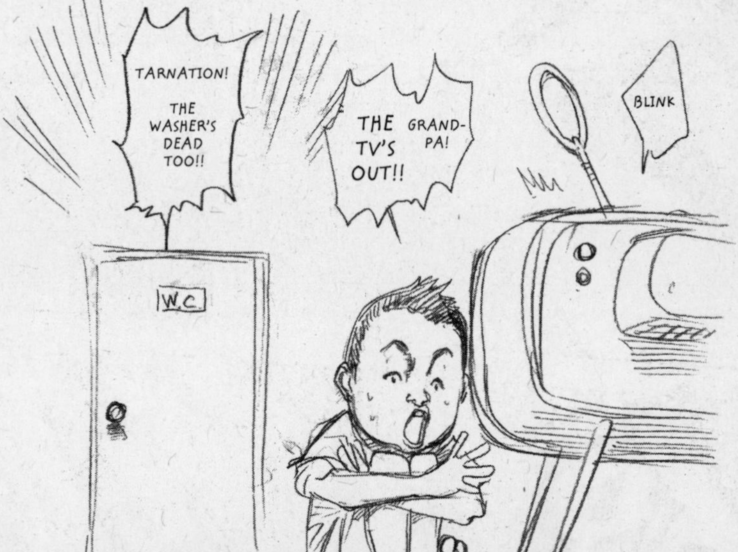
BLINK
GRAND-PA!
THE TV'S OUT!!
TARNATION!
THE WASHER'S DEAD TOO!!
W.C.

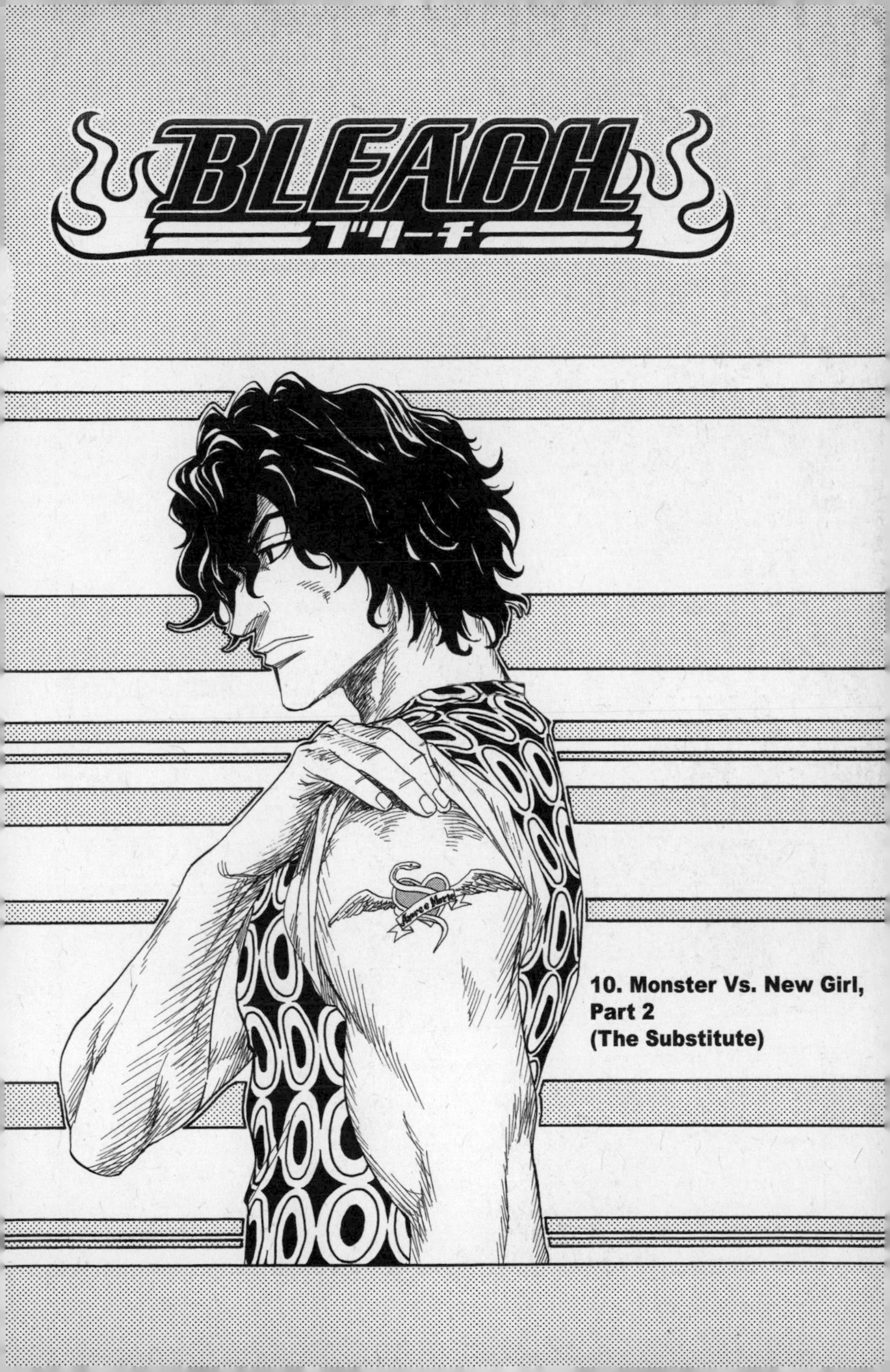
BLEACH
ブリーチ

10. Monster Vs. New Girl, Part 2 (The Substitute)

READ THIS WAY

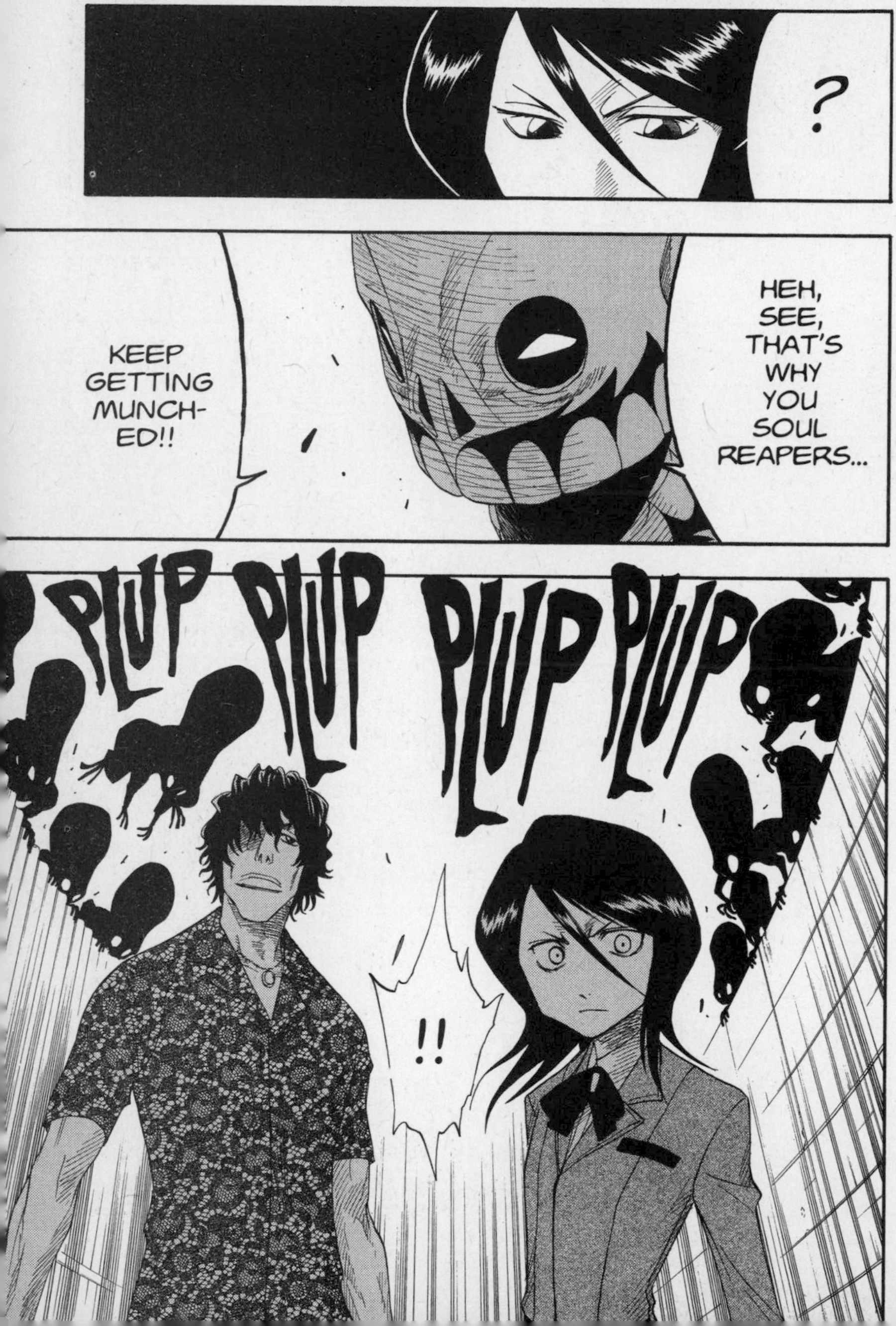
?
HEH, SEE, THAT'S WHY YOU SOUL REAPERS...
KEEP GETTING MUNCH-ED!!
PLUP PLUP PLUP PLUP
!!

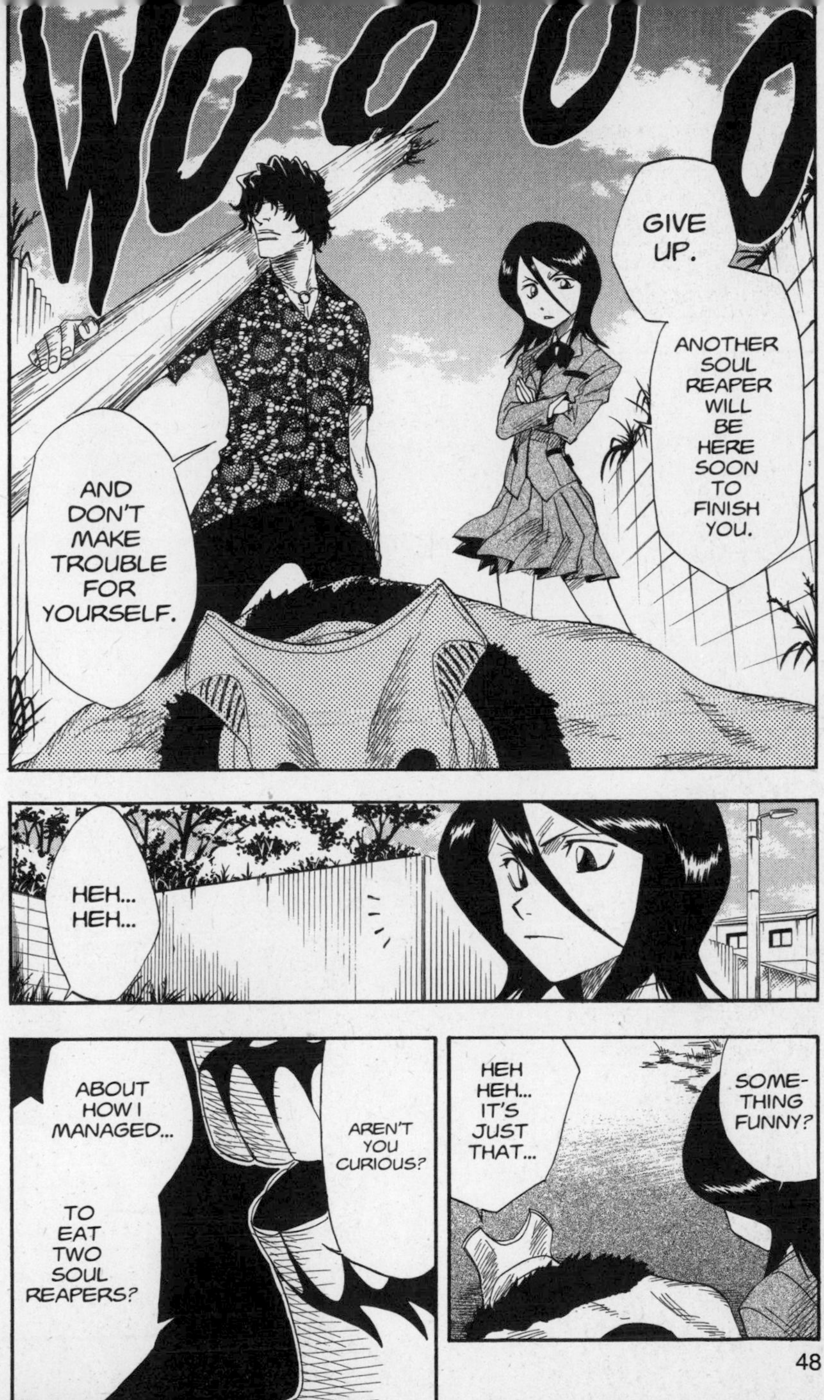
WOOOO
GIVE UP.
ANOTHER SOUL REAPER WILL BE HERE SOON TO FINISH YOU.
AND DON'T MAKE TROUBLE FOR YOURSELF.
HEH... HEH...
SOME-THING FUNNY?
HEH HEH... IT'S JUST THAT...
AREN'T YOU CURIOUS?
ABOUT HOW I MANAGED...
TO EAT TWO SOUL REAPERS?

10. Monster Vs. New Girl, Part 2 (The Substitute)

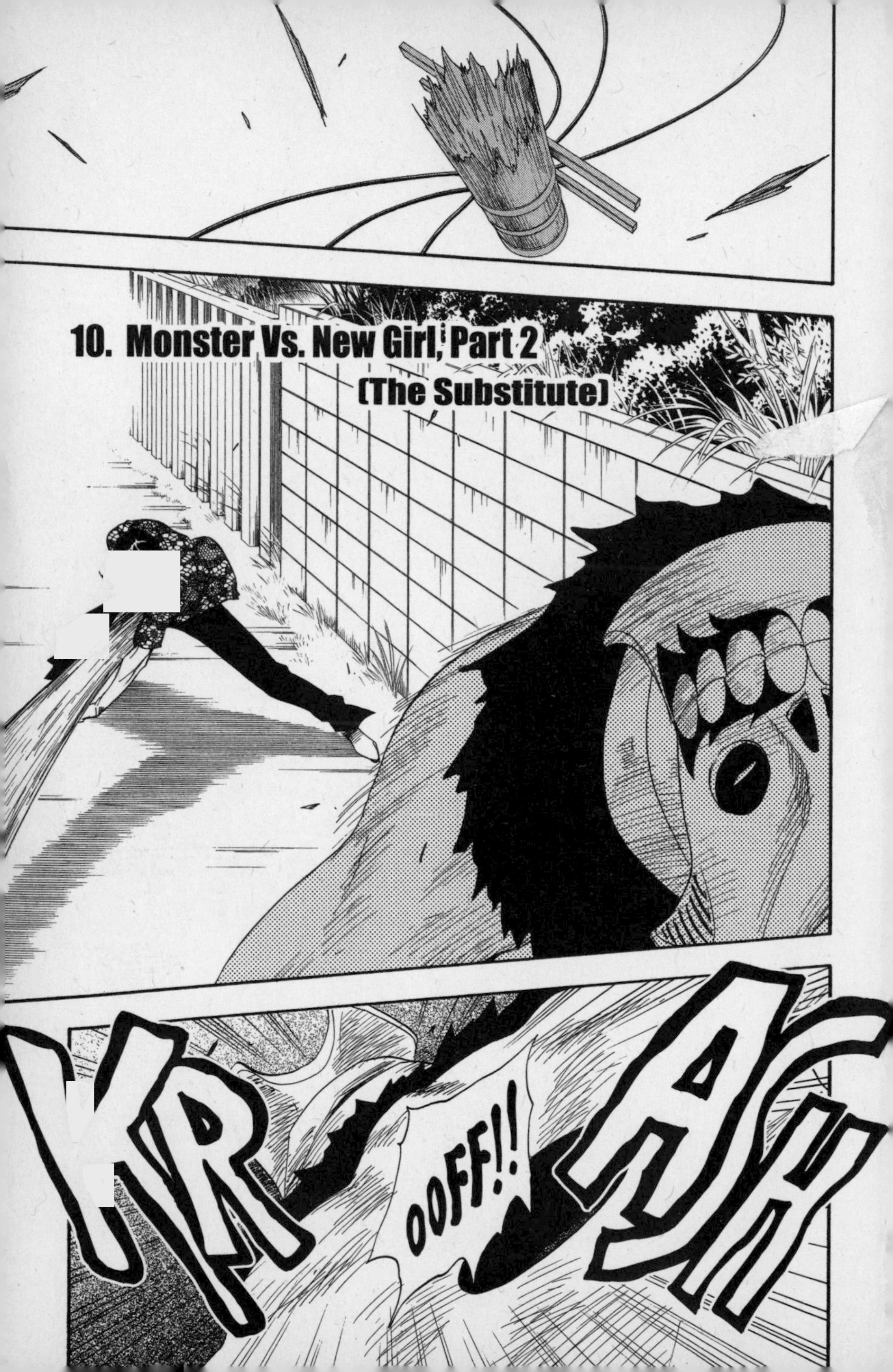
OOFF!!

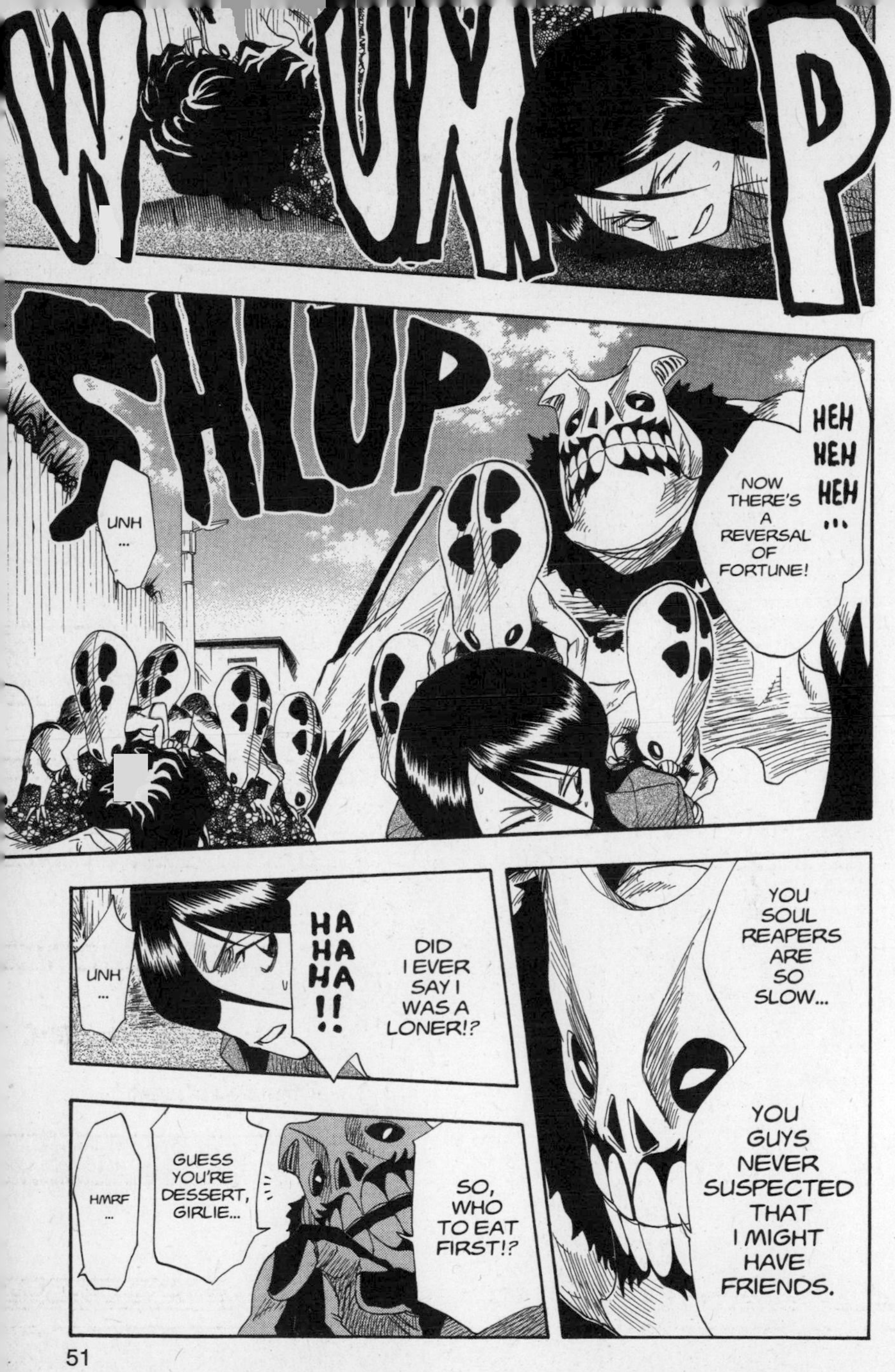
WHUMP
SHLUP
HEH HEH HEH ...
NOW THERE'S A REVERSAL OF FORTUNE!
UNH ...
YOU SOUL REAPERS ARE SO SLOW...
YOU GUYS NEVER SUSPECTED THAT I MIGHT HAVE FRIENDS.
HA HA HA!!
DID I EVER SAY I WAS A LONER!?
UNH ...
SO, WHO TO EAT FIRST!?
GUESS YOU'RE DESSERT, GIRLIE...
HMRF ...

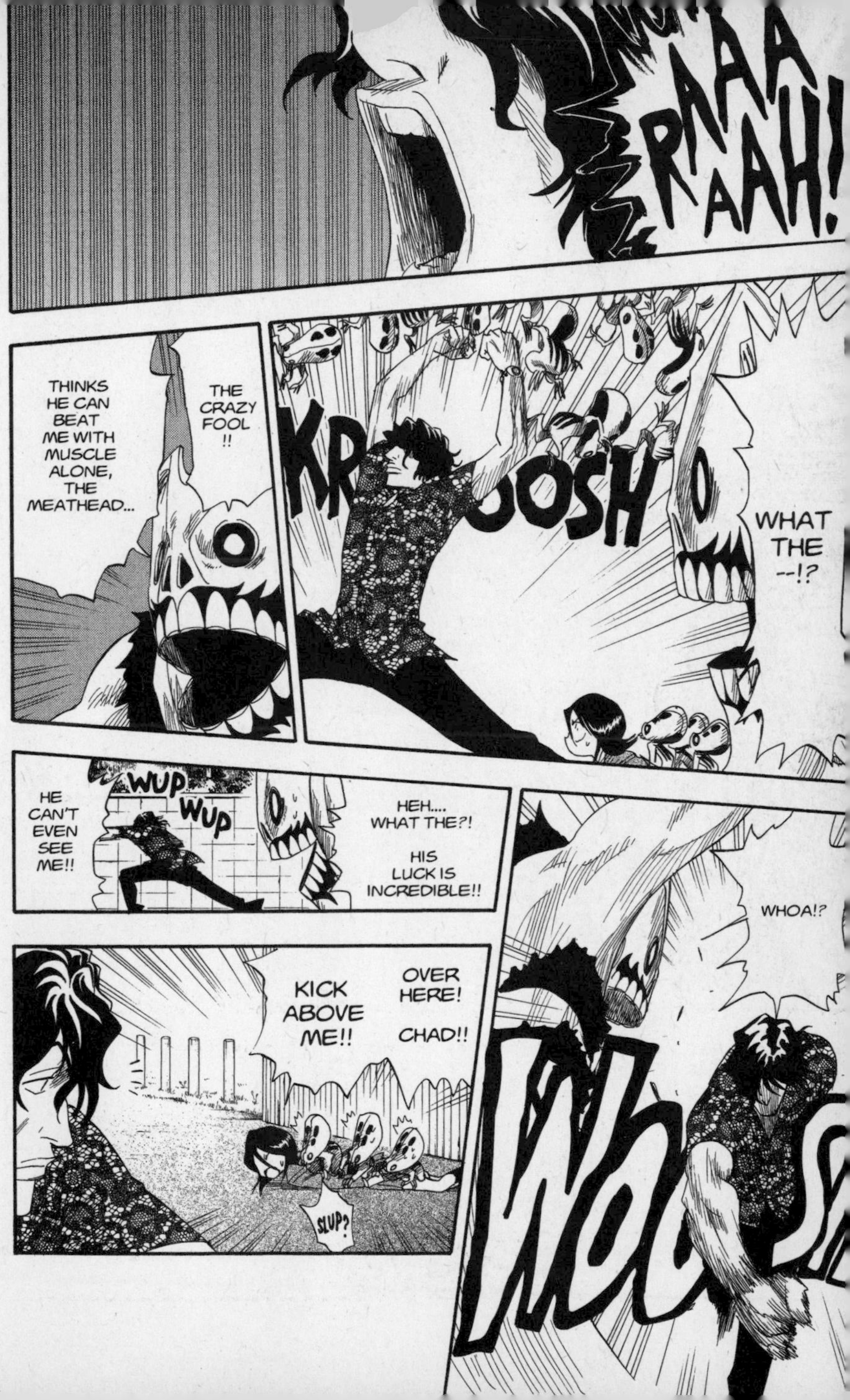
RAAAAAH!
KROOSH
WHAT THE --!?
THE CRAZY FOOL !!
THINKS HE CAN BEAT ME WITH MUSCLE ALONE, THE MEATHEAD...
WHOA!?
HEH.... WHAT THE?!
HIS LUCK IS INCREDIBLE!!
WUP WUP
HE CAN'T EVEN SEE ME!!
OVER HERE!
CHAD!!
KICK ABOVE ME!!
SLUP?

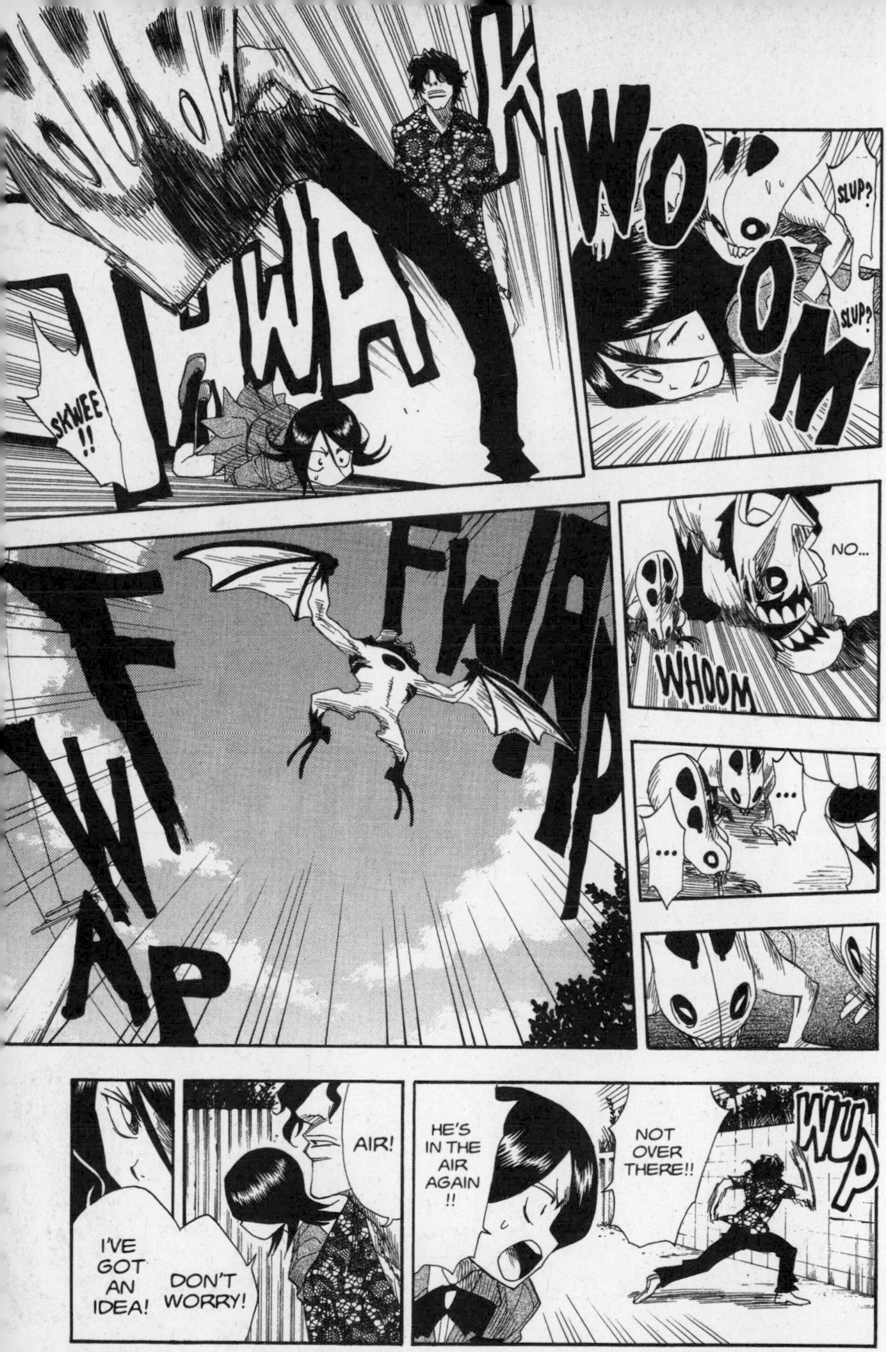
WOOOM
SLUP?
SLUP?
SKWEE !!
NO...
WHOOM
...
...
FWAP
WUP
NOT OVER THERE!!
HE'S IN THE AIR AGAIN !!
AIR!
DON'T WORRY!
I'VE GOT AN IDEA!

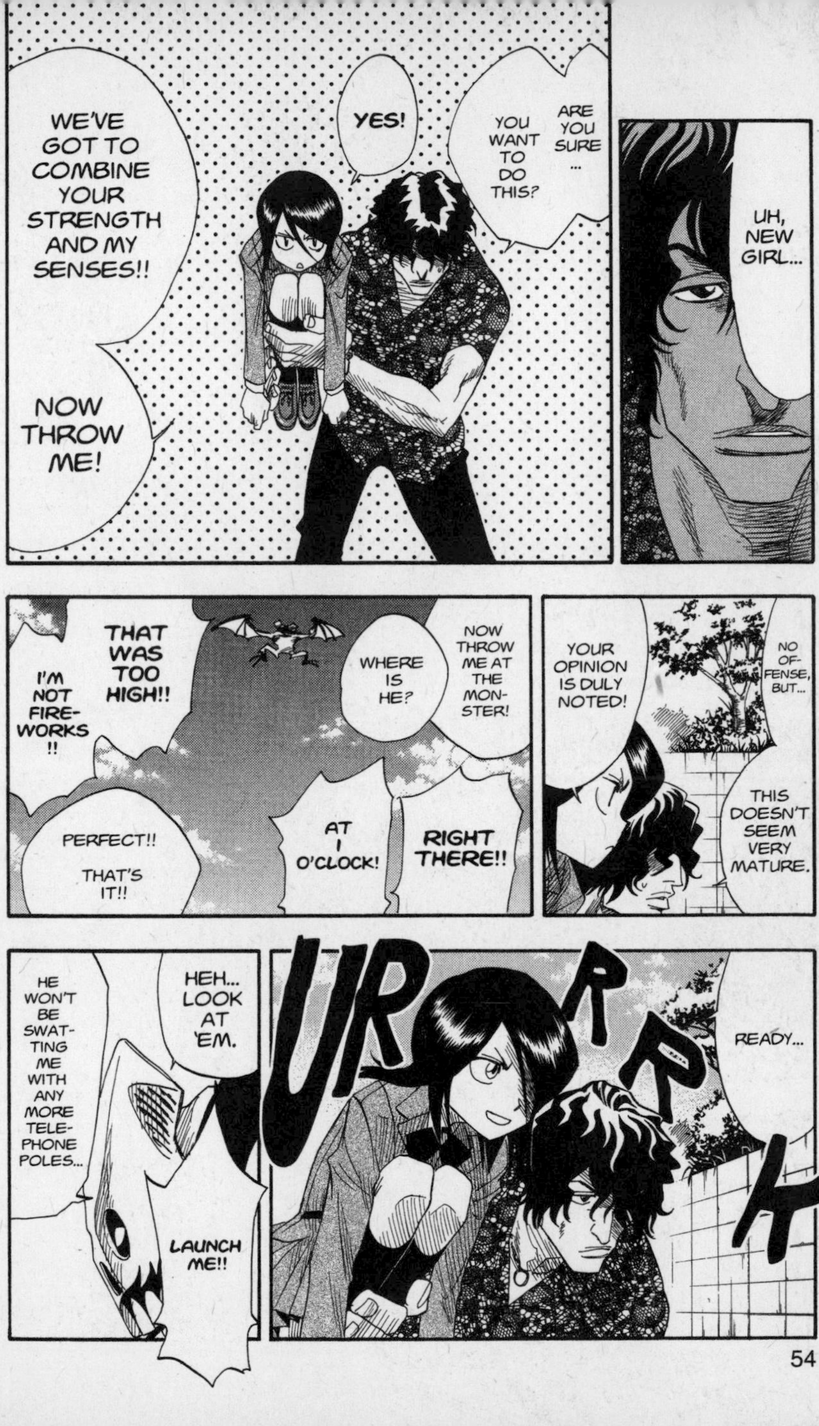
UH, NEW GIRL...
ARE YOU SURE...
YOU WANT TO DO THIS?
YES!
WE'VE GOT TO COMBINE YOUR STRENGTH AND MY SENSES!!
NOW THROW ME!
NO OFFENSE, BUT...
THIS DOESN'T SEEM VERY MATURE.
YOUR OPINION IS DULY NOTED!
NOW THROW ME AT THE MONSTER!
WHERE IS HE?
RIGHT THERE!!
AT 1 O'CLOCK!
THAT WAS TOO HIGH!!
I'M NOT FIREWORKS!!
PERFECT!!
THAT'S IT!!
READY...
URRRK
HEH... LOOK AT 'EM.
HE WON'T BE SWATTING ME WITH ANY MORE TELEPHONE POLES...
LAUNCH ME!!

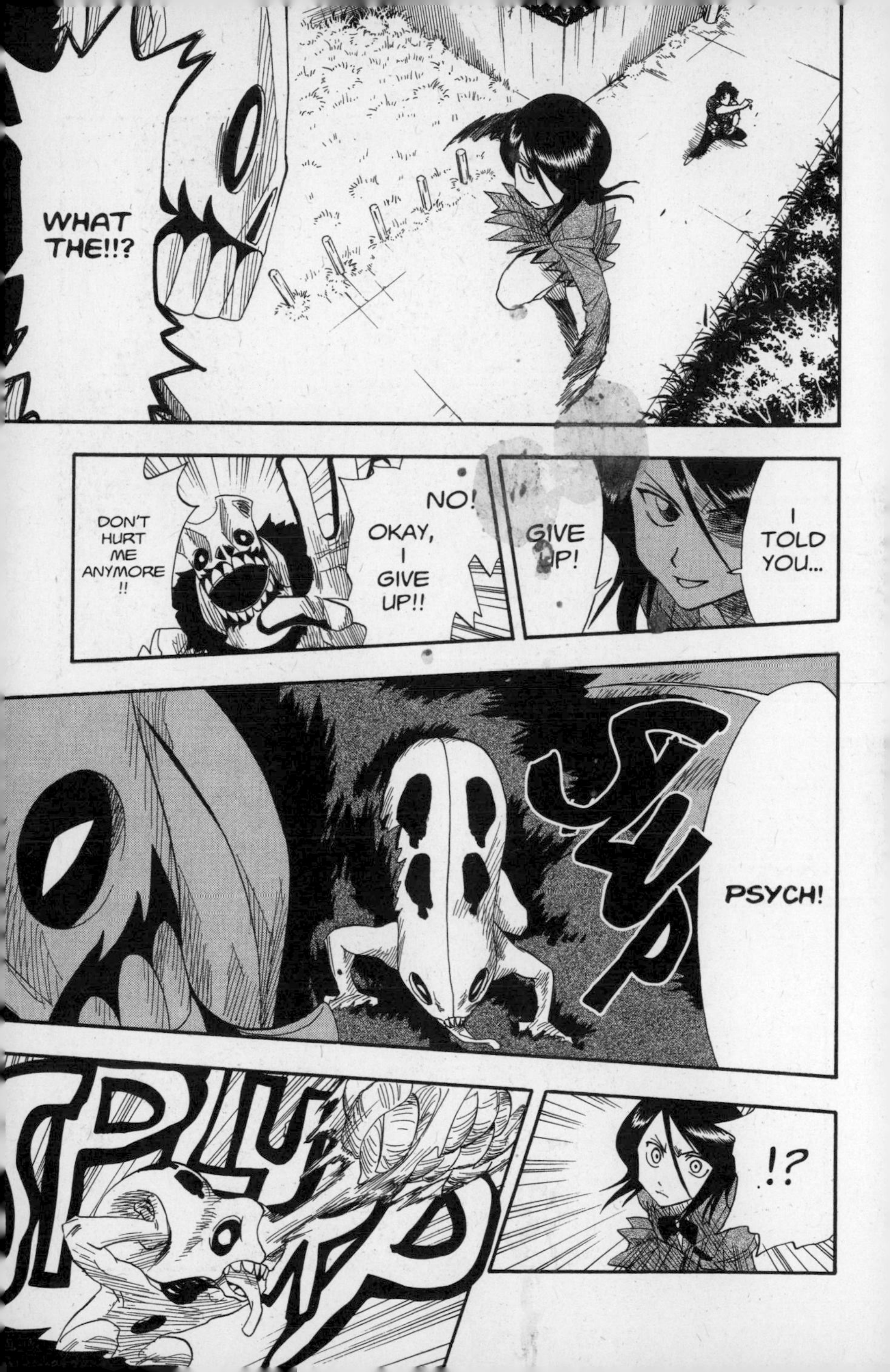
WHAT THE!!?
I TOLD YOU...
GIVE UP!
NO!
OKAY, I GIVE UP!!
DON'T HURT ME ANYMORE !!
PSYCH!
!?

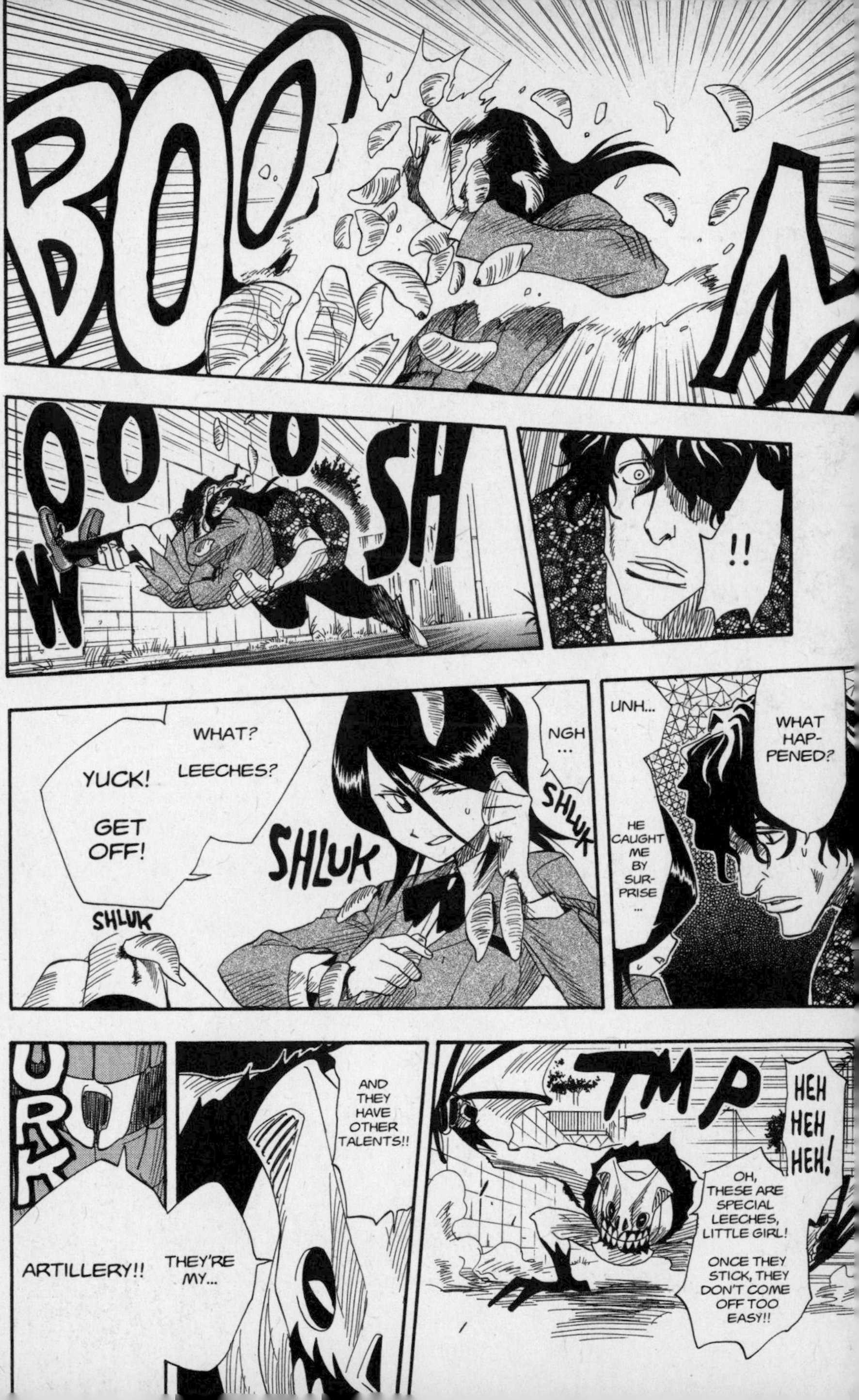
BOOOM
!!
WOOOSH
WHAT HAPPENED?
UNH...
HE CAUGHT ME BY SURPRISE...
NGH...
SHLUK
WHAT? LEECHES?
YUCK! GET OFF!
SHLUK
SHLUK
TMP
HEH HEH HEH!
OH, THESE ARE SPECIAL LEECHES, LITTLE GIRL!
ONCE THEY STICK, THEY DON'T COME OFF TOO EASY!!
AND THEY HAVE OTHER TALENTS!!
THEY'RE MY...
URK
ARTILLERY!!

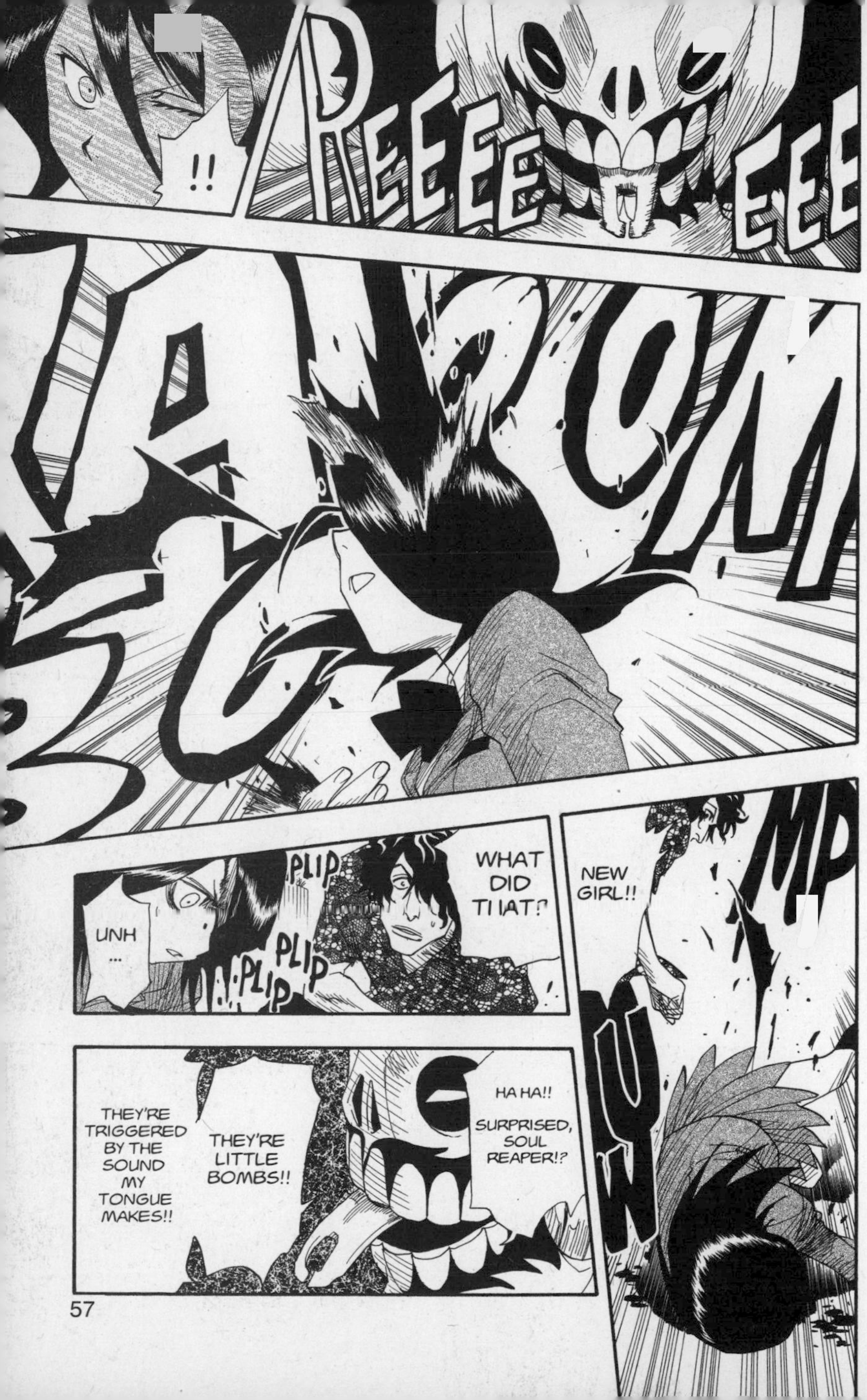
REEEE
EEE
!!
NEW GIRL!!
WHAT DID THAT!?
PLIP
PLIP
PLIP
UNH ...
HA HA!!
SURPRISED, SOUL REAPER!?
THEY'RE LITTLE BOMBS!!
THEY'RE TRIGGERED BY THE SOUND MY TONGUE MAKES!!

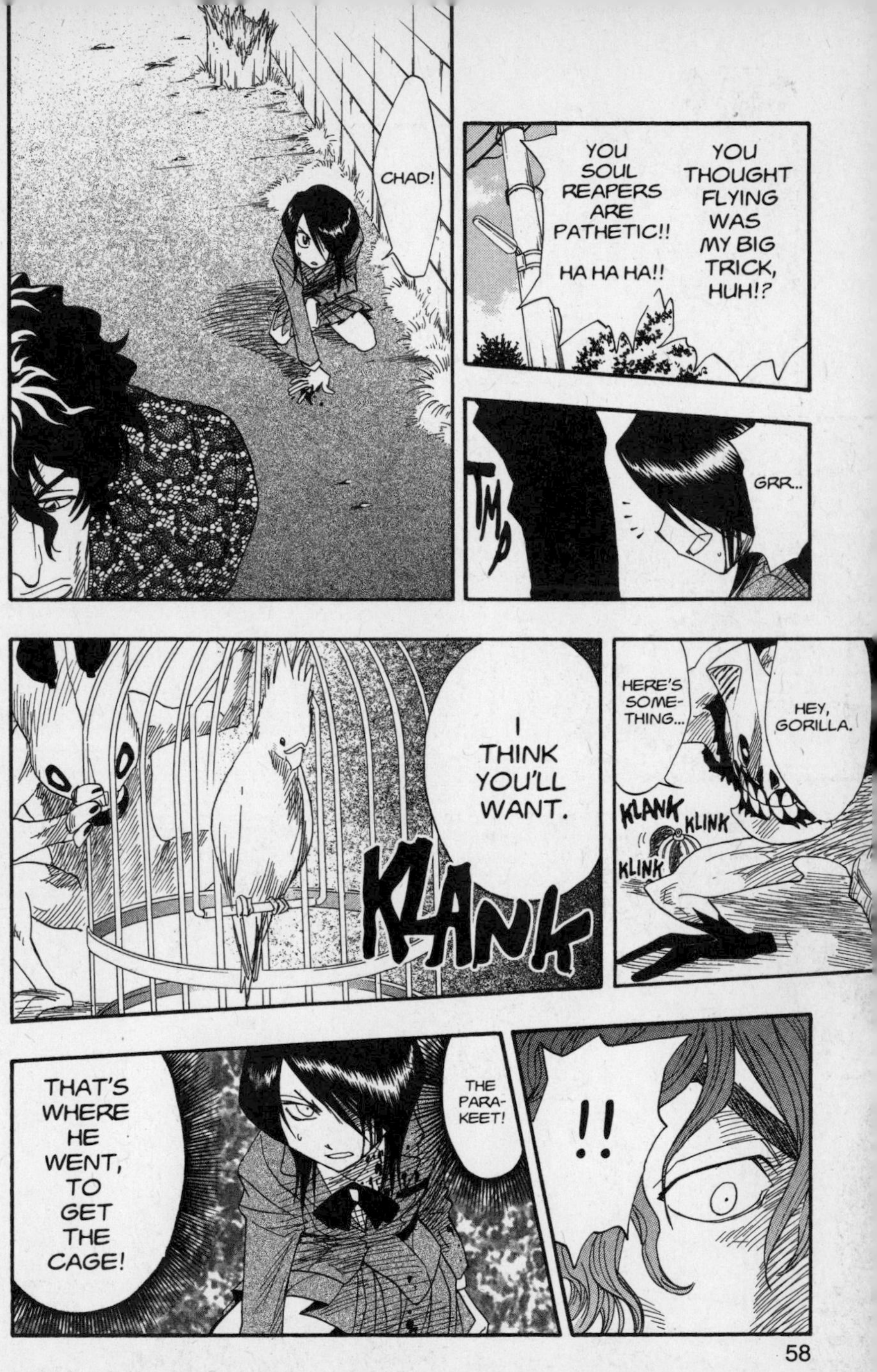
YOU THOUGHT FLYING WAS MY BIG TRICK, HUH!?
YOU SOUL REAPERS ARE PATHETIC!!
HA HA HA!!
GRR...
TMP
CHAD!
HEY, GORILLA.
HERE'S SOME-THING...
KLANK
KLINK
KLINK
I THINK YOU'LL WANT.
KLANK
!!
THE PARA-KEET!
THAT'S WHERE HE WENT, TO GET THE CAGE!

READ THIS WAY

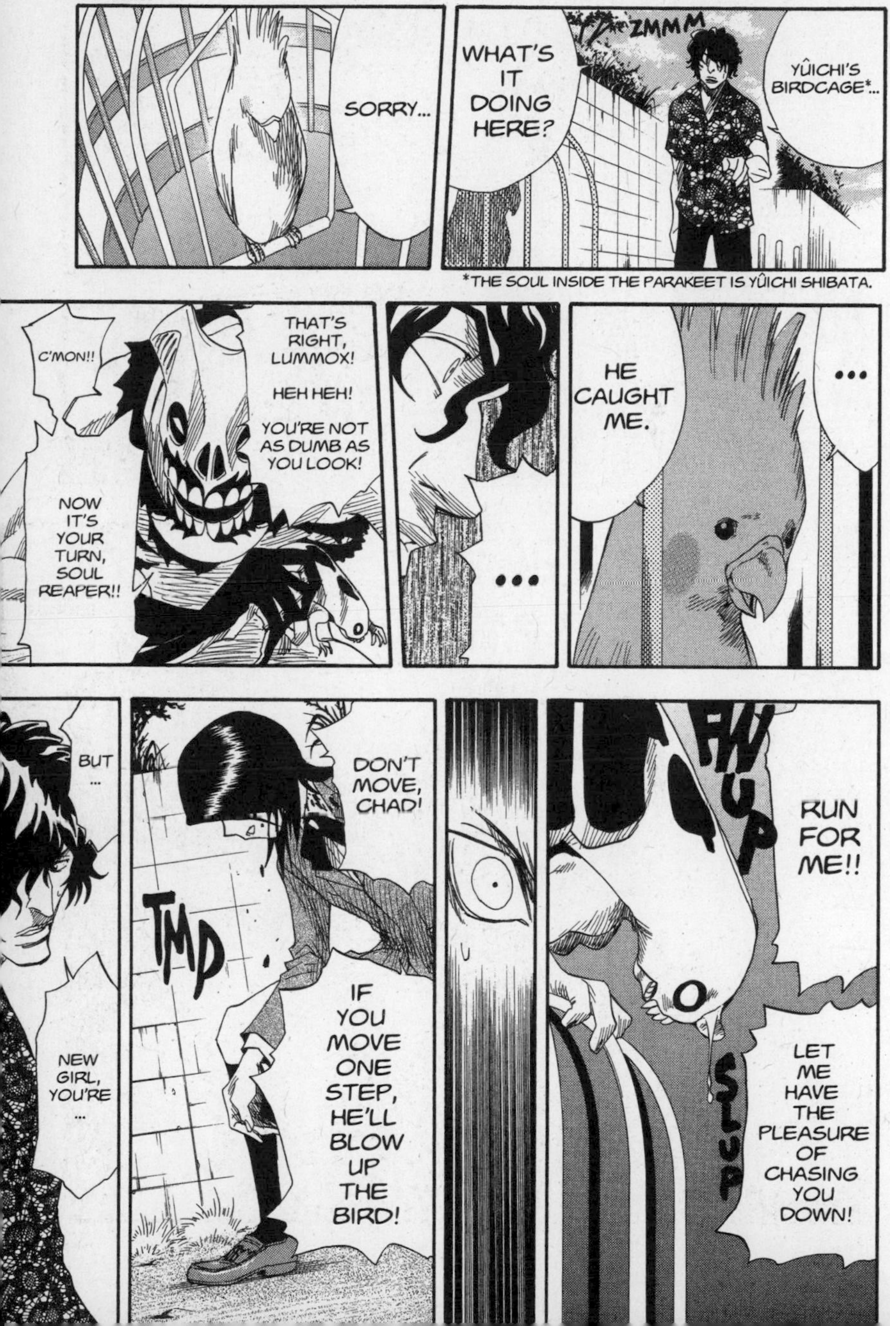
YÛICHI'S BIRDCAGE*...
ZMMM
WHAT'S IT DOING HERE?
SORRY...
*THE SOUL INSIDE THE PARAKEET IS YÛICHI SHIBATA.
...
HE CAUGHT ME.
...
THAT'S RIGHT, LUMMOX!
HEH HEH!
YOU'RE NOT AS DUMB AS YOU LOOK!
C'MON!!
NOW IT'S YOUR TURN, SOUL REAPER!!
RUN FOR ME!!
SLUP
LET ME HAVE THE PLEASURE OF CHASING YOU DOWN!
DON'T MOVE, CHAD!
TMP
IF YOU MOVE ONE STEP, HE'LL BLOW UP THE BIRD!
BUT ...
NEW GIRL, YOU'RE ...

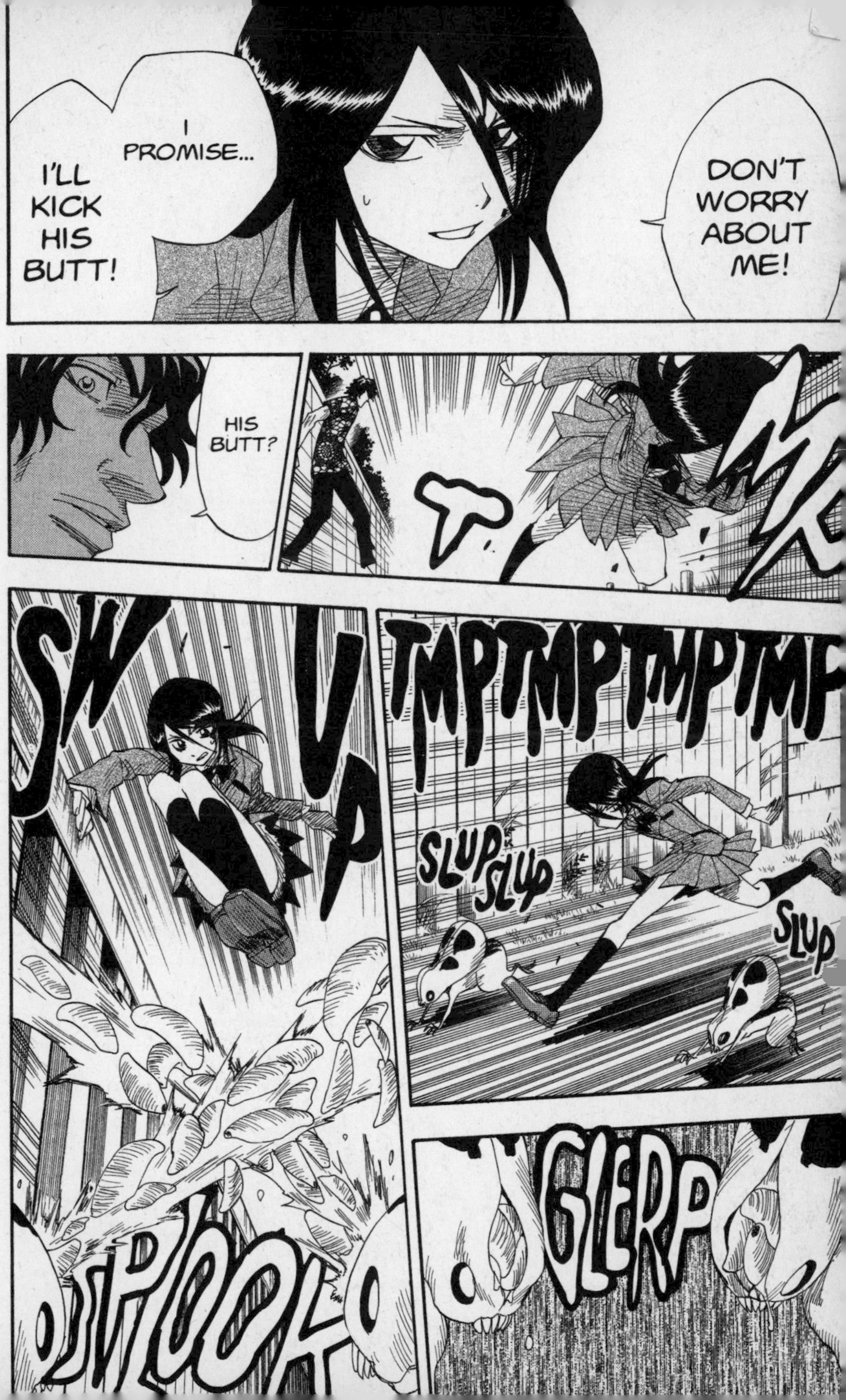
DON'T WORRY ABOUT ME!
I PROMISE...
I'LL KICK HIS BUTT!
HIS BUTT?
TMPTMPTMPTMP
SLUP SLUP
SLUP
GLERP
SWUP

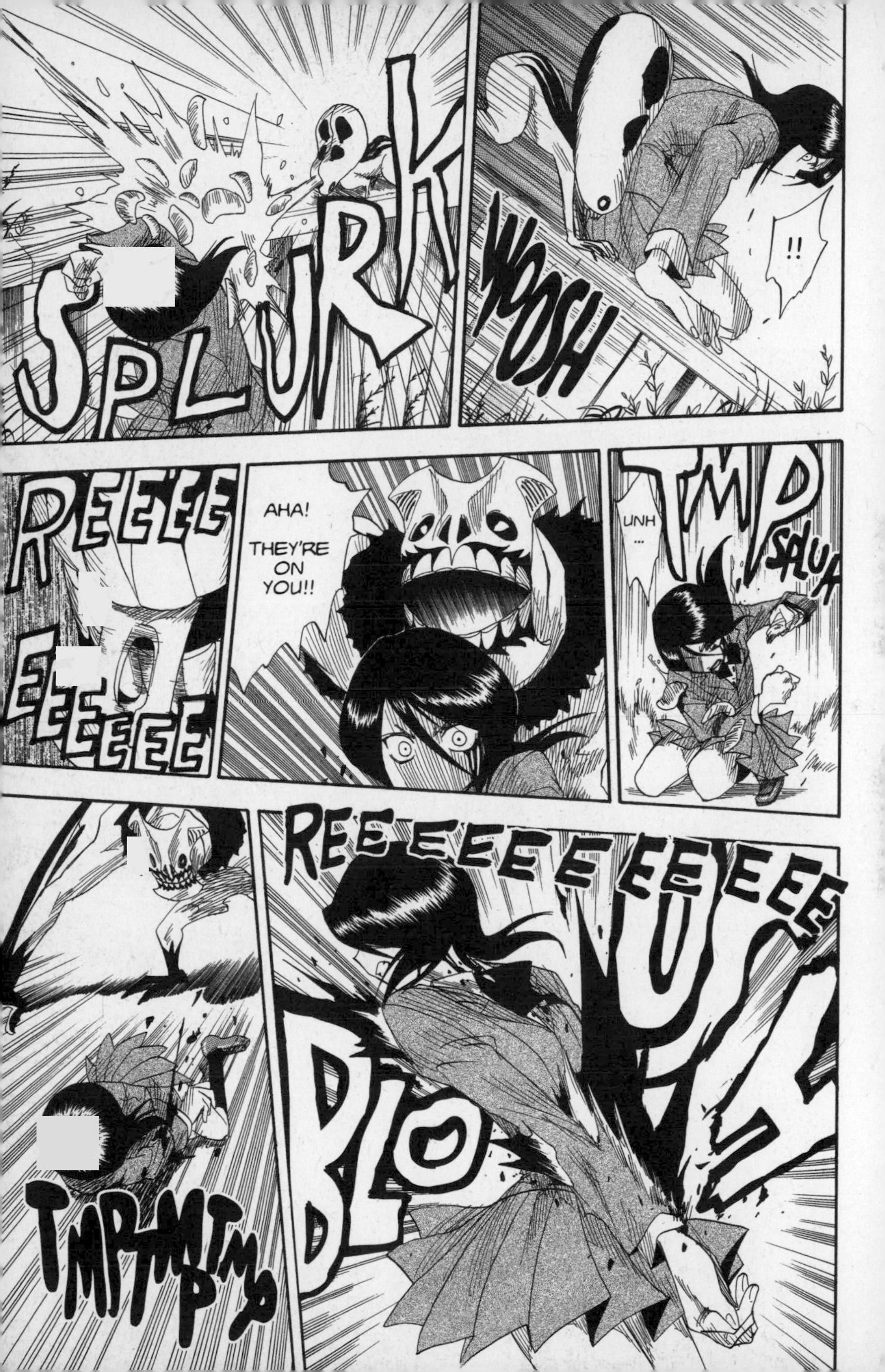
!!
WOOSH
SPLURK
TMP
UNH ...
AHA!
THEY'RE ON YOU!!

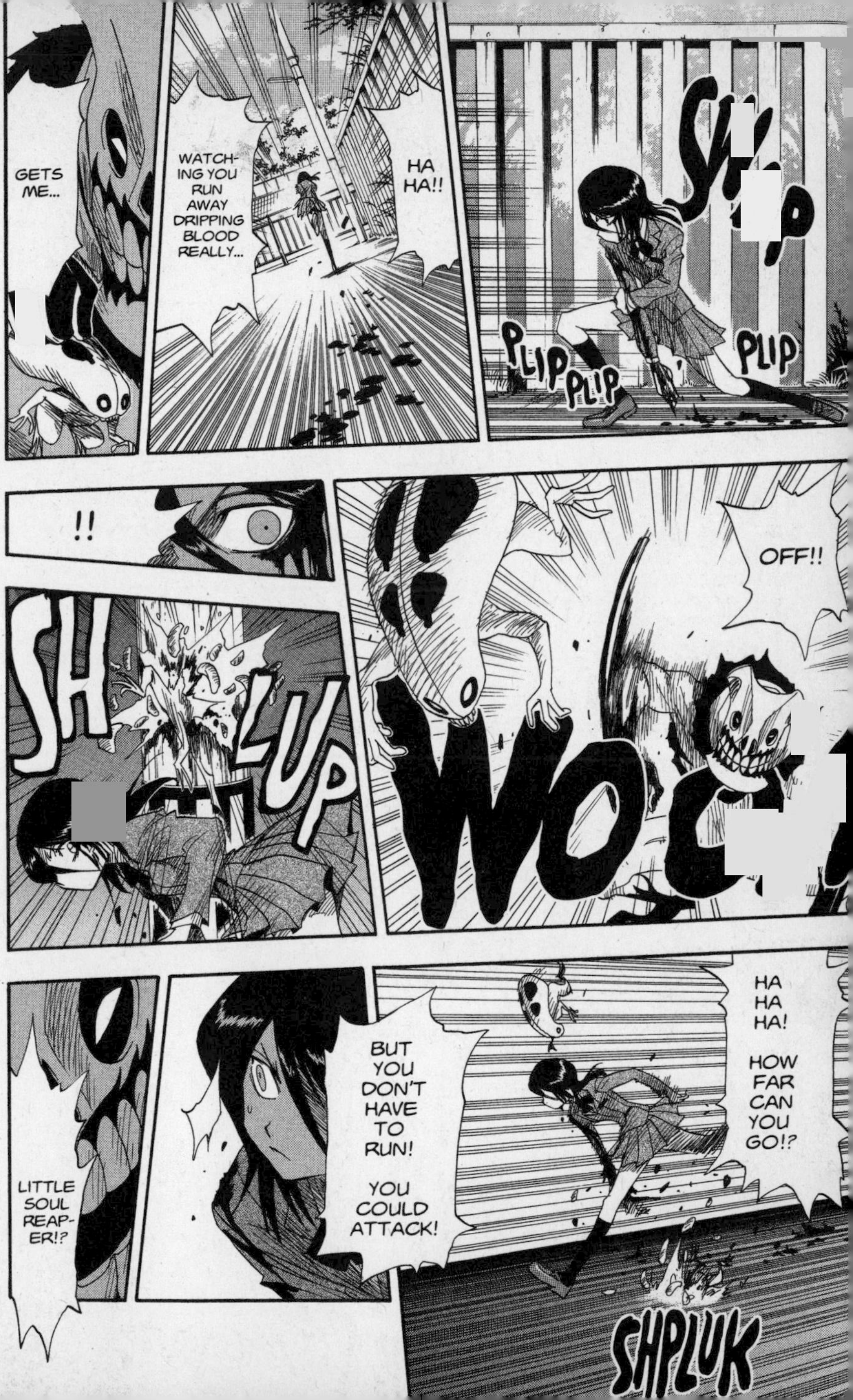
PLIP
PLIP
PLIP
HA HA!!
WATCHING YOU RUN AWAY DRIPPING BLOOD REALLY...
GETS ME...
OFF!!
!!
SHLUP
HA HA HA!
HOW FAR CAN YOU GO!?
SHPLUK
BUT YOU DON'T HAVE TO RUN!
YOU COULD ATTACK!
LITTLE SOUL REAPER!?

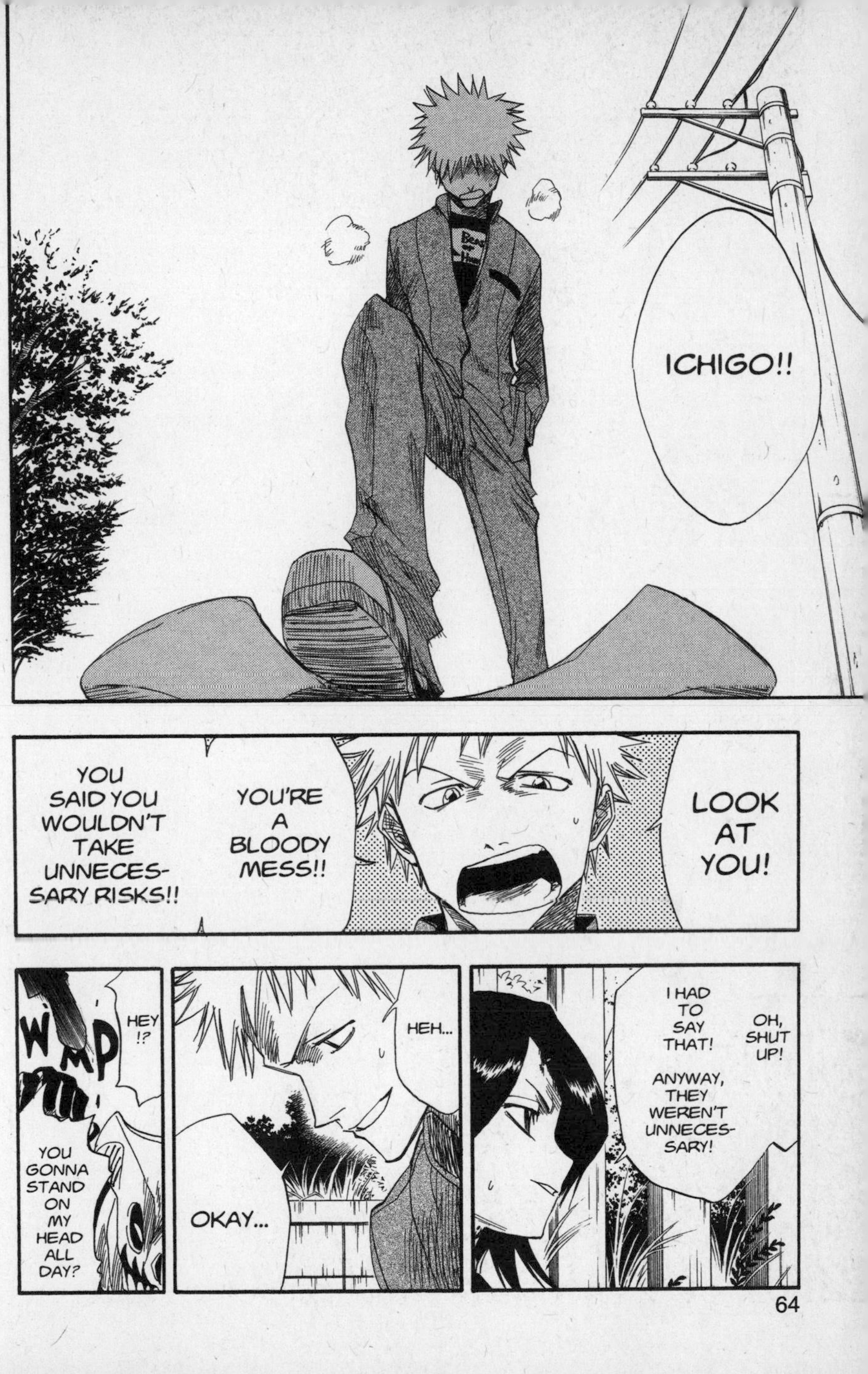
ICHIGO!!
LOOK AT YOU!
YOU'RE A BLOODY MESS!!
YOU SAID YOU WOULDN'T TAKE UNNECES-SARY RISKS!!
OH, SHUT UP!
I HAD TO SAY THAT!
ANYWAY, THEY WEREN'T UNNECES-SARY!
HEH...
OKAY...
HEY !?
WMP
YOU GONNA STAND ON MY HEAD ALL DAY?

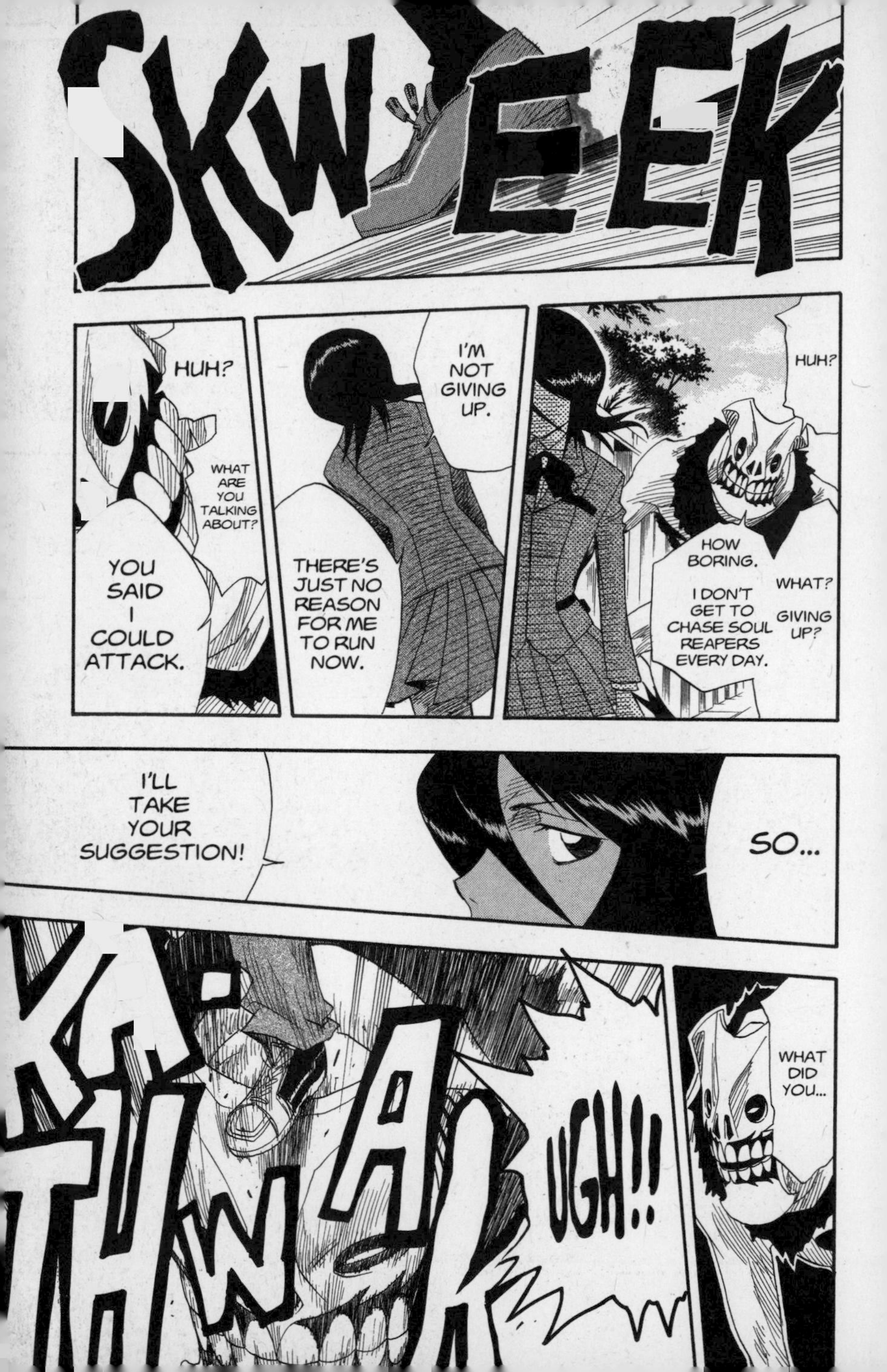
SKW EEK
HUH?
HOW BORING.
I DON'T GET TO CHASE SOUL REAPERS EVERY DAY.
WHAT?
GIVING UP?
I'M NOT GIVING UP.
THERE'S JUST NO REASON FOR ME TO RUN NOW.
HUH?
WHAT ARE YOU TALKING ABOUT?
YOU SAID I COULD ATTACK.
SO...
I'LL TAKE YOUR SUGGESTION!
WHAT DID YOU...
THWA
UGH!!

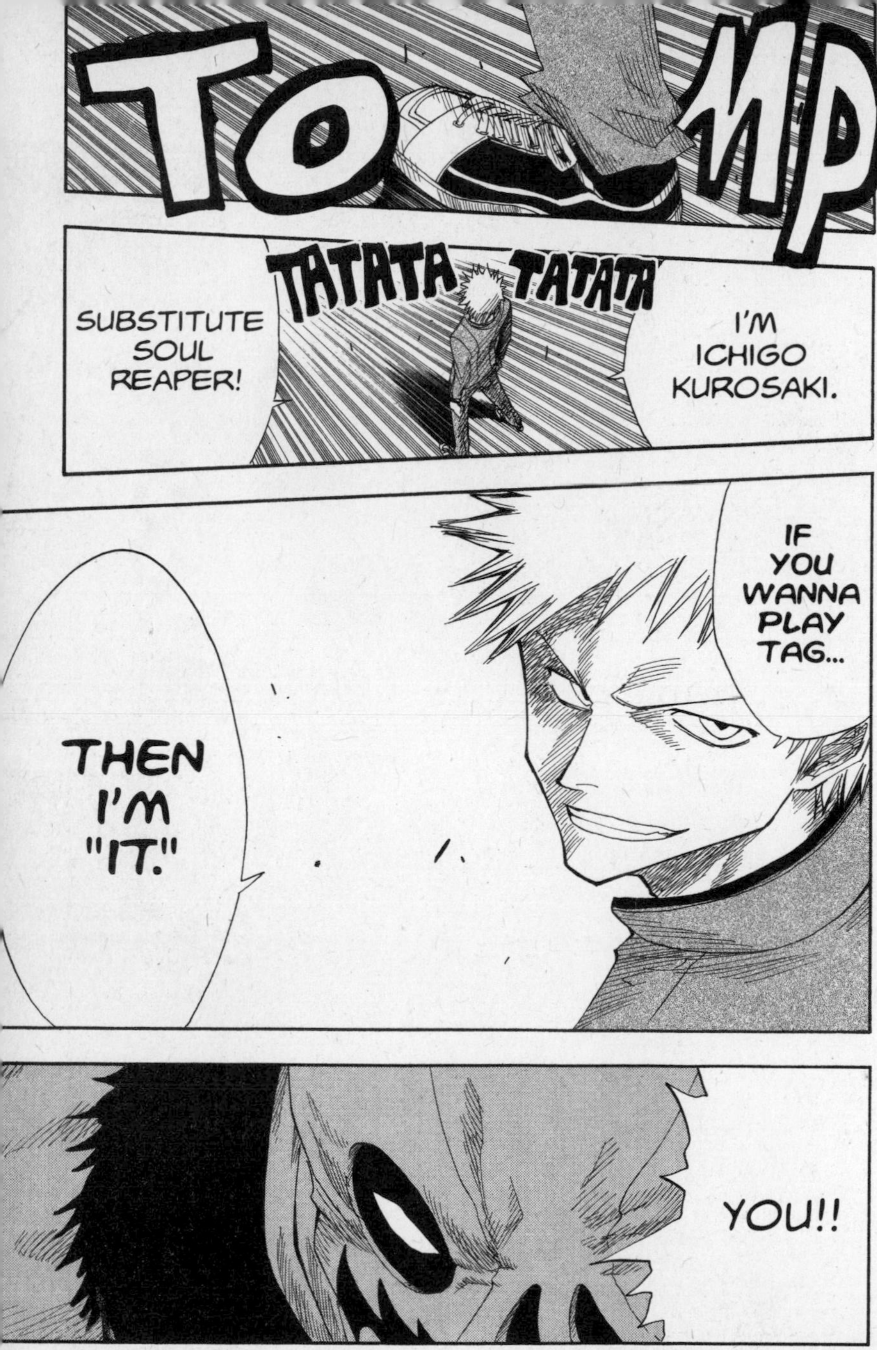
TOMP
TATATA TATATA
I'M ICHIGO KUROSAKI.
SUBSTITUTE SOUL REAPER!
IF YOU WANNA PLAY TAG...
THEN I'M "IT."
YOU!!

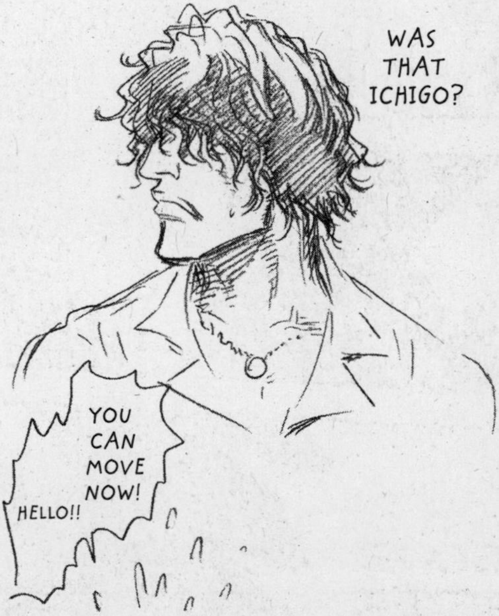
WAS THAT ICHIGO?
YOU CAN MOVE NOW!
HELLO!!

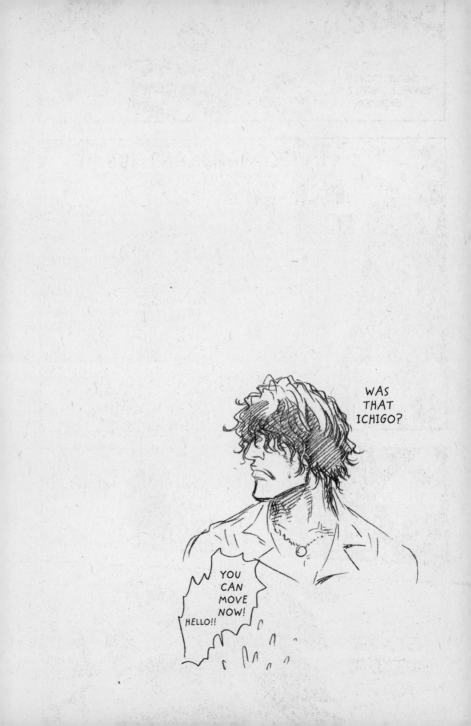

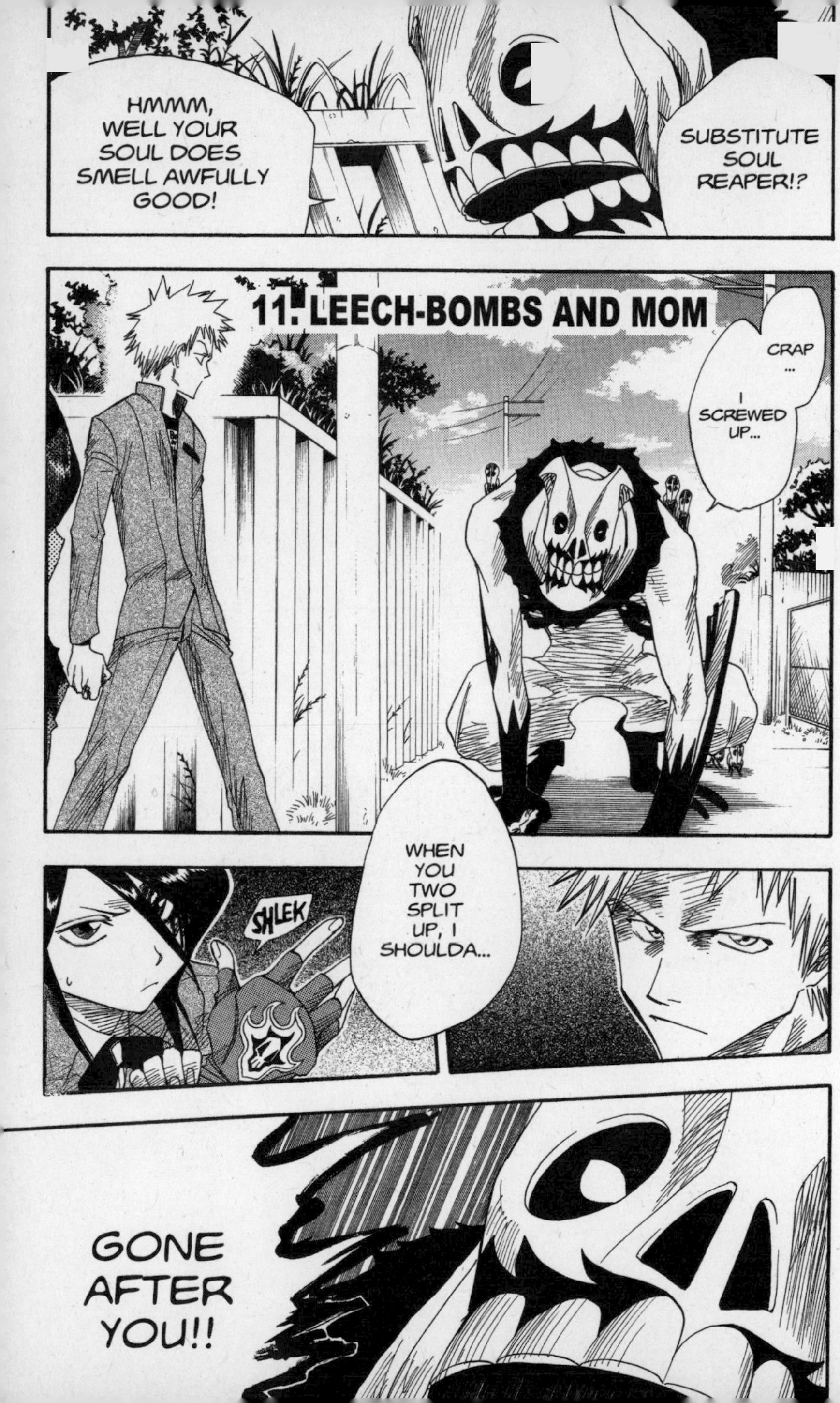
SUBSTITUTE SOUL REAPER!?
HMMM, WELL YOUR SOUL DOES SMELL AWFULLY GOOD!
11. LEECH-BOMBS AND MOM
CRAP ... I SCREWED UP...
WHEN YOU TWO SPLIT UP, I SHOULDA...
SHLEK
GONE AFTER YOU!!

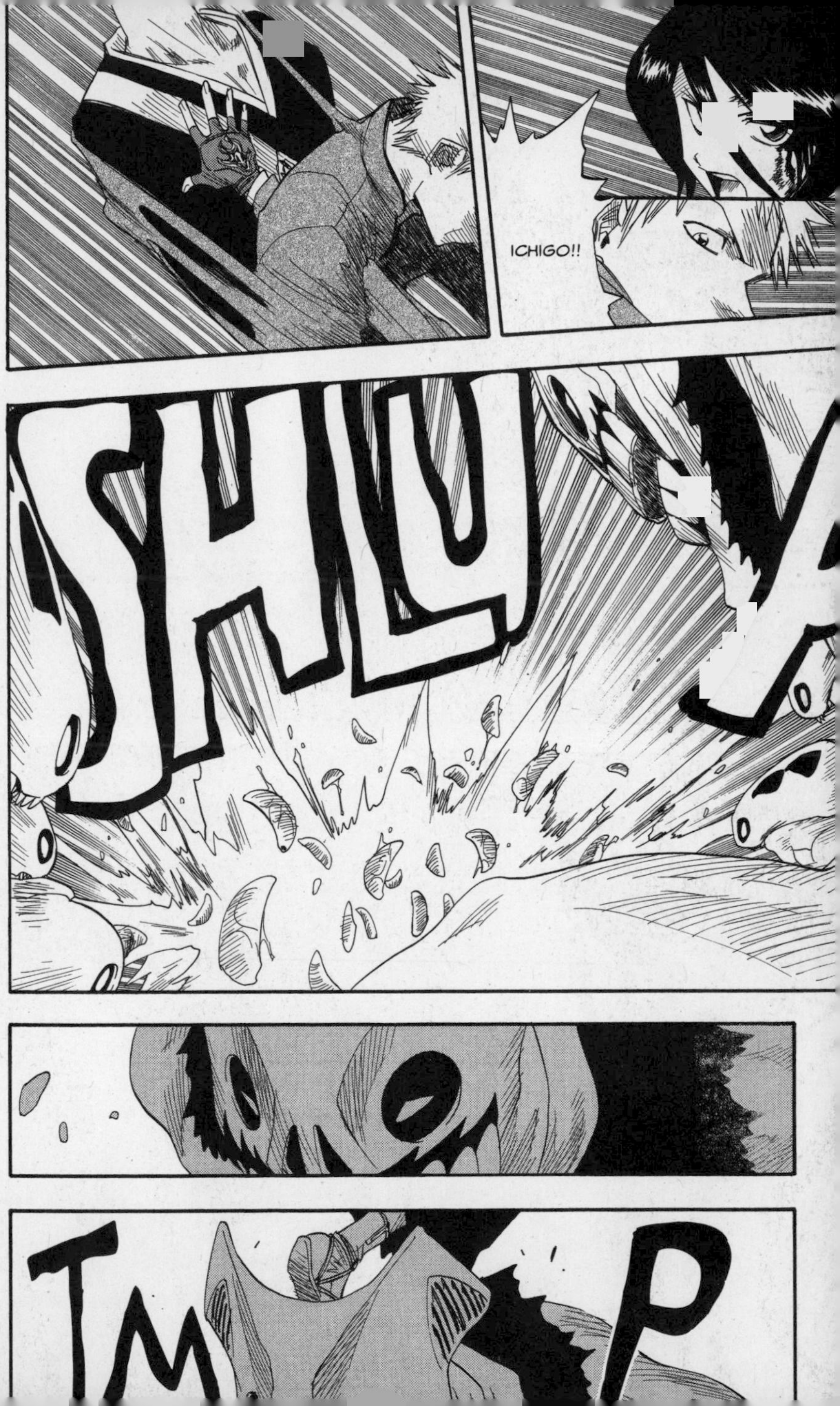
ICHIGO!!

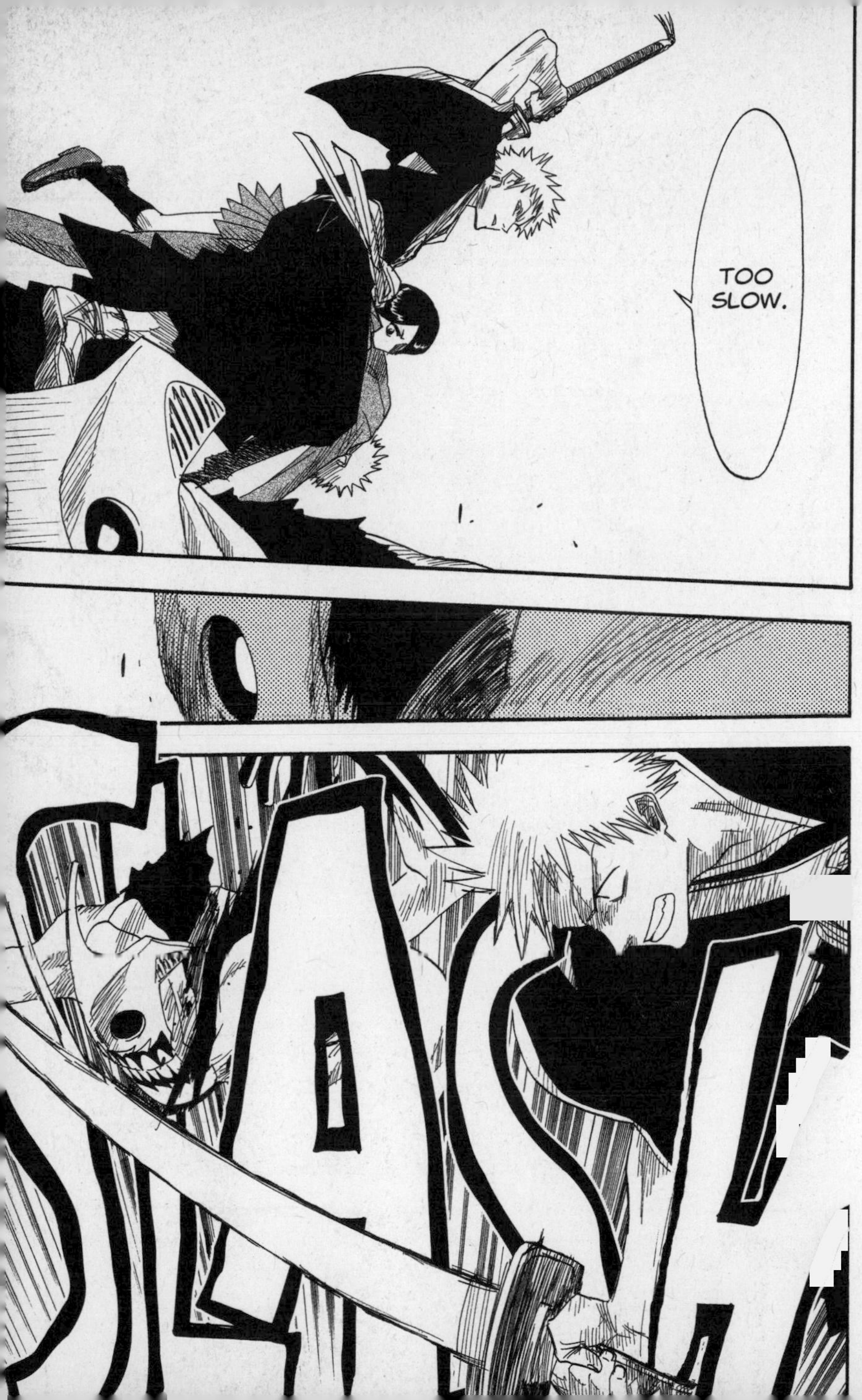
TOO
SLOW.

BLEACH

ブリーチ

11. LEECH-BOMBS AND MOM

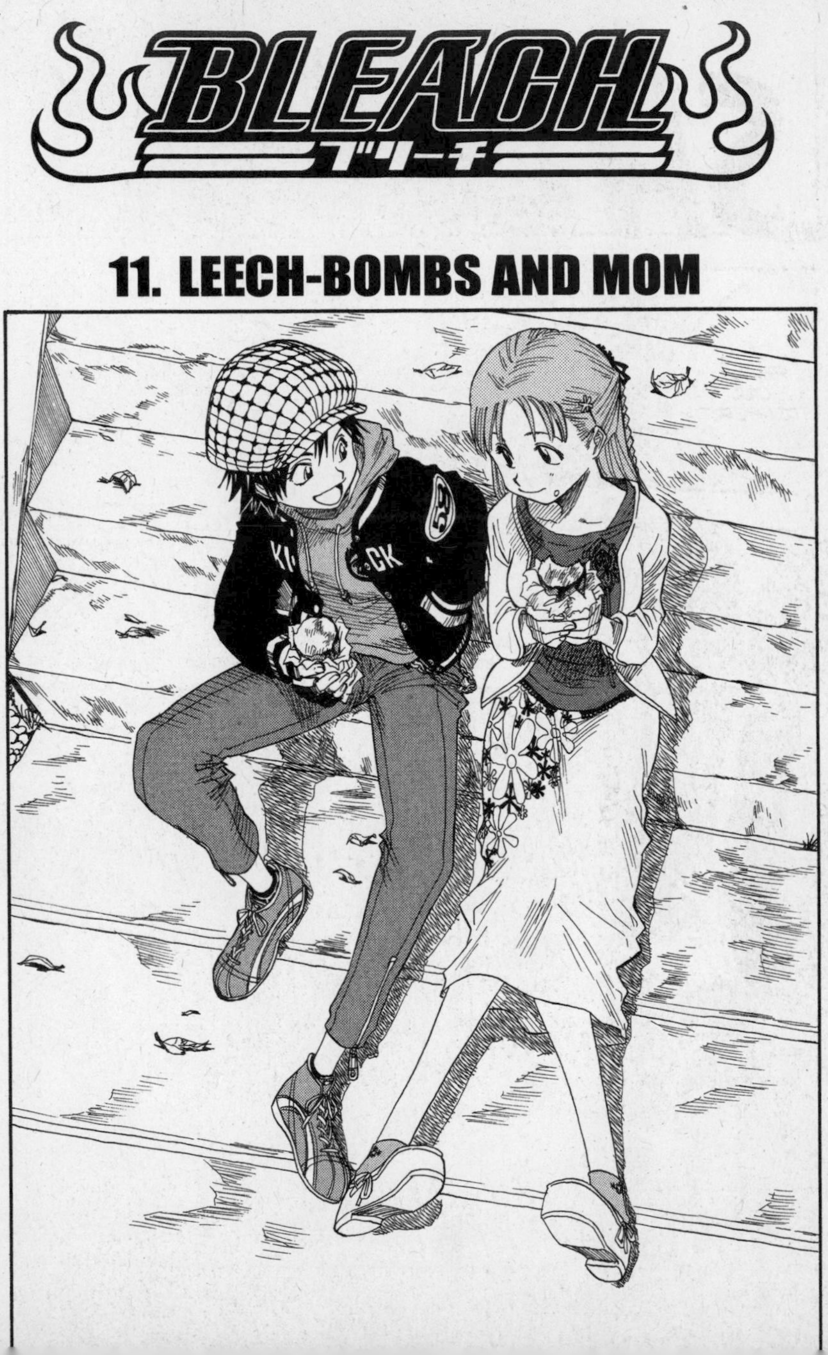

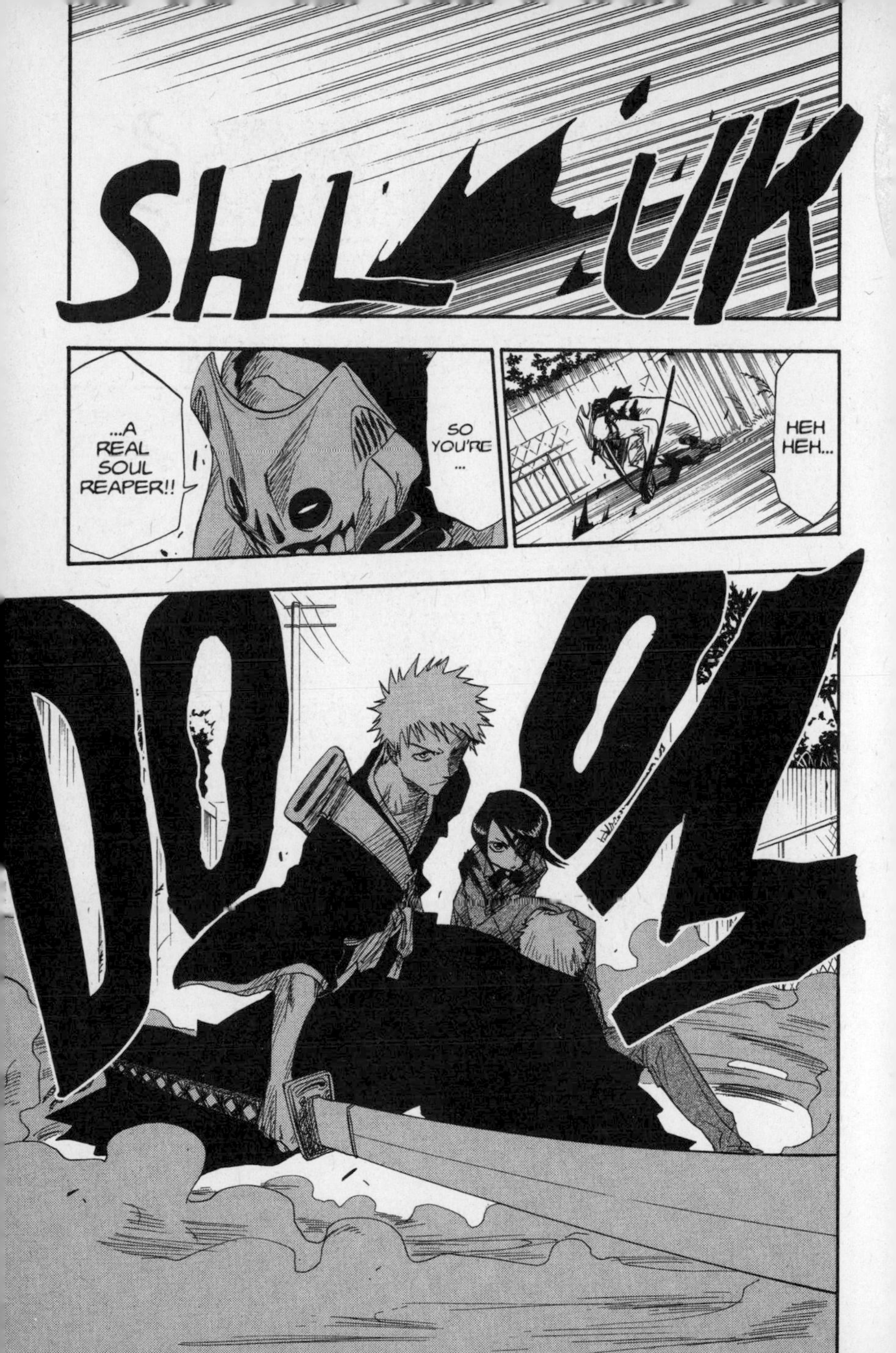
HEH HEH...
SO YOU'RE ...
...A REAL SOUL REAPER!!

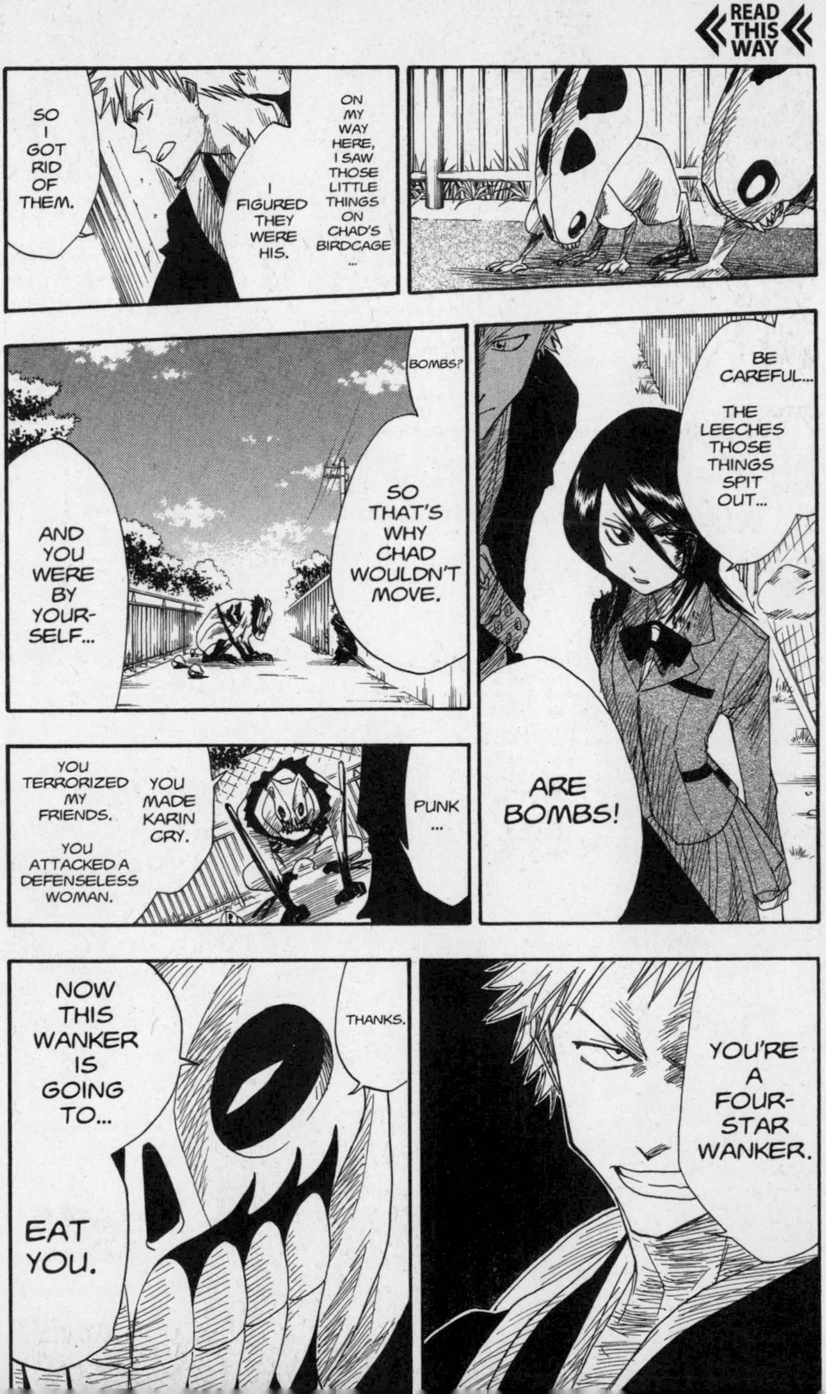
READ THIS WAY
ON MY WAY HERE, I SAW THOSE LITTLE THINGS ON CHAD'S BIRDCAGE...
I FIGURED THEY WERE HIS.
SO I GOT RID OF THEM.
BE CAREFUL...
THE LEECHES THOSE THINGS SPIT OUT...
ARE BOMBS!
BOMBS?
SO THAT'S WHY CHAD WOULDN'T MOVE.
AND YOU WERE BY YOURSELF...
PUNK...
YOU MADE KARIN CRY.
YOU TERRORIZED MY FRIENDS.
YOU ATTACKED A DEFENSELESS WOMAN.
YOU'RE A FOUR-STAR WANKER.
THANKS.
NOW THIS WANKER IS GOING TO...
EAT YOU.

READ THIS WAY

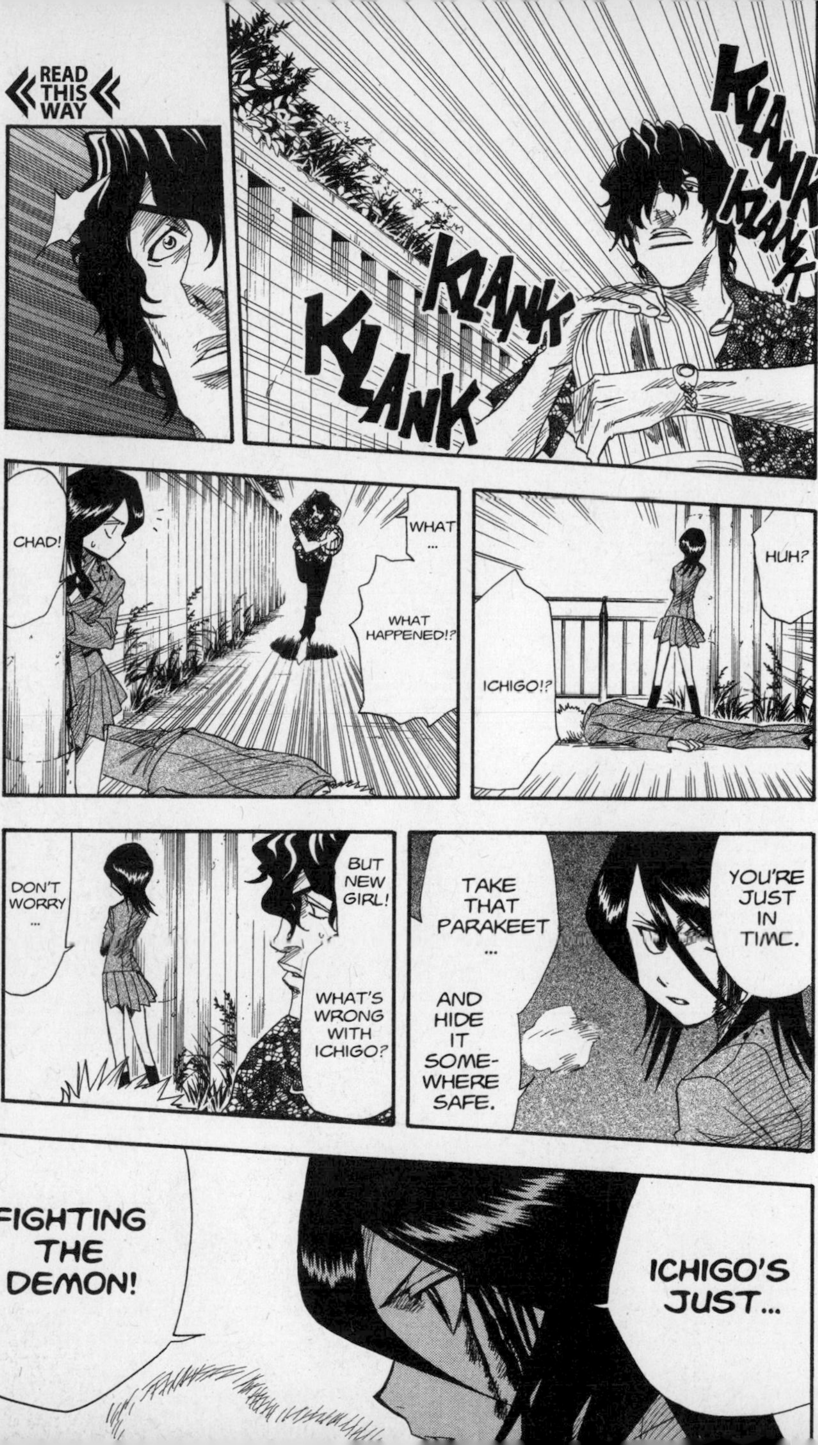
KLANK KLANK
KLANK KLANK
HUH?
ICHIGO!?
WHAT ...
WHAT HAPPENED!?
CHAD!
YOU'RE JUST IN TIMC.
TAKE THAT PARAKEET ...
AND HIDE IT SOME-WHERE SAFE.
BUT NEW GIRL!
WHAT'S WRONG WITH ICHIGO?
DON'T WORRY ...
ICHIGO'S JUST...
FIGHTING THE DEMON!

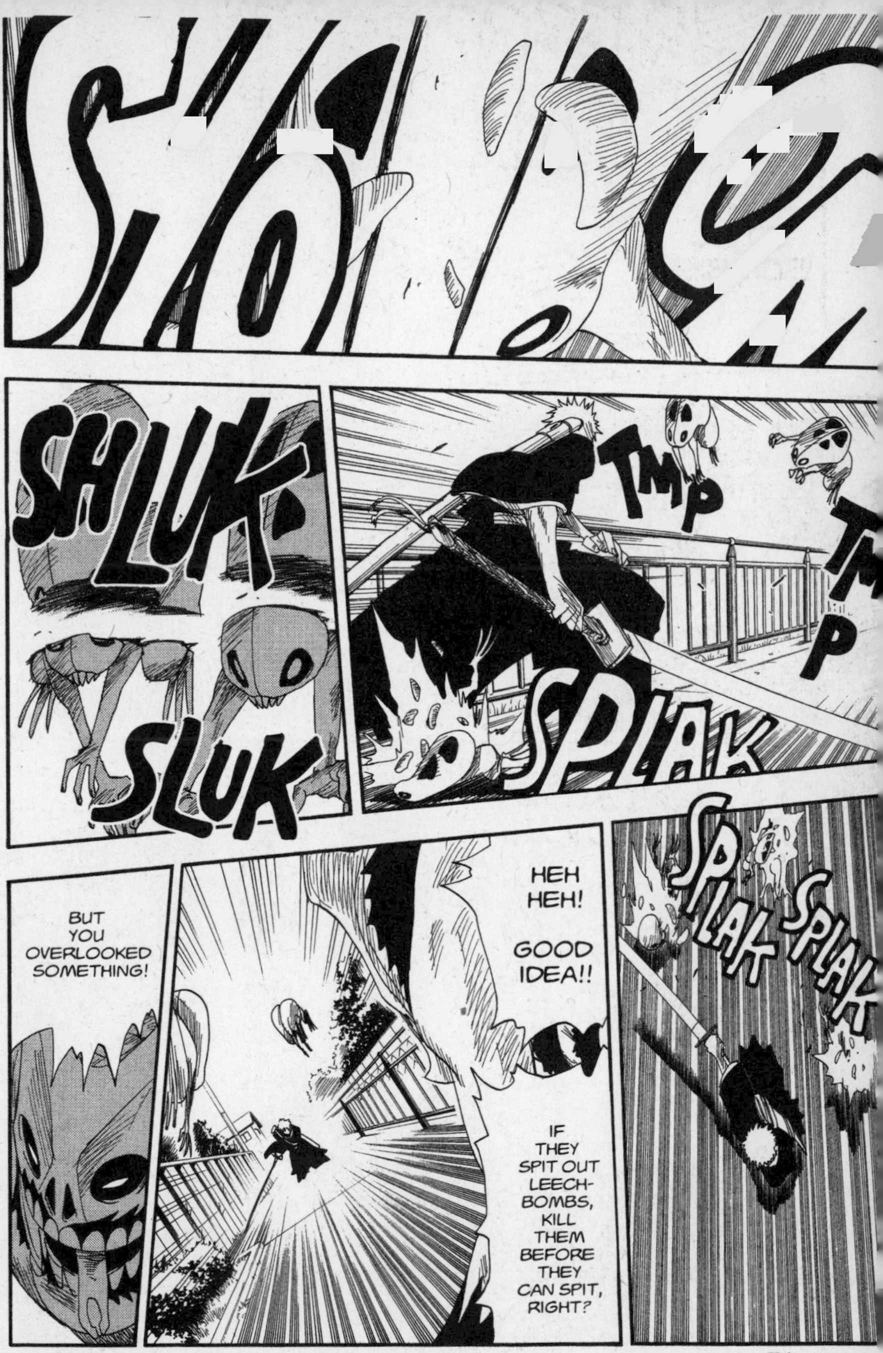
TMP
TMP
SPLAK
SHLUK
SLUK
SPLAK
SPLAK
SPLAK
HEH HEH!
GOOD IDEA!!
IF THEY SPIT OUT LEECH-BOMBS, KILL THEM BEFORE THEY CAN SPIT, RIGHT?
BUT YOU OVERLOOKED SOMETHING!

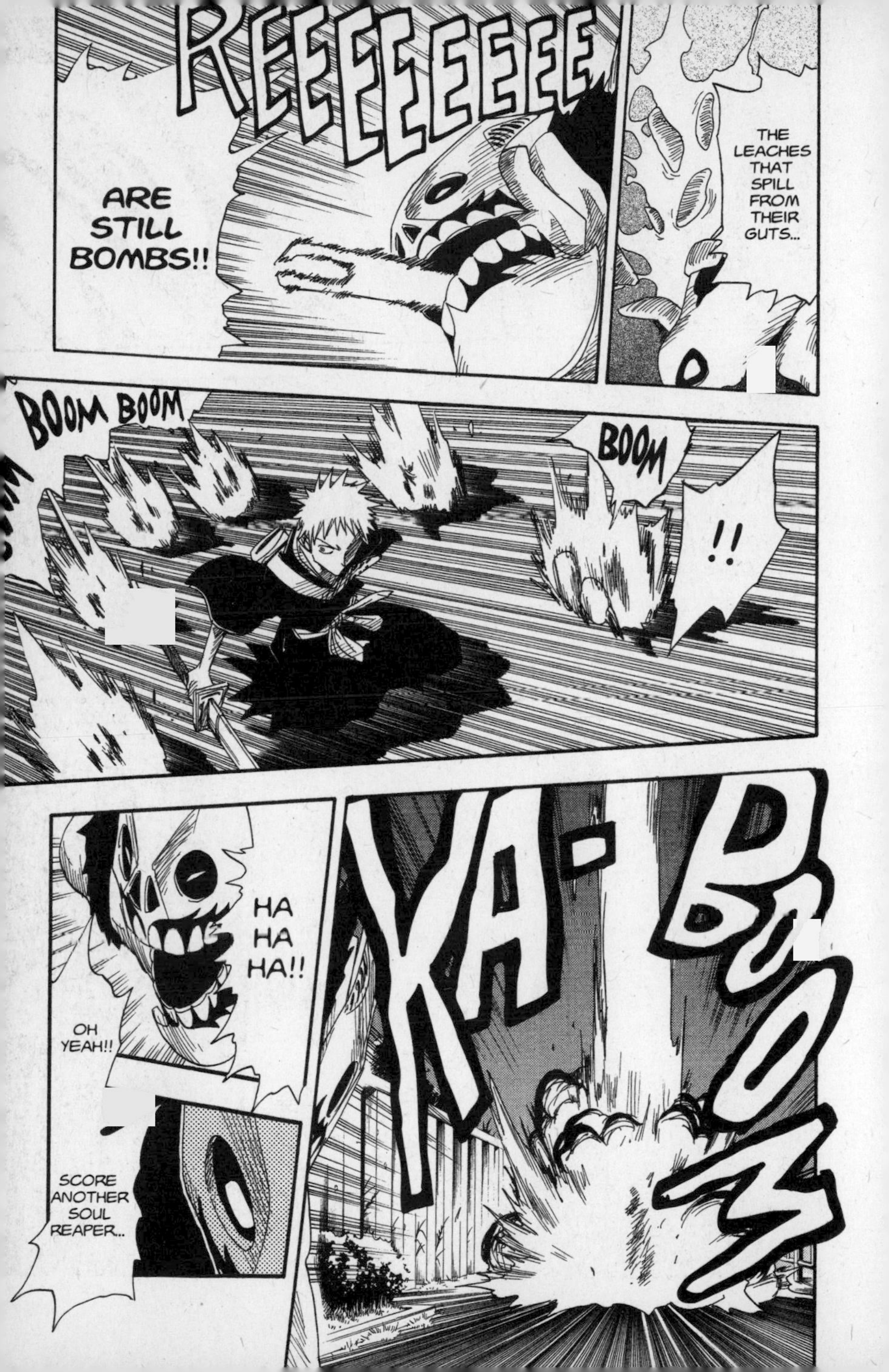
THE LEACHES THAT SPILL FROM THEIR GUTS...
REEEEEEEEE
ARE STILL BOMBS!!
BOOM
!!
BOOM BOOM
YA-BOOM
HA HA HA!!
OH YEAH!!
SCORE ANOTHER SOUL REAPER...

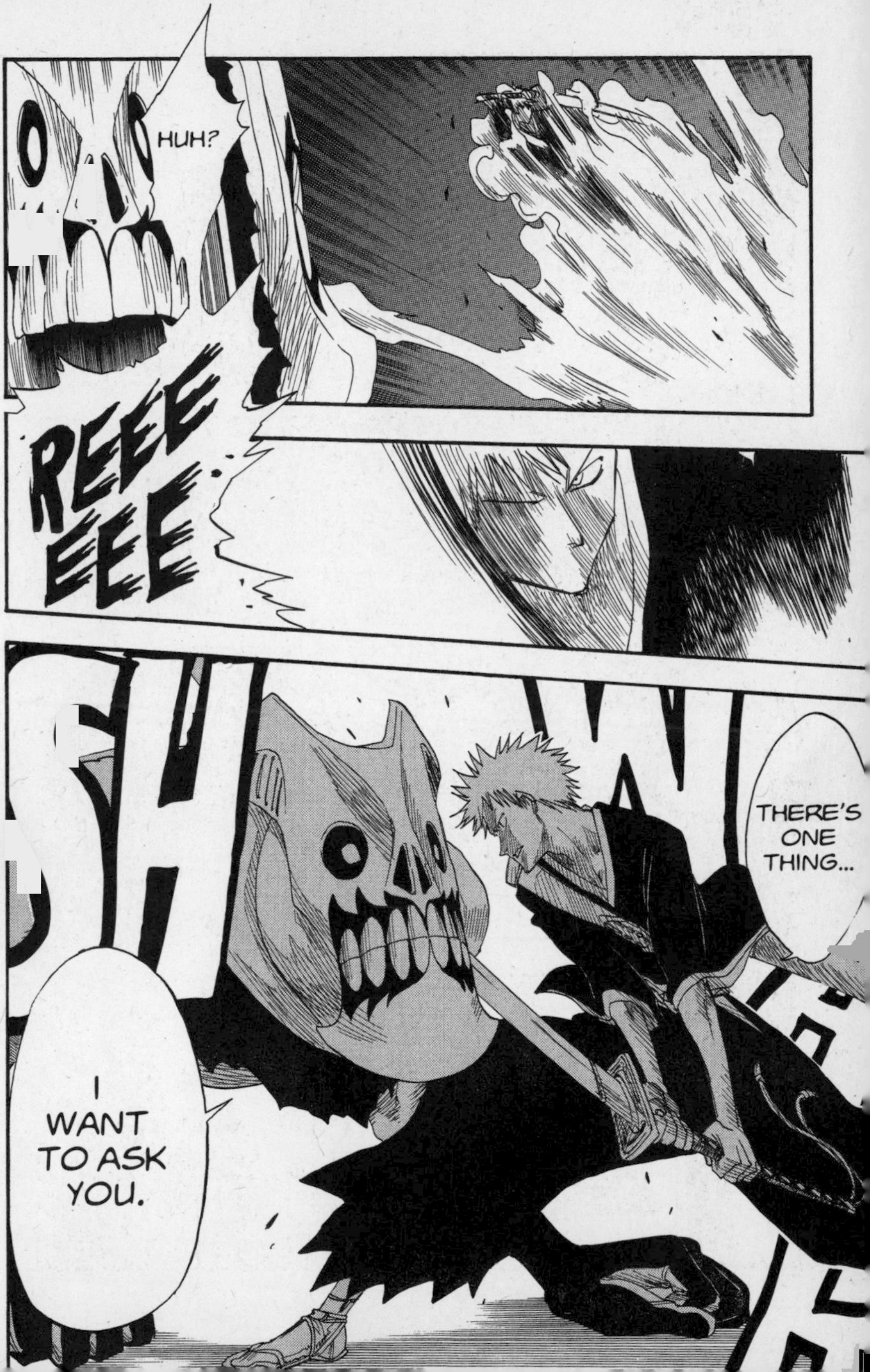
HUH?
REEEEEE
THERE'S ONE THING...
I WANT TO ASK YOU.

READ THIS WAY

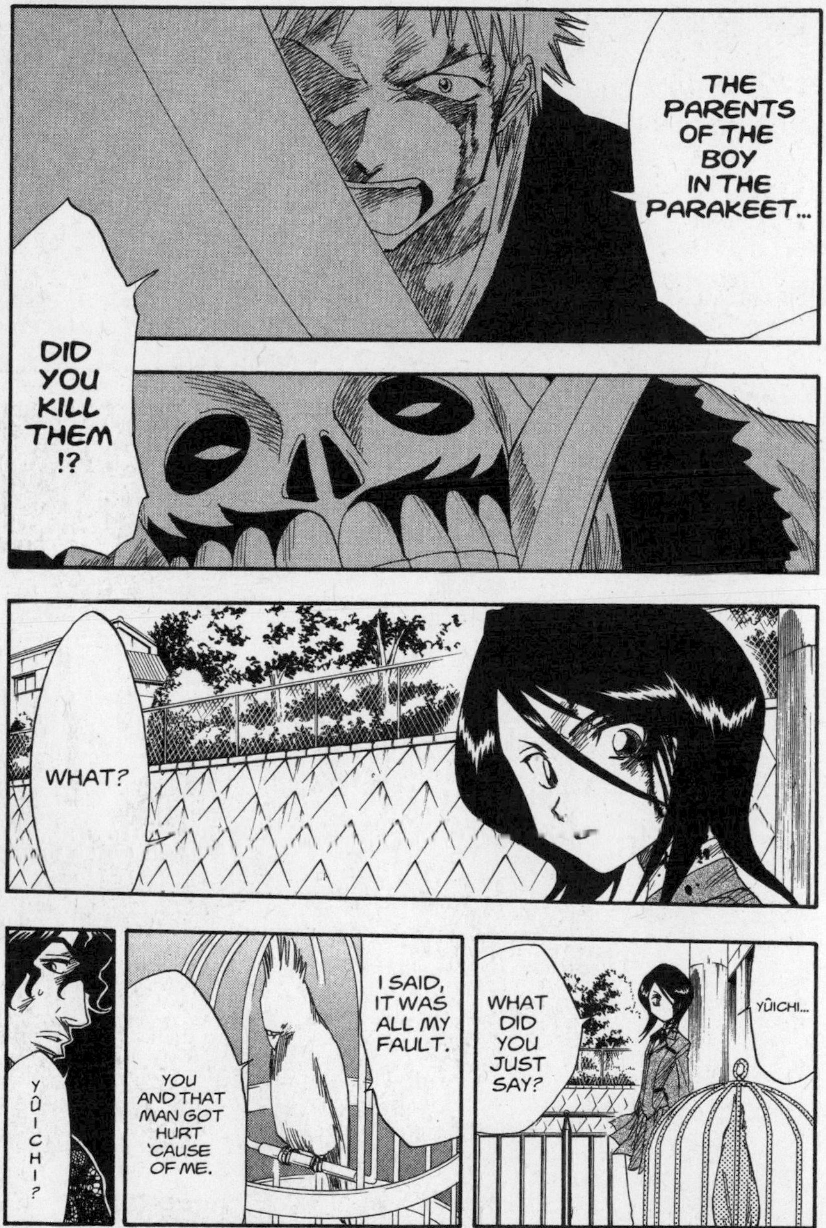
THE PARENTS OF THE BOY IN THE PARAKEET...
DID YOU KILL THEM!?
WHAT?
YÛICHI...
WHAT DID YOU JUST SAY?
I SAID, IT WAS ALL MY FAULT.
YOU AND THAT MAN GOT HURT 'CAUSE OF ME.
YÛICHI?

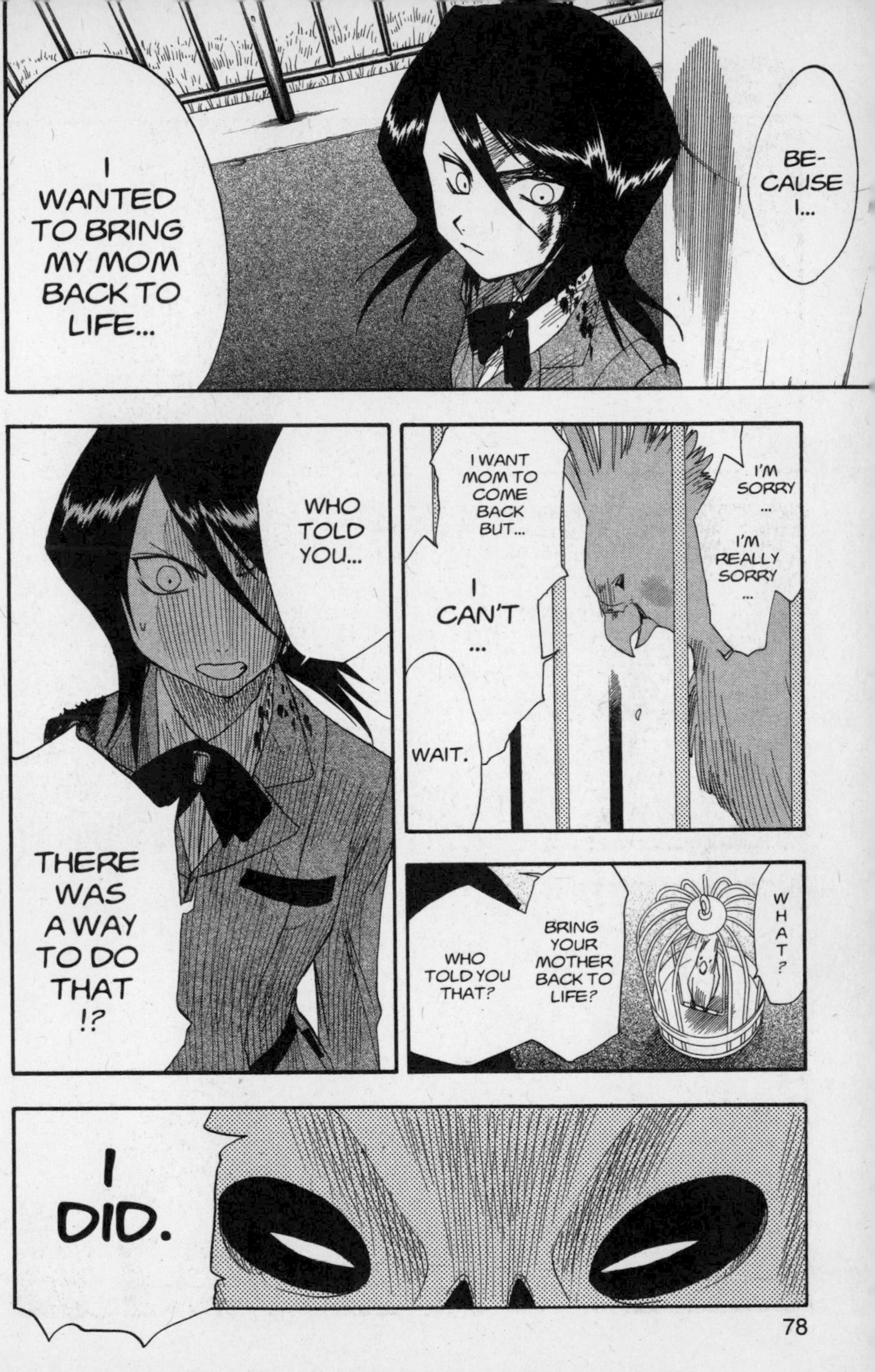
BE-CAUSE I...
I WANTED TO BRING MY MOM BACK TO LIFE...
I'M SORRY... I'M REALLY SORRY...
I WANT MOM TO COME BACK BUT... I CAN'T...
WAIT.
WHAT?
BRING YOUR MOTHER BACK TO LIFE?
WHO TOLD YOU THAT?
WHO TOLD YOU...
THERE WAS A WAY TO DO THAT!?
I DID.

READ THIS WAY

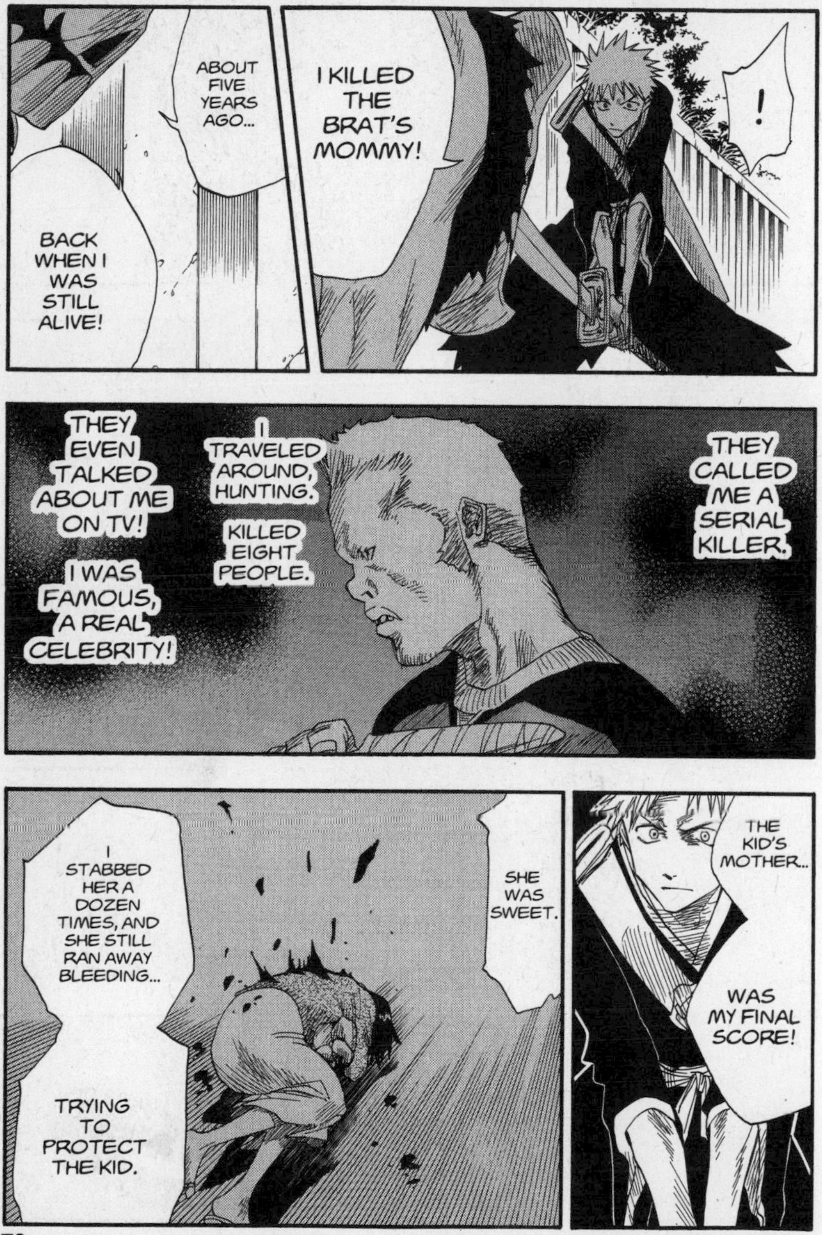

!
I KILLED THE BRAT'S MOMMY!
ABOUT FIVE YEARS AGO...
BACK WHEN I WAS STILL ALIVE!
THEY CALLED ME A SERIAL KILLER.
I TRAVELED AROUND, HUNTING.
KILLED EIGHT PEOPLE.
THEY EVEN TALKED ABOUT ME ON TV!
I WAS FAMOUS, A REAL CELEBRITY!
THE KID'S MOTHER...
WAS MY FINAL SCORE!
SHE WAS SWEET.
I STABBED HER A DOZEN TIMES, AND SHE STILL RAN AWAY BLEEDING...
TRYING TO PROTECT THE KID.

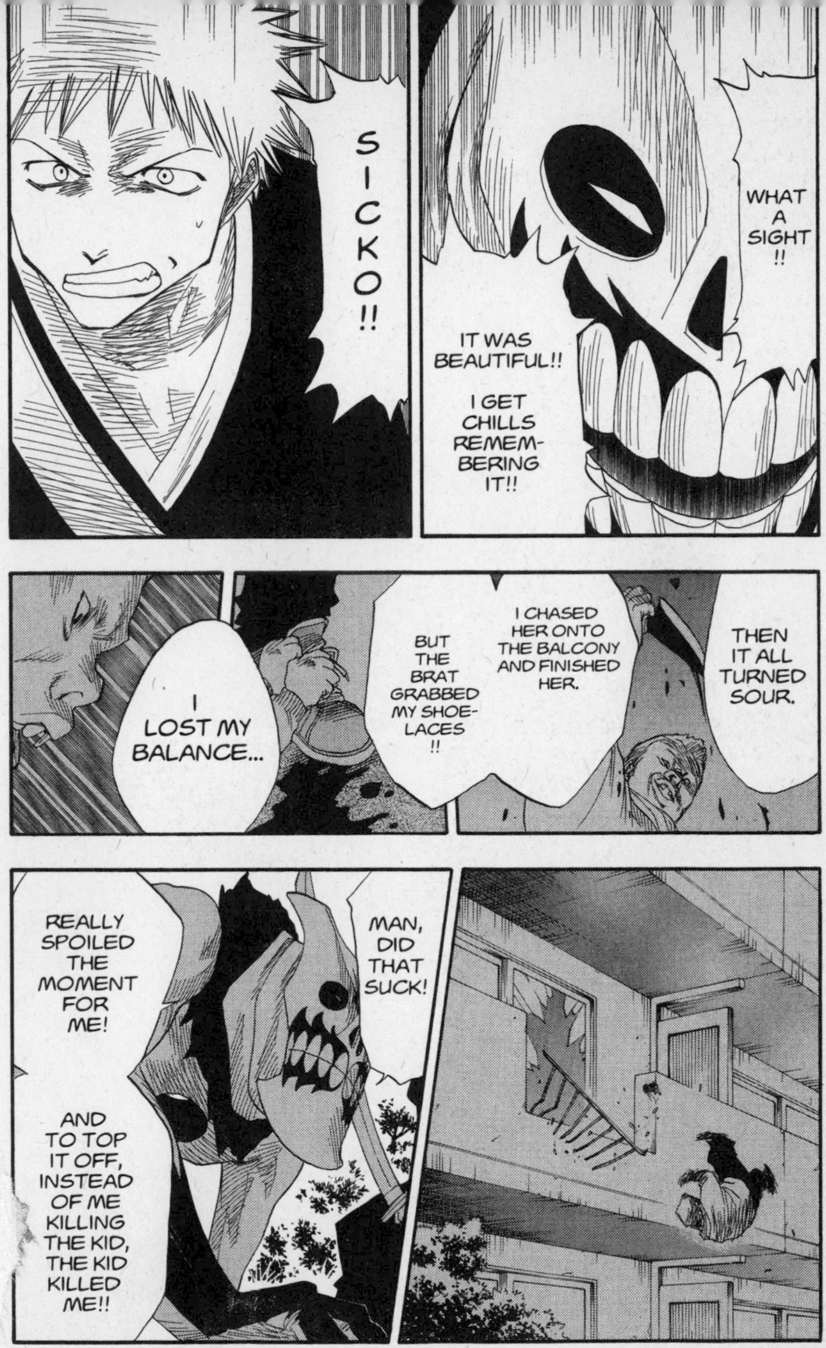
WHAT A SIGHT!!
IT WAS BEAUTIFUL!!
I GET CHILLS REMEMBERING IT!!
SICKO!!
THEN IT ALL TURNED SOUR.
I CHASED HER ONTO THE BALCONY AND FINISHED HER.
BUT THE BRAT GRABBED MY SHOELACES!!
I LOST MY BALANCE...
MAN, DID THAT SUCK!
REALLY SPOILED THE MOMENT FOR ME!
AND TO TOP IT OFF, INSTEAD OF ME KILLING THE KID, THE KID KILLED ME!!

READ THIS WAY

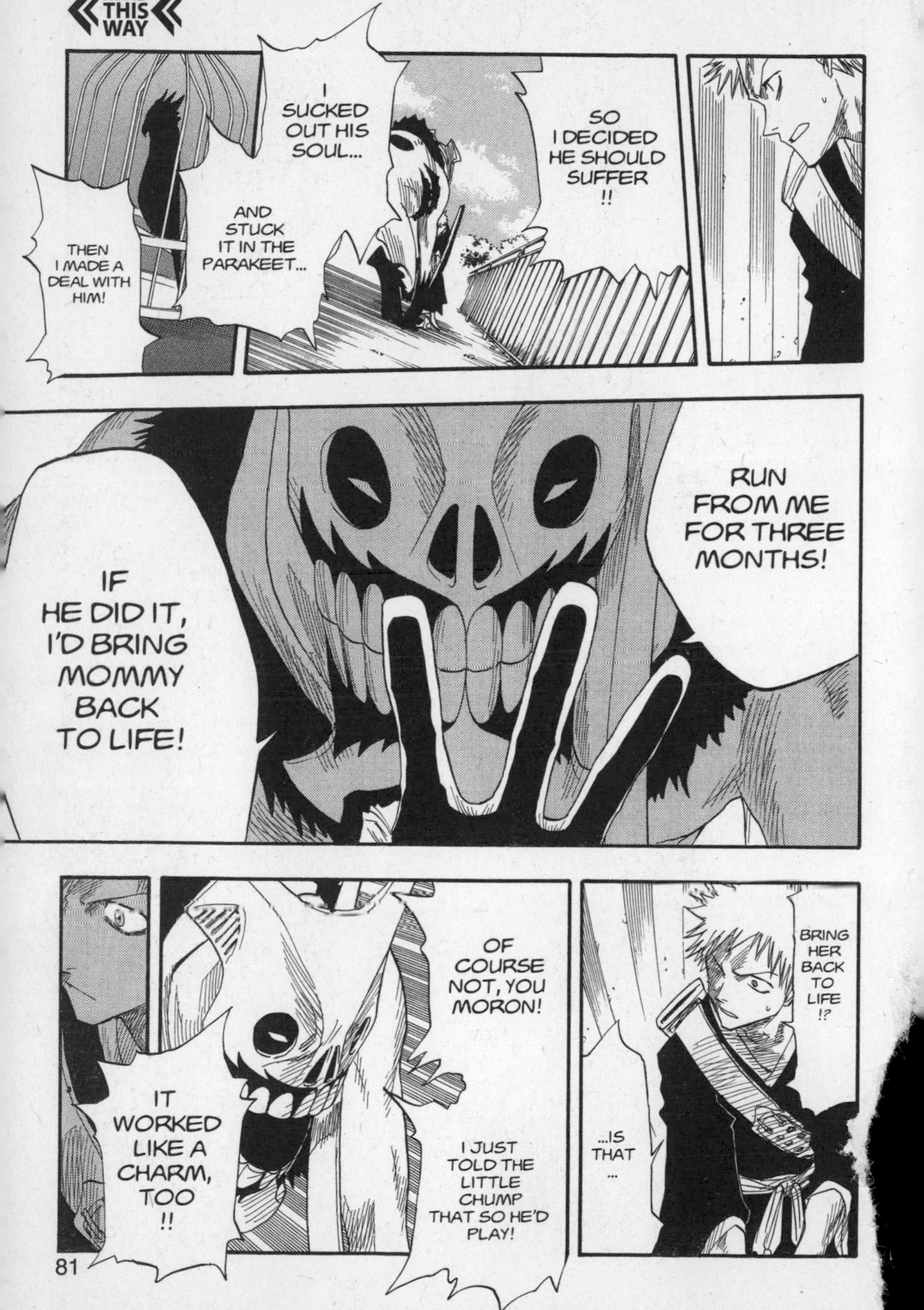
SO I DECIDED HE SHOULD SUFFER !!
I SUCKED OUT HIS SOUL...
AND STUCK IT IN THE PARAKEET...
THEN I MADE A DEAL WITH HIM!
RUN FROM ME FOR THREE MONTHS!
IF HE DID IT, I'D BRING MOMMY BACK TO LIFE!
BRING HER BACK TO LIFE !?
...IS THAT ...
OF COURSE NOT, YOU MORON!
I JUST TOLD THE LITTLE CHUMP THAT SO HE'D PLAY!
IT WORKED LIKE A CHARM, TOO !!

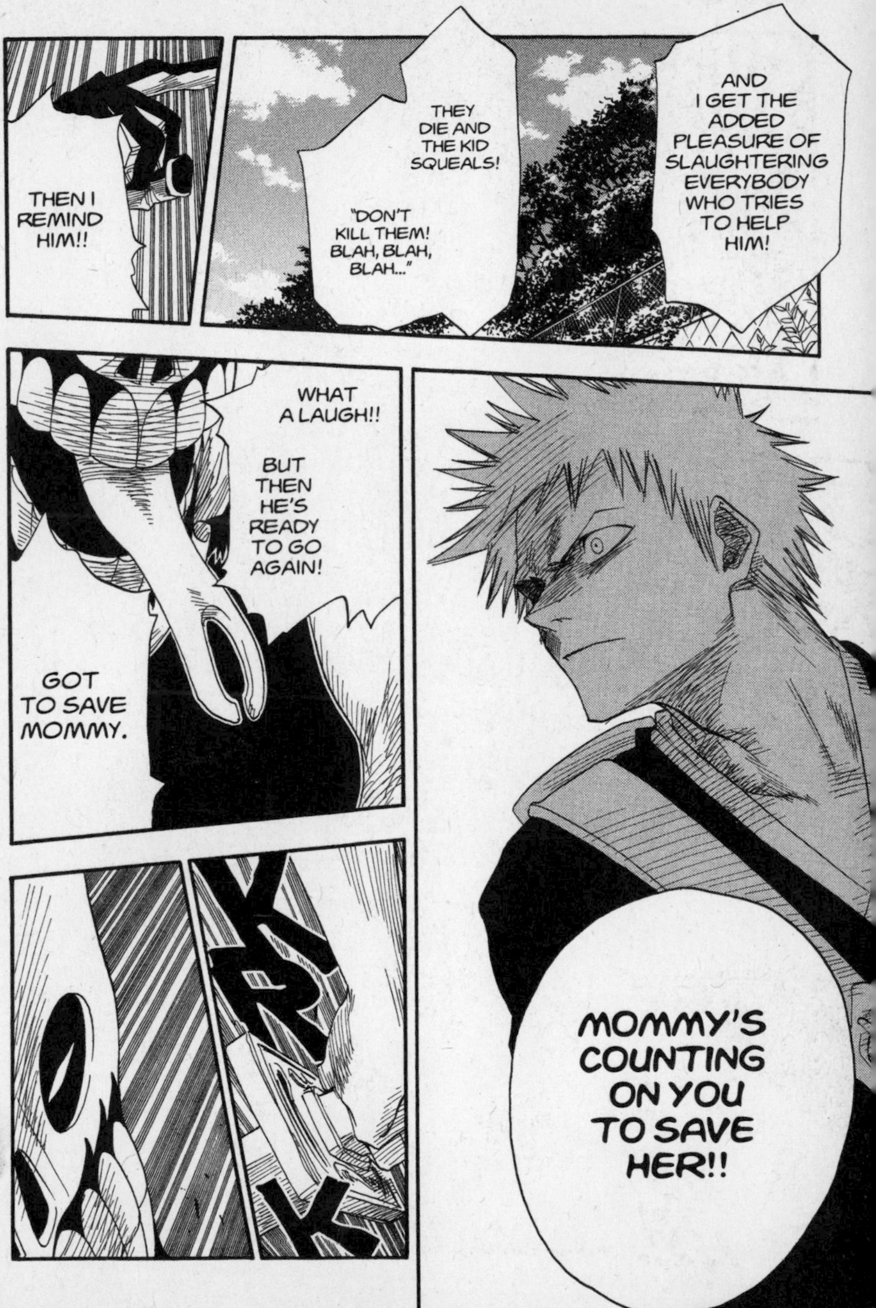
AND I GET THE ADDED PLEASURE OF SLAUGHTERING EVERYBODY WHO TRIES TO HELP HIM!
THEY DIE AND THE KID SQUEALS!
"DON'T KILL THEM! BLAH, BLAH, BLAH..."
THEN I REMIND HIM!!
MOMMY'S COUNTING ON YOU TO SAVE HER!!
WHAT A LAUGH!!
BUT THEN HE'S READY TO GO AGAIN!
GOT TO SAVE MOMMY.

READ THIS WAY

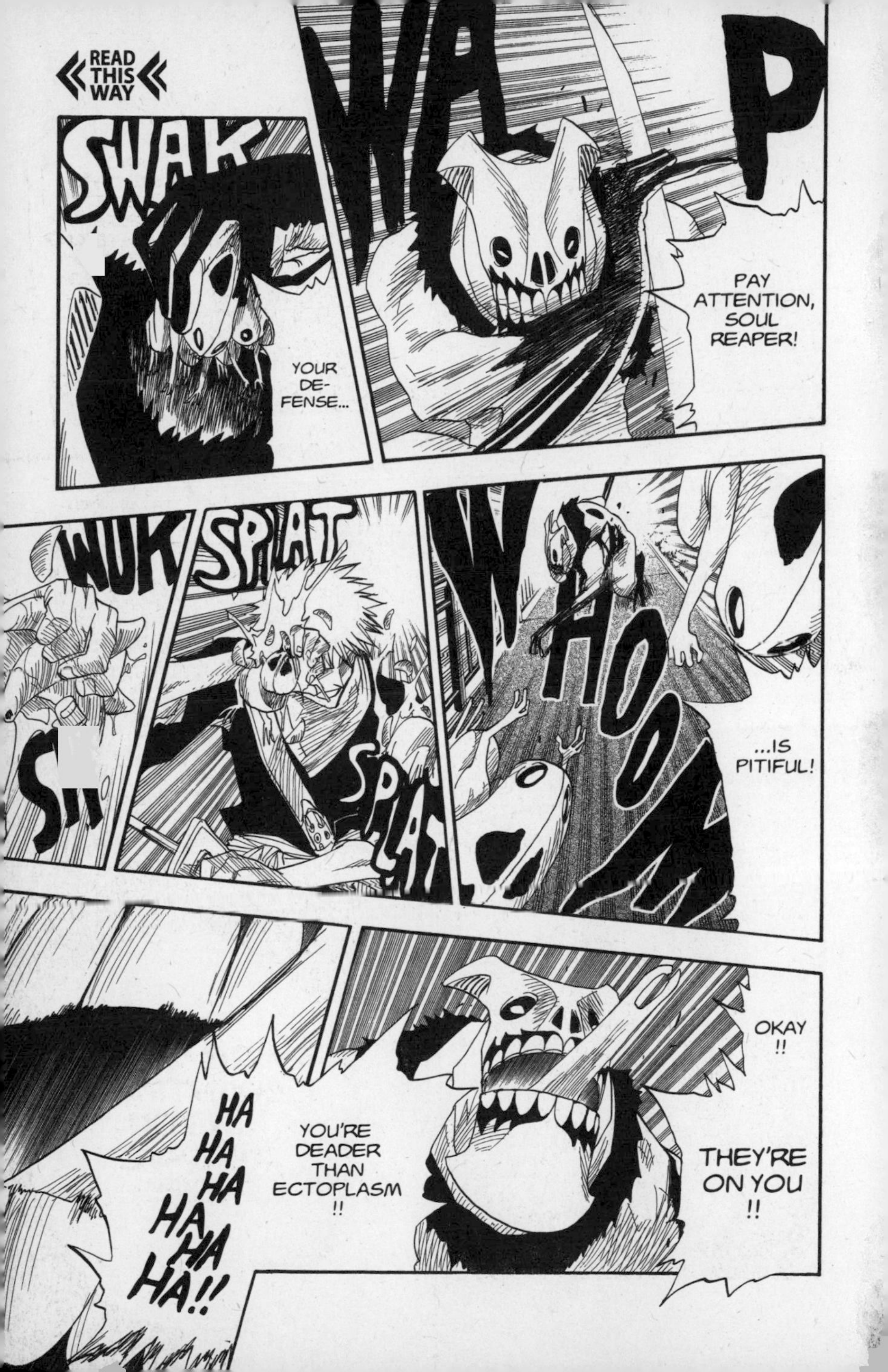
WAP
PAY ATTENTION, SOUL REAPER!
SWAK
YOUR DE-FENSE...
WHOOM
...IS PITIFUL!
SPLAT
WUK
SPLAT
OKAY !!
THEY'RE ON YOU !!
YOU'RE DEADER THAN ECTOPLASM !!
HA HA HA HA HA HA HA!!

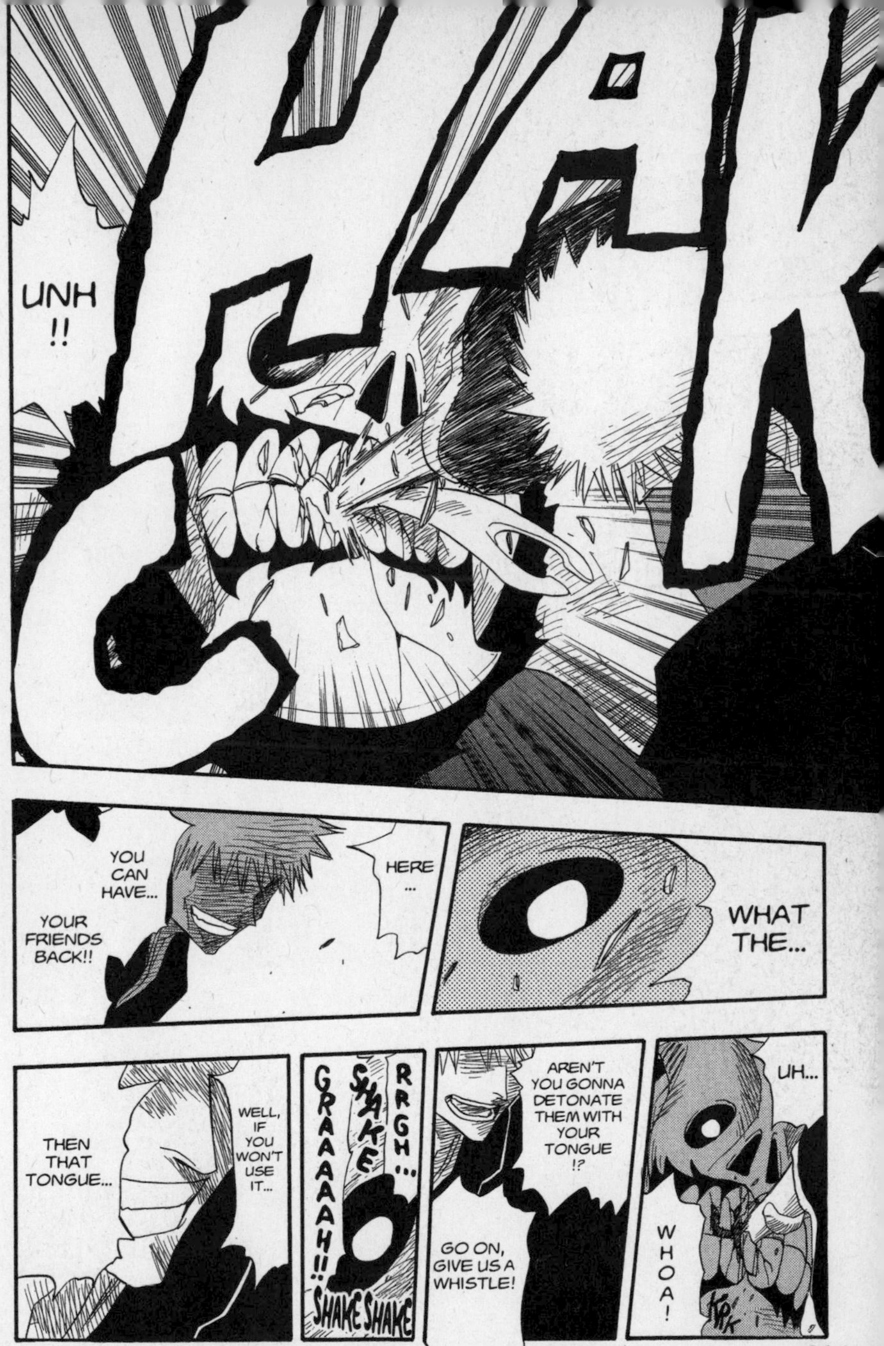
UNH !!
WHAT THE...
HERE ...
YOU CAN HAVE...
YOUR FRIENDS BACK!!
UH...
WHOA!
KRK
AREN'T YOU GONNA DETONATE THEM WITH YOUR TONGUE !?
GO ON, GIVE US A WHISTLE!
RRGH...
SHAKE
GRAAAAAAH!!
SHAKE SHAKE
WELL, IF YOU WON'T USE IT...
THEN THAT TONGUE...

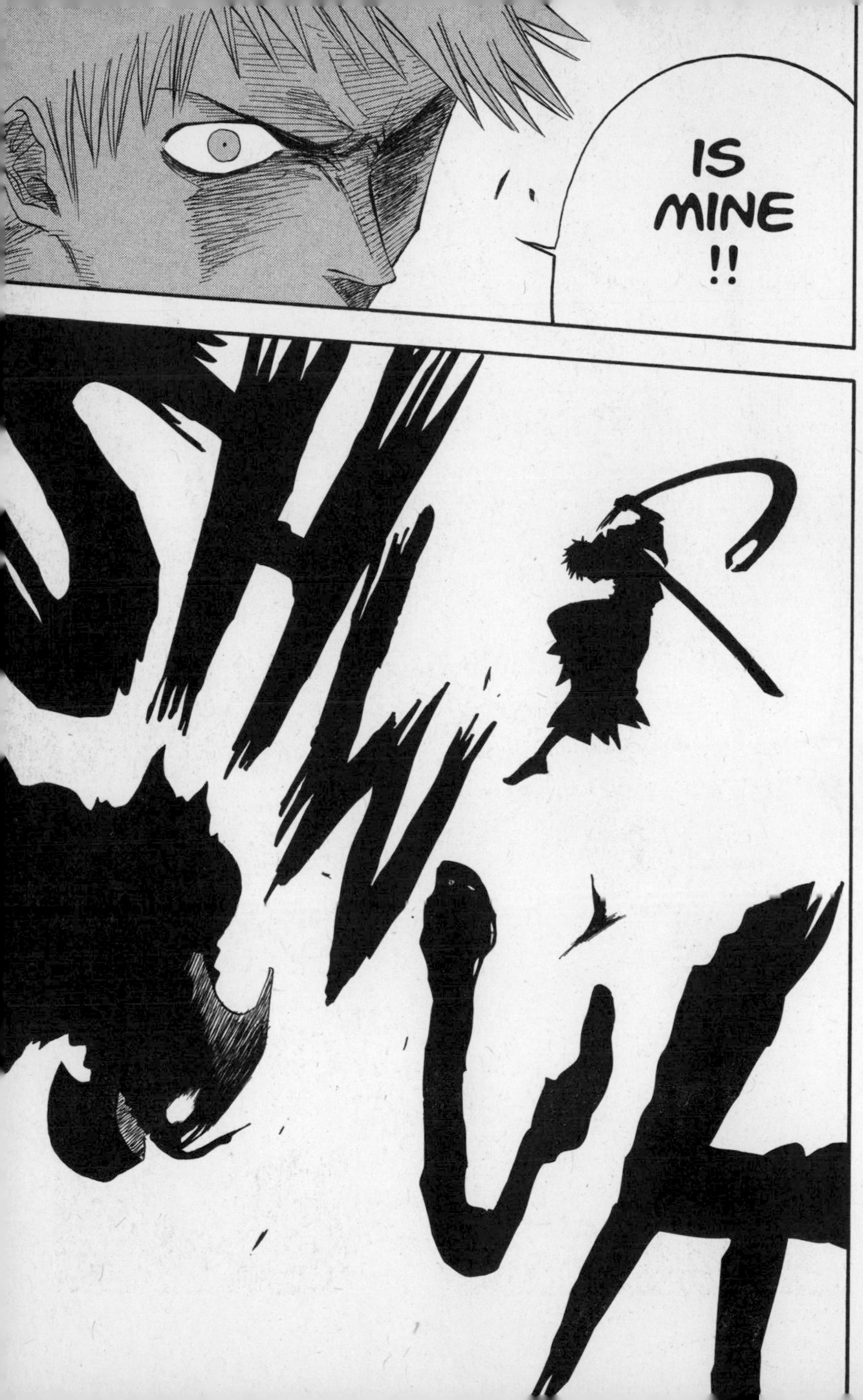
IS MINE !!
SHWUH

UH-OH.
THE TONGUE...

THESE GUYS AREN'T
HOLLOWS.
THEY'RE PARTS OF
A LARGER ENTITY,
LIKE A SECRETION.
THEY HAVE SOME
CONSCIOUSNESS
BUT DON'T FEEL
PAIN.

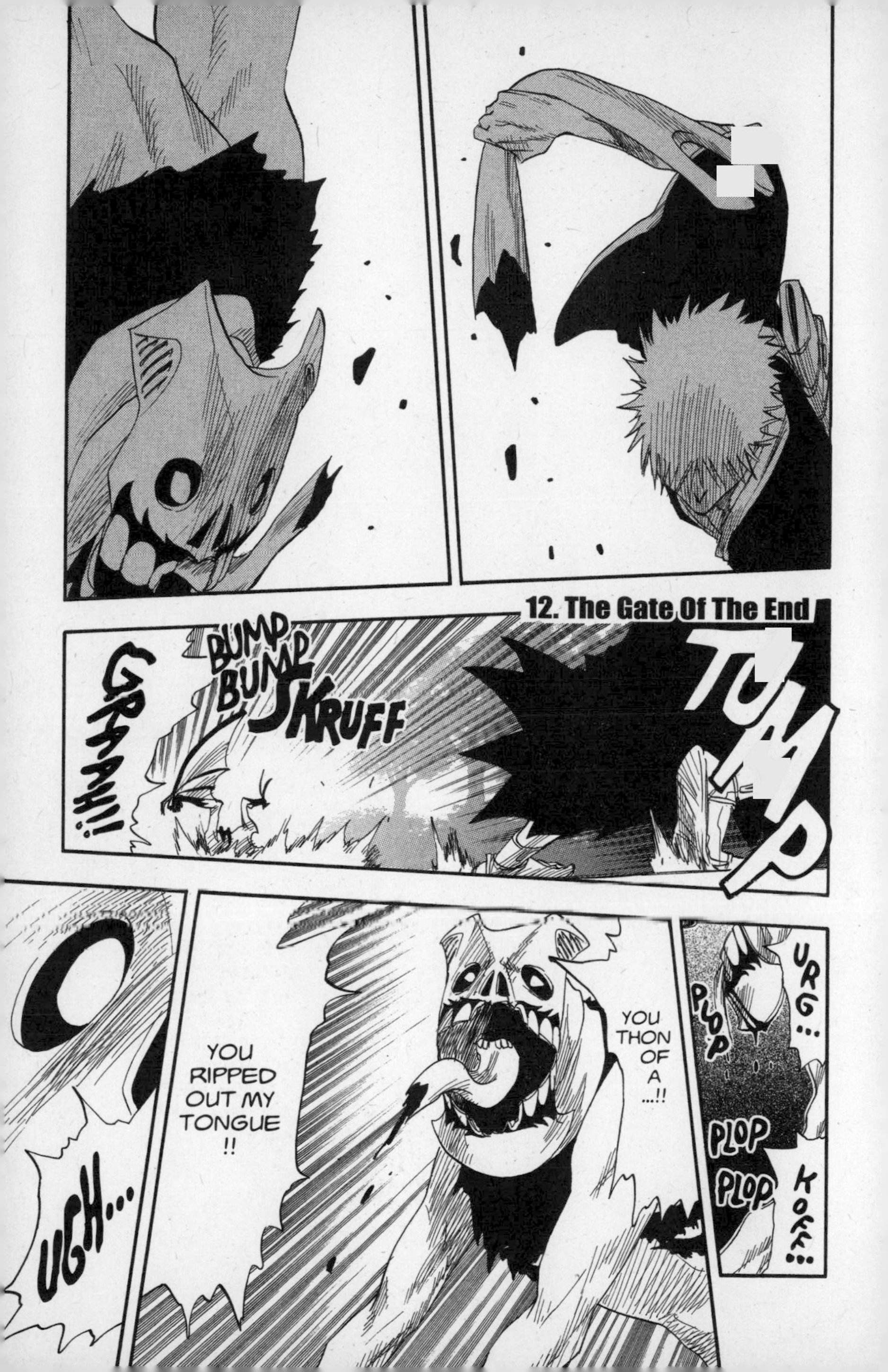
TUMP
SKRUFF
BUMP BUMP
GRAAAH!!!
URG...
PLOP
PLOP PLOP
KOFF...
YOU THON OF A ...!!
YOU RIPPED OUT MY TONGUE !!
UGH...

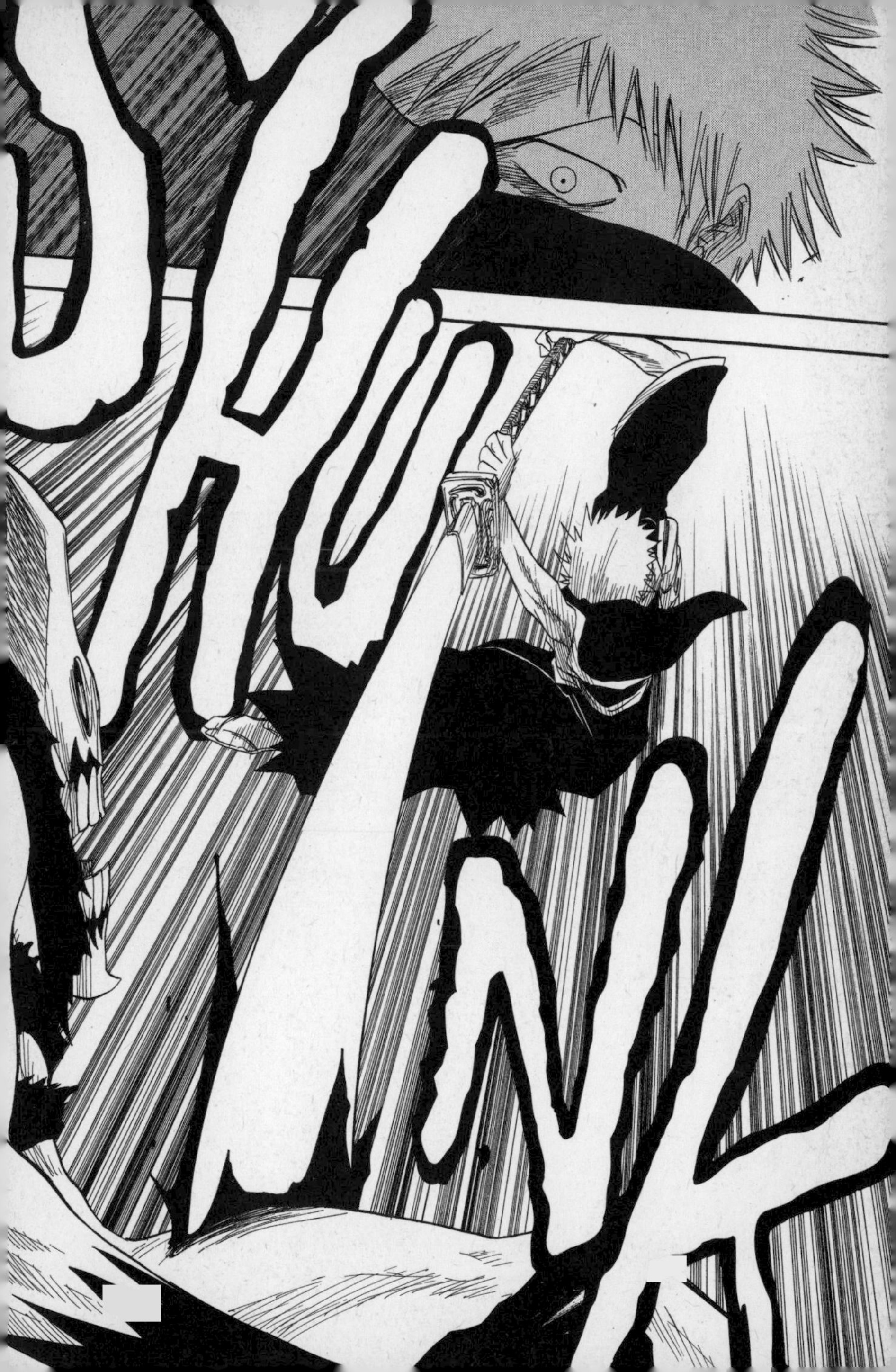

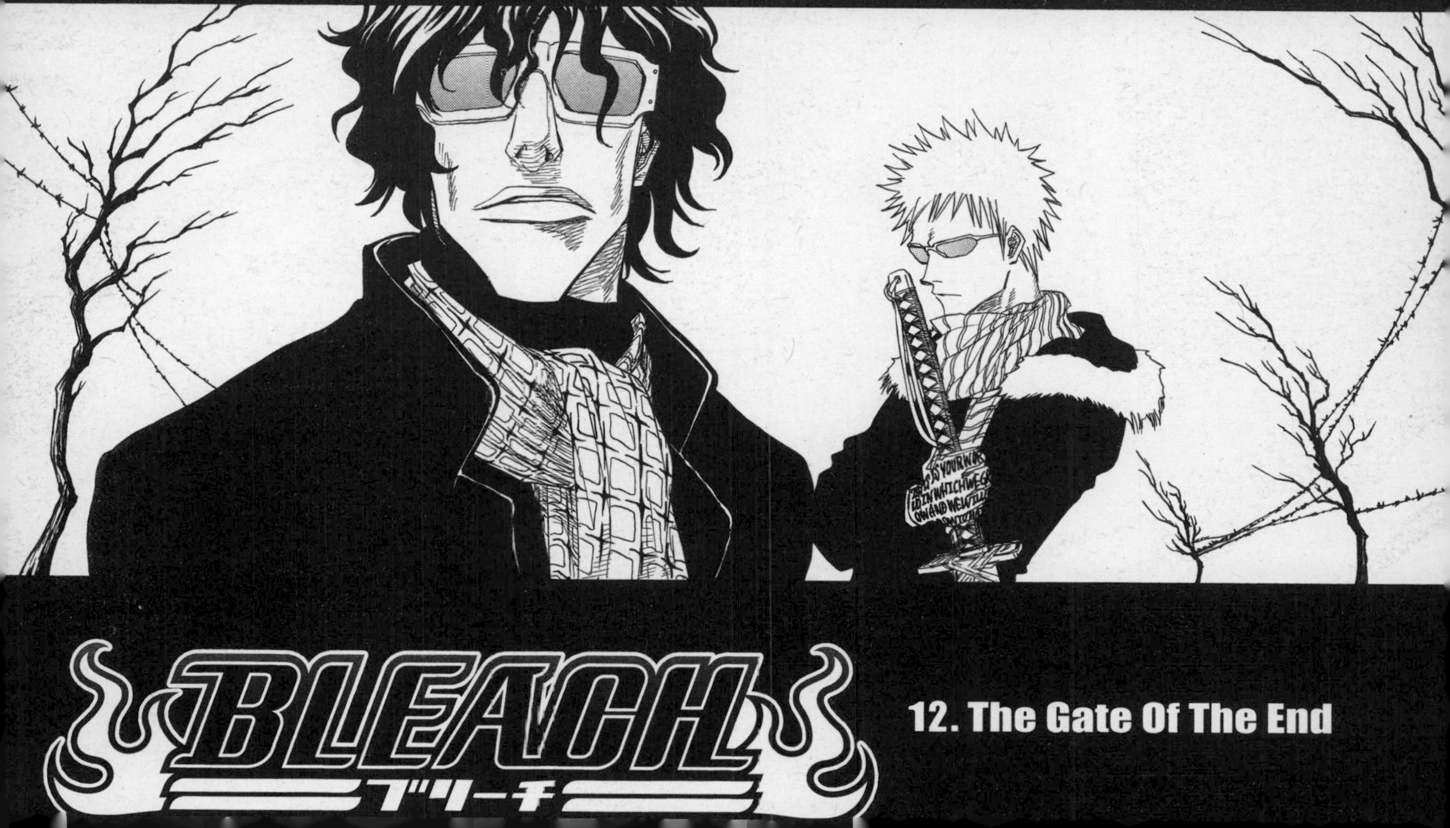

BLEACH

ブリーチ

12. The Gate Of The End

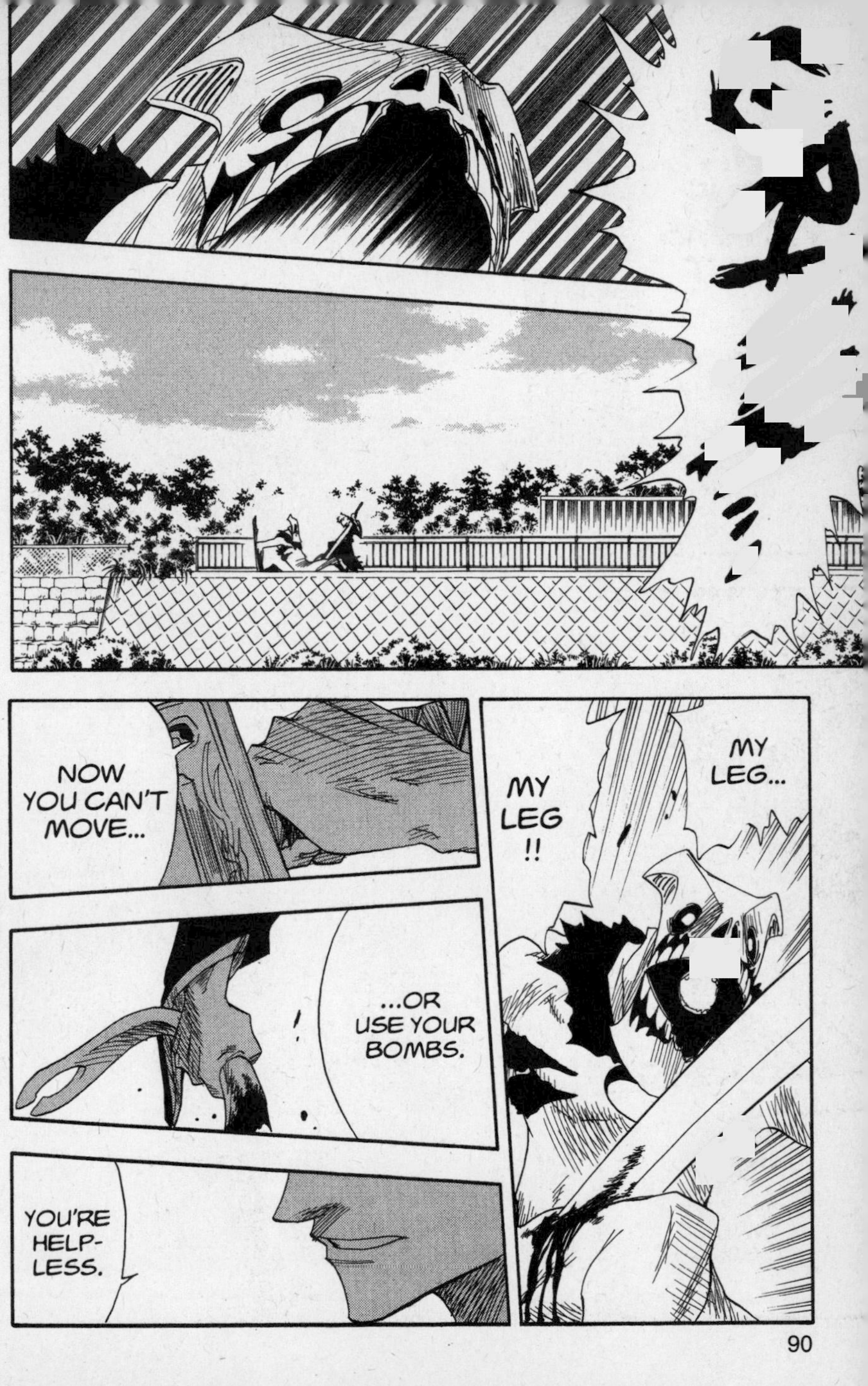
MY LEG...
MY LEG !!
NOW YOU CAN'T MOVE...
...OR USE YOUR BOMBS.
YOU'RE HELP-LESS.

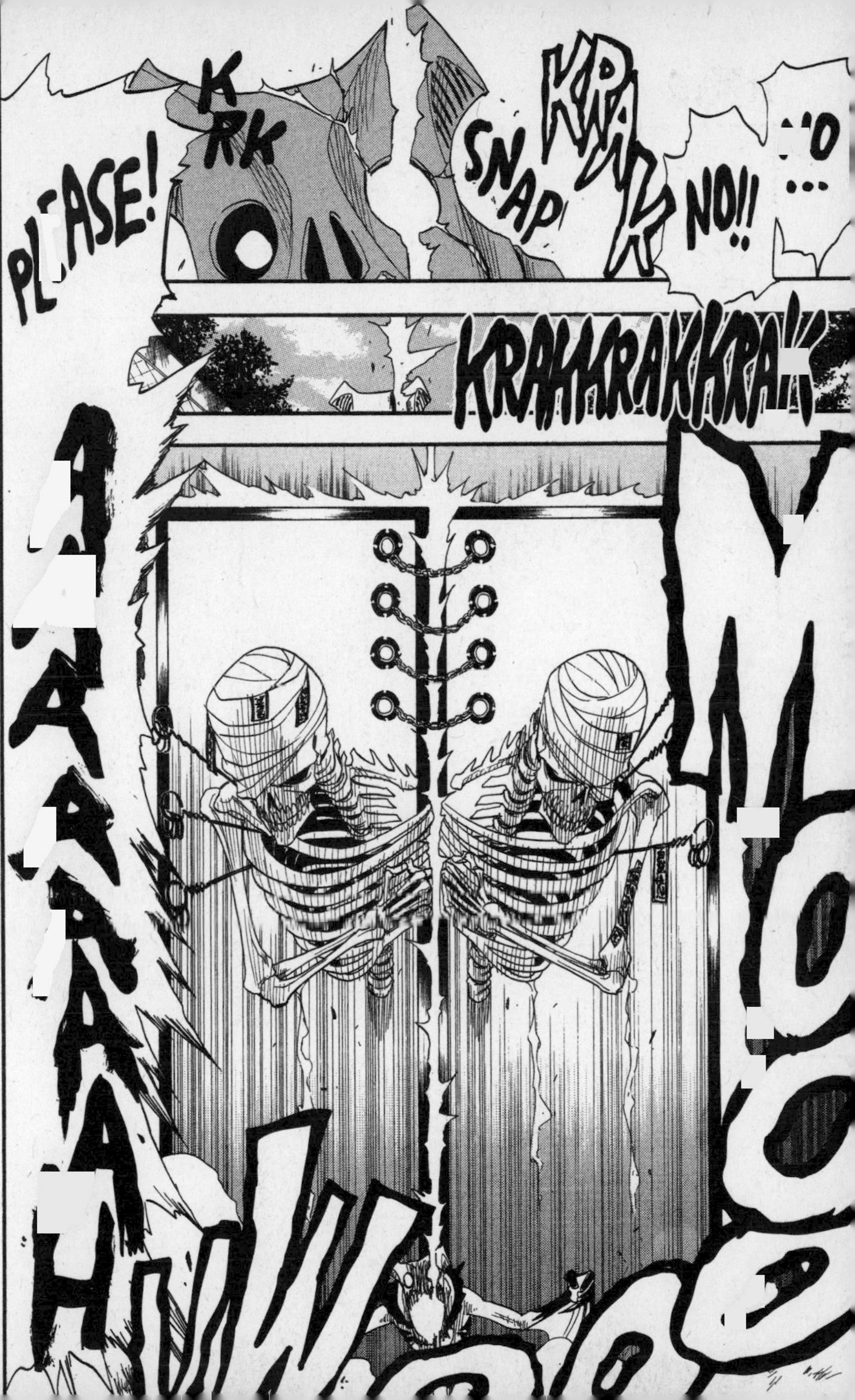
NO...
NO!!
KRAK
SNAP
KRK
RK
PLEASE!
KRAKKRAKKRAK
NOOOO
AAAAAAH

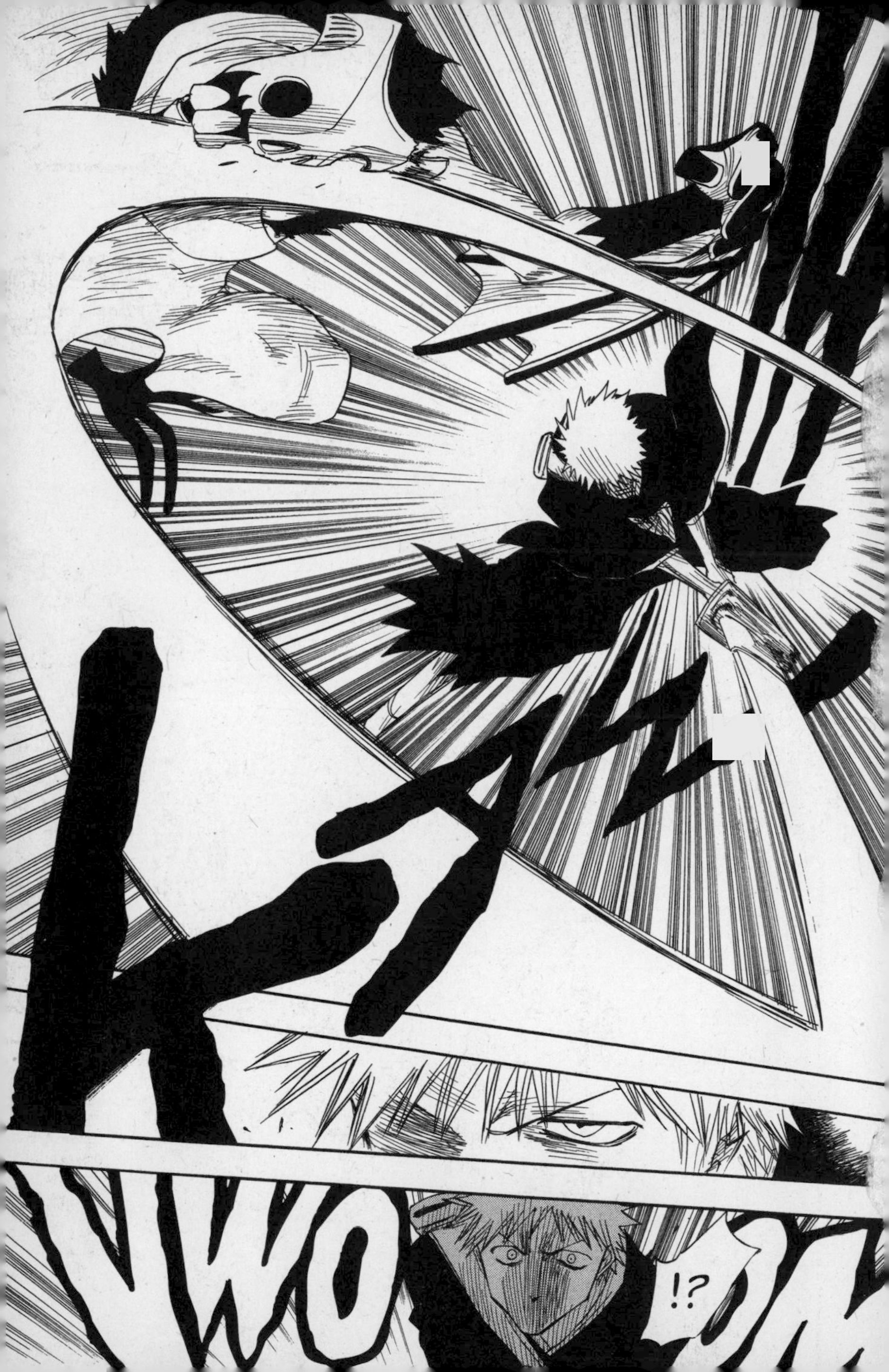
!?

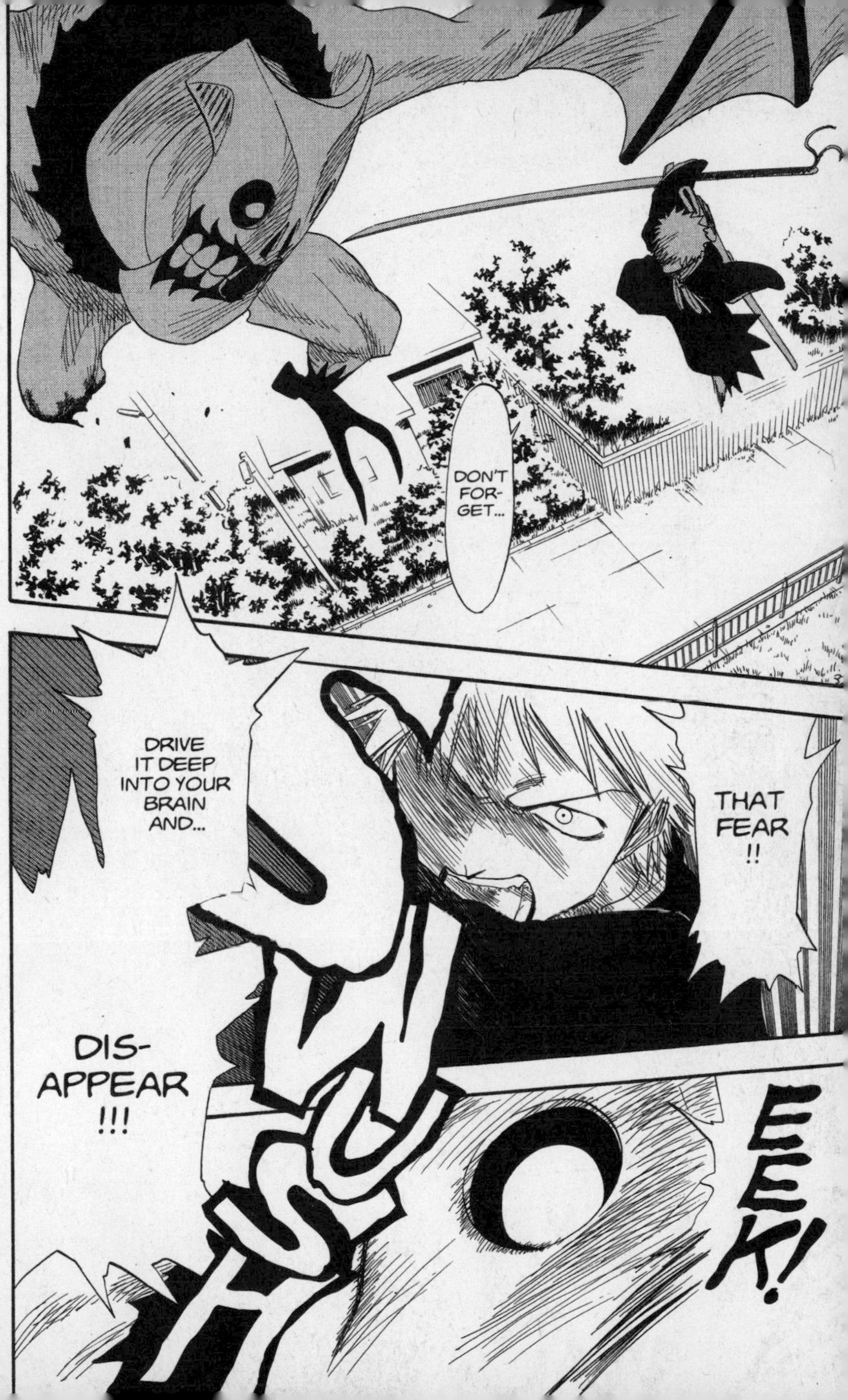
DON'T FORGET...
THAT FEAR !!
DRIVE IT DEEP INTO YOUR BRAIN AND...
DIS-APPEAR !!!
EEK!

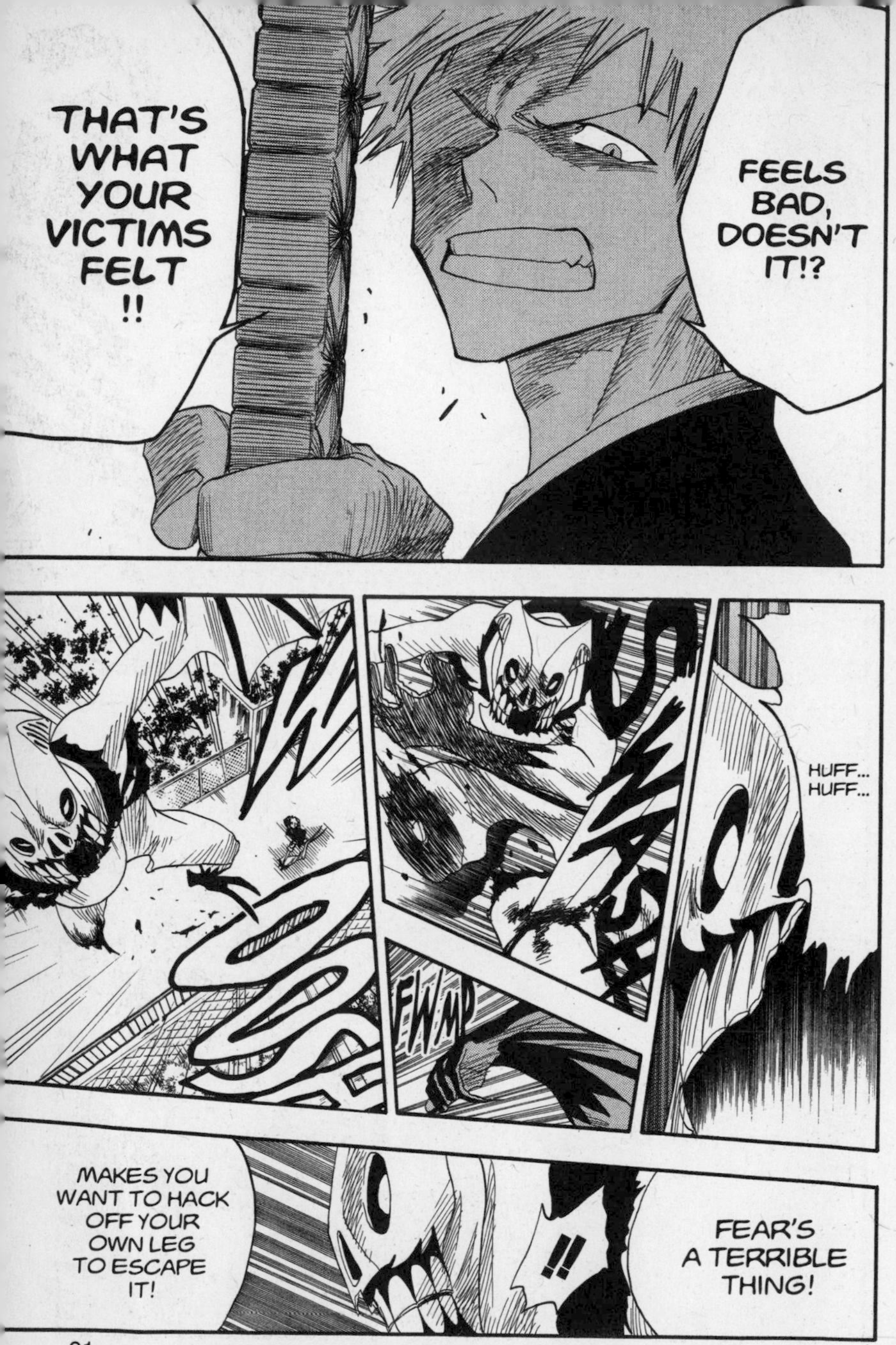

FEELS BAD, DOESN'T IT!?
THAT'S WHAT YOUR VICTIMS FELT !!
HUFF... HUFF...
SWASH
FWMP
FEAR'S A TERRIBLE THING!
!!
MAKES YOU WANT TO HACK OFF YOUR OWN LEG TO ESCAPE IT!

READ THIS WAY

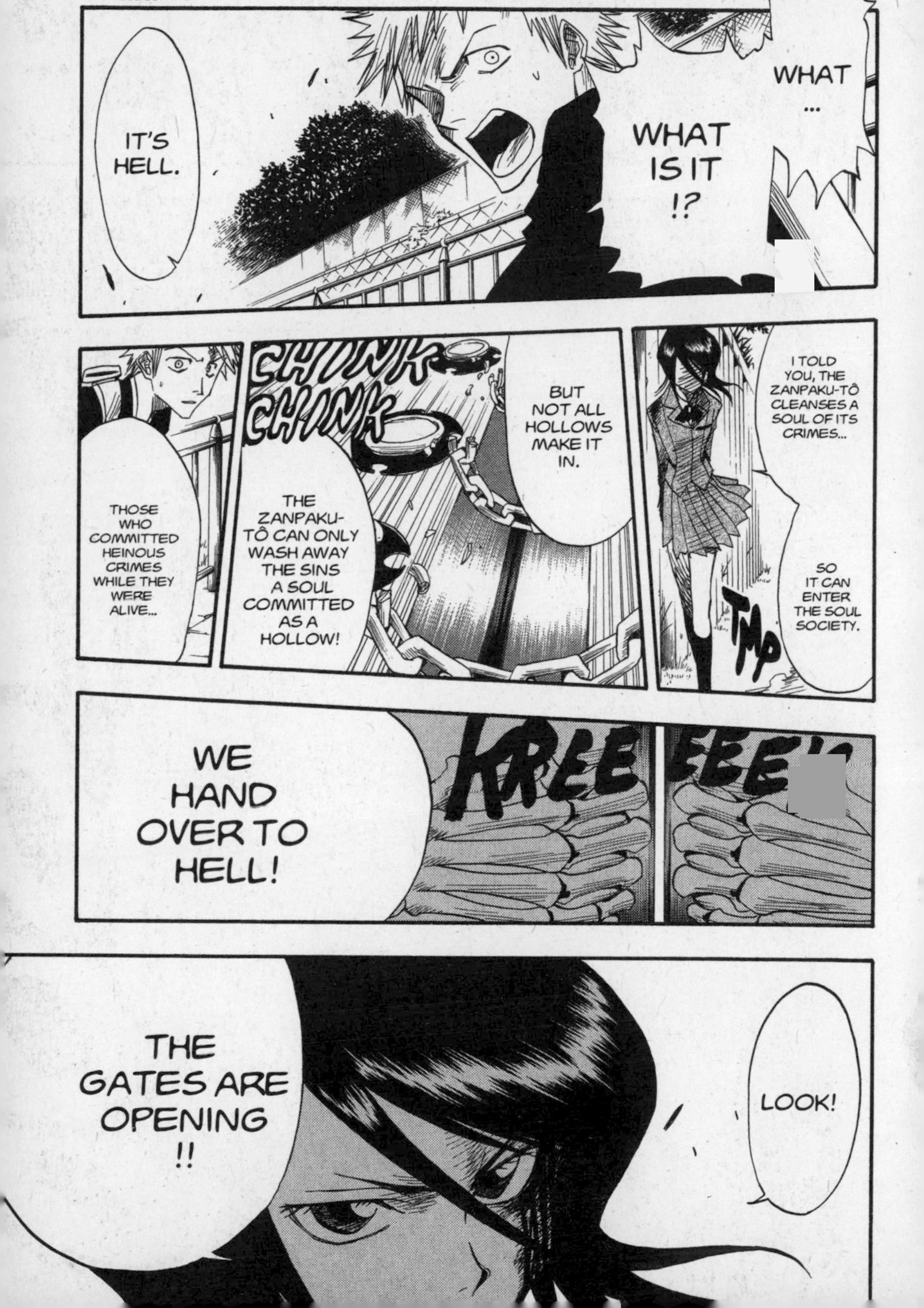
WHAT ...
WHAT IS IT !?
IT'S HELL.
I TOLD YOU, THE ZANPAKU-TÔ CLEANSES A SOUL OF ITS CRIMES...
SO IT CAN ENTER THE SOUL SOCIETY.
TMP
CHINK CHINK
BUT NOT ALL HOLLOWS MAKE IT IN.
THE ZANPAKU-TÔ CAN ONLY WASH AWAY THE SINS A SOUL COMMITTED AS A HOLLOW!
THOSE WHO COMMITTED HEINOUS CRIMES WHILE THEY WERE ALIVE...
KREEEEE
WE HAND OVER TO HELL!
LOOK!
THE GATES ARE OPENING !!

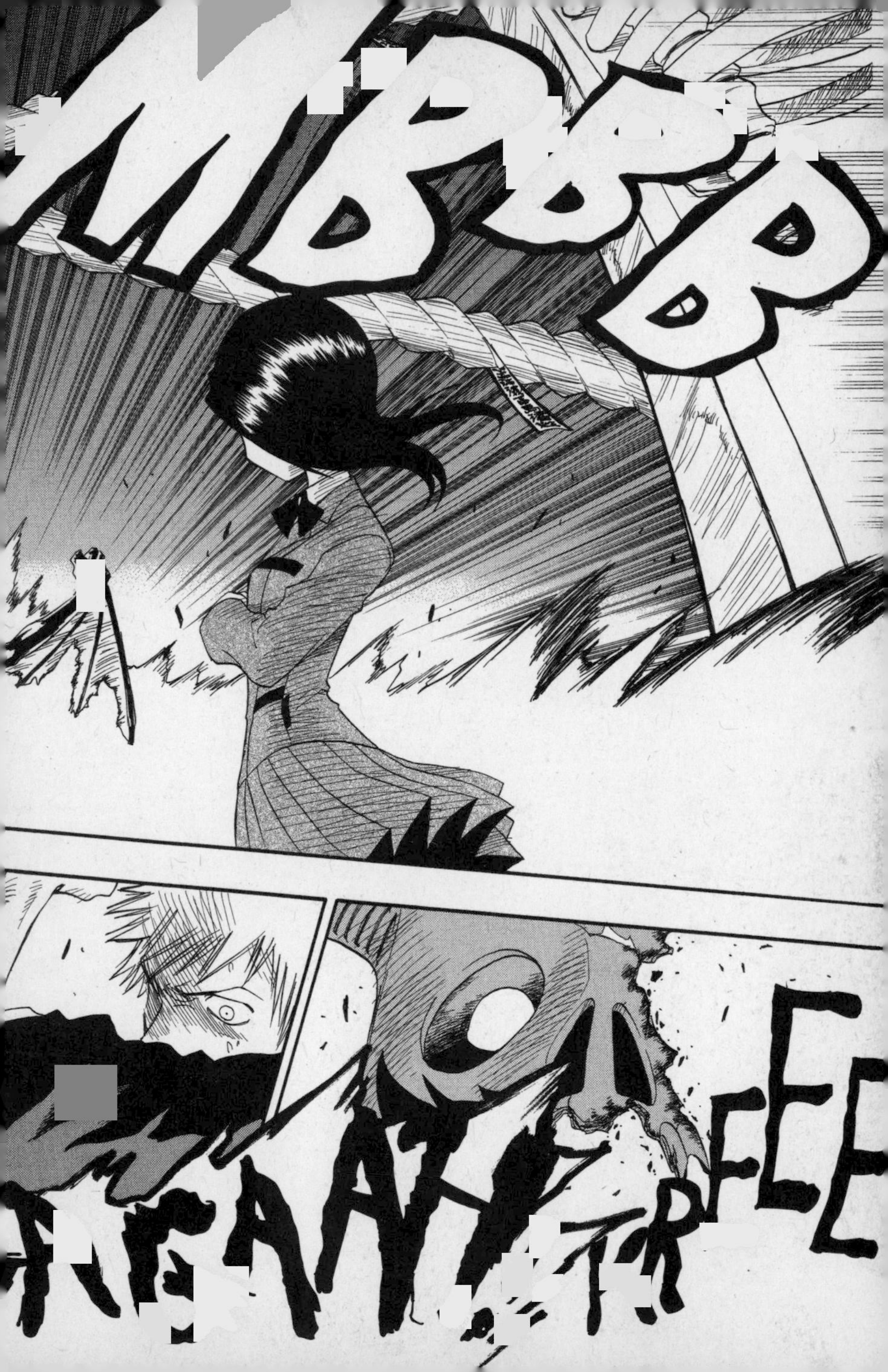

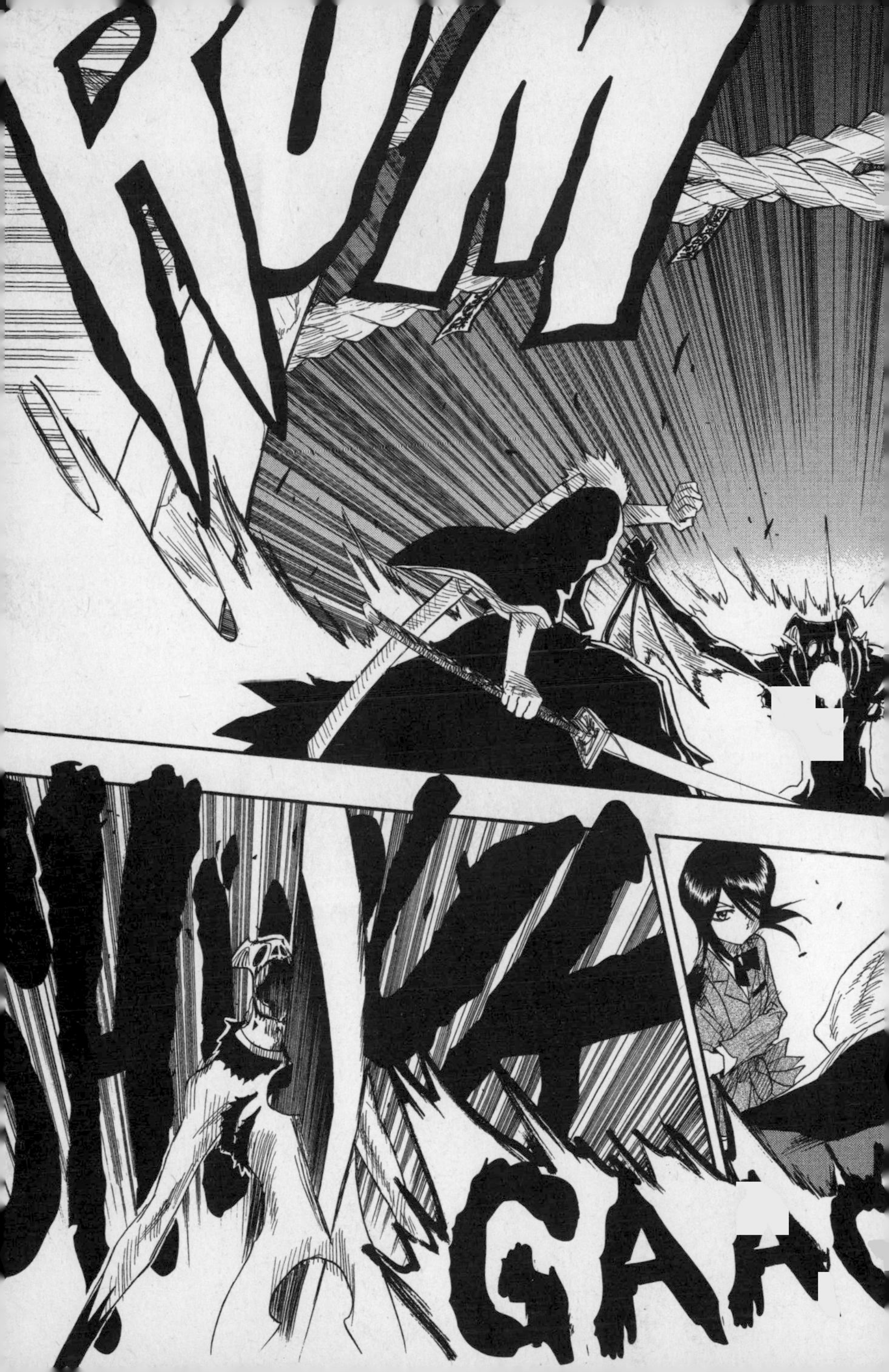

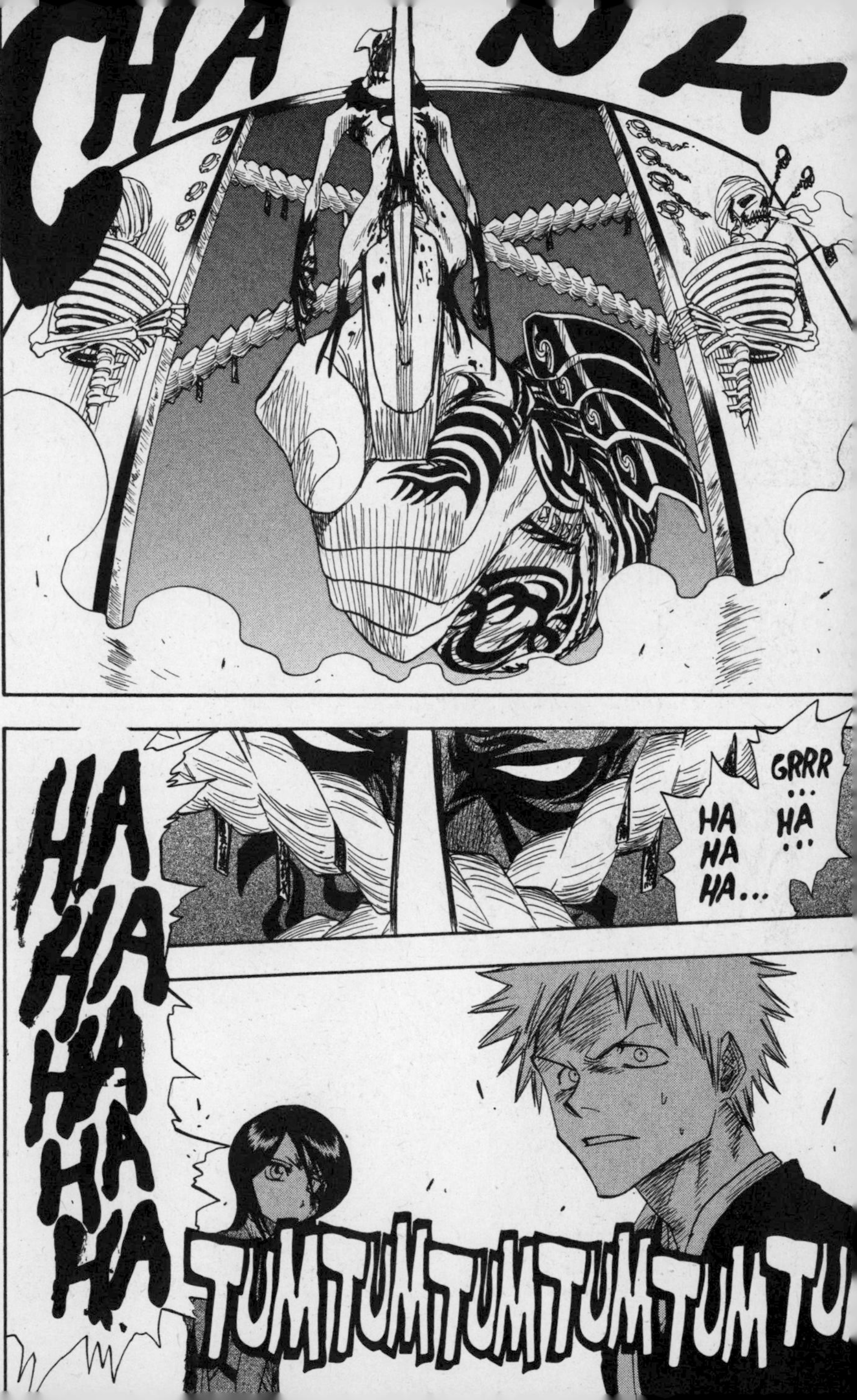
CHA
NK
GRRR... HA...
HA HA HA...
HAHAHAHAHAHAHA
TUM TUM TUM TUM TUM TU

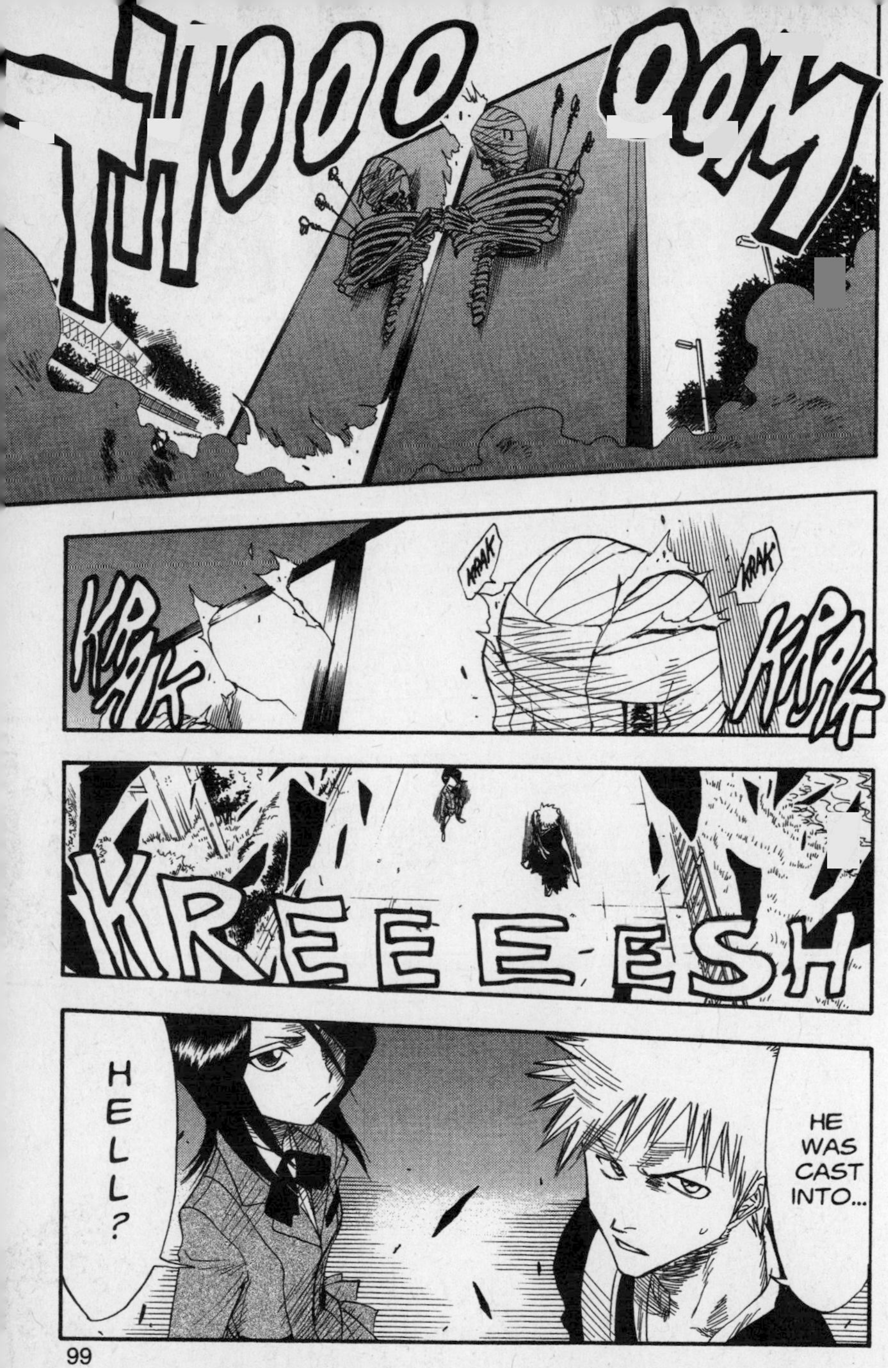
THOOOOOM
KRAK
KRAK
KRAK
KRAK
KREEEESH
HE WAS CAST INTO...
HELL?

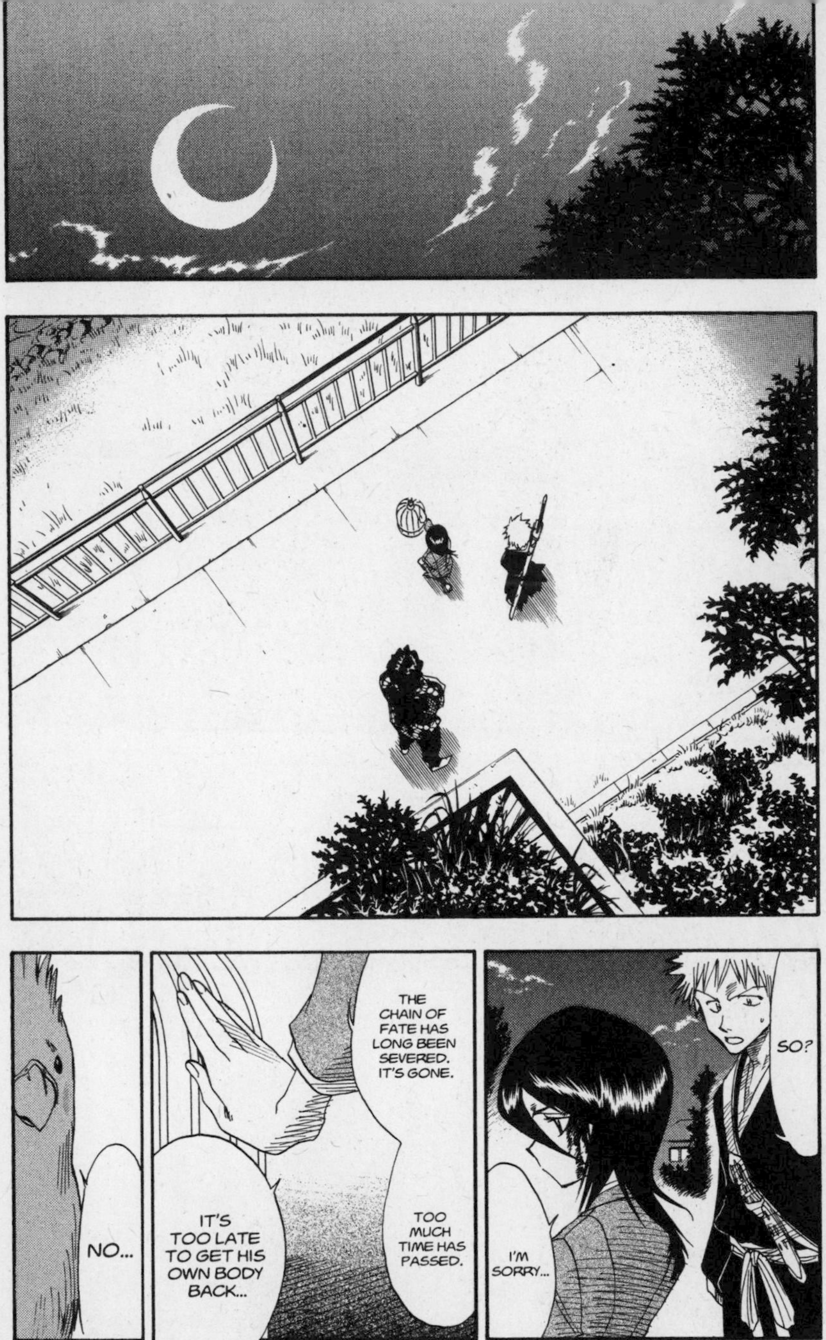
SO?
I'M SORRY...
THE CHAIN OF FATE HAS LONG BEEN SEVERED. IT'S GONE.
TOO MUCH TIME HAS PASSED.
IT'S TOO LATE TO GET HIS OWN BODY BACK...
NO...

READ THIS WAY

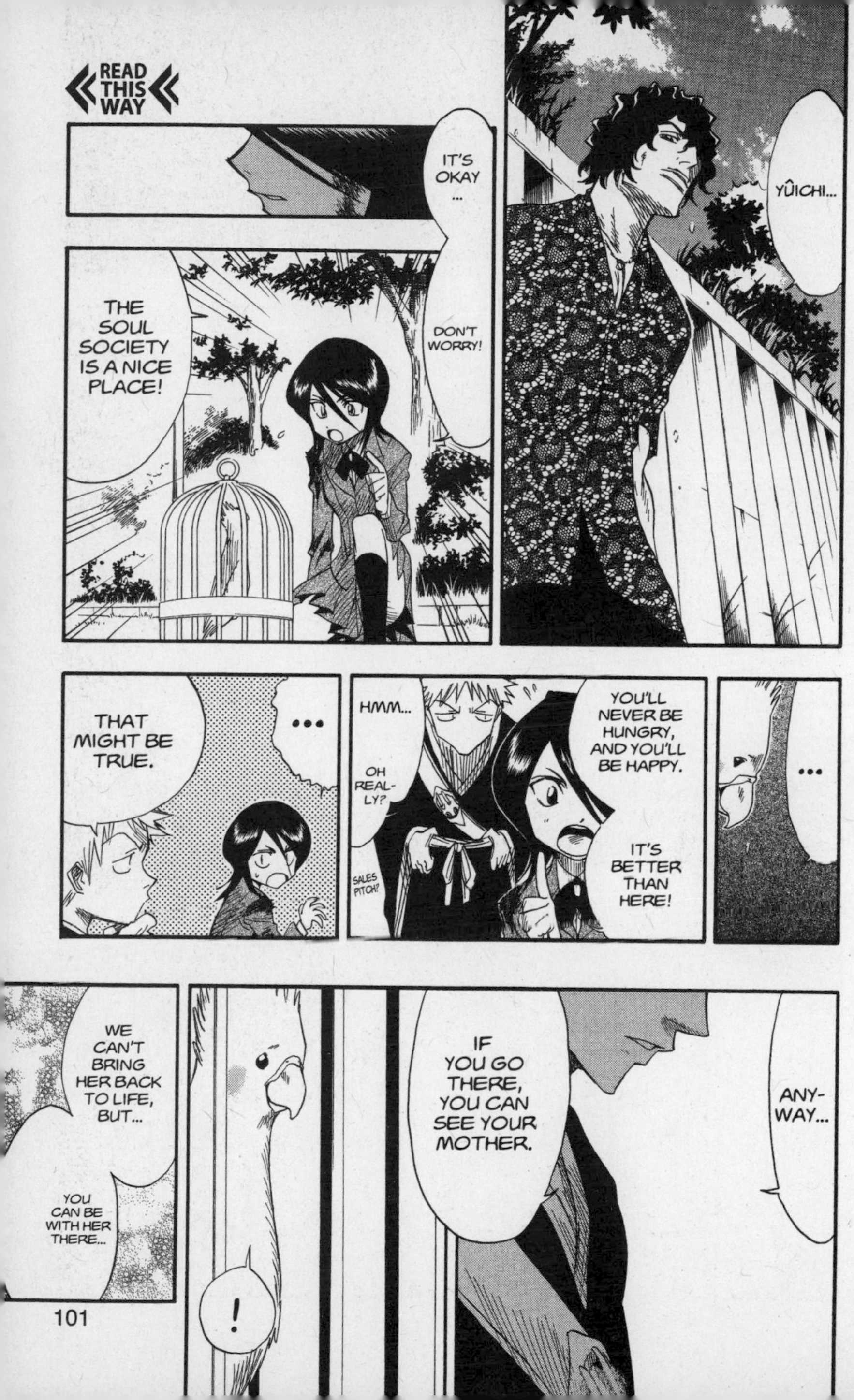

YÛICHI...
IT'S OKAY ...
DON'T WORRY!
THE SOUL SOCIETY IS A NICE PLACE!
...
YOU'LL NEVER BE HUNGRY, AND YOU'LL BE HAPPY.
IT'S BETTER THAN HERE!
HMM...
OH REAL-LY?
SALES PITCH?
...
THAT MIGHT BE TRUE.
ANY-WAY...
IF YOU GO THERE, YOU CAN SEE YOUR MOTHER.
!
WE CAN'T BRING HER BACK TO LIFE, BUT...
YOU CAN BE WITH HER THERE...

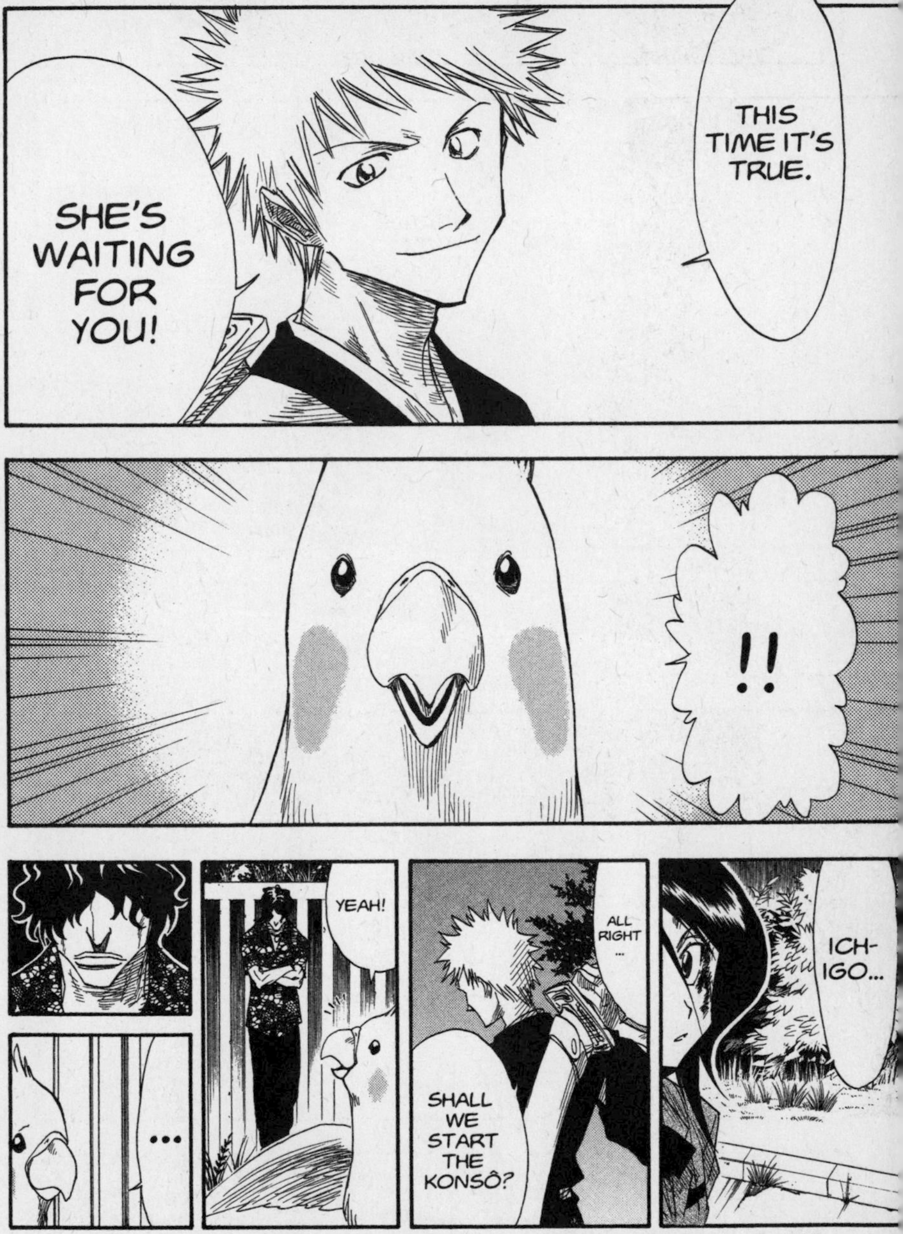
THIS TIME IT'S TRUE.
SHE'S WAITING FOR YOU!
!!
ICH-IGO...
ALL RIGHT...
SHALL WE START THE KONSÔ?
YEAH!
...

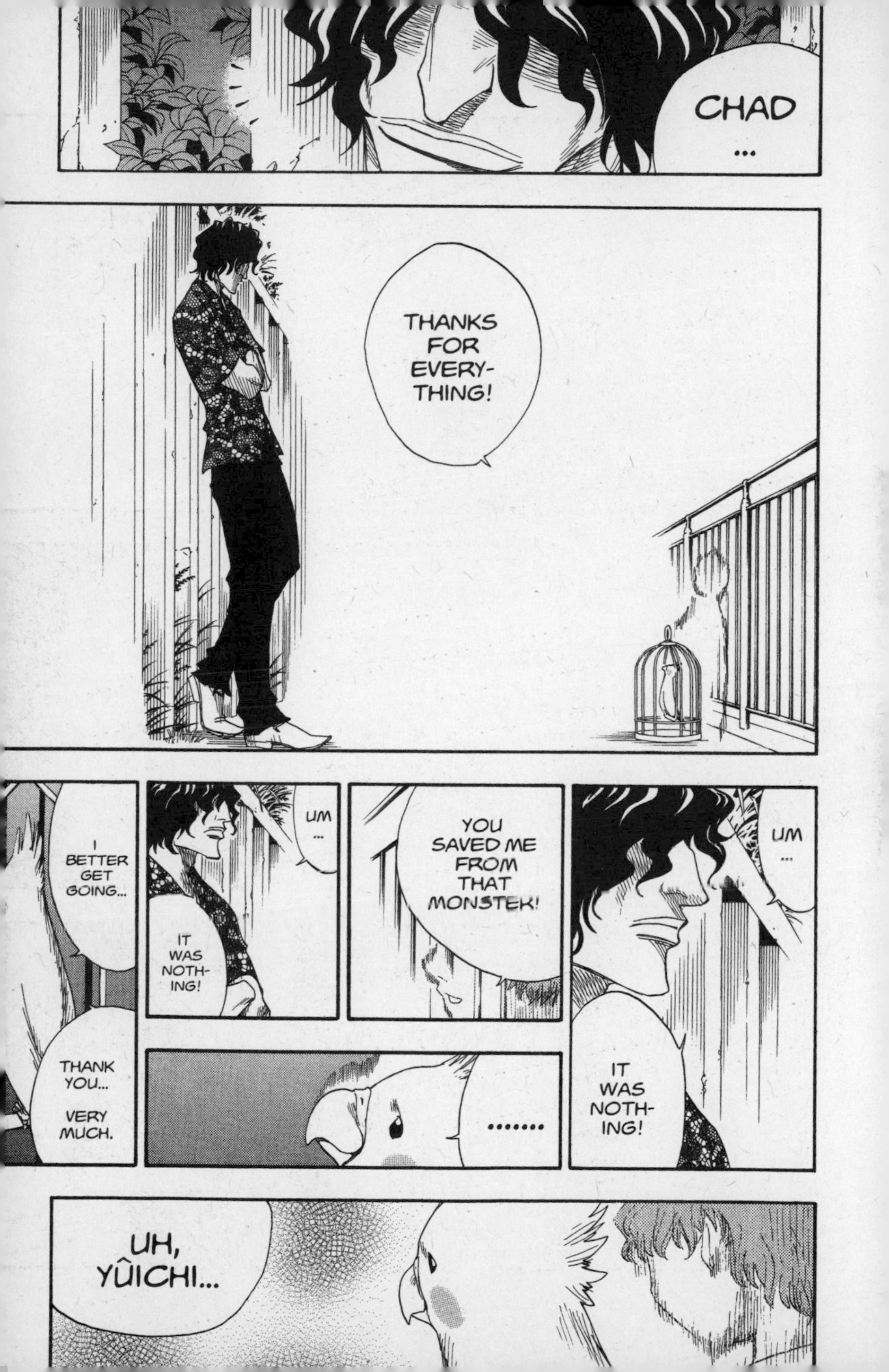
CHAD ...
THANKS FOR EVERY-THING!
UM ...
IT WAS NOTH-ING!
YOU SAVED ME FROM THAT MONSTER!
UM ...
IT WAS NOTH-ING!
....
I BETTER GET GOING...
THANK YOU... VERY MUCH.
UH, YÛICHI...

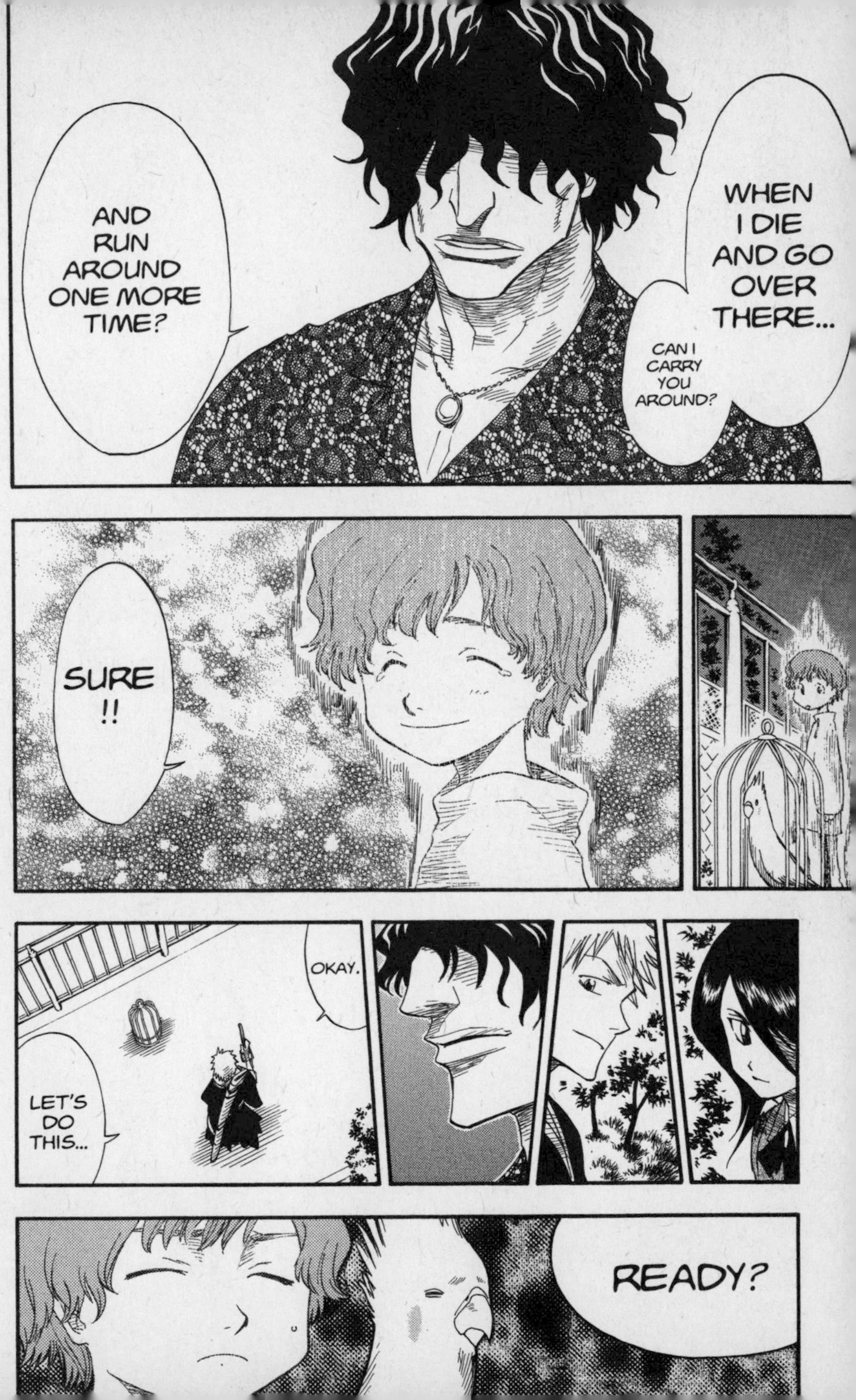
WHEN I DIE AND GO OVER THERE...
CAN I CARRY YOU AROUND?
AND RUN AROUND ONE MORE TIME?
SURE !!
OKAY.
LET'S DO THIS...
READY?

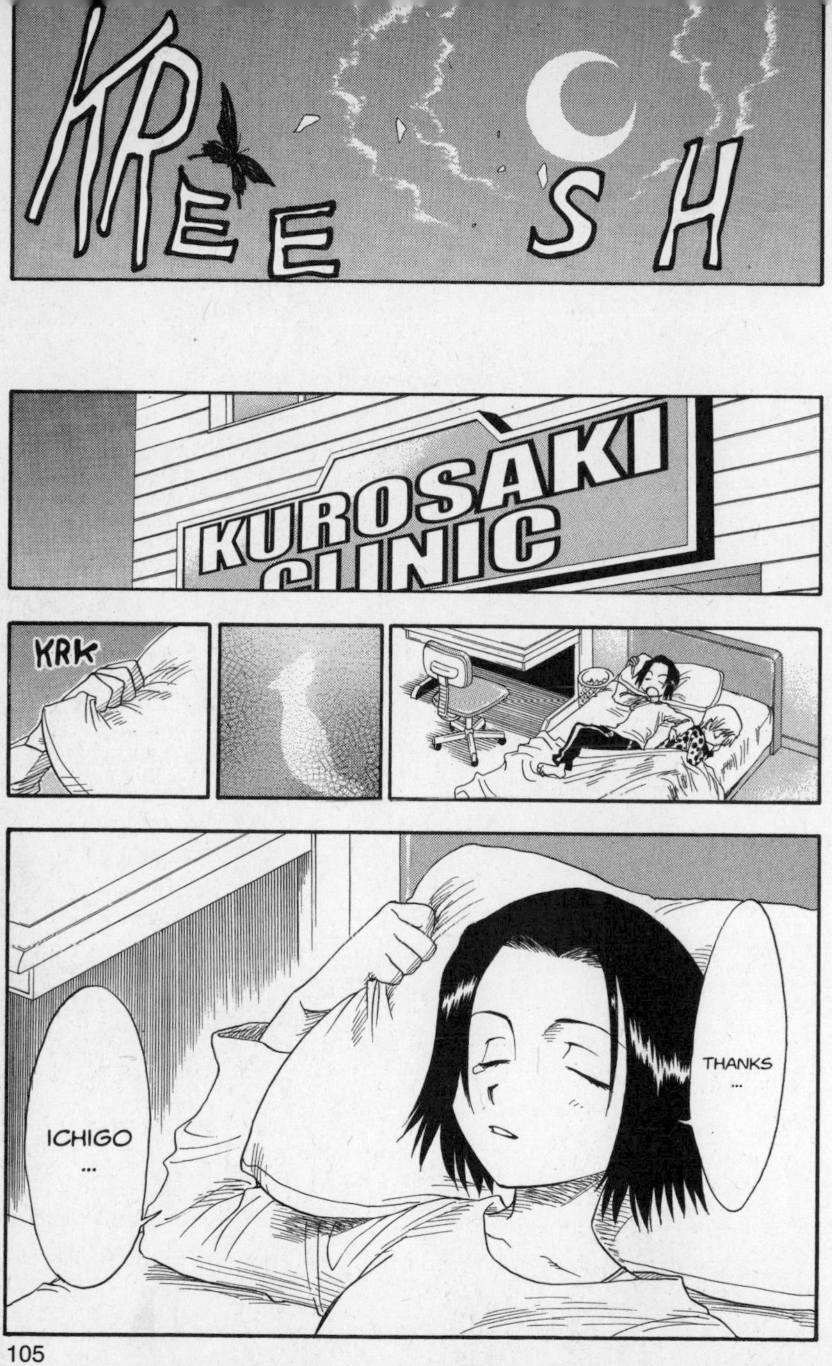
KREESH
KUROSAKI CLINIC
KRK
THANKS ...
ICHIGO ...

13. BAD STANDARD

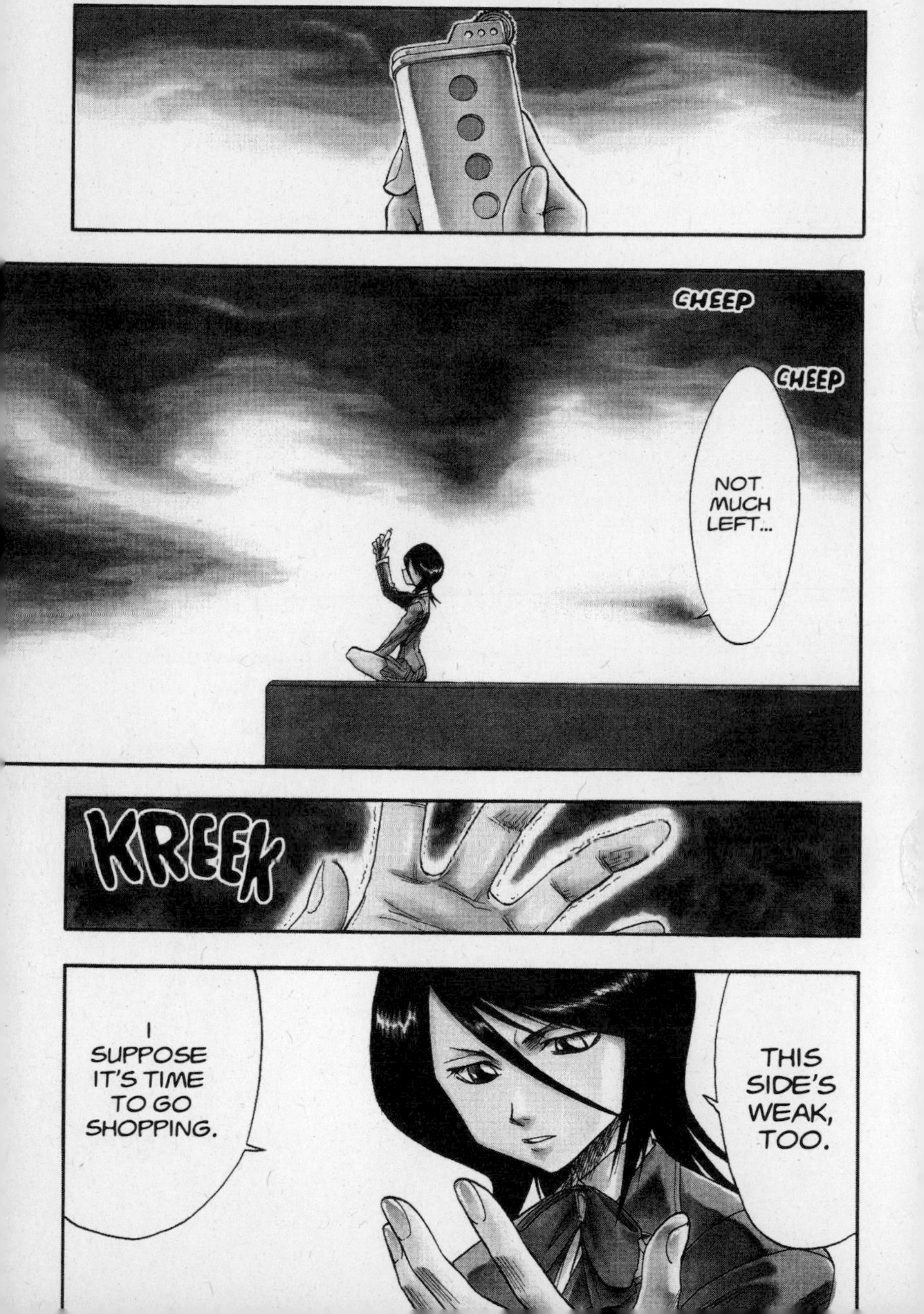
CHEEP
CHEEP
NOT MUCH LEFT...
KREEK
THIS SIDE'S WEAK, TOO.
I SUPPOSE IT'S TIME TO GO SHOPPING.

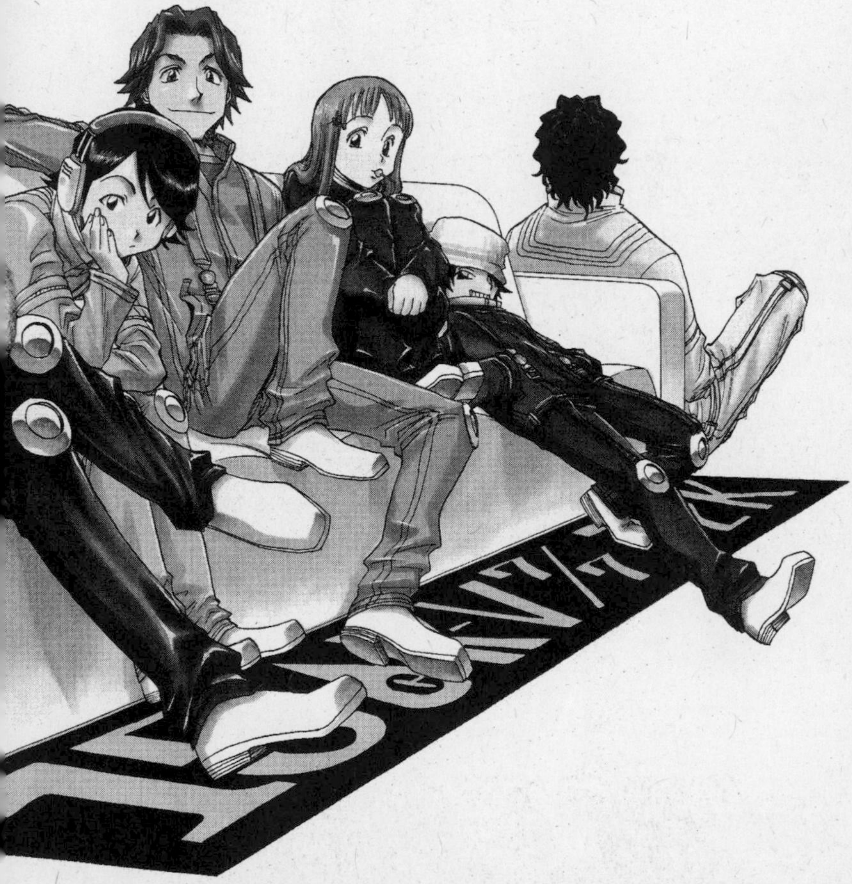

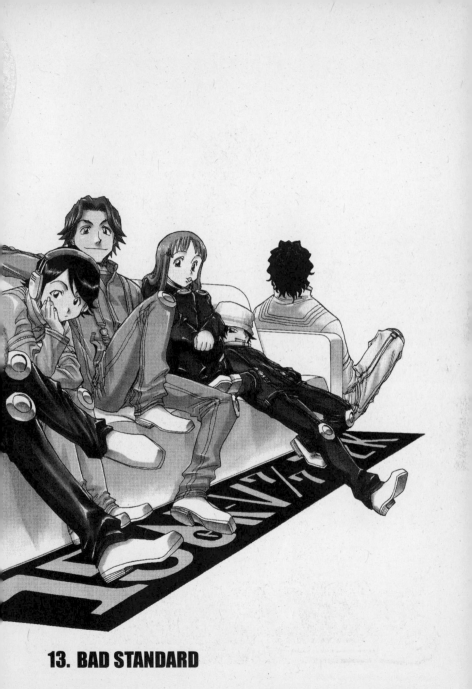

13. BAD STANDARD

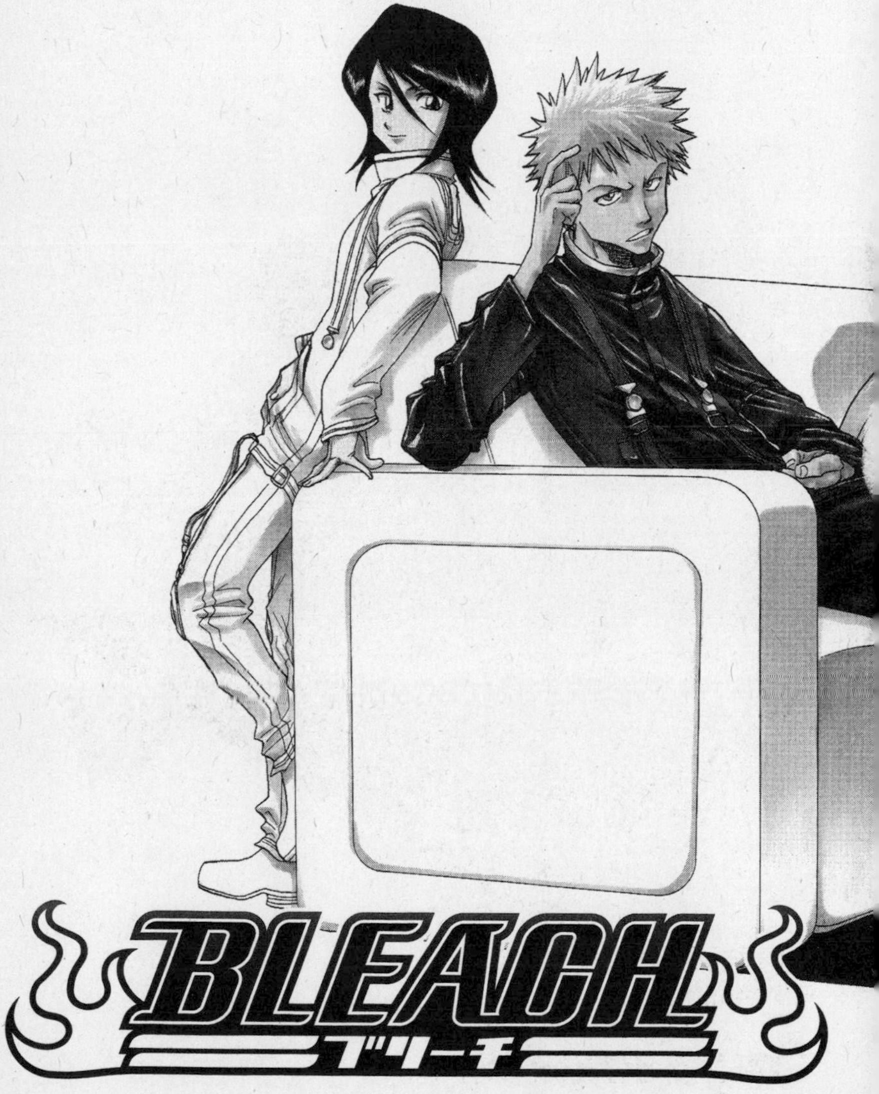

BLEACH
ブリーチ

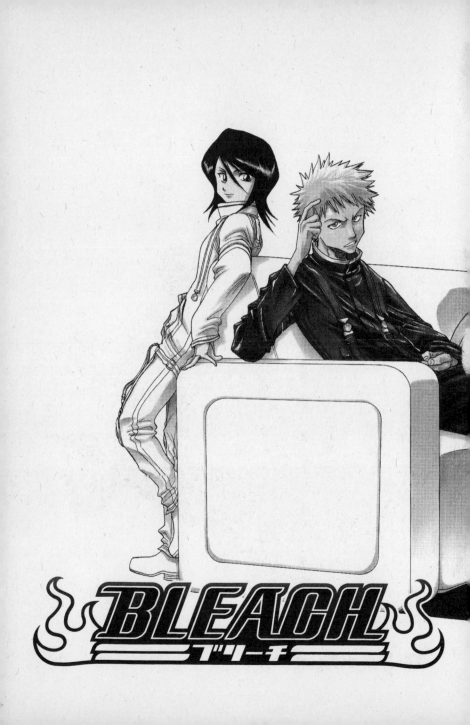

READ THIS WAY

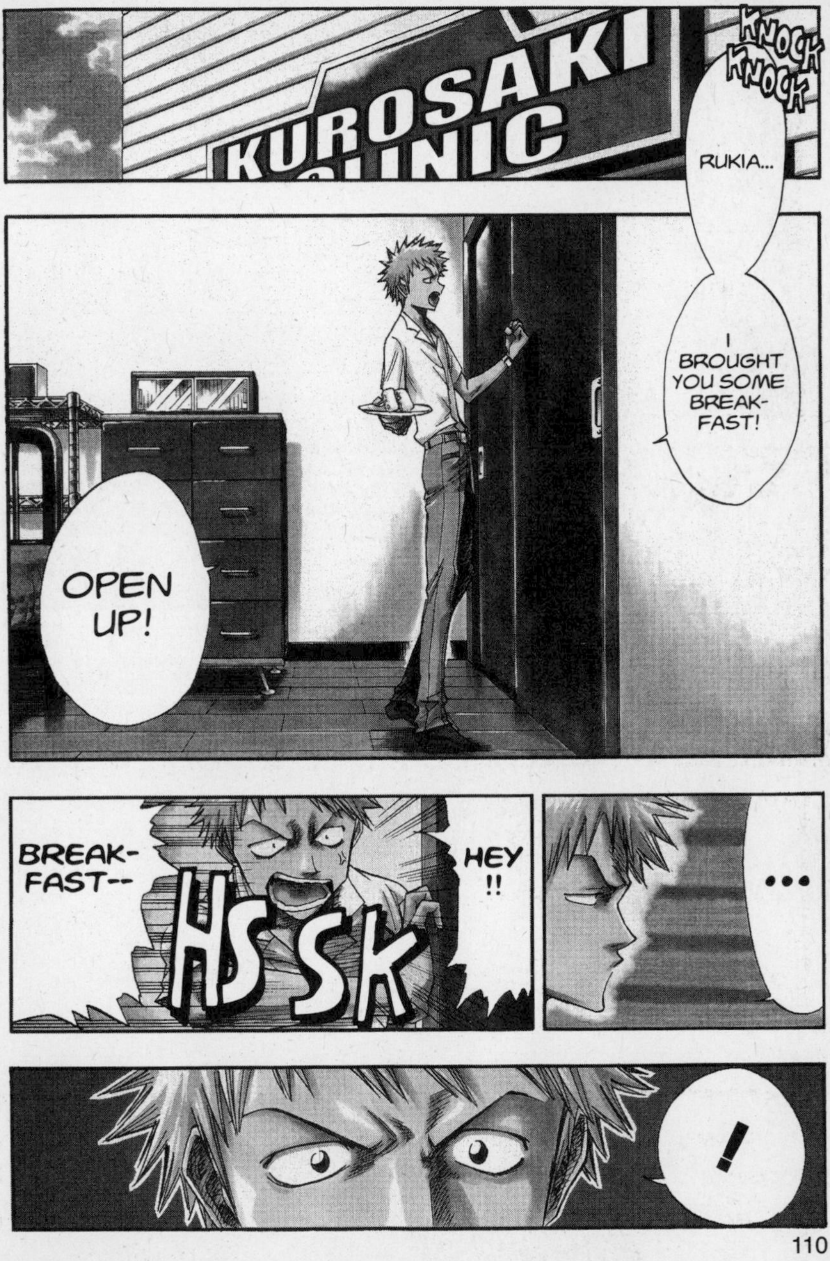
KNOCK KNOCK
RUKIA...
I BROUGHT YOU SOME BREAK-FAST!
OPEN UP!
...
HEY !!
HSSK
BREAK-FAST--
!

READ THIS WAY

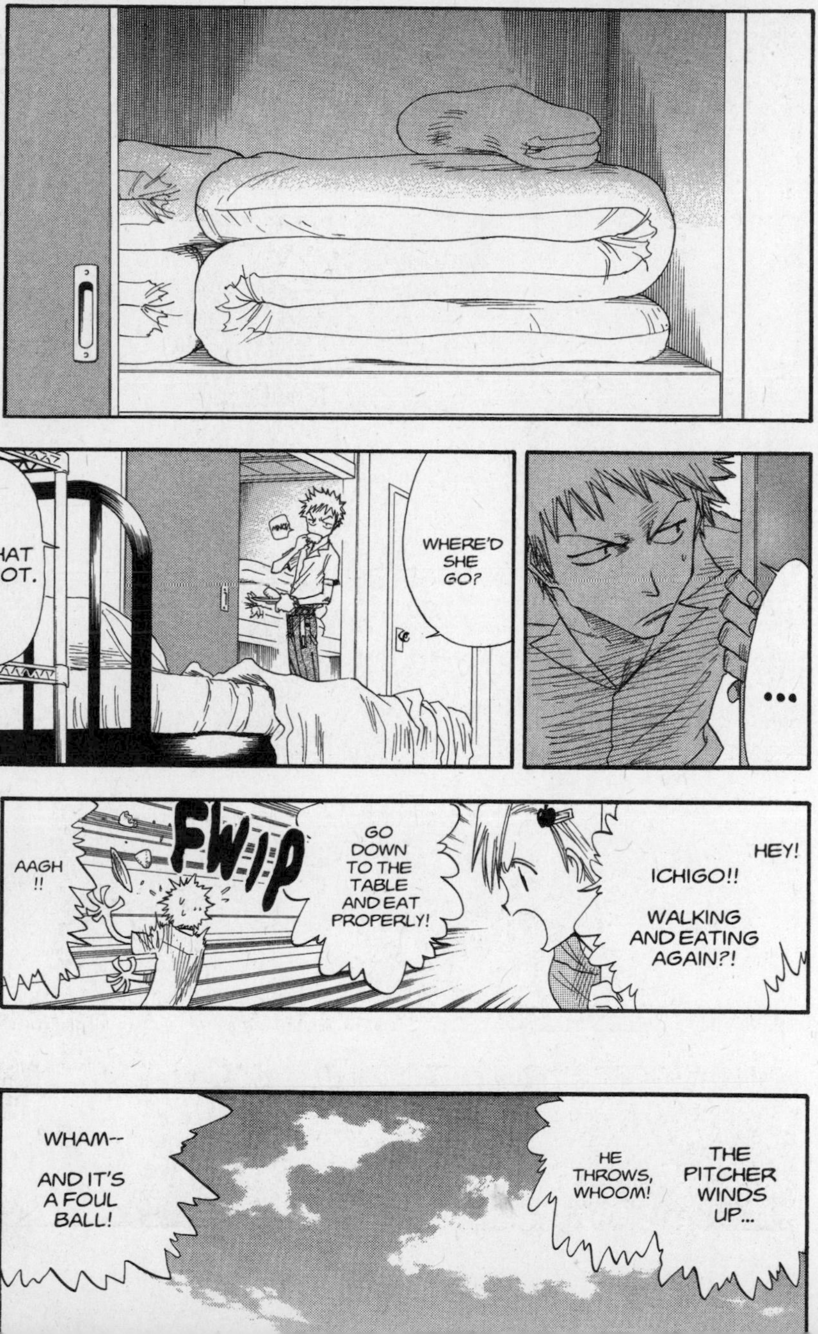
...
WHERE'D SHE GO?
THAT IDIOT.
HEY!
ICHIGO!!
WALKING AND EATING AGAIN?!
GO DOWN TO THE TABLE AND EAT PROPERLY!
FWIP
AAGH!!
THE PITCHER WINDS UP...
HE THROWS, WHOOM!
WHAM--
AND IT'S A FOUL BALL!

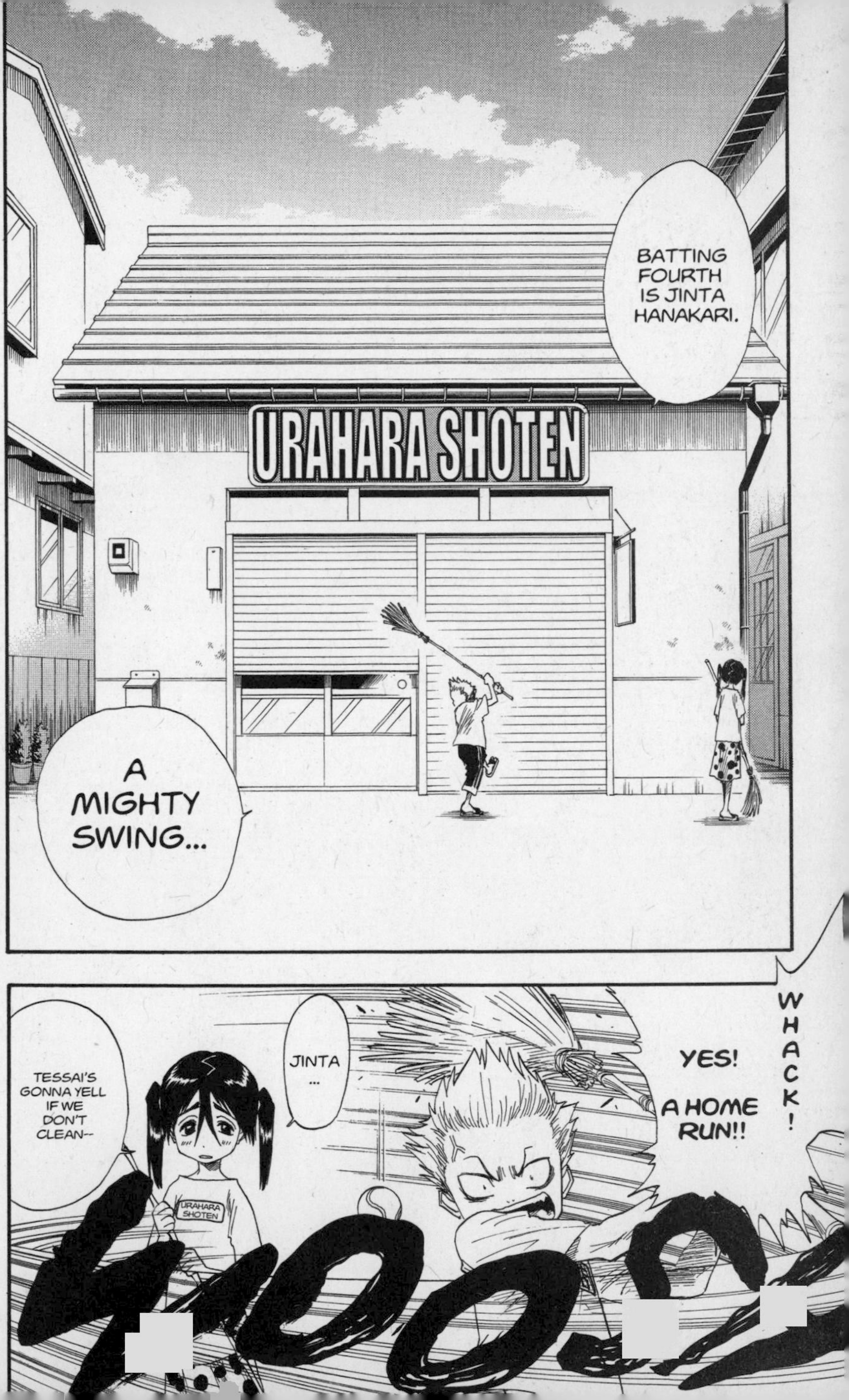
BATTING FOURTH IS JINTA HANAKARI.
A MIGHTY SWING...
URAHARA SHOTEN
WHACK!
YES!
A HOME RUN!!
JINTA ...
TESSAI'S GONNA YELL IF WE DON'T CLEAN--
URAHARA SHOTEN

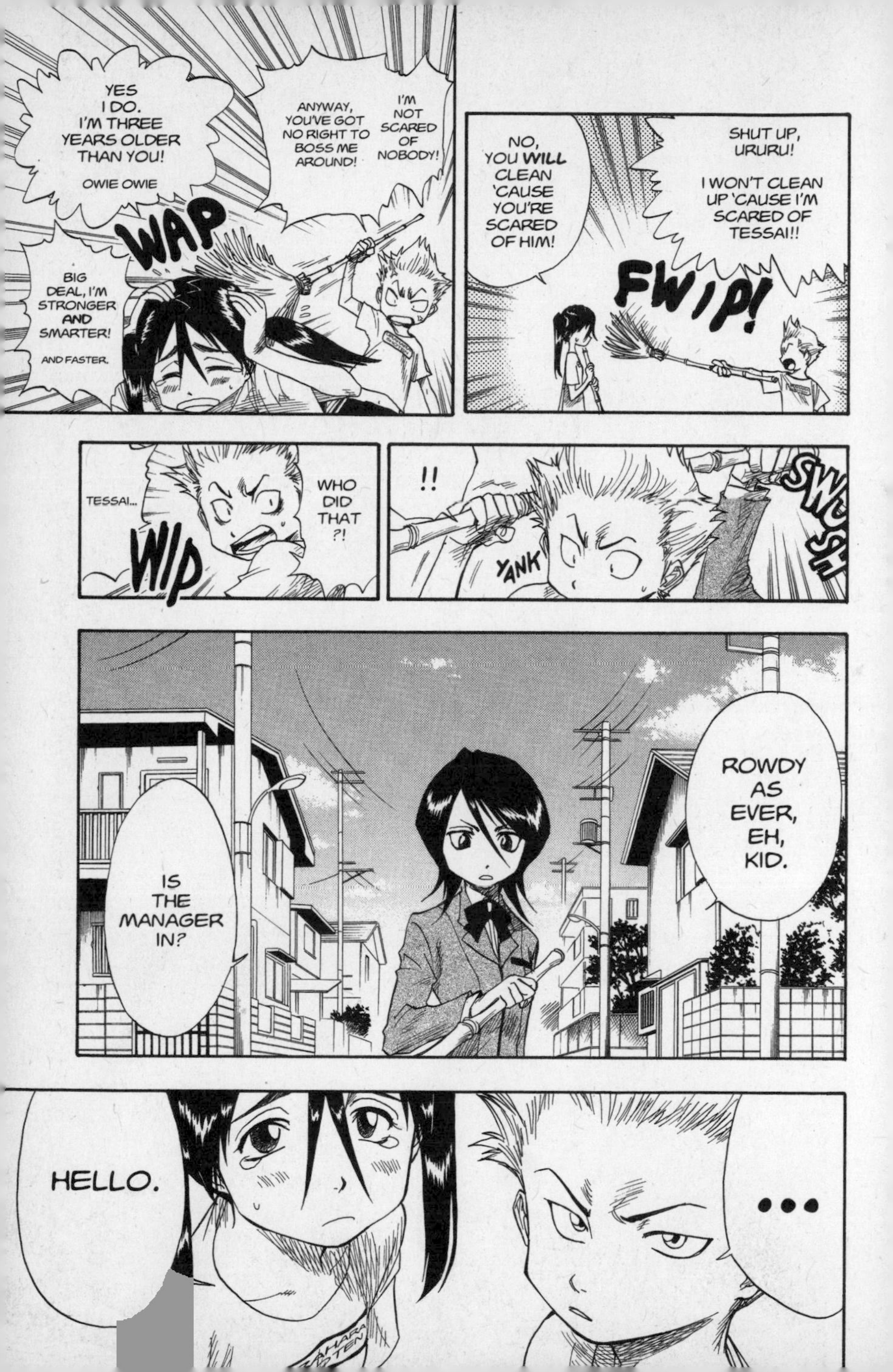
SHUT UP, URURU!
I WON'T CLEAN UP 'CAUSE I'M SCARED OF TESSAI!!
NO, YOU WILL CLEAN 'CAUSE YOU'RE SCARED OF HIM!
FWIP!
I'M NOT SCARED OF NOBODY!
ANYWAY, YOU'VE GOT NO RIGHT TO BOSS ME AROUND!
YES I DO. I'M THREE YEARS OLDER THAN YOU!
OWIE OWIE
WAP
BIG DEAL, I'M STRONGER AND SMARTER!
AND FASTER.
!!
SWISH
YANK
WHO DID THAT ?!
TESSAI...
WIP
ROWDY AS EVER, EH, KID.
IS THE MANAGER IN?
...
HELLO.

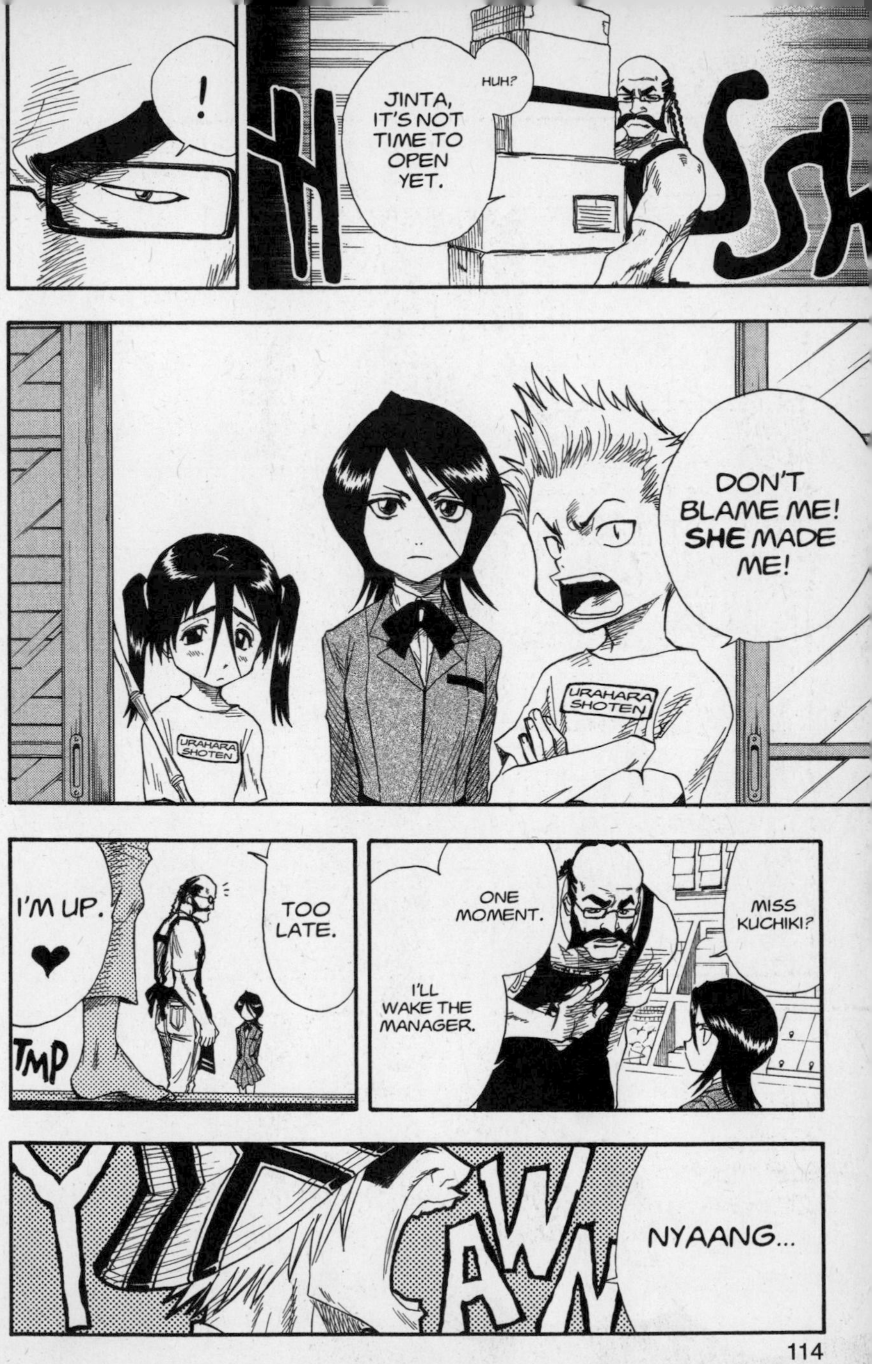
SSH
HUH?
JINTA, IT'S NOT TIME TO OPEN YET.
!
DON'T BLAME ME! SHE MADE ME!
MISS KUCHIKI?
ONE MOMENT.
I'LL WAKE THE MANAGER.
TOO LATE.
I'M UP. ♥
TMP
NYAANG...
YAWN

READ THIS WAY

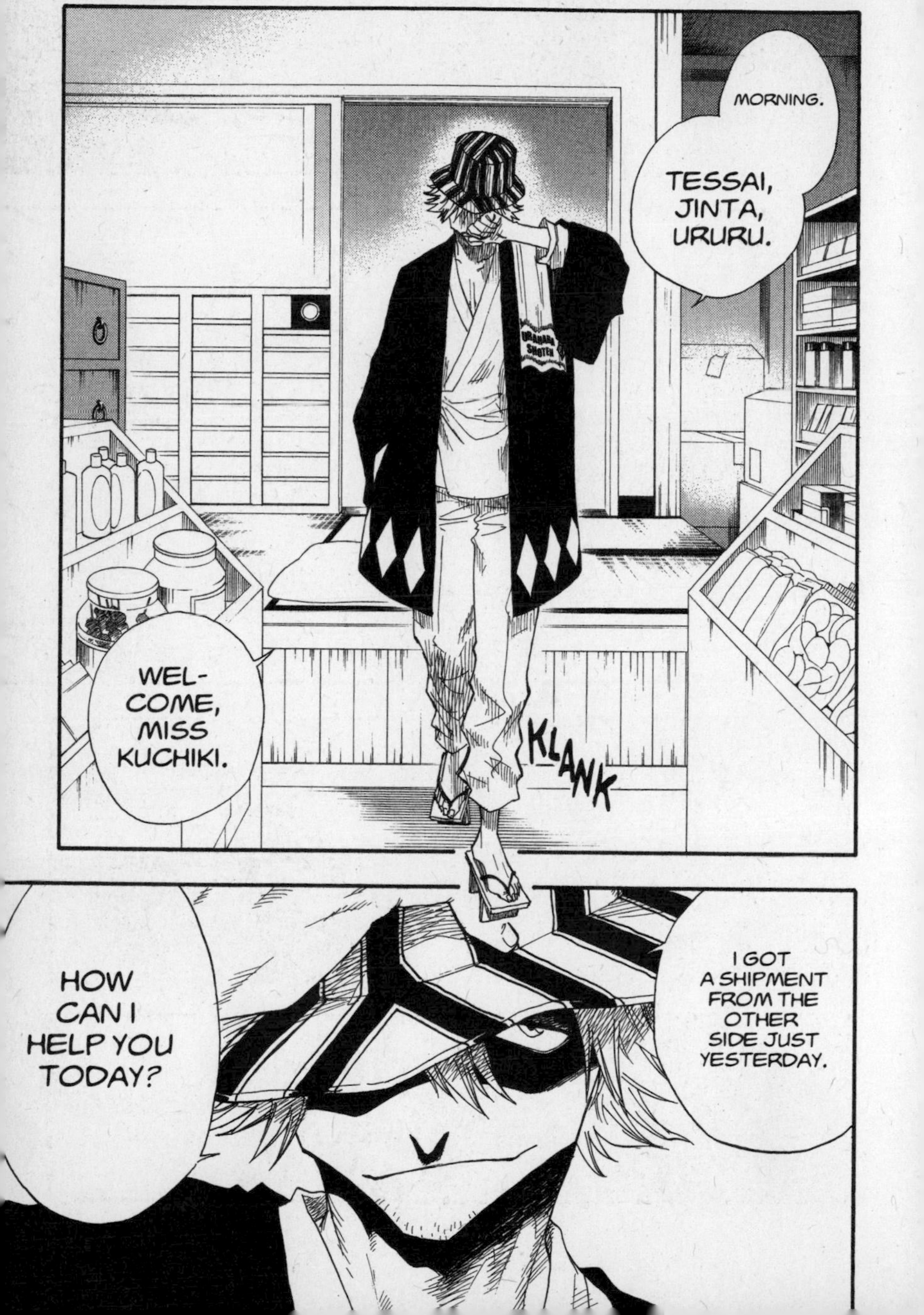
MORNING.
TESSAI, JINTA, URURU.
WEL-COME, MISS KUCHIKI.
KLANK
I GOT A SHIPMENT FROM THE OTHER SIDE JUST YESTERDAY.
HOW CAN I HELP YOU TODAY?

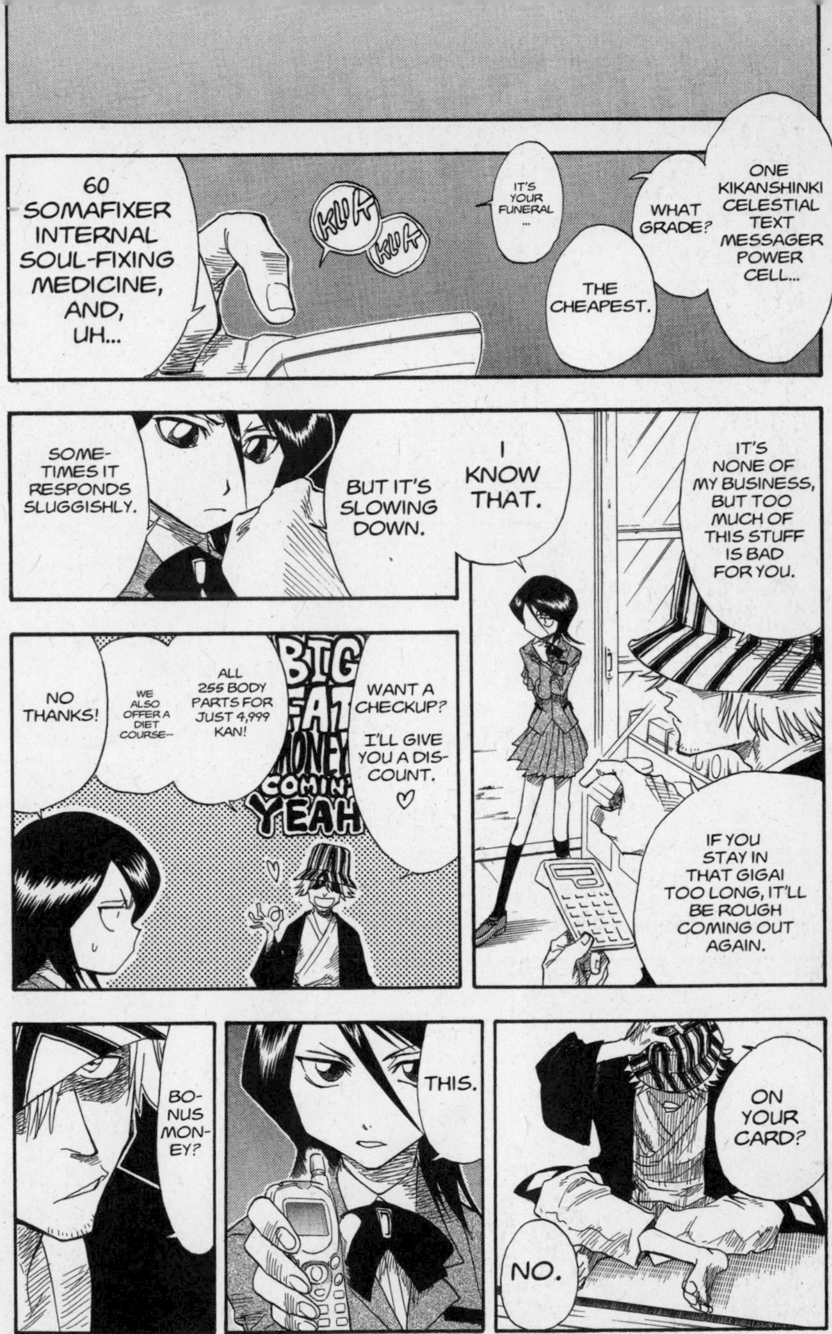
ONE KIKANSHINKI CELESTIAL TEXT MESSAGER POWER CELL...
WHAT GRADE?
THE CHEAPEST.
IT'S YOUR FUNERAL...
KLIK
KLIK
60 SOMAFIXER INTERNAL SOUL-FIXING MEDICINE, AND, UH...
IT'S NONE OF MY BUSINESS, BUT TOO MUCH OF THIS STUFF IS BAD FOR YOU.
I KNOW THAT.
IF YOU STAY IN THAT GIGAI TOO LONG, IT'LL BE ROUGH COMING OUT AGAIN.
BUT IT'S SLOWING DOWN.
SOME-TIMES IT RESPONDS SLUGGISHLY.
WANT A CHECKUP? I'LL GIVE YOU A DIS-COUNT. ♡
BIG FAT MONEY COMIN' YEAH
ALL 255 BODY PARTS FOR JUST 4,999 KAN!
WE ALSO OFFER A DIET COURSE--
NO THANKS!
ON YOUR CARD?
NO.
THIS.
BO-NUS MON-EY?

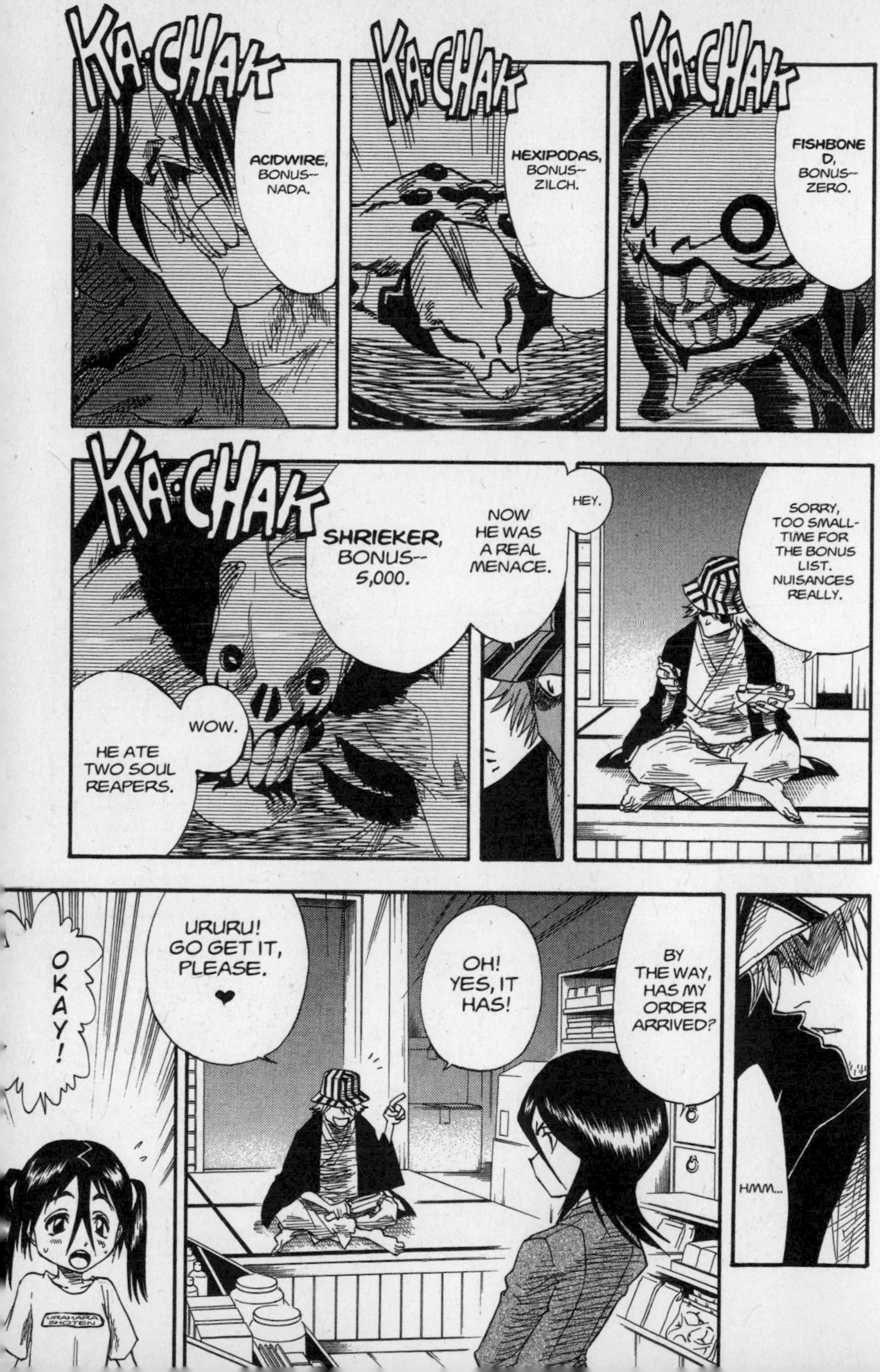
KA-CHAK
FISHBONE D, BONUS--ZERO.
KA-CHAK
HEXIPODAS, BONUS--ZILCH.
KA-CHAK
ACIDWIRE, BONUS--NADA.
SORRY, TOO SMALL-TIME FOR THE BONUS LIST. NUISANCES REALLY.
HEY.
KA-CHAK
SHRIEKER, BONUS--5,000.
NOW HE WAS A REAL MENACE.
WOW.
HE ATE TWO SOUL REAPERS.
HMM...
BY THE WAY, HAS MY ORDER ARRIVED?
OH! YES, IT HAS!
URURU! GO GET IT, PLEASE. ❤
OKAY!
URAHARA SHOTEN

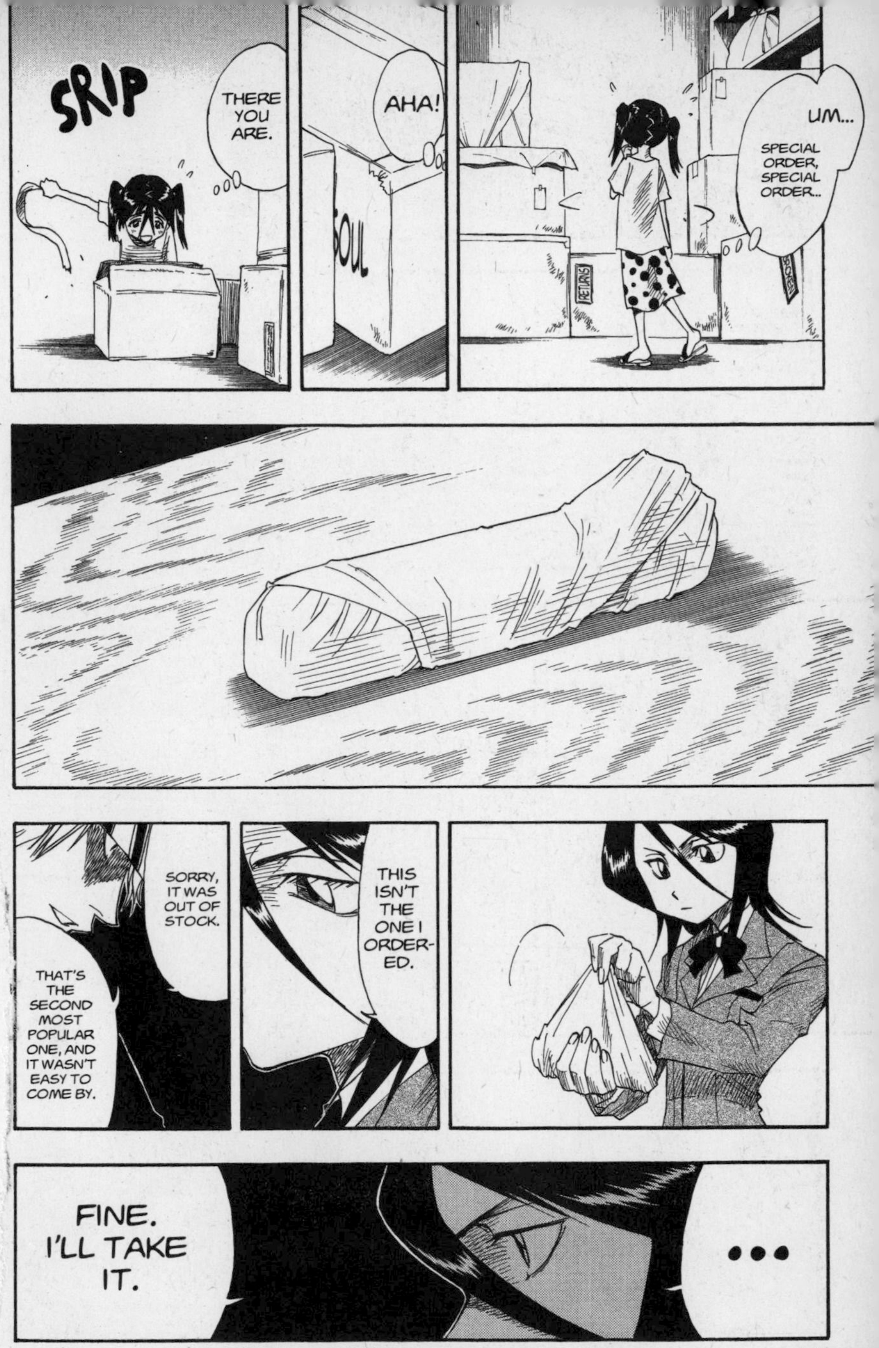
UM...
SPECIAL ORDER, SPECIAL ORDER...
RETURNS
AHA!
SOUL
SRIP
THERE YOU ARE.
THIS ISN'T THE ONE I ORDER-ED.
SORRY, IT WAS OUT OF STOCK.
THAT'S THE SECOND MOST POPULAR ONE, AND IT WASN'T EASY TO COME BY.
•••
FINE. I'LL TAKE IT.

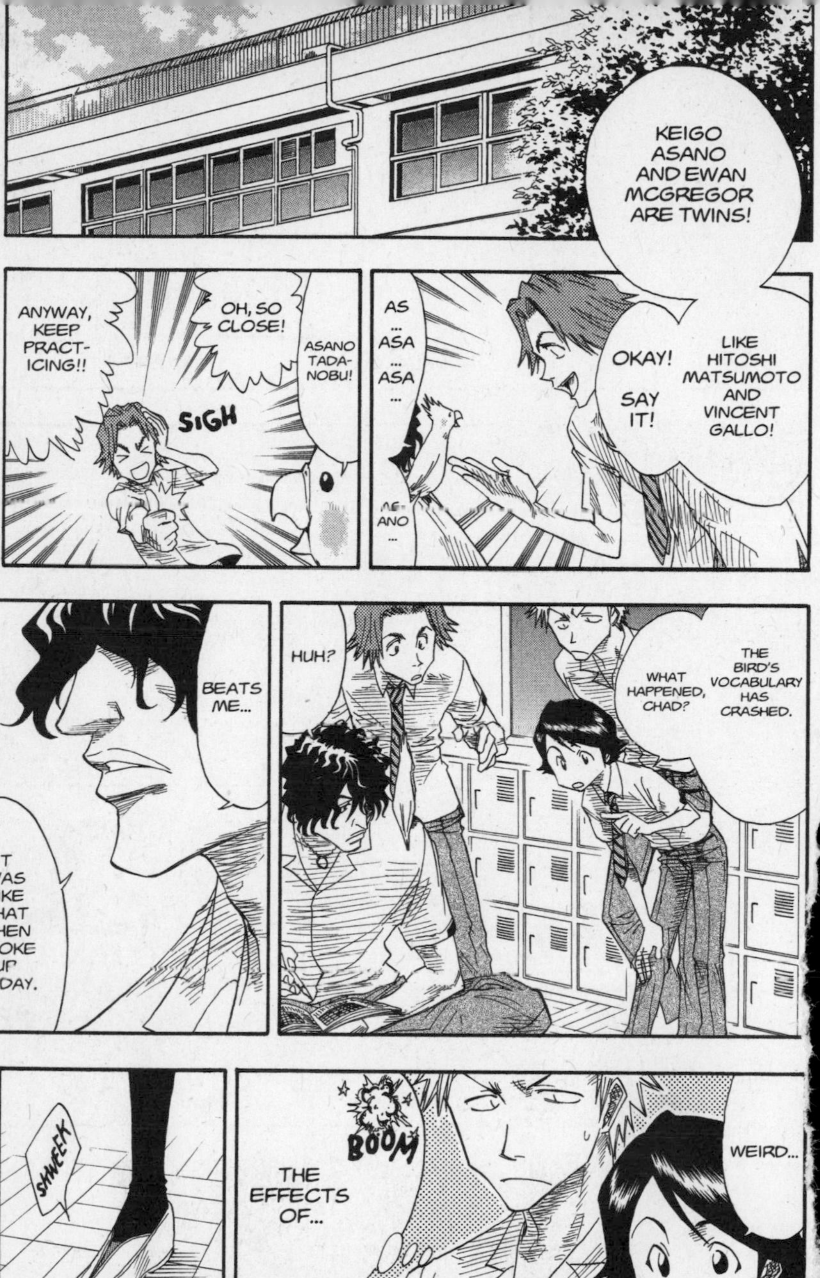
KEIGO ASANO AND EWAN MCGREGOR ARE TWINS!
LIKE HITOSHI MATSUMOTO AND VINCENT GALLO!
OKAY! SAY IT!
AS ... ASA ... ASA ...
ANO ...
ASANO TADA-NOBU!
OH, SO CLOSE!
SIGH
ANYWAY, KEEP PRACT-ICING!!
THE BIRD'S VOCABULARY HAS CRASHED.
WHAT HAPPENED, CHAD?
HUH?
BEATS ME...
IT WAS LIKE THAT WHEN I WOKE UP TODAY.
WEIRD...
BOOM
THE EFFECTS OF...
SHWEEK

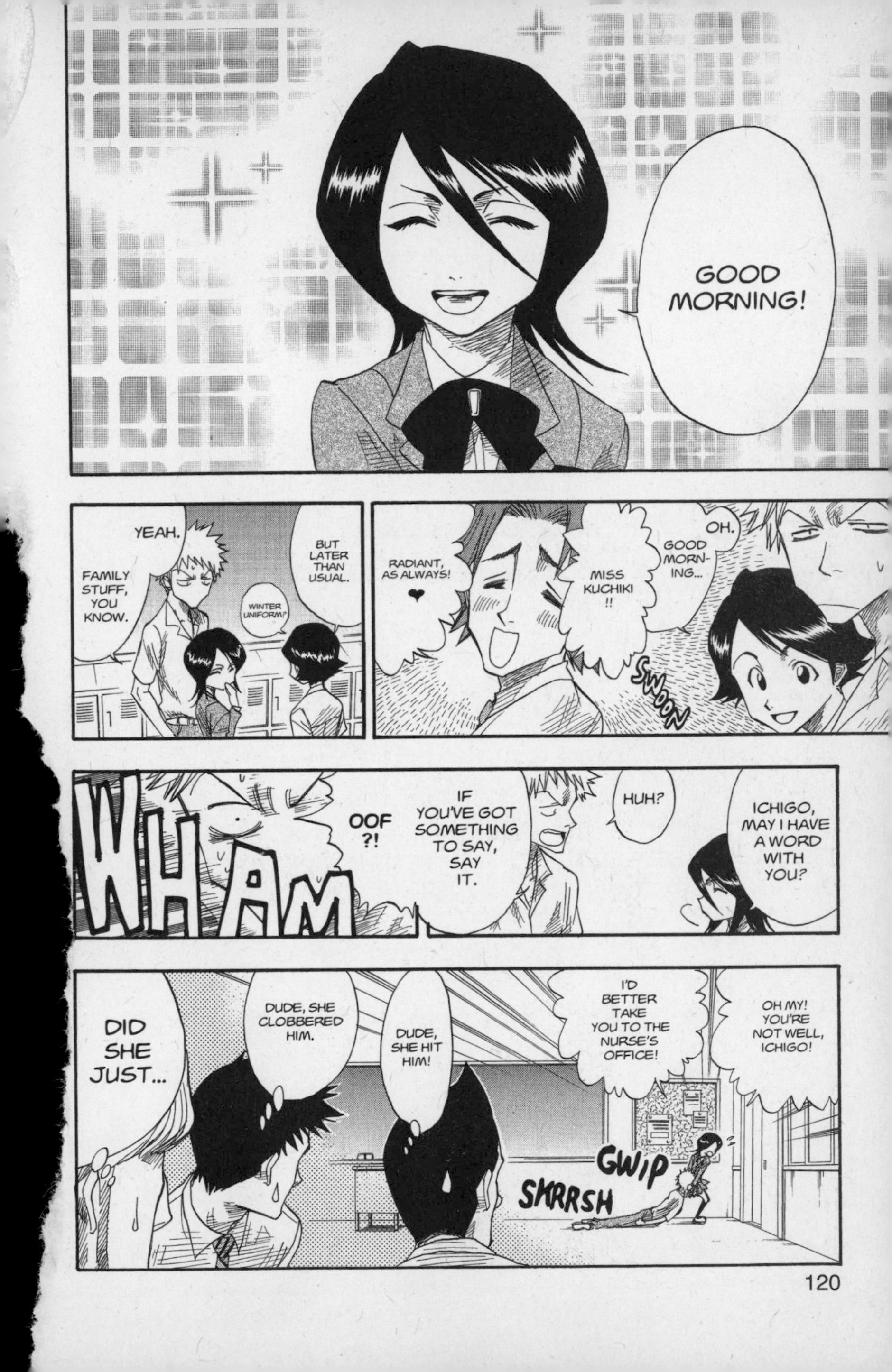
GOOD MORNING!
OH.
GOOD MORNING...
MISS KUCHIKI !!
RADIANT, AS ALWAYS! ♥
SWOON
BUT LATER THAN USUAL.
WINTER UNIFORM?
YEAH.
FAMILY STUFF, YOU KNOW.
ICHIGO, MAY I HAVE A WORD WITH YOU?
HUH?
IF YOU'VE GOT SOMETHING TO SAY, SAY IT.
OOF ?!
WHAM
OH MY! YOU'RE NOT WELL, ICHIGO!
I'D BETTER TAKE YOU TO THE NURSE'S OFFICE!
GWIP
SKRRSH
DUDE, SHE HIT HIM!
DUDE, SHE CLOBBERED HIM.
DID SHE JUST...

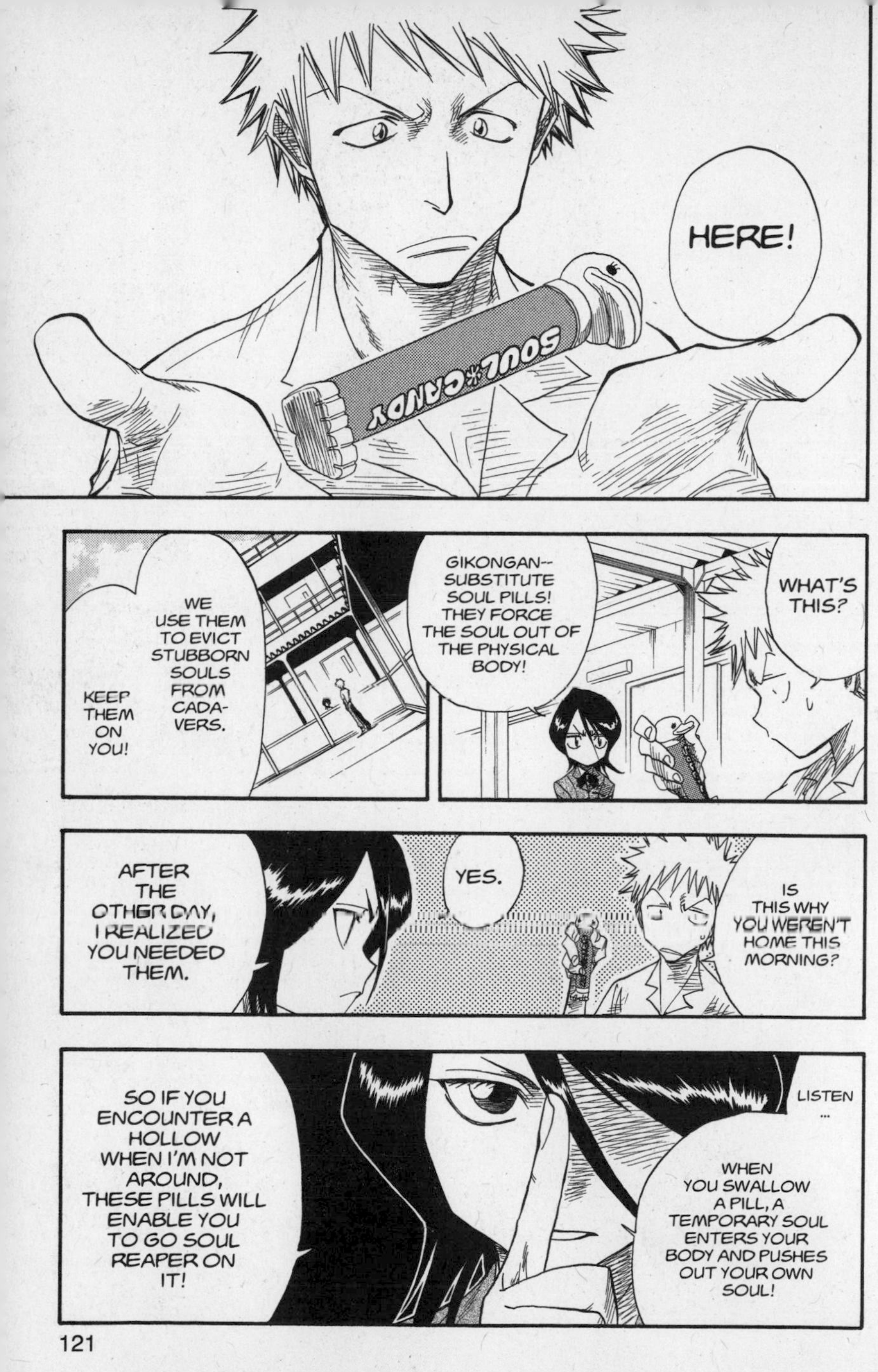
HERE!
SOUL CANDY
WHAT'S THIS?
GIKONGAN-- SUBSTITUTE SOUL PILLS! THEY FORCE THE SOUL OUT OF THE PHYSICAL BODY!
WE USE THEM TO EVICT STUBBORN SOULS FROM CADAVERS.
KEEP THEM ON YOU!
IS THIS WHY YOU WEREN'T HOME THIS MORNING?
YES.
AFTER THE OTHER DAY, I REALIZED YOU NEEDED THEM.
LISTEN...
WHEN YOU SWALLOW A PILL, A TEMPORARY SOUL ENTERS YOUR BODY AND PUSHES OUT YOUR OWN SOUL!
SO IF YOU ENCOUNTER A HOLLOW WHEN I'M NOT AROUND, THESE PILLS WILL ENABLE YOU TO GO SOUL REAPER ON IT!

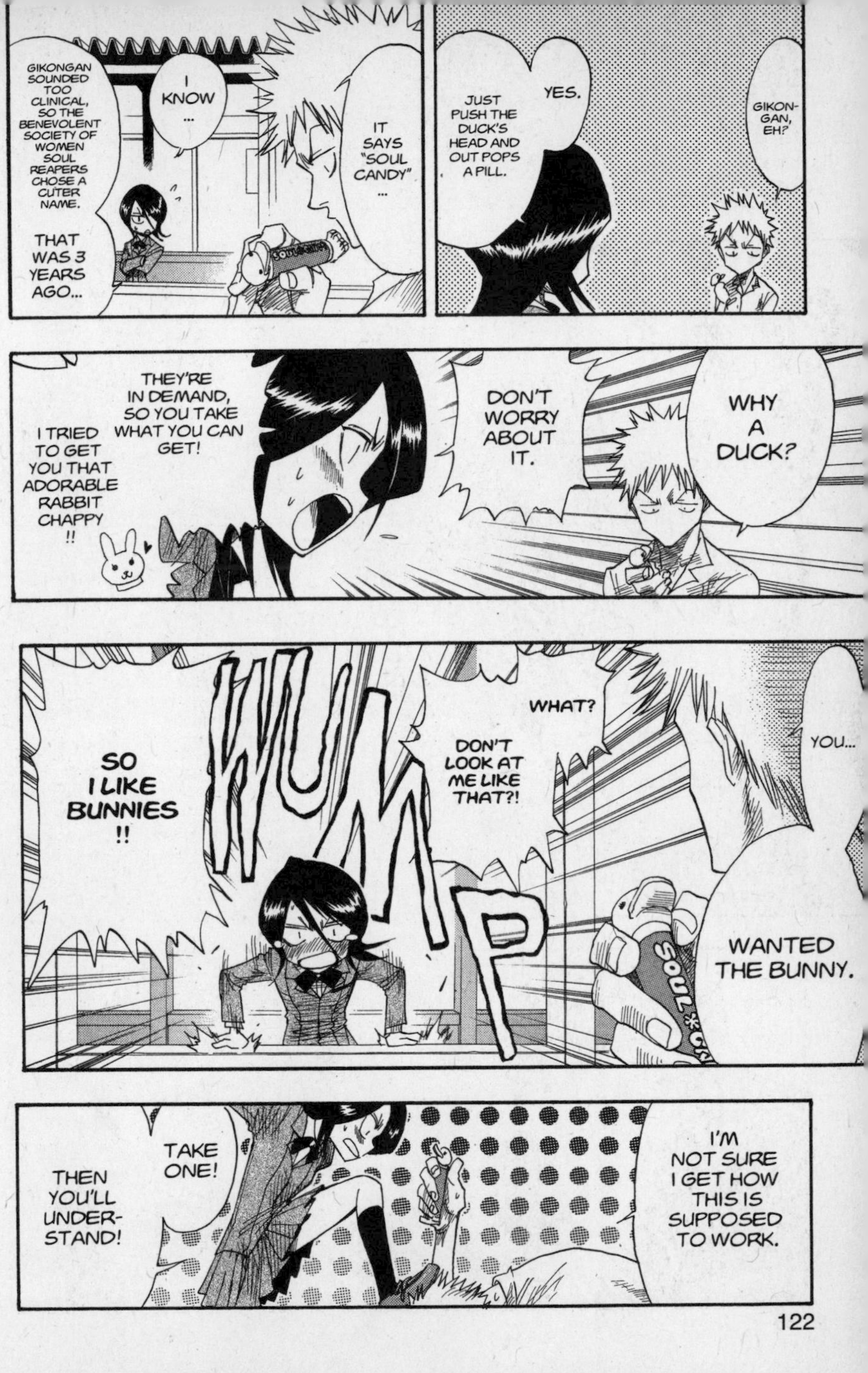
GIKON-GAN, EH?
YES.
JUST PUSH THE DUCK'S HEAD AND OUT POPS A PILL.
IT SAYS "SOUL CANDY" ...
I KNOW ...
GIKONGAN SOUNDED TOO CLINICAL, SO THE BENEVOLENT SOCIETY OF WOMEN SOUL REAPERS CHOSE A CUTER NAME.
THAT WAS 3 YEARS AGO...
WHY A DUCK?
DON'T WORRY ABOUT IT.
THEY'RE IN DEMAND, SO YOU TAKE WHAT YOU CAN GET!
I TRIED TO GET YOU THAT ADORABLE RABBIT CHAPPY !!
YOU...
WANTED THE BUNNY.
WHAT?
DON'T LOOK AT ME LIKE THAT?!
WUMP
SO I LIKE BUNNIES !!
I'M NOT SURE I GET HOW THIS IS SUPPOSED TO WORK.
TAKE ONE!
THEN YOU'LL UNDER-STAND!

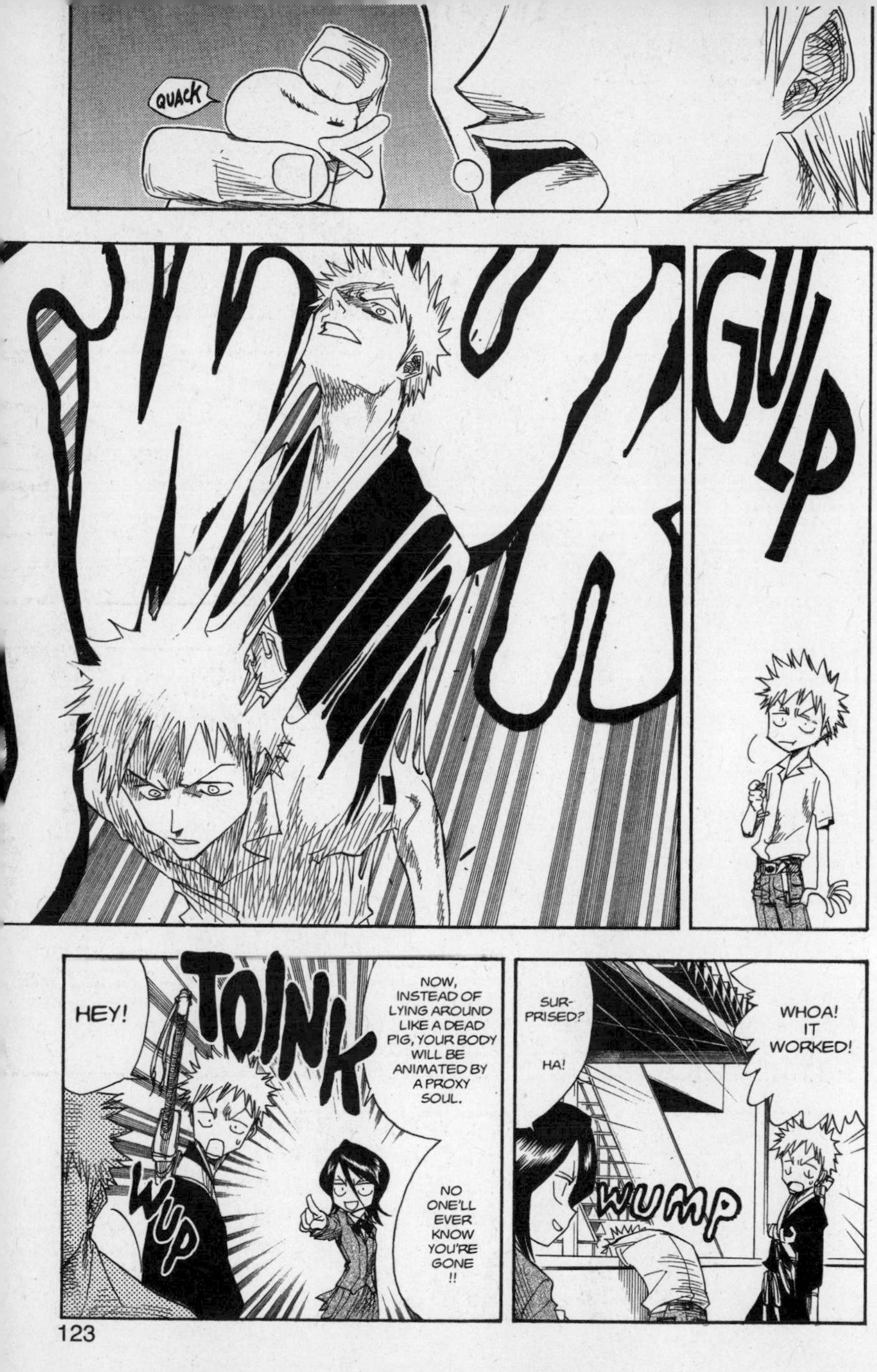
QUACK
GULP
WHOA! IT WORKED!
SUR-PRISED?
HA!
WUMP
NOW, INSTEAD OF LYING AROUND LIKE A DEAD PIG, YOUR BODY WILL BE ANIMATED BY A PROXY SOUL.
NO ONE'LL EVER KNOW YOU'RE GONE !!
TOINK
HEY!
WUP

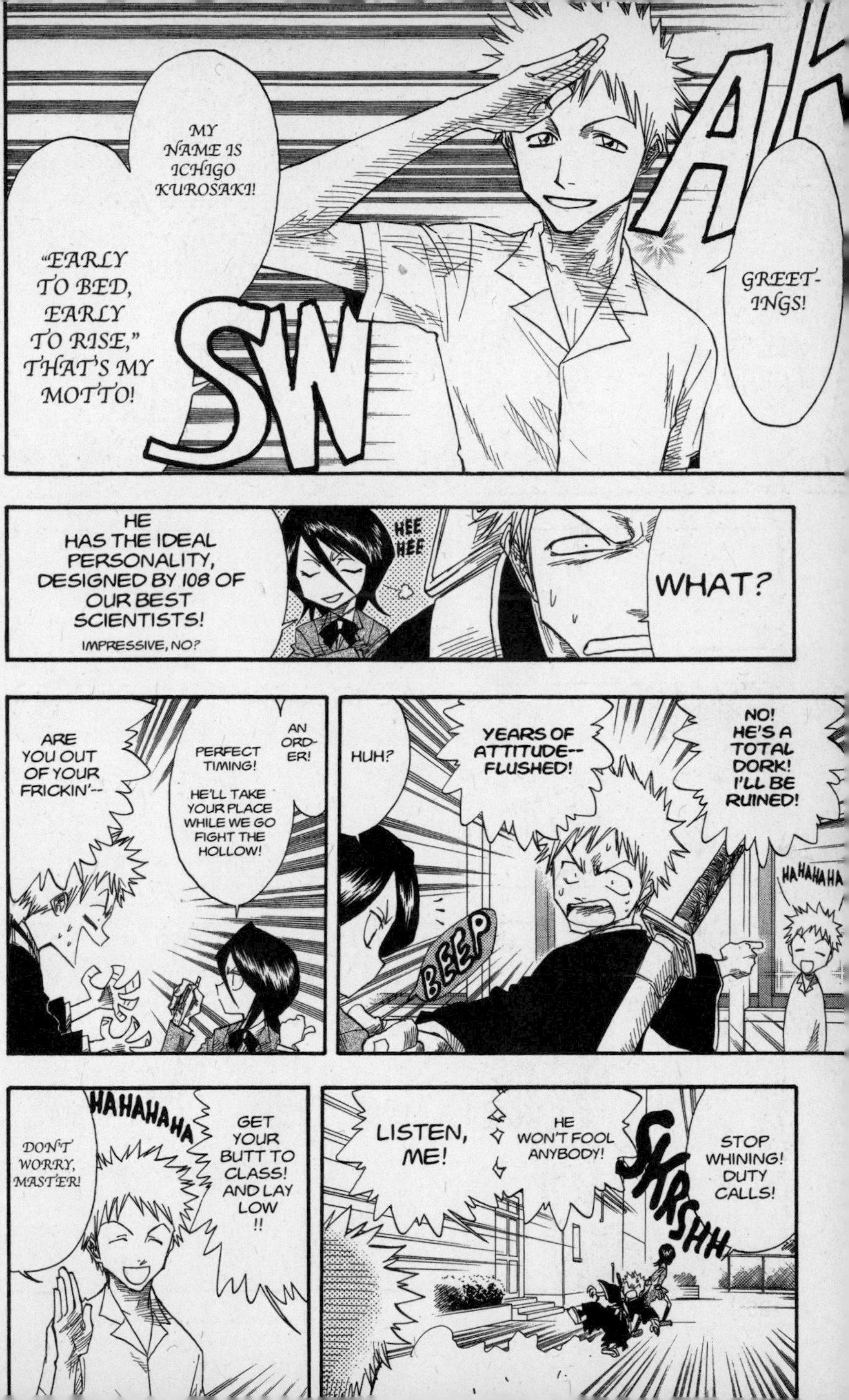
GREETINGS!
AK
MY NAME IS ICHIGO KUROSAKI!
"EARLY TO BED, EARLY TO RISE," THAT'S MY MOTTO!
SW
WHAT?
HEE HEE
HE HAS THE IDEAL PERSONALITY, DESIGNED BY 108 OF OUR BEST SCIENTISTS!
IMPRESSIVE, NO?
NO! HE'S A TOTAL DORK! I'LL BE RUINED!
HAHAHAHA
YEARS OF ATTITUDE--FLUSHED!
HUH?
BEEP
AN ORDER!
PERFECT TIMING!
HE'LL TAKE YOUR PLACE WHILE WE GO FIGHT THE HOLLOW!
ARE YOU OUT OF YOUR FRICKIN'--
STOP WHINING! DUTY CALLS!
SHRSHH
HE WON'T FOOL ANYBODY!
LISTEN, ME!
GET YOUR BUTT TO CLASS! AND LAY LOW !!
HAHAHAHA
DON'T WORRY, MASTER!

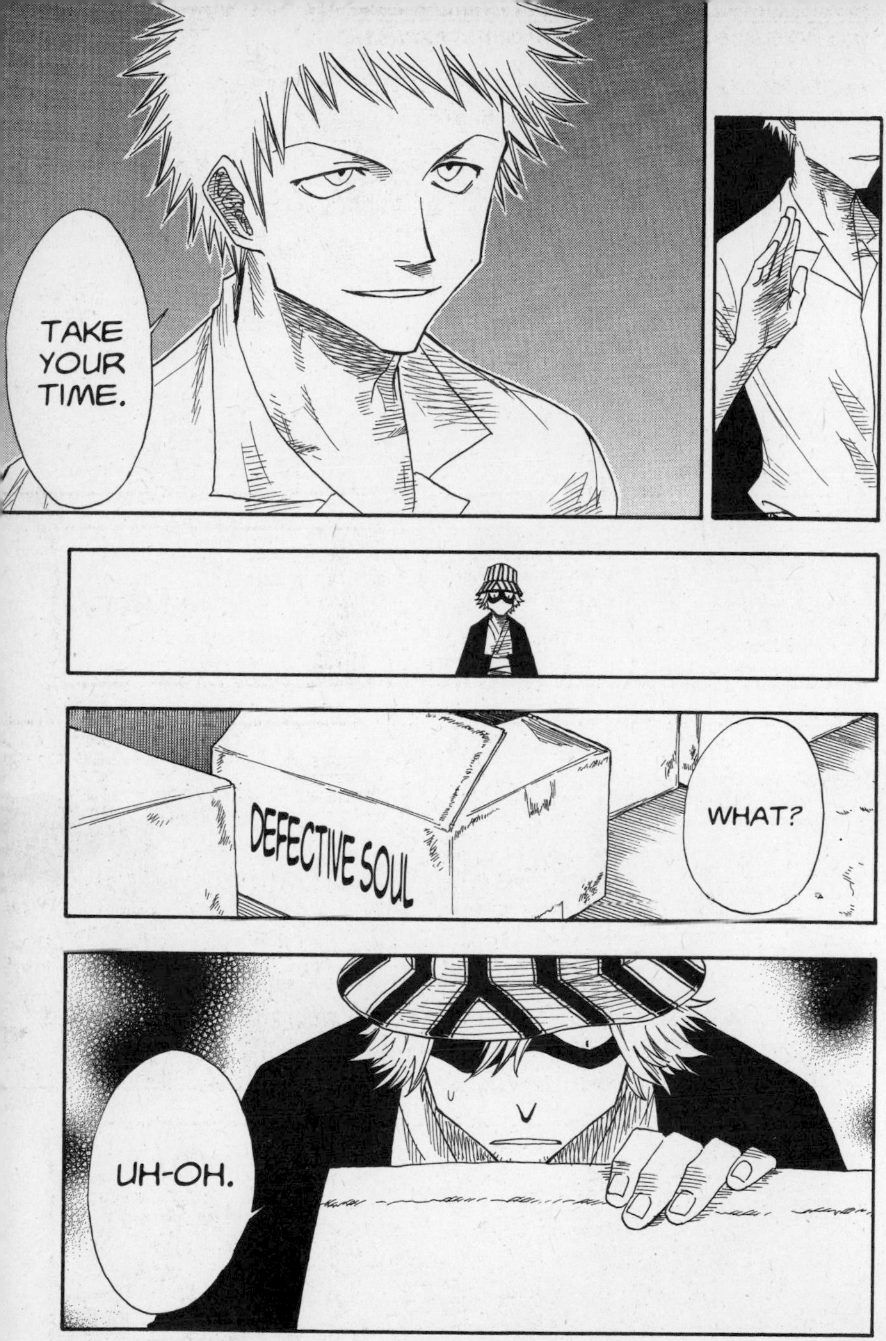
TAKE YOUR TIME.
WHAT?
DEFECTIVE SOUL
UH-OH.

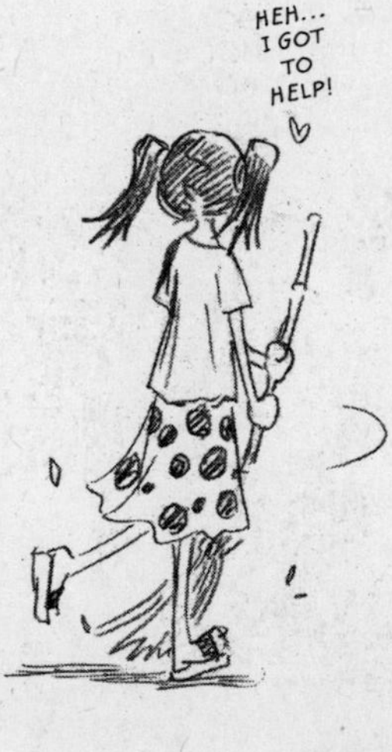
HEH...
I GOT
TO
HELP!

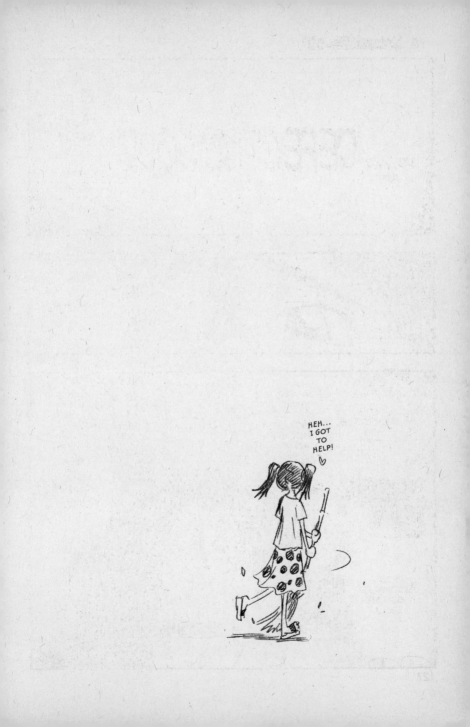

14. School Daze!!!

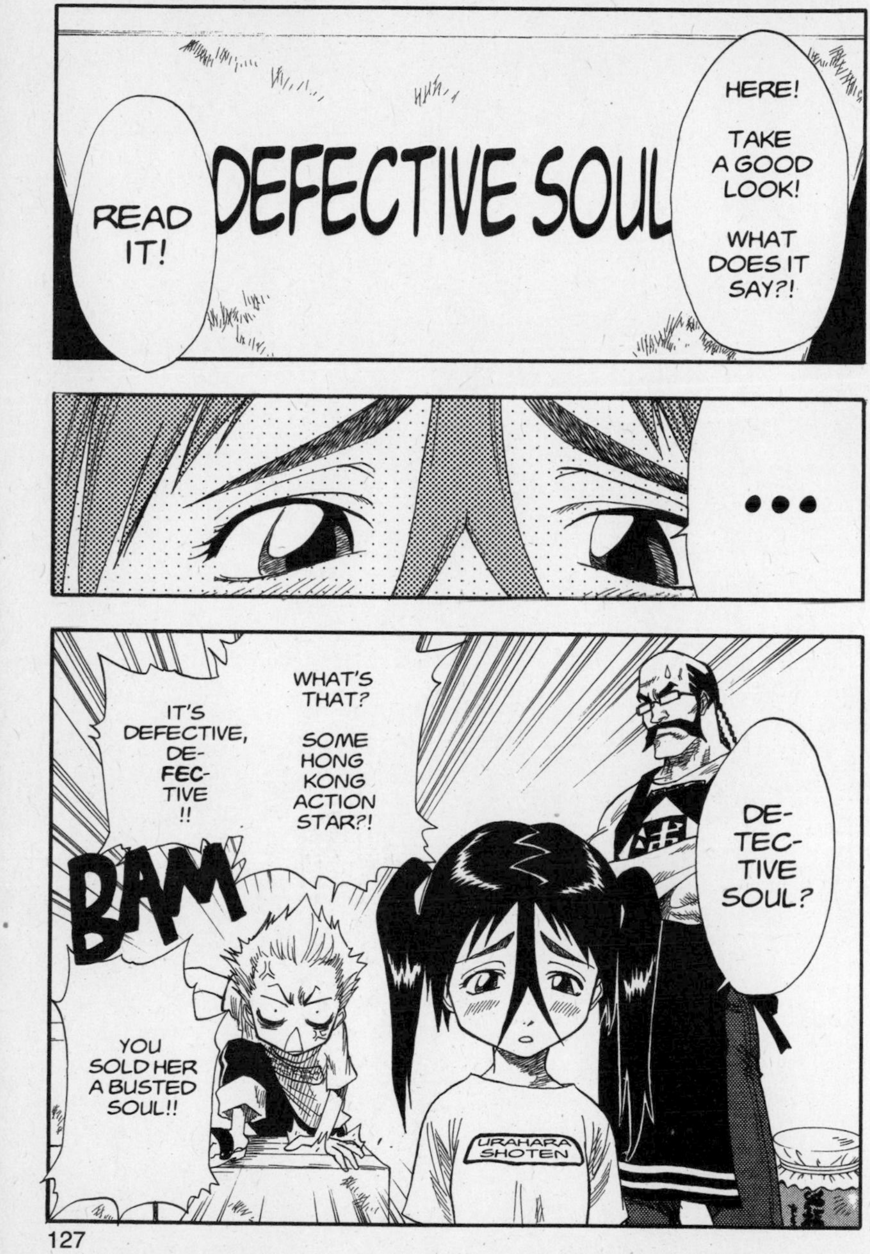
HERE! TAKE A GOOD LOOK! WHAT DOES IT SAY?!
DEFECTIVE SOUL
READ IT!
...
DE-TEC-TIVE SOUL?
WHAT'S THAT? SOME HONG KONG ACTION STAR?!
IT'S DEFECTIVE, DE-FEC-TIVE!!
BAM
URAHARA SHOTEN
YOU SOLD HER A BUSTED SOUL!!

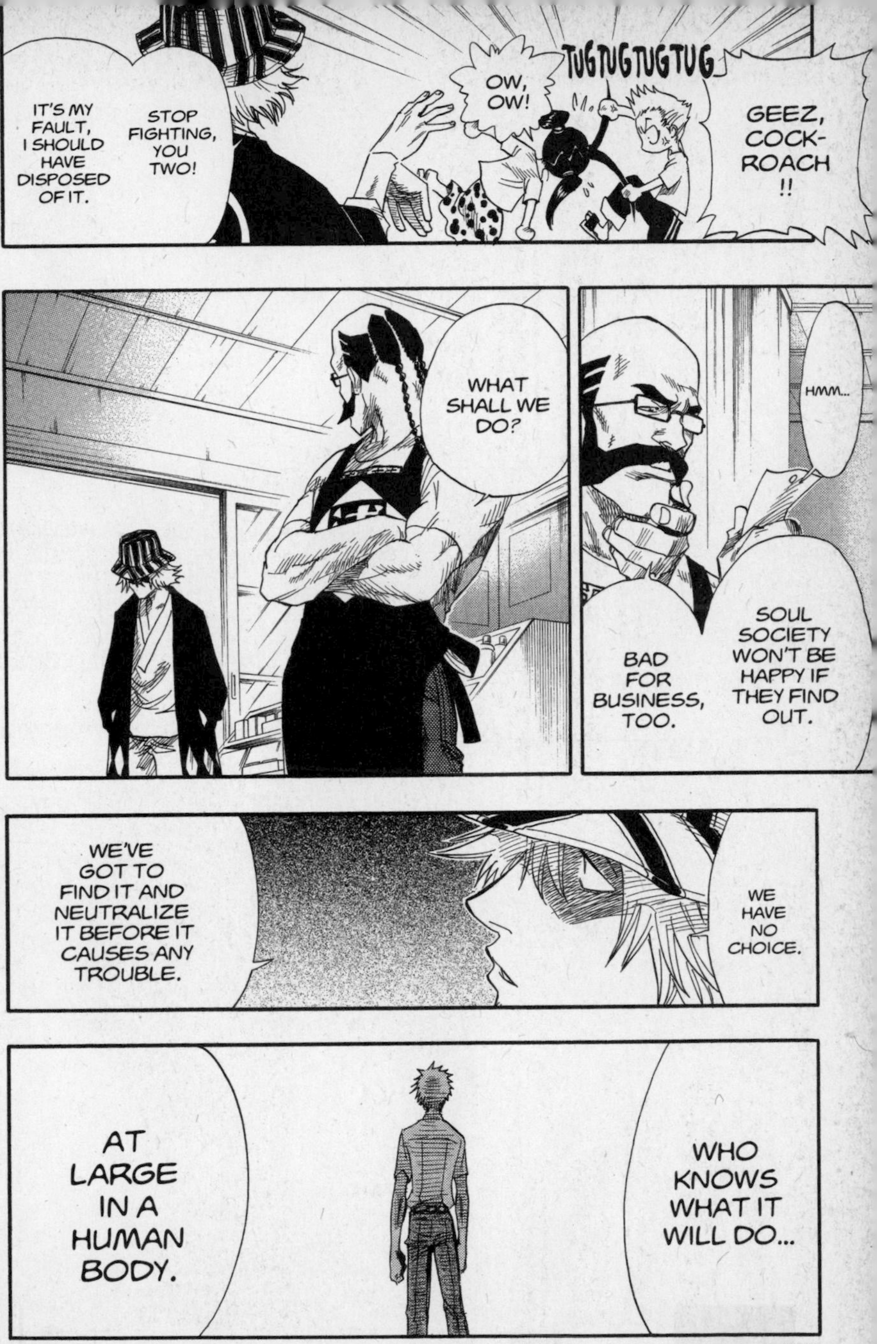
GEEZ, COCKROACH!!
TUGTUGTUGTUG
OW, OW!
STOP FIGHTING, YOU TWO!
IT'S MY FAULT, I SHOULD HAVE DISPOSED OF IT.
HMM...
SOUL SOCIETY WON'T BE HAPPY IF THEY FIND OUT.
BAD FOR BUSINESS, TOO.
WHAT SHALL WE DO?
WE HAVE NO CHOICE.
WE'VE GOT TO FIND IT AND NEUTRALIZE IT BEFORE IT CAUSES ANY TROUBLE.
WHO KNOWS WHAT IT WILL DO...
AT LARGE IN A HUMAN BODY.

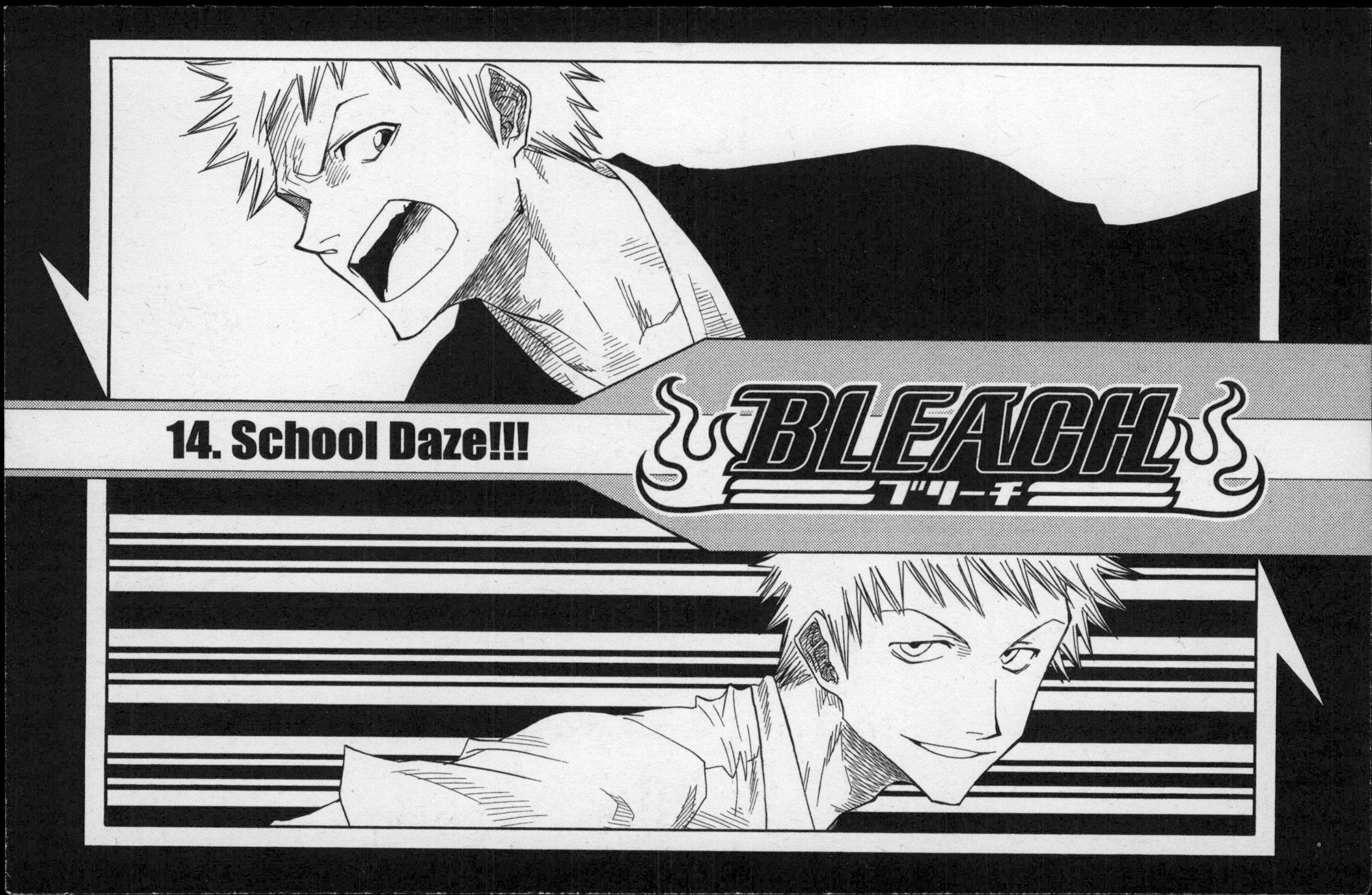
14. School Daze!!!
BLEACH
ブリーチ

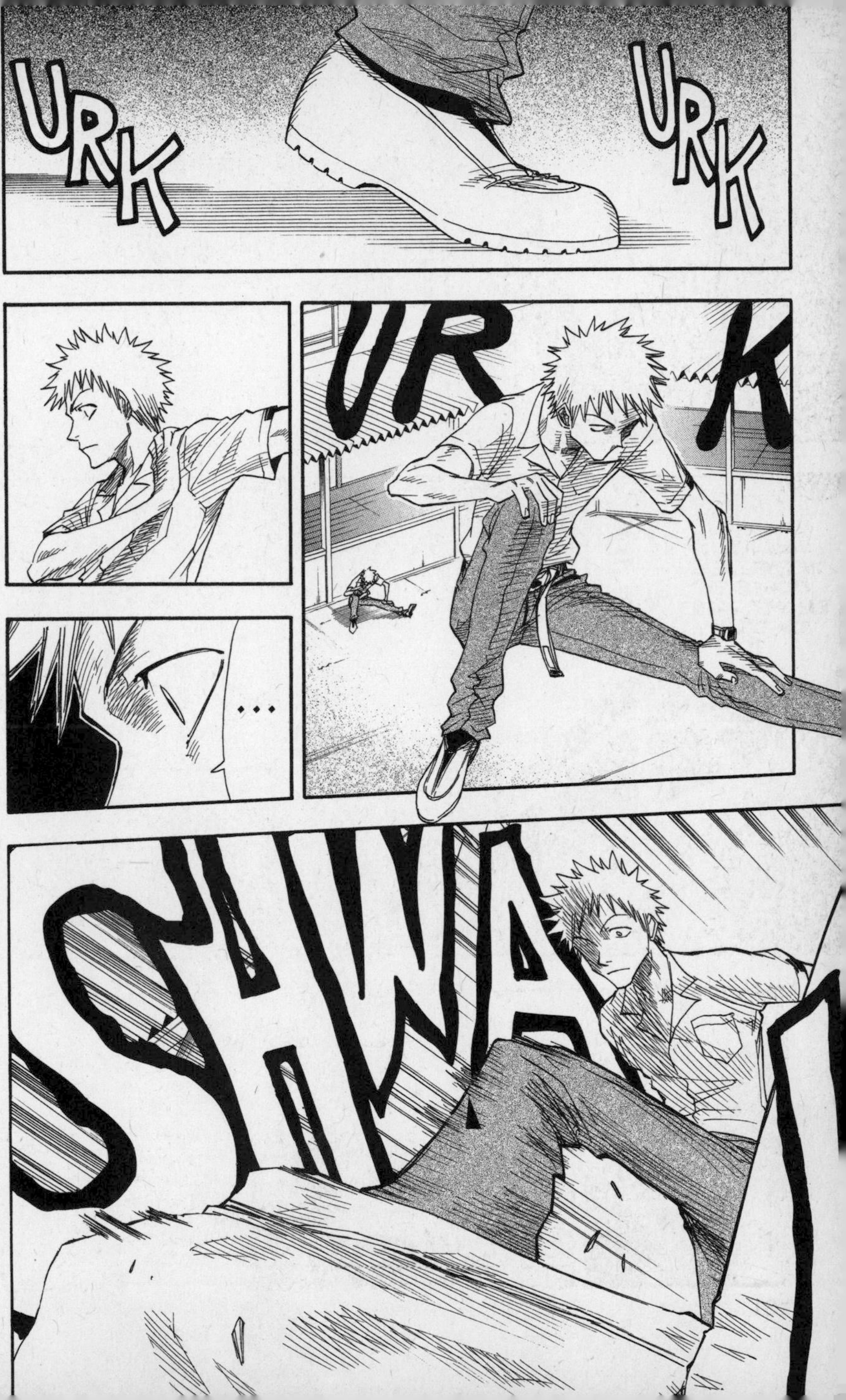
URK
URK
URK
...
SHWA

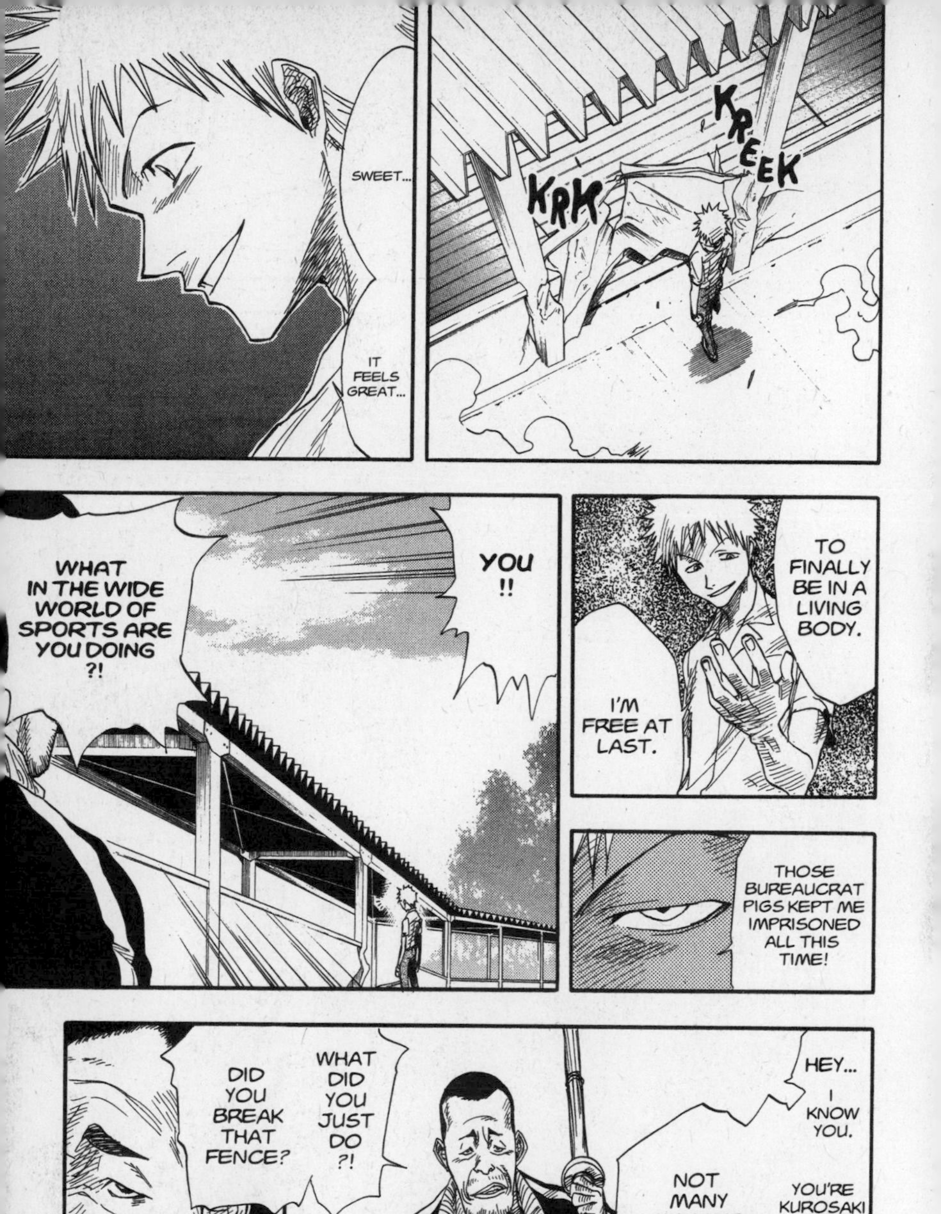
KREEK
KRK
SWEET...
IT FEELS GREAT...
TO FINALLY BE IN A LIVING BODY.
I'M FREE AT LAST.
THOSE BUREAUCRAT PIGS KEPT ME IMPRISONED ALL THIS TIME!
YOU !!
WHAT IN THE WIDE WORLD OF SPORTS ARE YOU DOING ?!
HEY...
I KNOW YOU.
YOU'RE KUROSAKI FROM I-3!
NOT MANY HUMANS WITH HAIR THAT COLOR, THANK THE GODS.
WHAT DID YOU JUST DO ?!
DID YOU BREAK THAT FENCE?

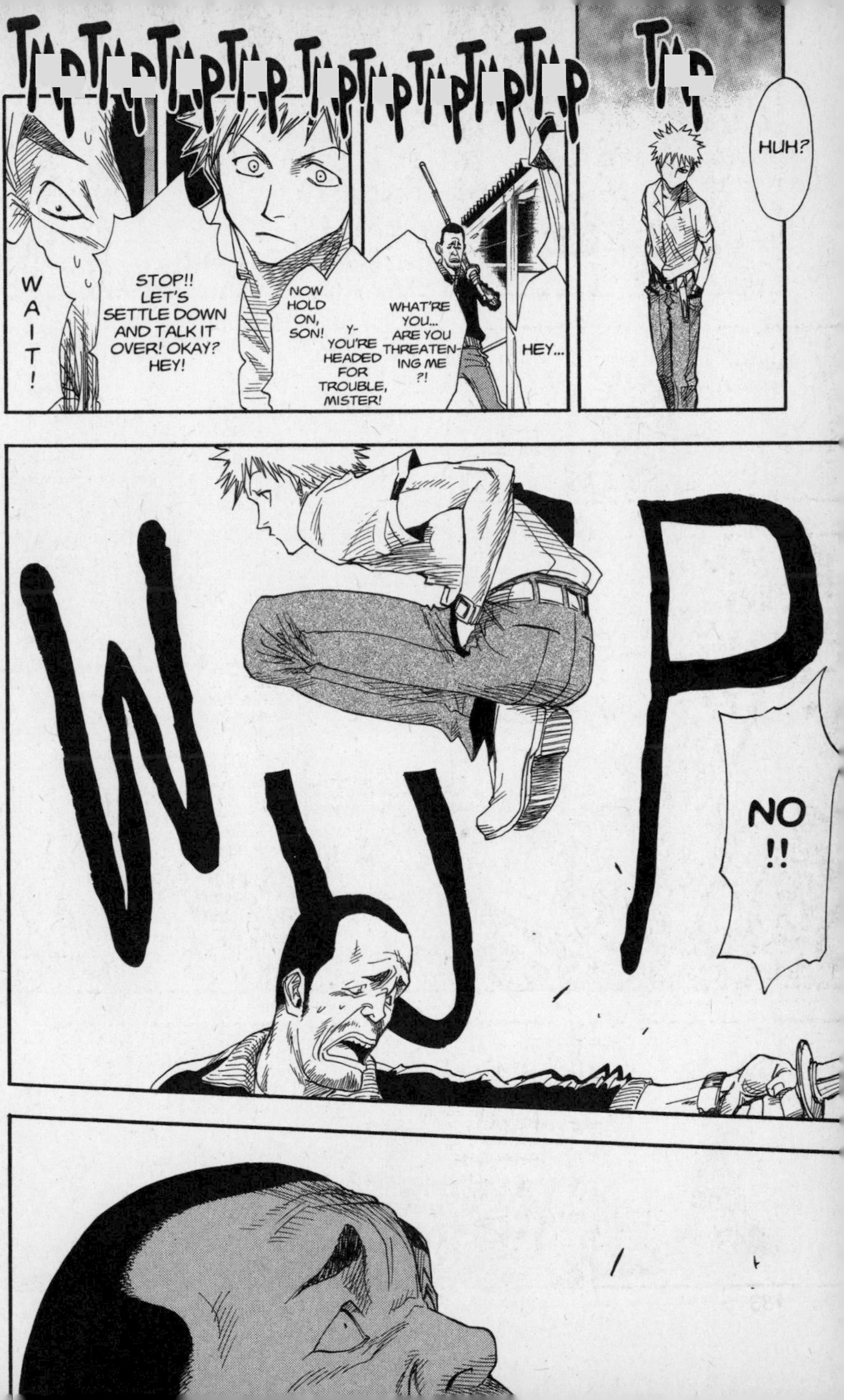
HUH?
HEY...
WHAT'RE YOU... ARE YOU THREATENING ME?!
Y- YOU'RE HEADED FOR TROUBLE, MISTER!
NOW HOLD ON, SON!
STOP!! LET'S SETTLE DOWN AND TALK IT OVER! OKAY? HEY!
WAIT!
NO!!

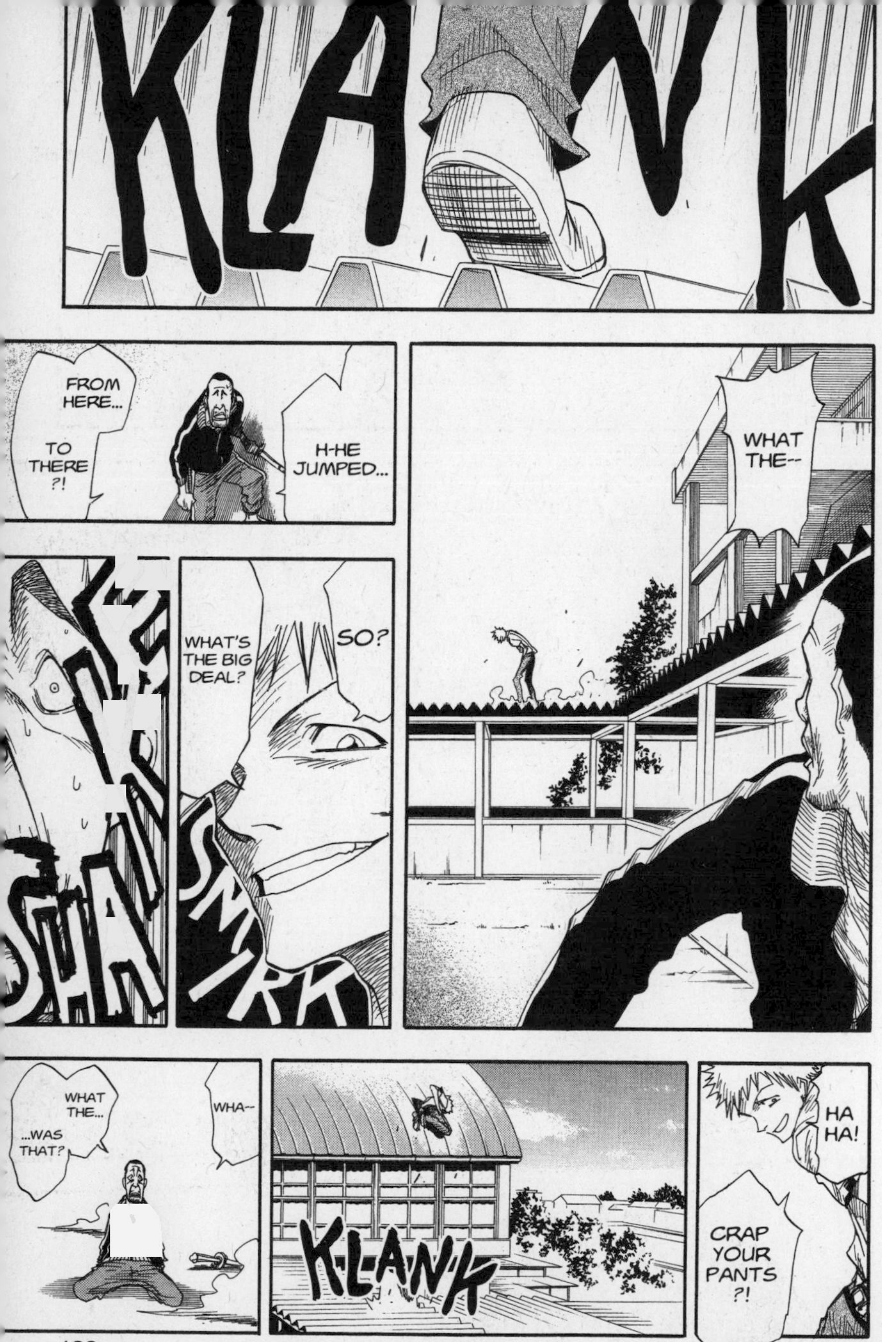
KLANK
WHAT THE--
H-HE JUMPED...
FROM HERE...
TO THERE?!
SO?
WHAT'S THE BIG DEAL?
SMIRK
HA HA!
CRAP YOUR PANTS?!
KLANK
WHA--
WHAT THE...
...WAS THAT?

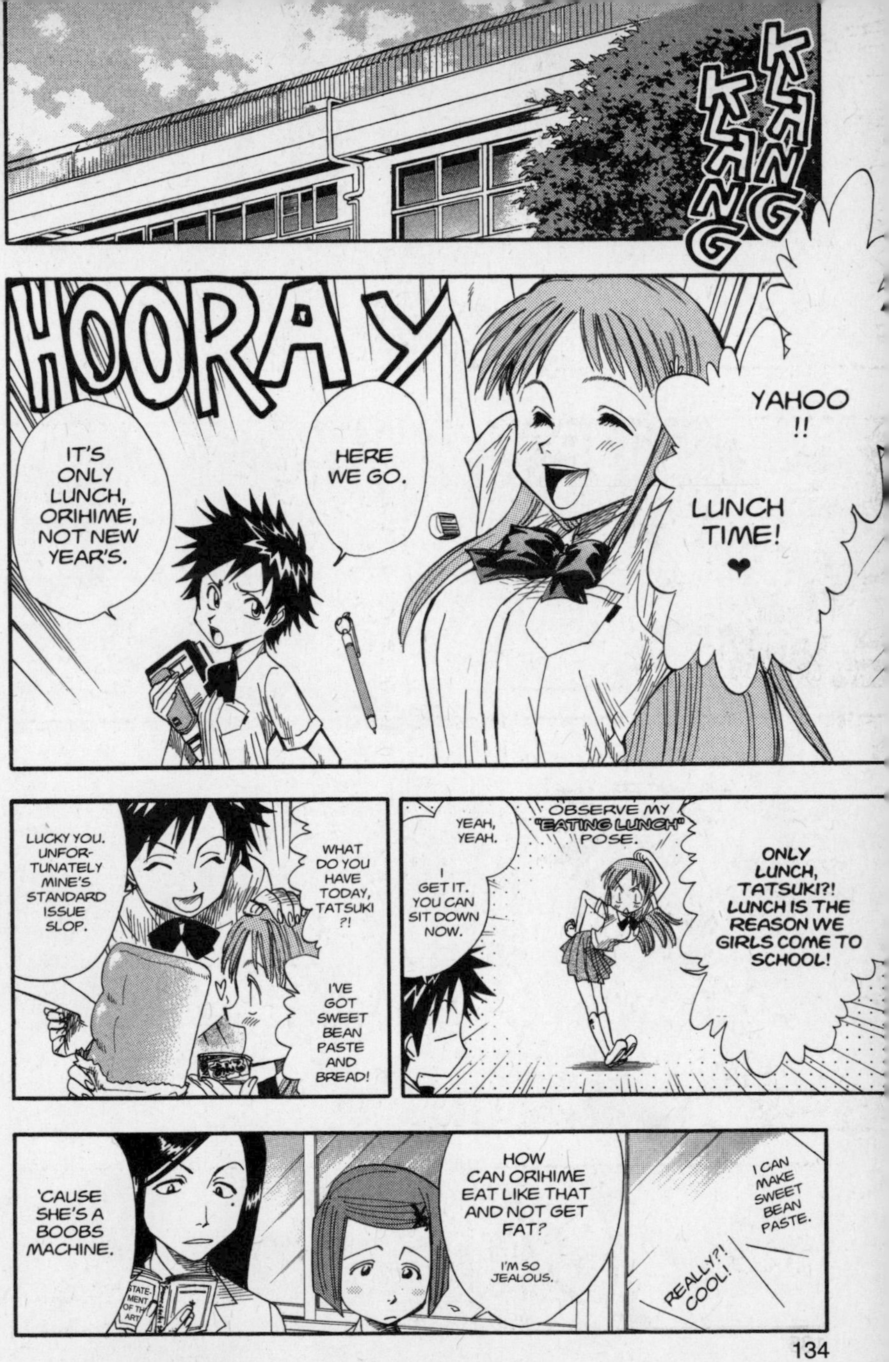
KLANG
KLANG
YAHOO!!
LUNCH TIME! ❤
HOORAY
HERE WE GO.
IT'S ONLY LUNCH, ORIHIME, NOT NEW YEAR'S.
ONLY LUNCH, TATSUKI?! LUNCH IS THE REASON WE GIRLS COME TO SCHOOL!
OBSERVE MY "EATING LUNCH" POSE.
YEAH, YEAH.
I GET IT. YOU CAN SIT DOWN NOW.
WHAT DO YOU HAVE TODAY, TATSUKI?!
I'VE GOT SWEET BEAN PASTE AND BREAD!
LUCKY YOU. UNFORTUNATELY MINE'S STANDARD ISSUE SLOP.
I CAN MAKE SWEET BEAN PASTE.
REALLY?! COOL!
HOW CAN ORIHIME EAT LIKE THAT AND NOT GET FAT?
I'M SO JEALOUS.
'CAUSE SHE'S A BOOBS MACHINE.
STATEMENT OF THE ART

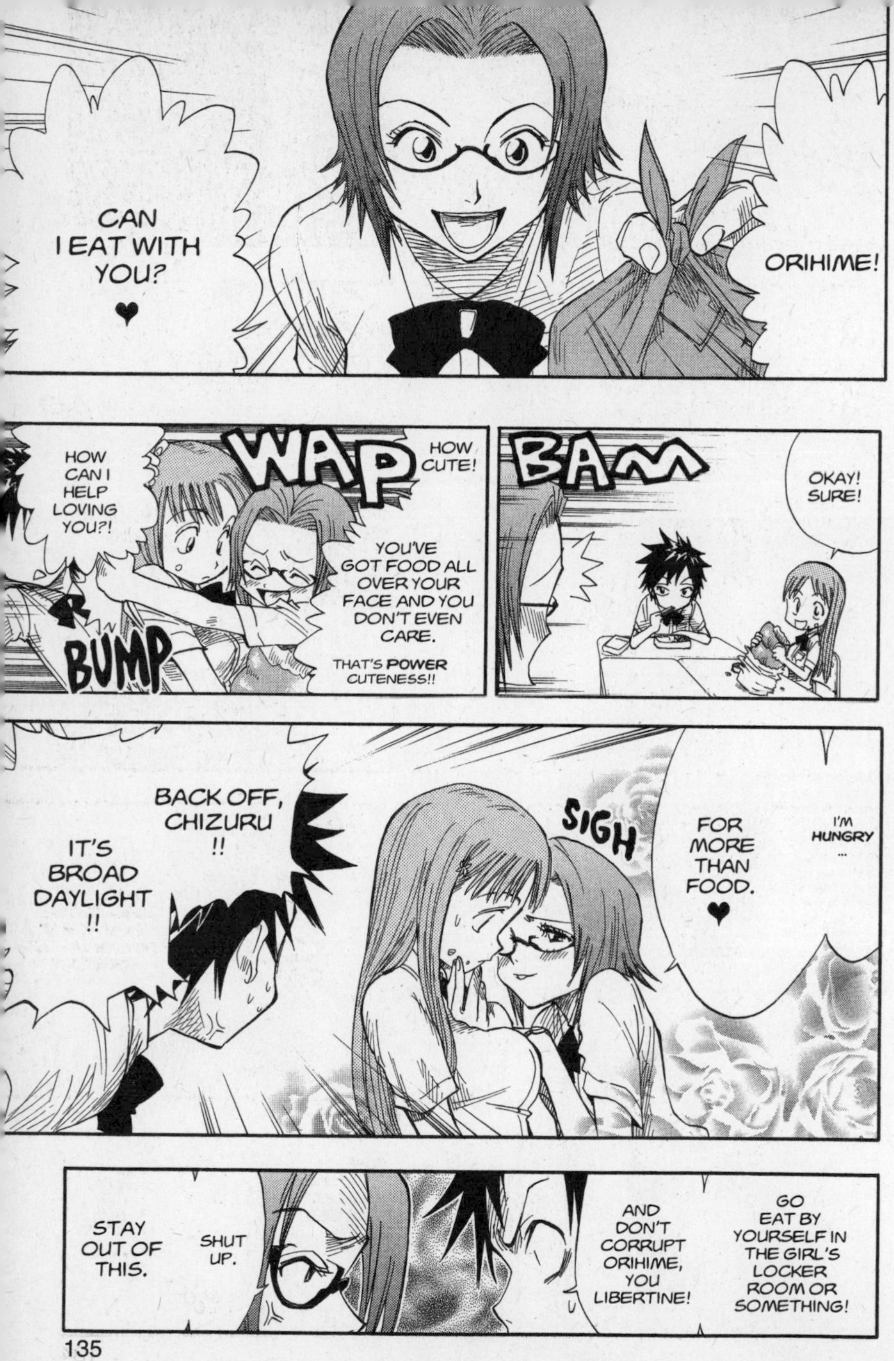

ORIHIME!
CAN I EAT WITH YOU? ♥
BAM
OKAY! SURE!
WAP
HOW CUTE!
YOU'VE GOT FOOD ALL OVER YOUR FACE AND YOU DON'T EVEN CARE.
THAT'S **POWER** CUTENESS!!
HOW CAN I HELP LOVING YOU?!
BUMP
I'M **HUNGRY** ...
FOR MORE THAN FOOD. ♥
SIGH
BACK OFF, CHIZURU !!
IT'S BROAD DAYLIGHT !!
GO EAT BY YOURSELF IN THE GIRL'S LOCKER ROOM OR SOMETHING!
AND DON'T CORRUPT ORIHIME, YOU LIBERTINE!
SHUT UP.
STAY OUT OF THIS.

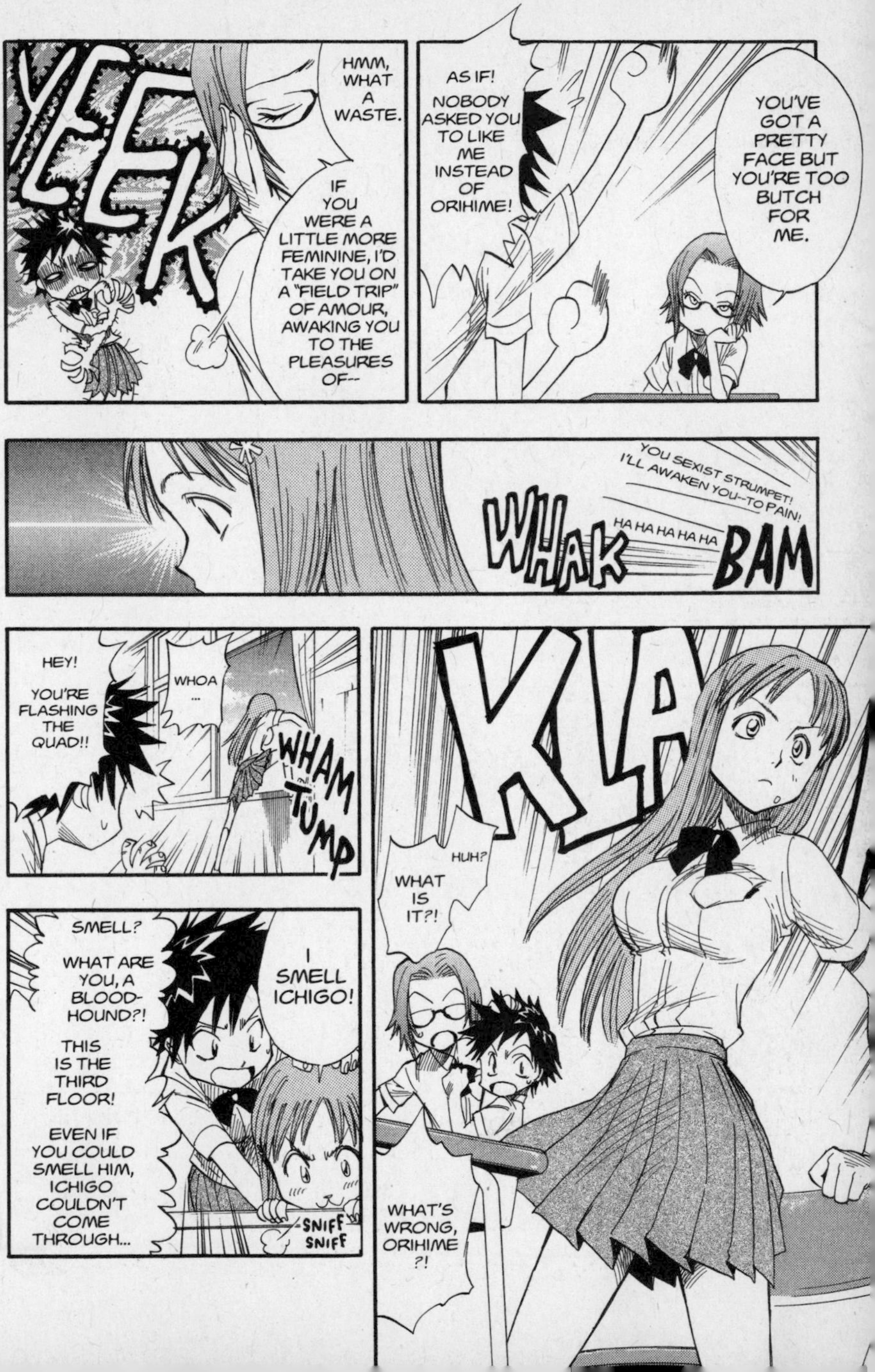
YOU'VE GOT A PRETTY FACE BUT YOU'RE TOO BUTCH FOR ME.
AS IF! NOBODY ASKED YOU TO LIKE ME INSTEAD OF ORIHIME!
HMM, WHAT A WASTE.
IF YOU WERE A LITTLE MORE FEMININE, I'D TAKE YOU ON A "FIELD TRIP" OF AMOUR, AWAKING YOU TO THE PLEASURES OF--
YEEK
YOU SEXIST STRUMPET! I'LL AWAKEN YOU--TO PAIN!
BAM
HA HA HA HA HA
WHAK
KIA
HUH?
WHAT IS IT?!
WHAT'S WRONG, ORIHIME ?!
HEY!
YOU'RE FLASHING THE QUAD!!
WHOA ...
WHAM
TUMP
I SMELL ICHIGO!
SMELL?
WHAT ARE YOU, A BLOOD-HOUND?!
THIS IS THE THIRD FLOOR!
EVEN IF YOU COULD SMELL HIM, ICHIGO COULDN'T COME THROUGH...
SNIFF SNIFF

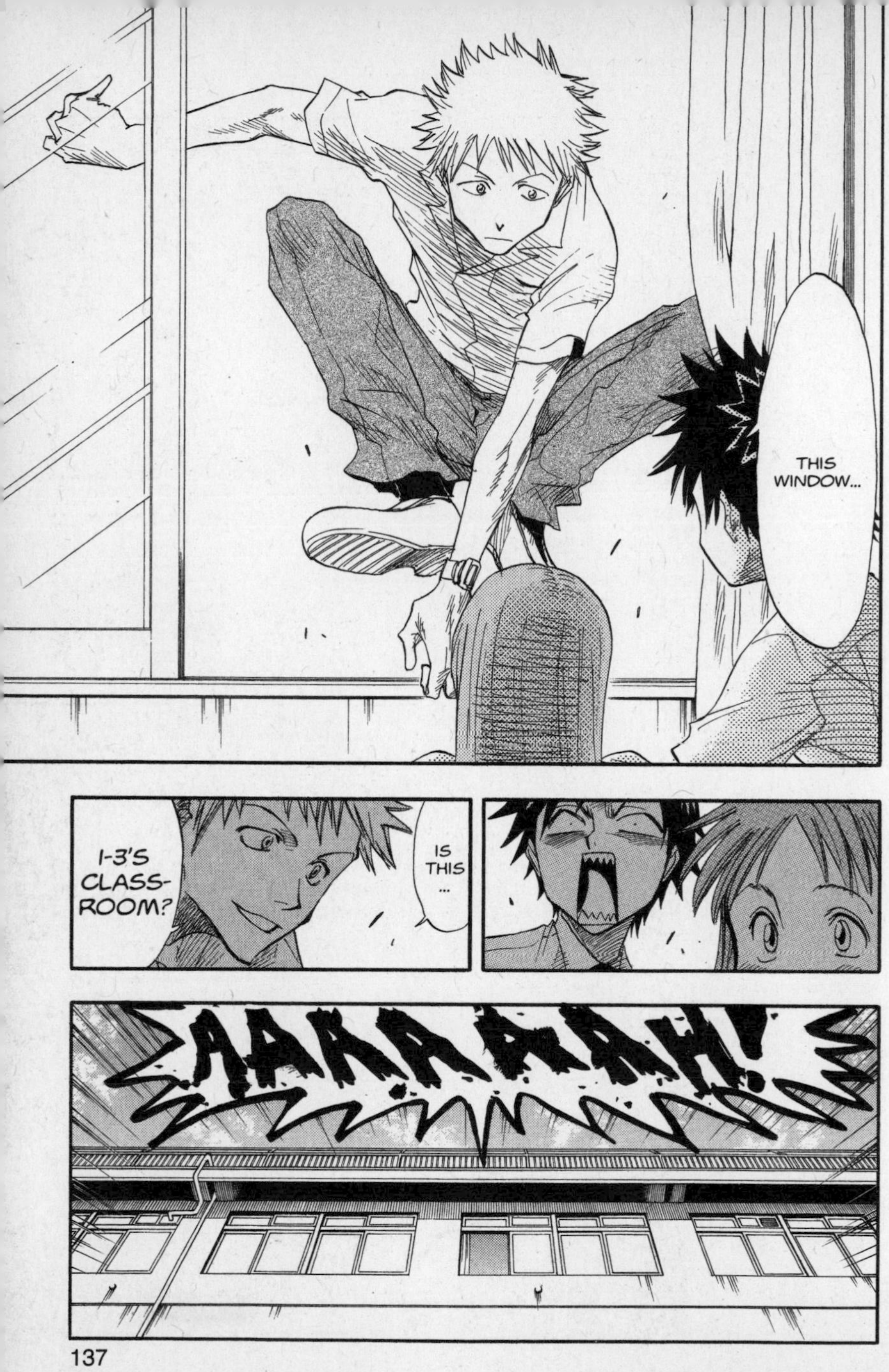
THIS WINDOW...
IS THIS ...
I-3'S CLASSROOM?
AARRRAH!

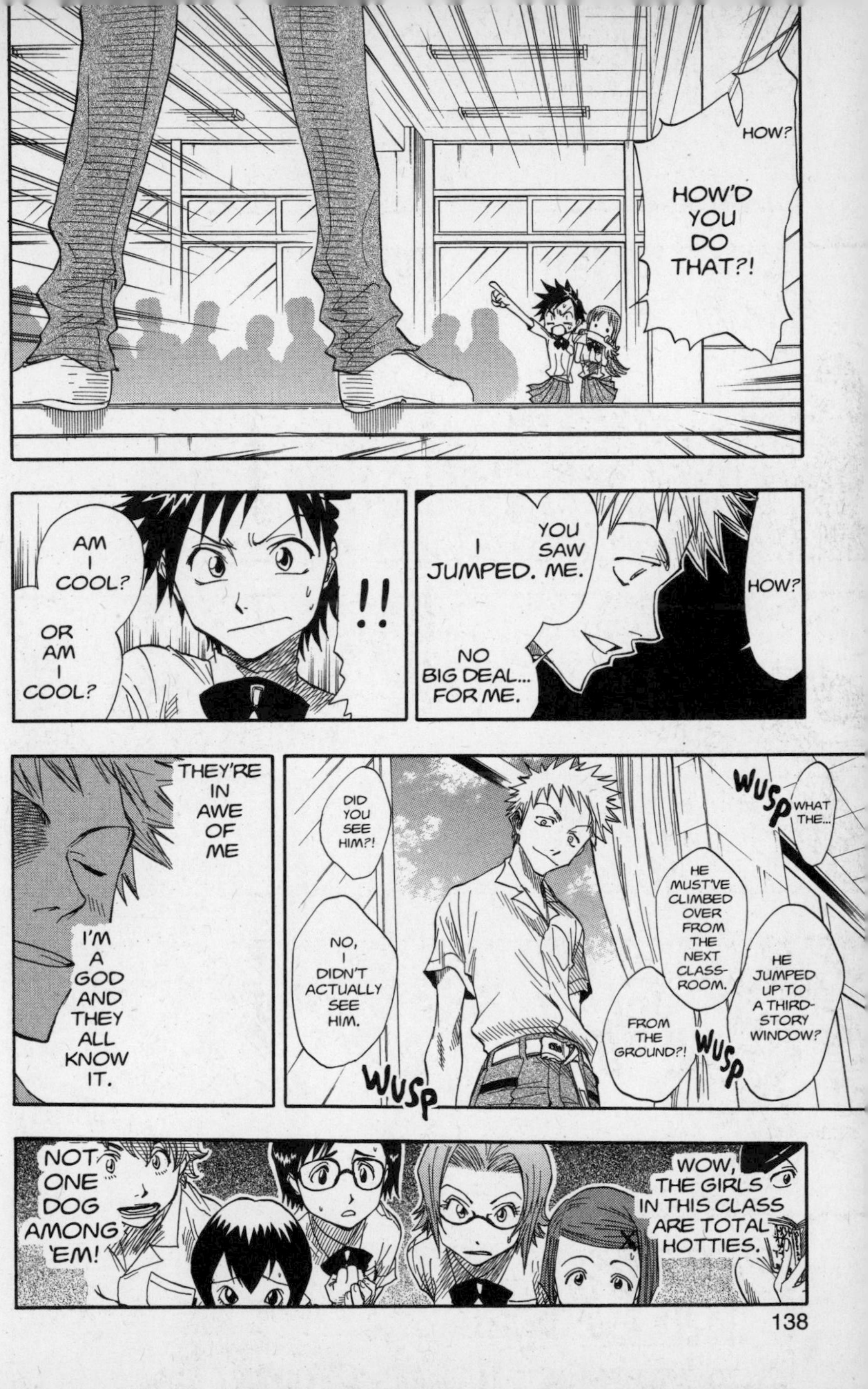
HOW?
HOW'D YOU DO THAT?!
HOW?
YOU SAW ME.
I JUMPED.
NO BIG DEAL... FOR ME.
!!
AM I COOL?
OR AM I COOL?
WUSP
WHAT THE...
HE JUMPED UP TO A THIRD-STORY WINDOW?
HE MUST'VE CLIMBED OVER FROM THE NEXT CLASSROOM.
FROM THE GROUND?!
WUSP
DID YOU SEE HIM?!
NO, I DIDN'T ACTUALLY SEE HIM.
WUSP
THEY'RE IN AWE OF ME
I'M A GOD AND THEY ALL KNOW IT.
WOW, THE GIRLS IN THIS CLASS ARE TOTAL HOTTIES.
NOT ONE DOG AMONG 'EM!

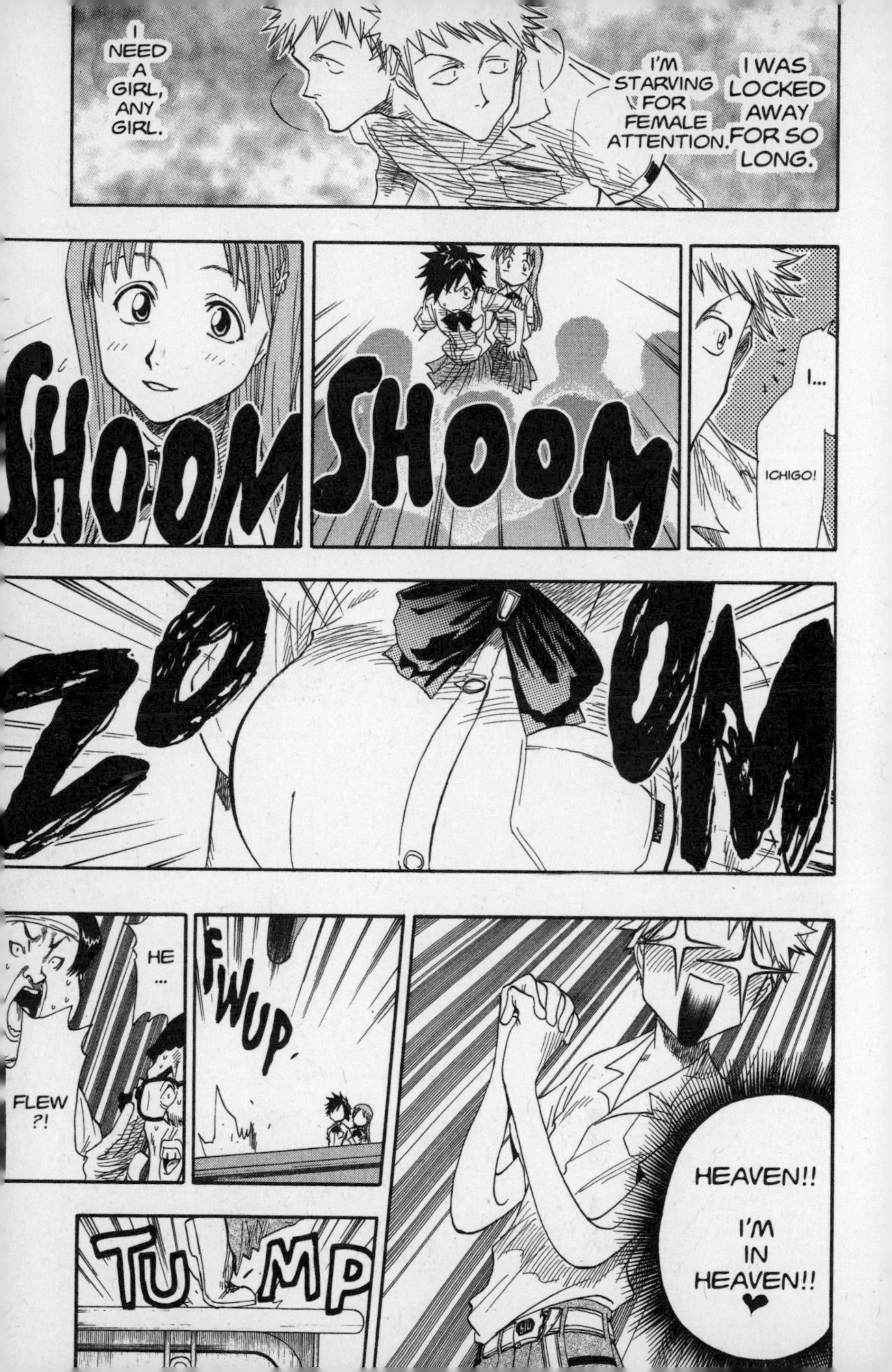
I WAS LOCKED AWAY FOR SO LONG.
I'M STARVING FOR FEMALE ATTENTION.
I NEED A GIRL, ANY GIRL.
I...
ICHIGO!
SHOOM
SHOOM
ZOOM
HEAVEN!!
I'M IN HEAVEN!! ❤
FWUP
HE ... FLEW ?!
TUMP

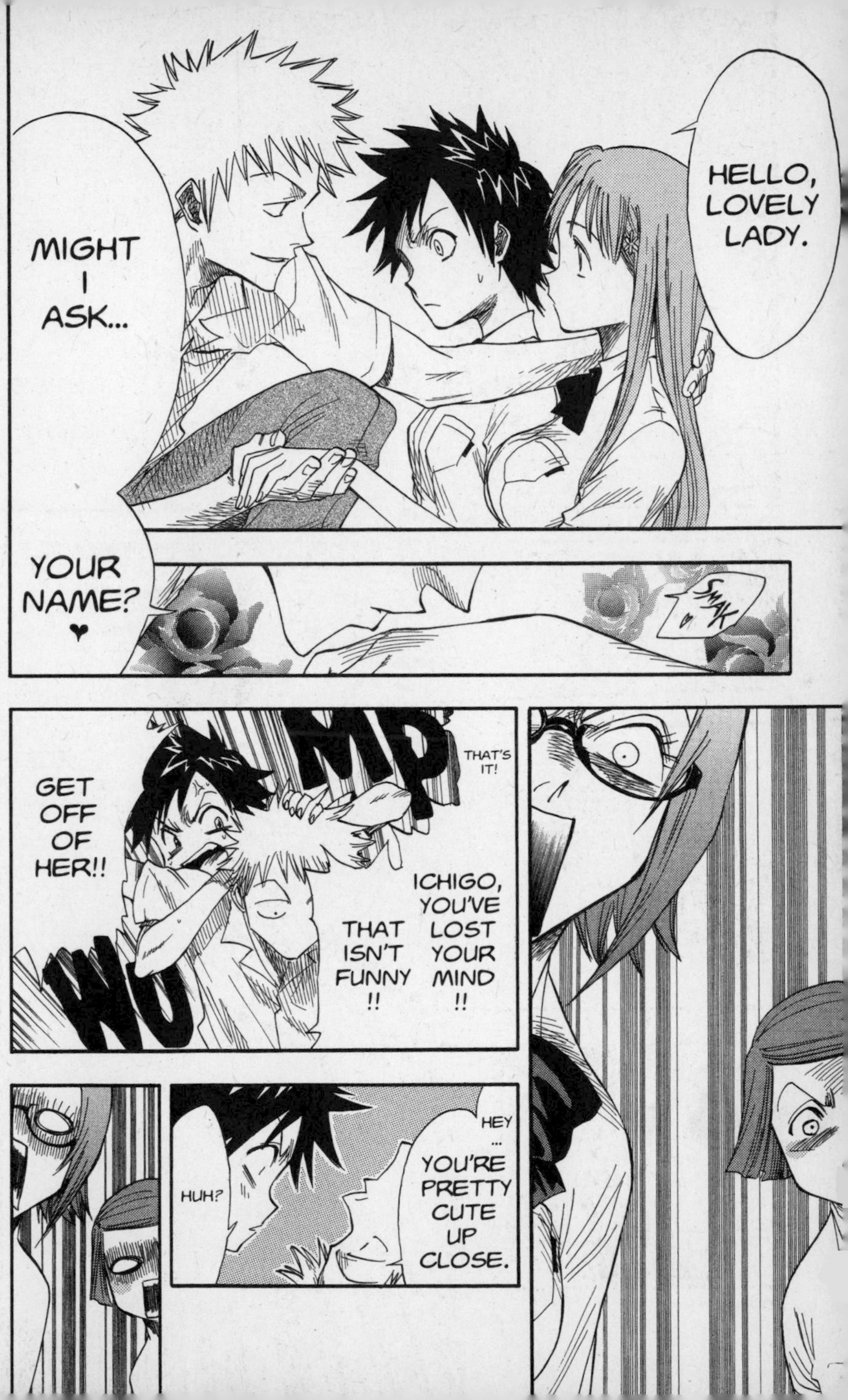
HELLO, LOVELY LADY.
MIGHT I ASK...
YOUR NAME? ♥
SMAK
THAT'S IT!
WHOMP
GET OFF OF HER!!
ICHIGO, YOU'VE LOST YOUR MIND!!
THAT ISN'T FUNNY!!
HEY... YOU'RE PRETTY CUTE UP CLOSE.
HUH?

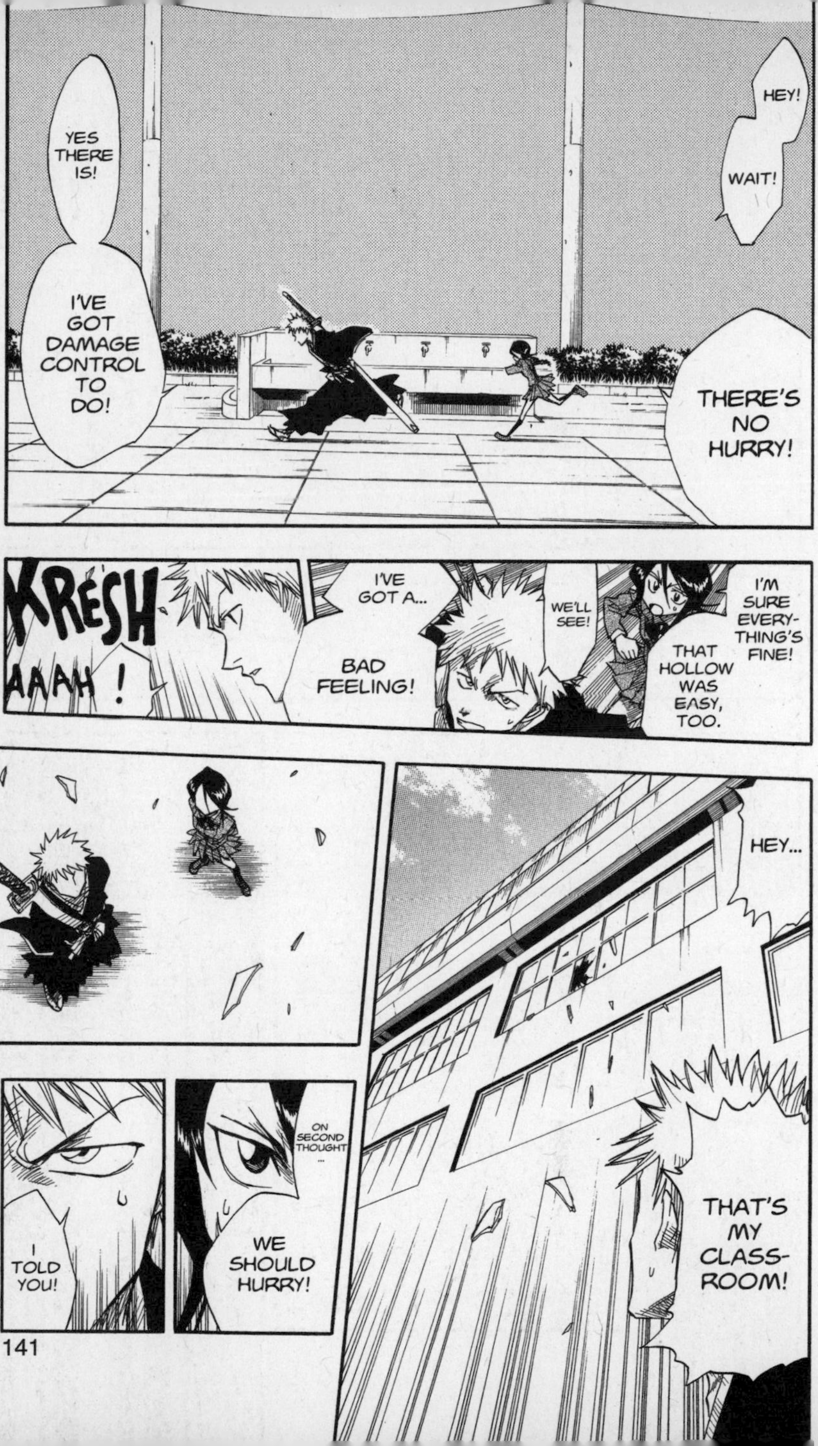
HEY!
WAIT!
THERE'S NO HURRY!
YES THERE IS!
I'VE GOT DAMAGE CONTROL TO DO!
I'M SURE EVERYTHING'S FINE!
THAT HOLLOW WAS EASY, TOO.
WE'LL SEE!
I'VE GOT A...
BAD FEELING!
KRESH
AAAH!
HEY...
THAT'S MY CLASSROOM!
ON SECOND THOUGHT...
WE SHOULD HURRY!
I TOLD YOU!

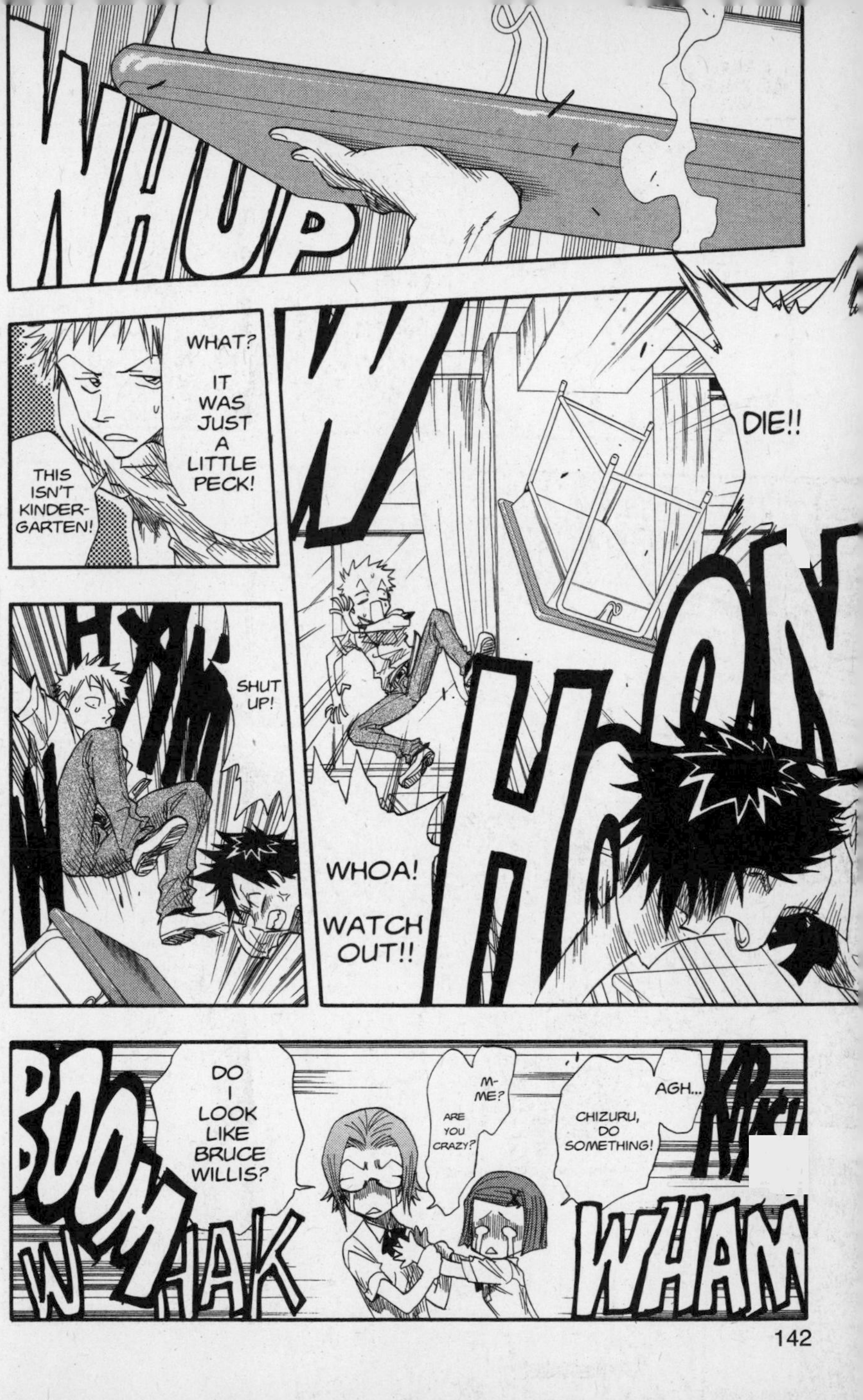
WHUP
DIE!!
WHOA!
WATCH OUT!!
WHAT?
IT WAS JUST A LITTLE PECK!
THIS ISN'T KINDER-GARTEN!
SHUT UP!
WHAM
AGH...
CHIZURU, DO SOMETHING!
M-ME?
ARE YOU CRAZY?
DO I LOOK LIKE BRUCE WILLIS?
BOOM
WHAK

READ THIS WAY

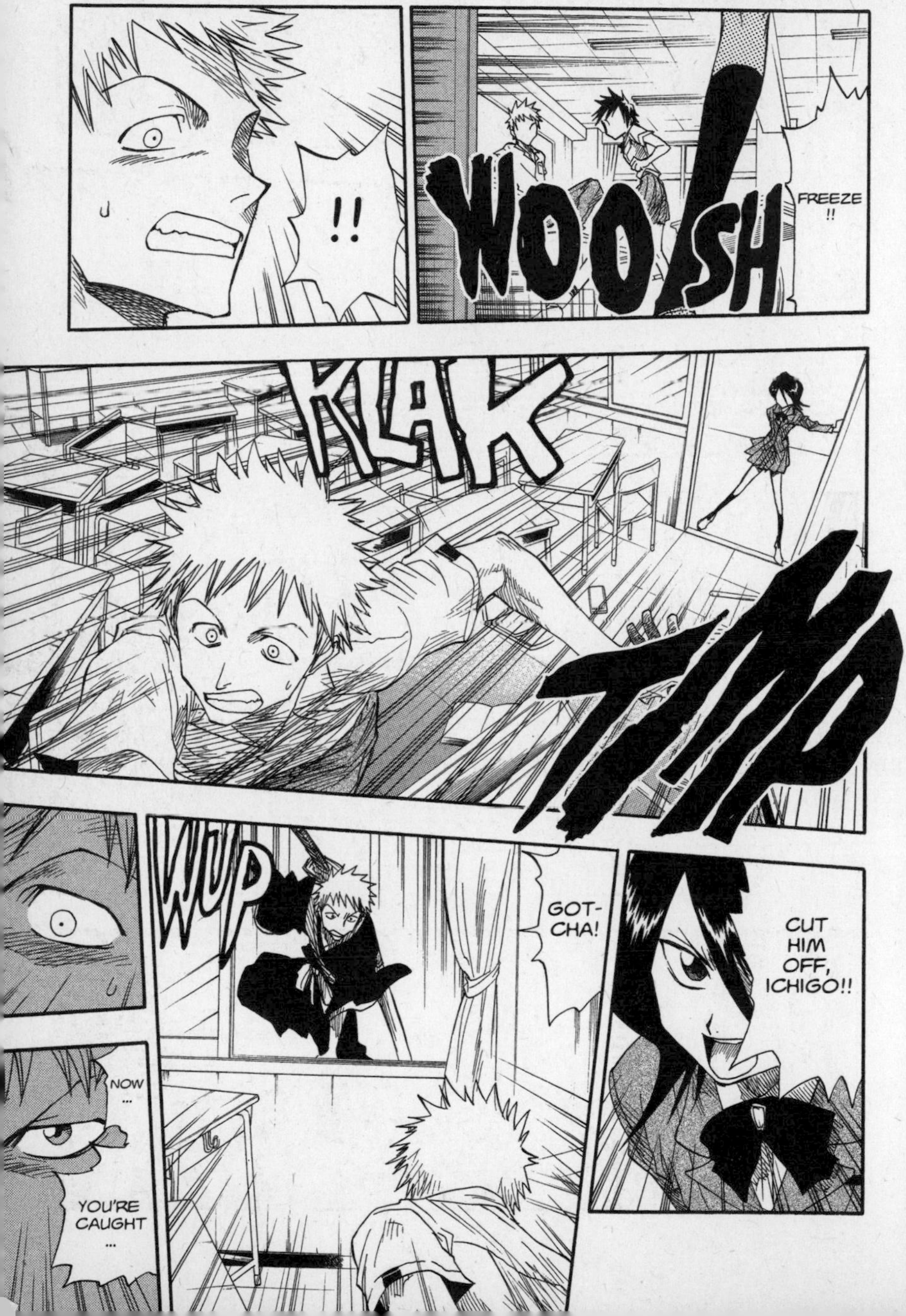
WOOSH
FREEZE !!
!!
KLAK
THUD
CUT HIM OFF, ICHIGO!!
GOT-CHA!
WUP
NOW ...
YOU'RE CAUGHT ...

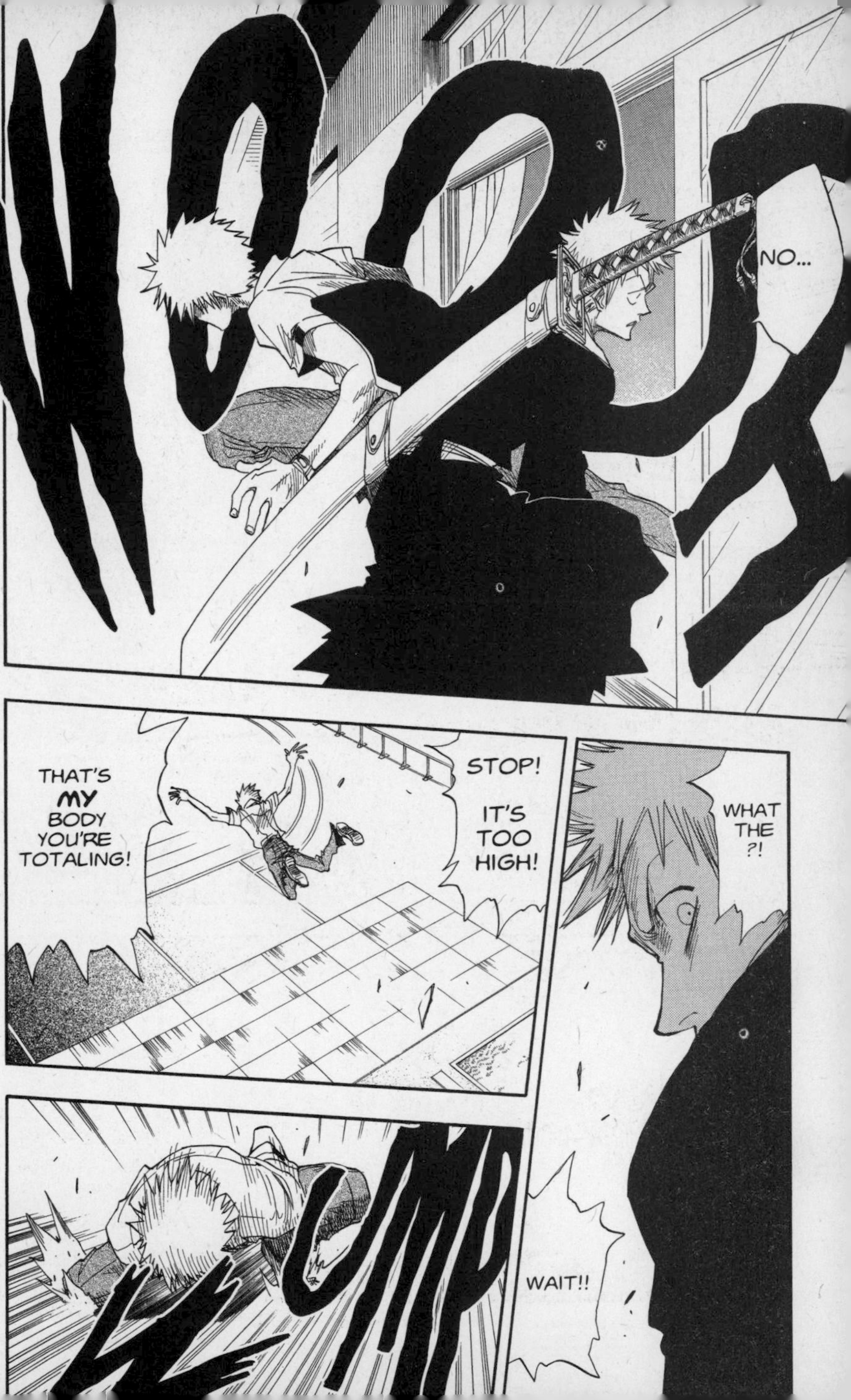
NO...
WHAT THE ?!
WAIT!!
STOP!
IT'S TOO HIGH!
THAT'S MY BODY YOU'RE TOTALING!

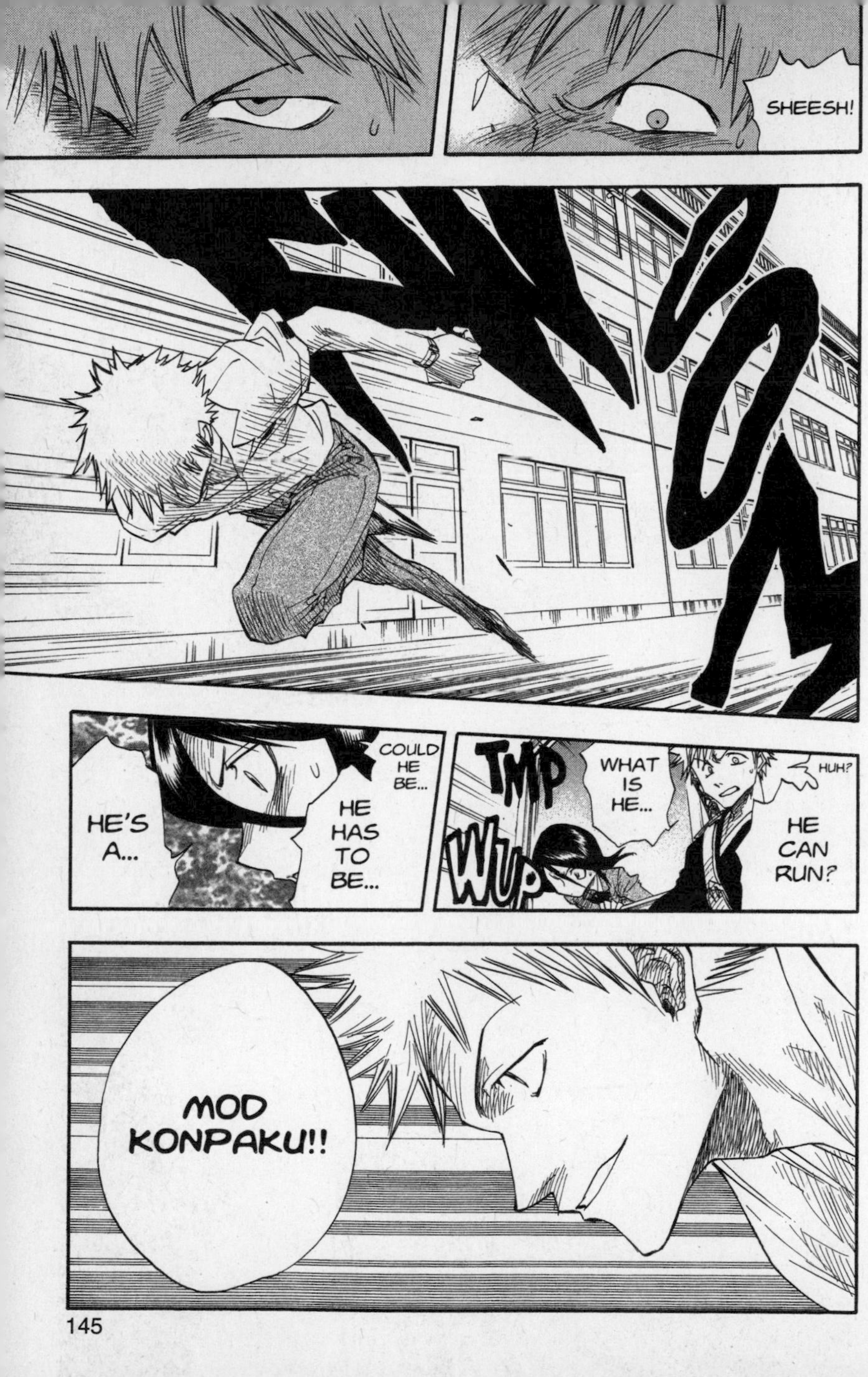

SHEESH!
HUH?
WHAT IS HE...
HE CAN RUN?
TMP
WUP
COULD HE BE...
HE HAS TO BE...
HE'S A...
MOD KONPAKU!!

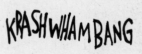

I THINK IT WAS...
RUKIA?

WHAT WAS THAT?

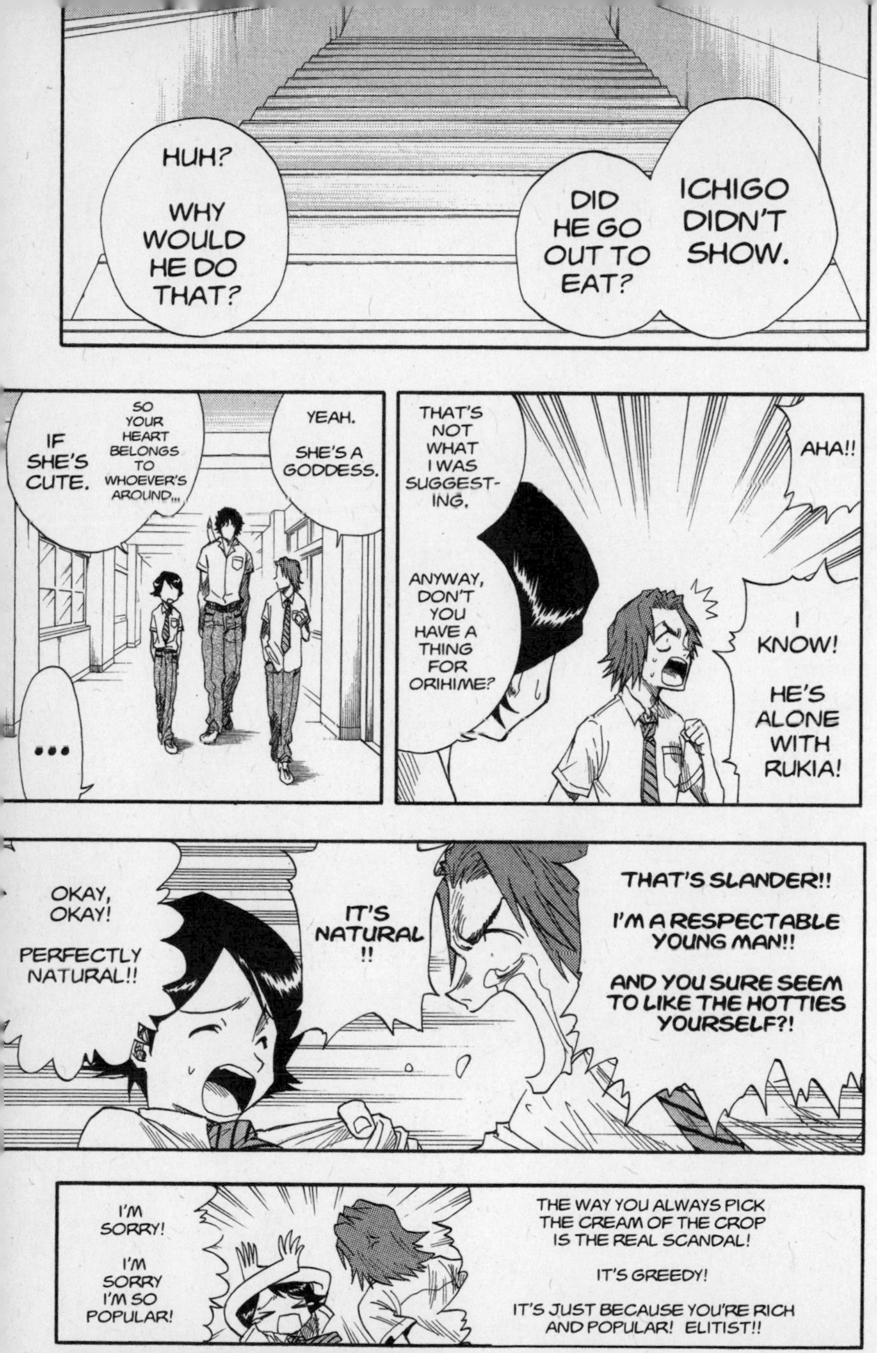
ICHIGO DIDN'T SHOW.
DID HE GO OUT TO EAT?
HUH? WHY WOULD HE DO THAT?
AHA!! I KNOW! HE'S ALONE WITH RUKIA!
THAT'S NOT WHAT I WAS SUGGEST-ING.
ANYWAY, DON'T YOU HAVE A THING FOR ORIHIME?
YEAH. SHE'S A GODDESS.
SO YOUR HEART BELONGS TO WHOEVER'S AROUND...
IF SHE'S CUTE.
...
THAT'S SLANDER!! I'M A RESPECTABLE YOUNG MAN!! AND YOU SURE SEEM TO LIKE THE HOTTIES YOURSELF?!
IT'S NATURAL!!
OKAY, OKAY! PERFECTLY NATURAL!!
THE WAY YOU ALWAYS PICK THE CREAM OF THE CROP IS THE REAL SCANDAL! IT'S GREEDY! IT'S JUST BECAUSE YOU'RE RICH AND POPULAR! ELITIST!!
I'M SORRY! I'M SORRY I'M SO POPULAR!

15. Jumpin' Jack, Jolted

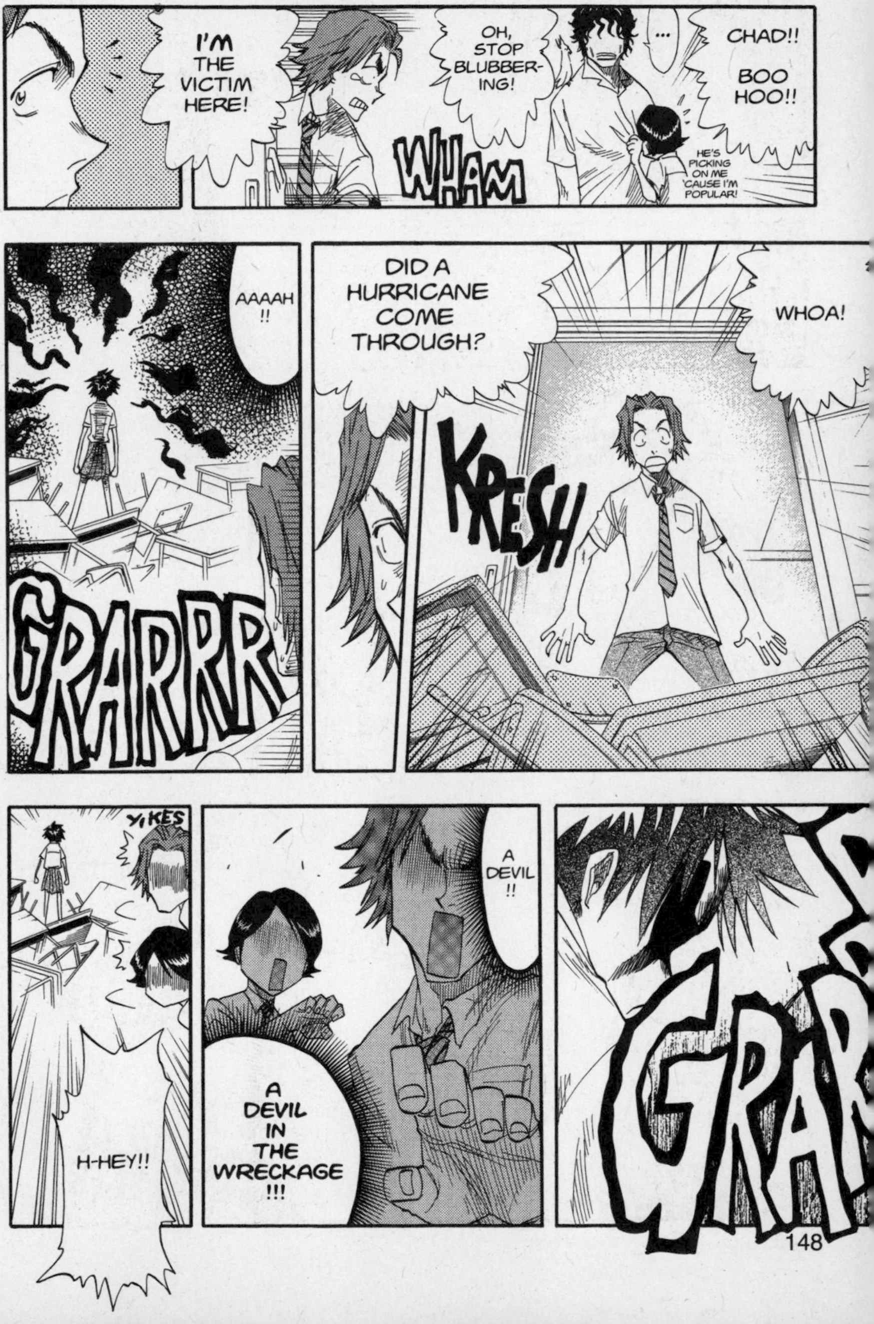
CHAD!!
BOO HOO!!
HE'S PICKING ON ME 'CAUSE I'M POPULAR!
...
OH, STOP BLUBBERING!
WHAM
I'M THE VICTIM HERE!
WHOA!
DID A HURRICANE COME THROUGH?
KRESH
AAAAH!!
GRARRR
GRAR
A DEVIL!!
A DEVIL IN THE WRECKAGE!!!
YIKES
H-HEY!!

READ THIS WAY

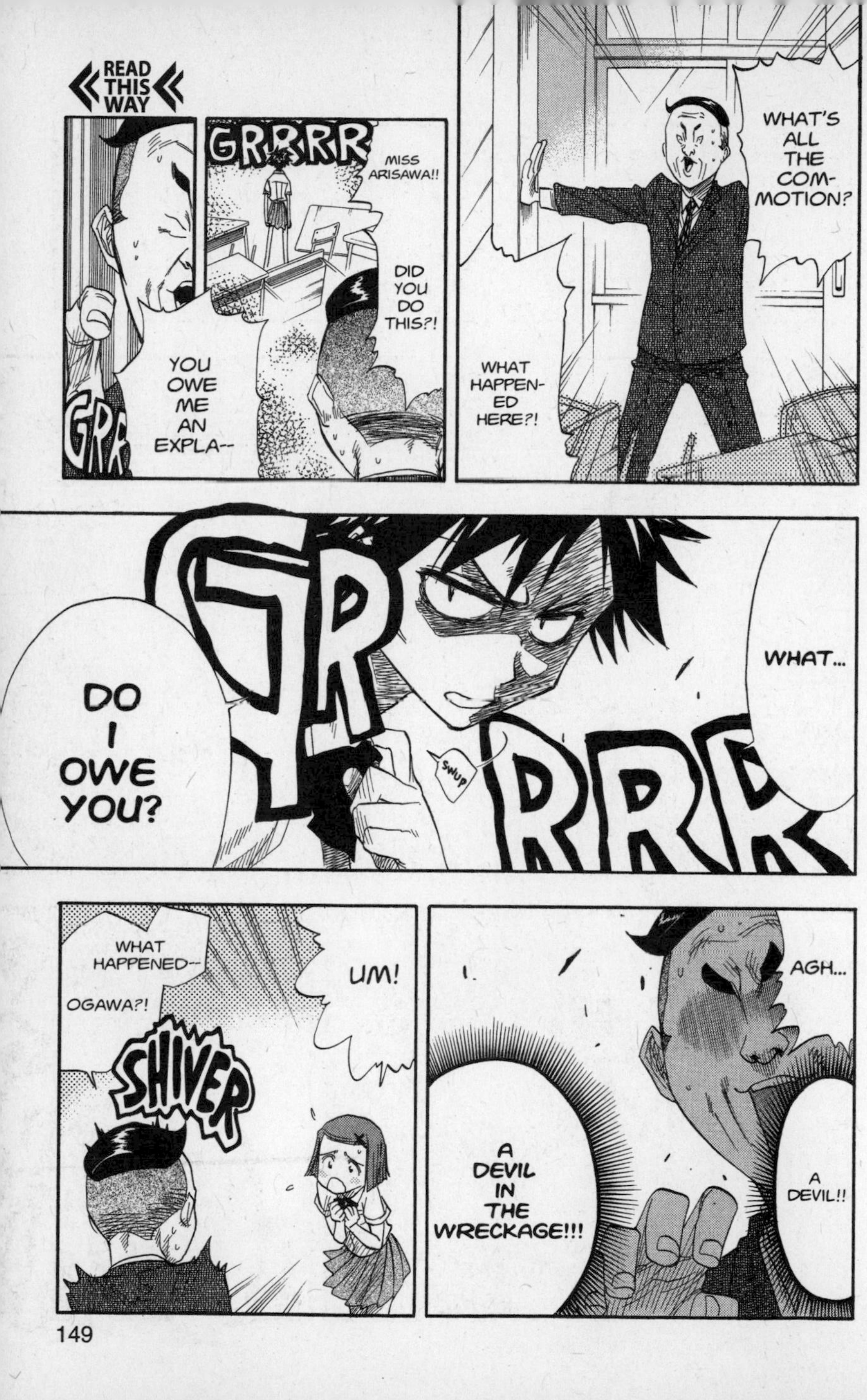
WHAT'S ALL THE COM-MOTION?
WHAT HAPPEN-ED HERE?!
GRRRR
MISS ARISAWA!!
DID YOU DO THIS?!
YOU OWE ME AN EXPLA--
GRR
WHAT...
GRRRR
SWUP
DO I OWE YOU?
AGH...
A DEVIL!!
A DEVIL IN THE WRECKAGE!!!
UM!
WHAT HAPPENED--
OGAWA?!
SHIVER

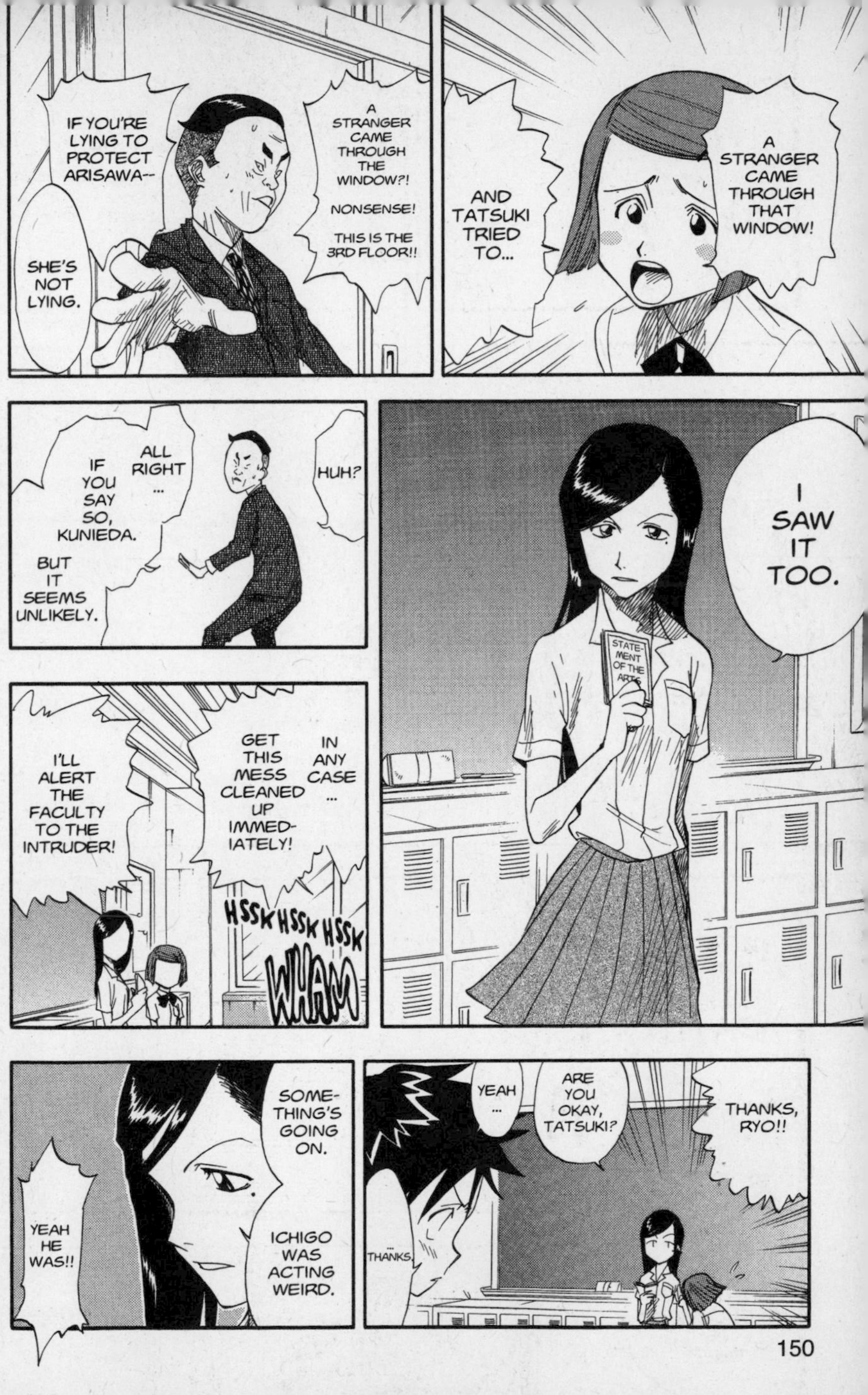

A STRANGER CAME THROUGH THAT WINDOW!
AND TATSUKI TRIED TO...
A STRANGER CAME THROUGH THE WINDOW?!
NONSENSE!
THIS IS THE 3RD FLOOR!!
IF YOU'RE LYING TO PROTECT ARISAWA--
SHE'S NOT LYING.
I SAW IT TOO.
STATE-MENT OF THE ARTS
HUH?
ALL RIGHT...
IF YOU SAY SO, KUNIEDA.
BUT IT SEEMS UNLIKELY.
IN ANY CASE...
GET THIS MESS CLEANED UP IMMEDIATELY!
I'LL ALERT THE FACULTY TO THE INTRUDER!
HSSK HSSK HSSK
WHAM
THANKS, RYO!!
ARE YOU OKAY, TATSUKI?
YEAH...
...THANKS.
SOME-THING'S GOING ON.
ICHIGO WAS ACTING WEIRD.
YEAH HE WAS!!

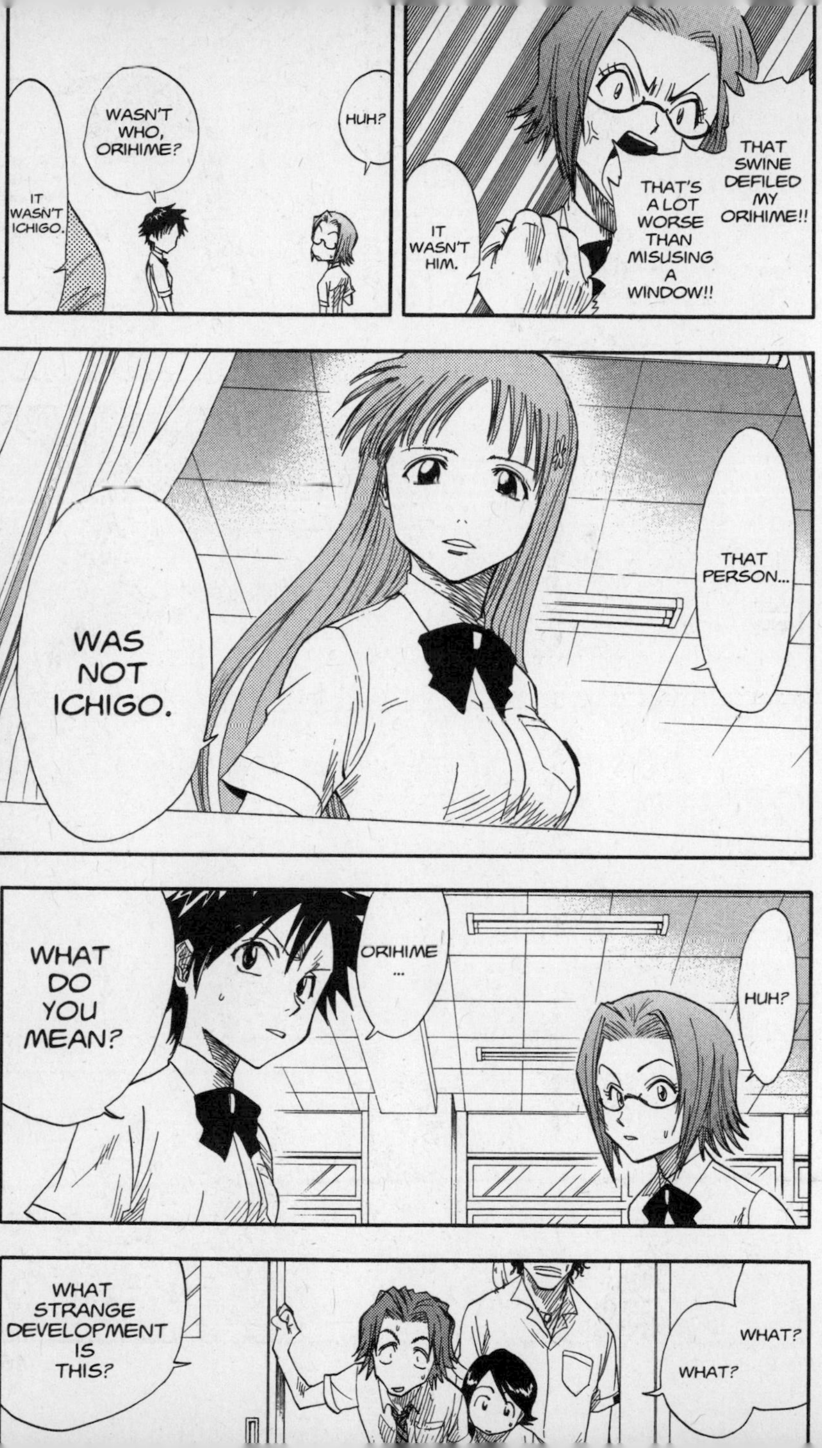
THAT SWINE DEFILED MY ORIHIME!!
THAT'S A LOT WORSE THAN MISUSING A WINDOW!!
IT WASN'T HIM.
HUH?
WASN'T WHO, ORIHIME?
IT WASN'T ICHIGO.
THAT PERSON...
WAS NOT ICHIGO.
HUH?
ORIHIME...
WHAT DO YOU MEAN?
WHAT?
WHAT?
WHAT STRANGE DEVELOPMENT IS THIS?

15. Jumpin' Jack, Jolted

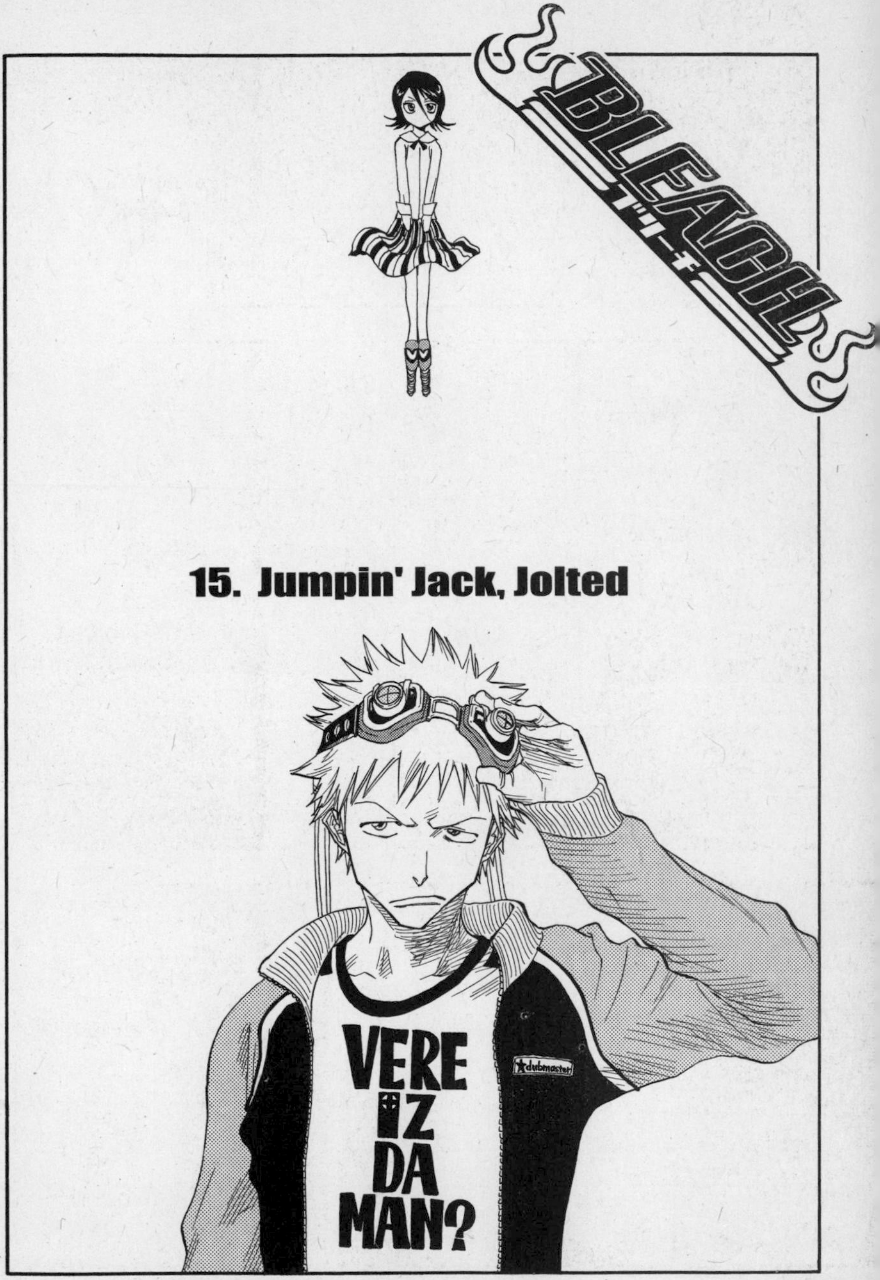
BLEACH
VERE IZ DA MAN?
dubmaster

READ THIS WAY

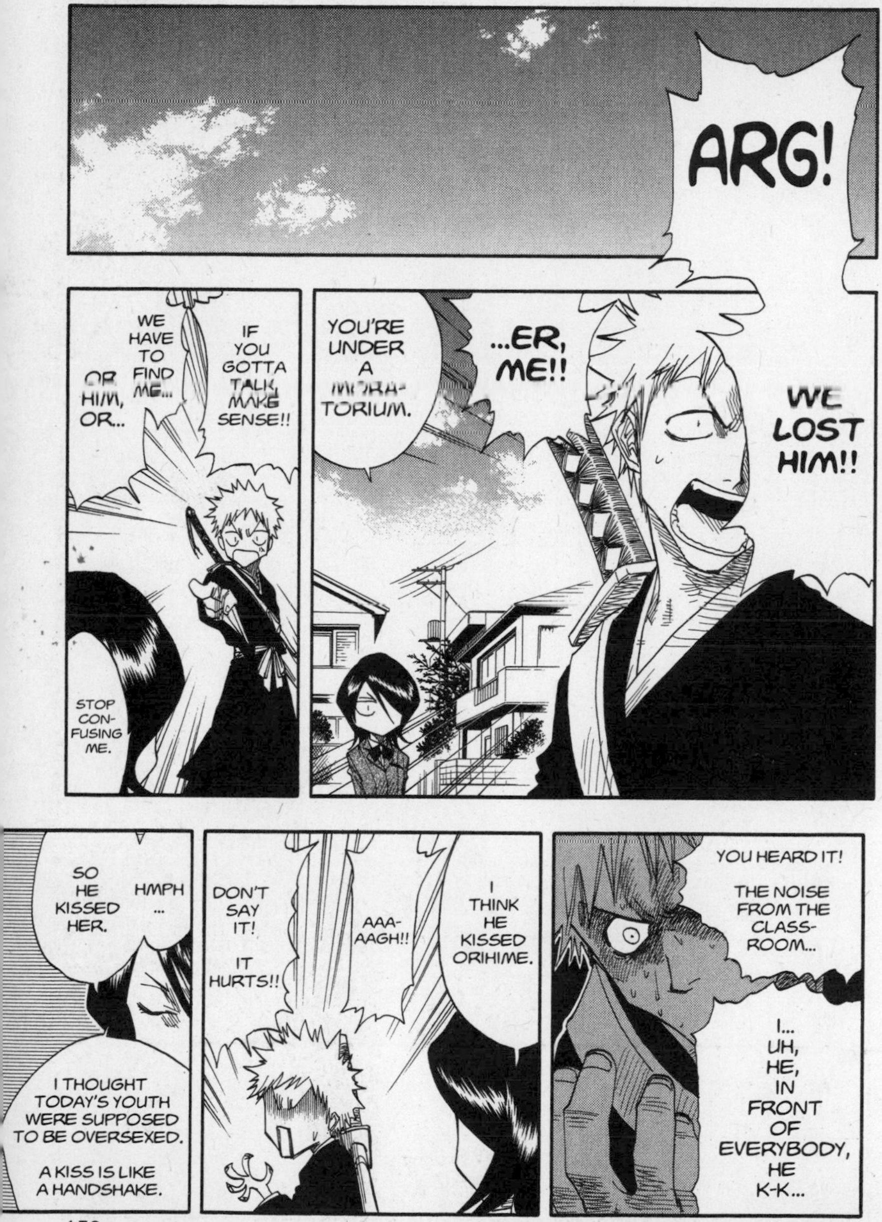

ARG!
WE LOST HIM!!
...ER, ME!!
YOU'RE UNDER A MORA-TORIUM.
IF YOU GOTTA TALK, MAKE SENSE!!
WE HAVE TO FIND ME... OR HIM, OR...
STOP CON-FUSING ME.
YOU HEARD IT!
THE NOISE FROM THE CLASS-ROOM...
I... UH, HE, IN FRONT OF EVERYBODY, HE K-K...
I THINK HE KISSED ORIHIME.
AAA-AAGH!!
DON'T SAY IT!
IT HURTS!!
HMPH...
SO HE KISSED HER.
I THOUGHT TODAY'S YOUTH WERE SUPPOSED TO BE OVERSEXED.
A KISS IS LIKE A HANDSHAKE.

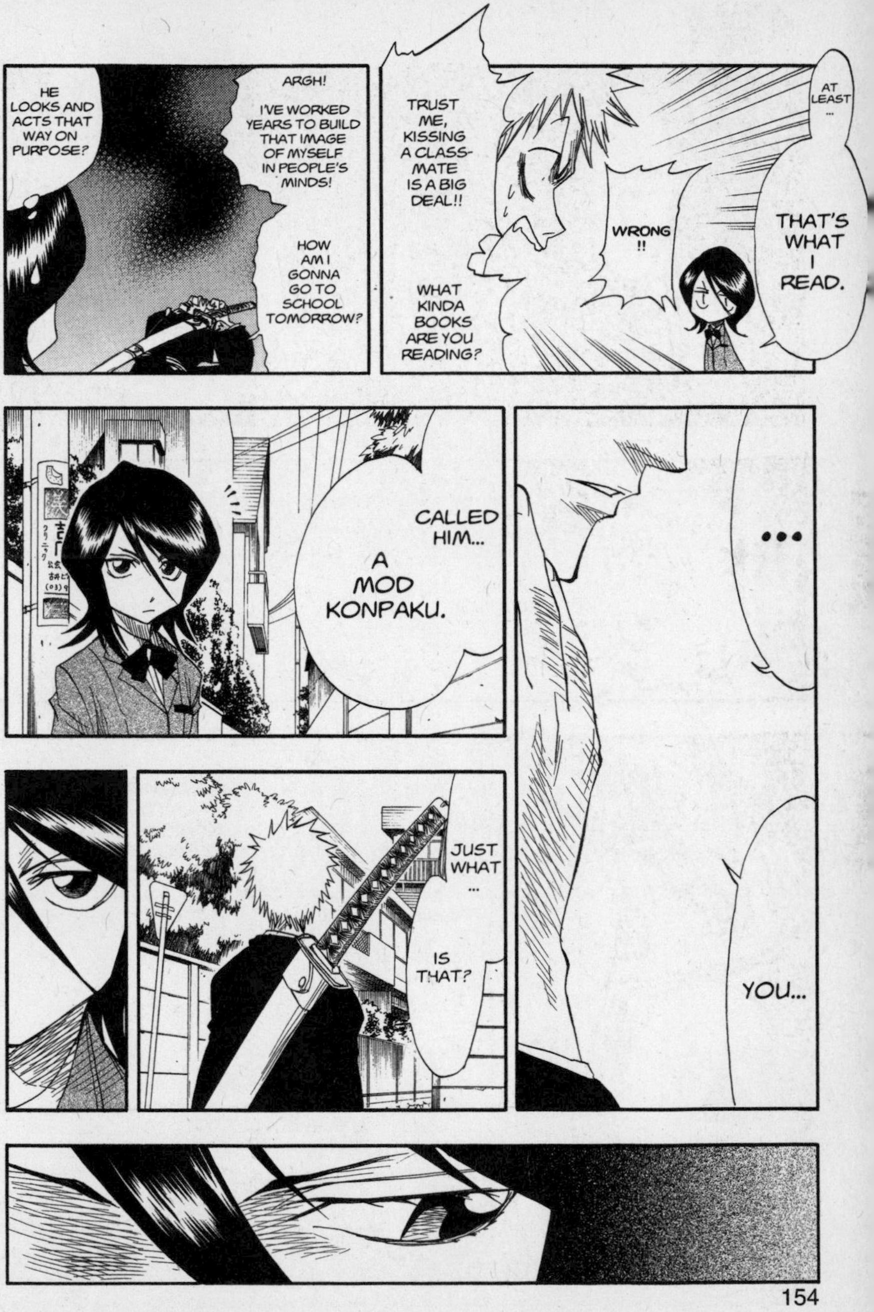

AT LEAST ...
THAT'S WHAT I READ.
TRUST ME, KISSING A CLASSMATE IS A BIG DEAL!!
WRONG !!
WHAT KINDA BOOKS ARE YOU READING?
ARGH!
I'VE WORKED YEARS TO BUILD THAT IMAGE OF MYSELF IN PEOPLE'S MINDS!
HOW AM I GONNA GO TO SCHOOL TOMORROW?
HE LOOKS AND ACTS THAT WAY ON PURPOSE?
...
YOU...
CALLED HIM...
A MOD KONPAKU.
JUST WHAT ...
IS THAT?

READ THIS WAY

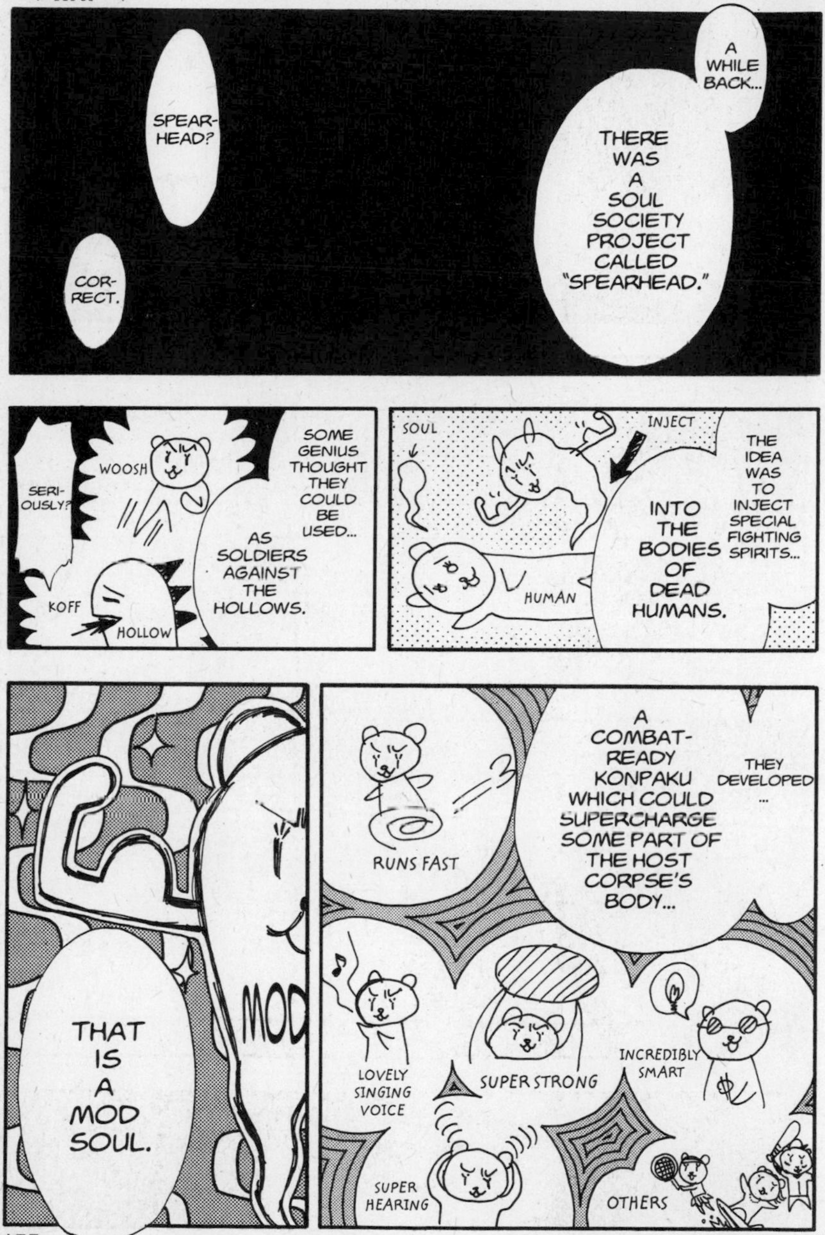

A WHILE BACK...
THERE WAS A SOUL SOCIETY PROJECT CALLED "SPEARHEAD."
SPEAR-HEAD?
COR-RECT.
THE IDEA WAS TO INJECT SPECIAL FIGHTING SPIRITS...
INTO THE BODIES OF DEAD HUMANS.
INJECT
SOUL
HUMAN
SOME GENIUS THOUGHT THEY COULD BE USED...
AS SOLDIERS AGAINST THE HOLLOWS.
WOOSH
SERI-OUSLY?
KOFF
HOLLOW
THEY DEVELOPED...
A COMBAT-READY KONPAKU WHICH COULD SUPERCHARGE SOME PART OF THE HOST CORPSE'S BODY...
RUNS FAST
INCREDIBLY SMART
SUPER STRONG
LOVELY SINGING VOICE
SUPER HEARING
OTHERS
MOD
THAT IS A MOD SOUL.

READ THIS WAY

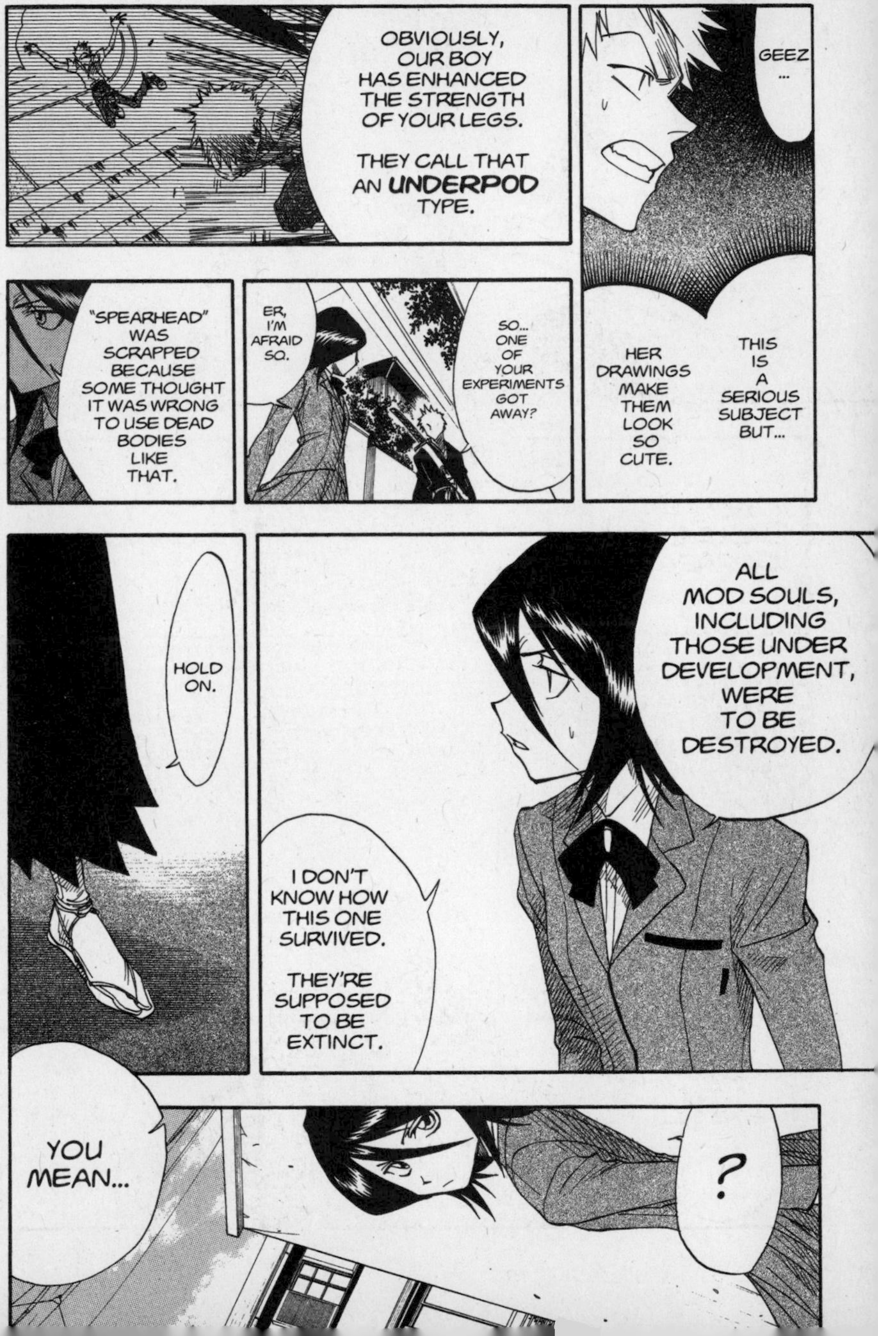
GEEZ...
THIS IS A SERIOUS SUBJECT BUT...
HER DRAWINGS MAKE THEM LOOK SO CUTE.
OBVIOUSLY, OUR BOY HAS ENHANCED THE STRENGTH OF YOUR LEGS.
THEY CALL THAT AN UNDERPOD TYPE.
SO... ONE OF YOUR EXPERIMENTS GOT AWAY?
ER, I'M AFRAID SO.
"SPEARHEAD" WAS SCRAPPED BECAUSE SOME THOUGHT IT WAS WRONG TO USE DEAD BODIES LIKE THAT.
ALL MOD SOULS, INCLUDING THOSE UNDER DEVELOPMENT, WERE TO BE DESTROYED.
I DON'T KNOW HOW THIS ONE SURVIVED.
THEY'RE SUPPOSED TO BE EXTINCT.
HOLD ON.
?
YOU MEAN...

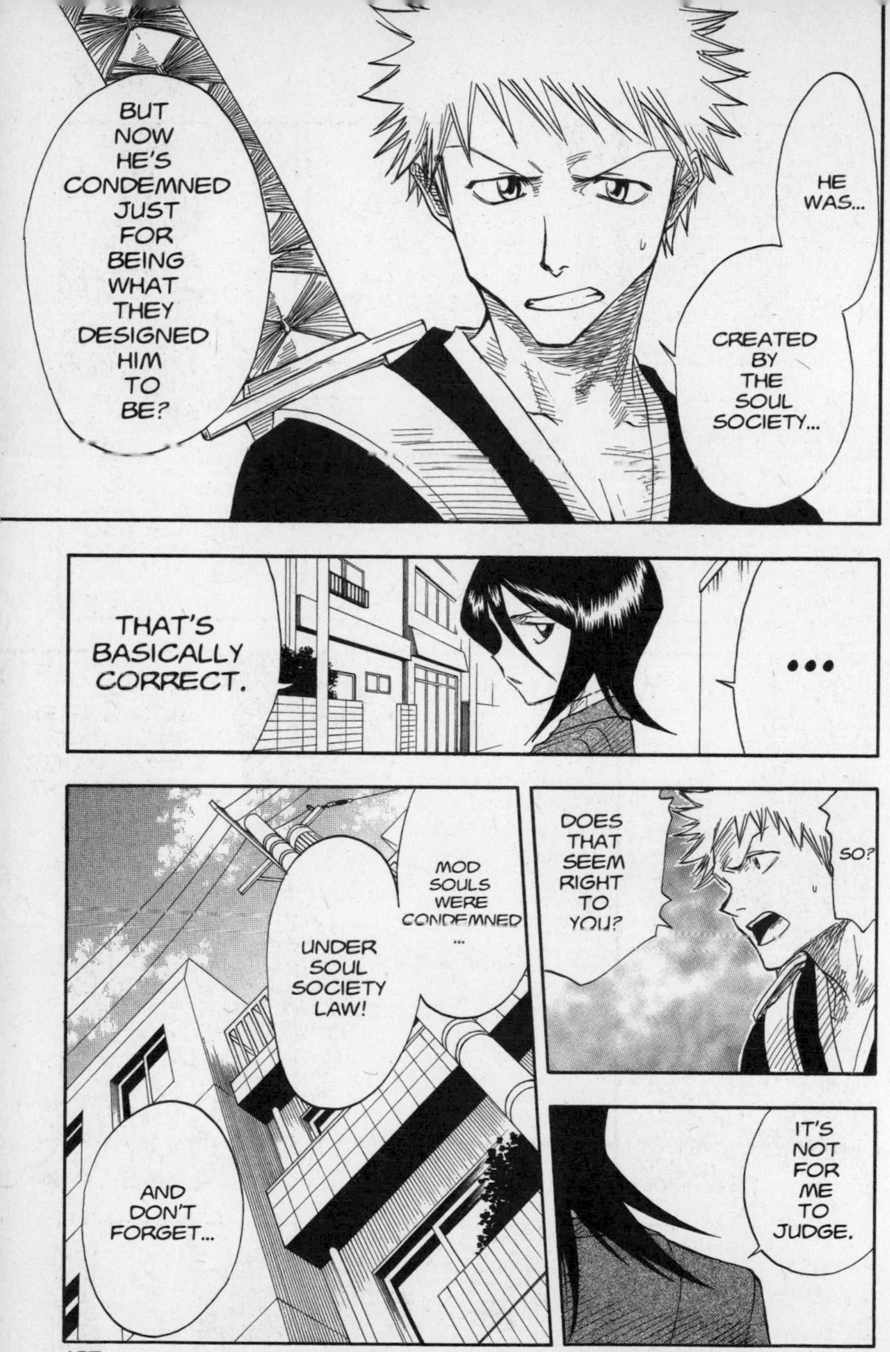
HE WAS...
CREATED BY THE SOUL SOCIETY...
BUT NOW HE'S CONDEMNED JUST FOR BEING WHAT THEY DESIGNED HIM TO BE?
...
THAT'S BASICALLY CORRECT.
SO?
DOES THAT SEEM RIGHT TO YOU?
IT'S NOT FOR ME TO JUDGE.
MOD SOULS WERE CONDEMNED...
UNDER SOUL SOCIETY LAW!
AND DON'T FORGET...

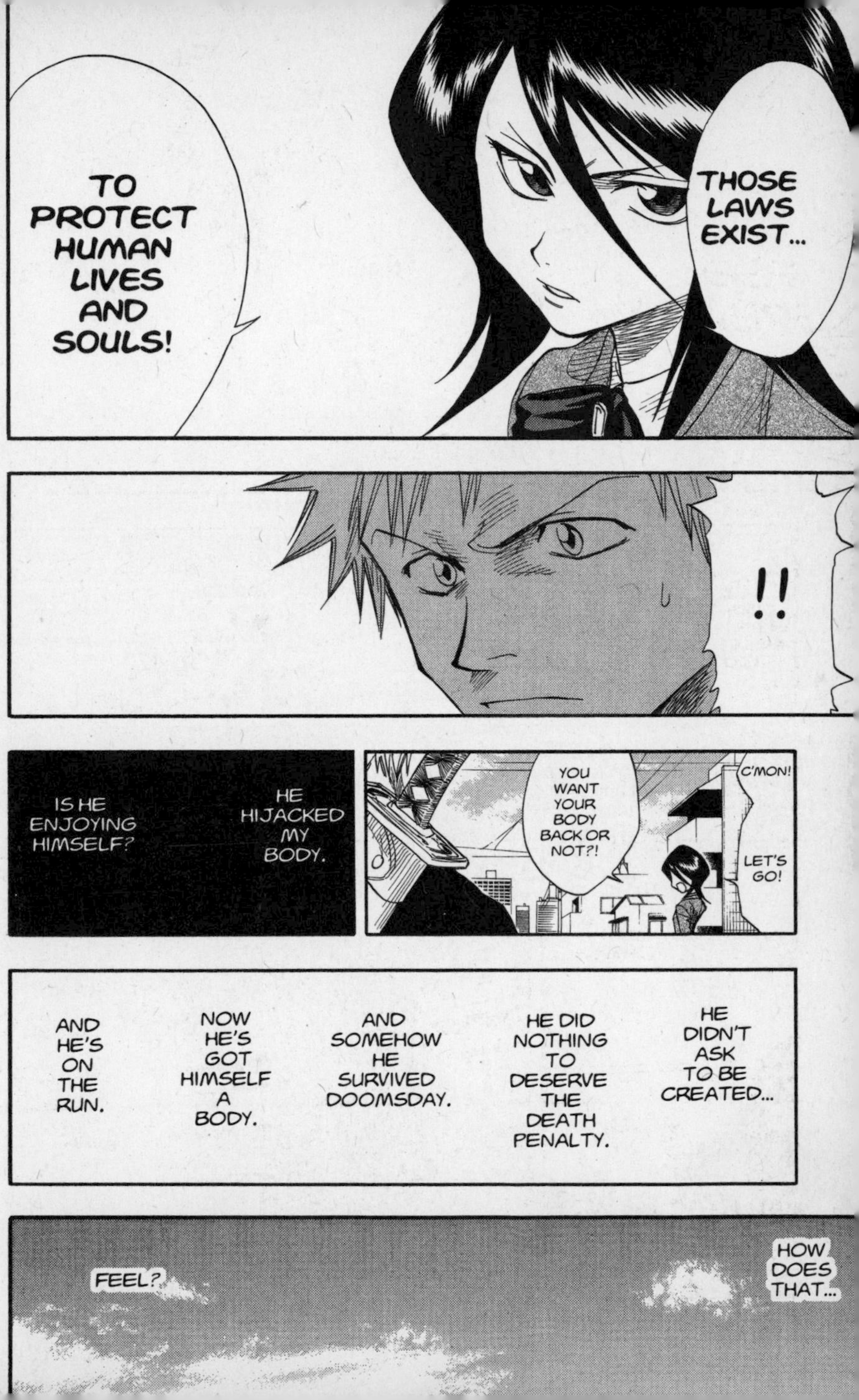
THOSE LAWS EXIST...
TO PROTECT HUMAN LIVES AND SOULS!
!!
C'MON!
YOU WANT YOUR BODY BACK OR NOT?!
LET'S GO!
HE HIJACKED MY BODY.
IS HE ENJOYING HIMSELF?
HE DIDN'T ASK TO BE CREATED...
HE DID NOTHING TO DESERVE THE DEATH PENALTY.
AND SOMEHOW HE SURVIVED DOOMSDAY.
NOW HE'S GOT HIMSELF A BODY.
AND HE'S ON THE RUN.
HOW DOES THAT...
FEEL?

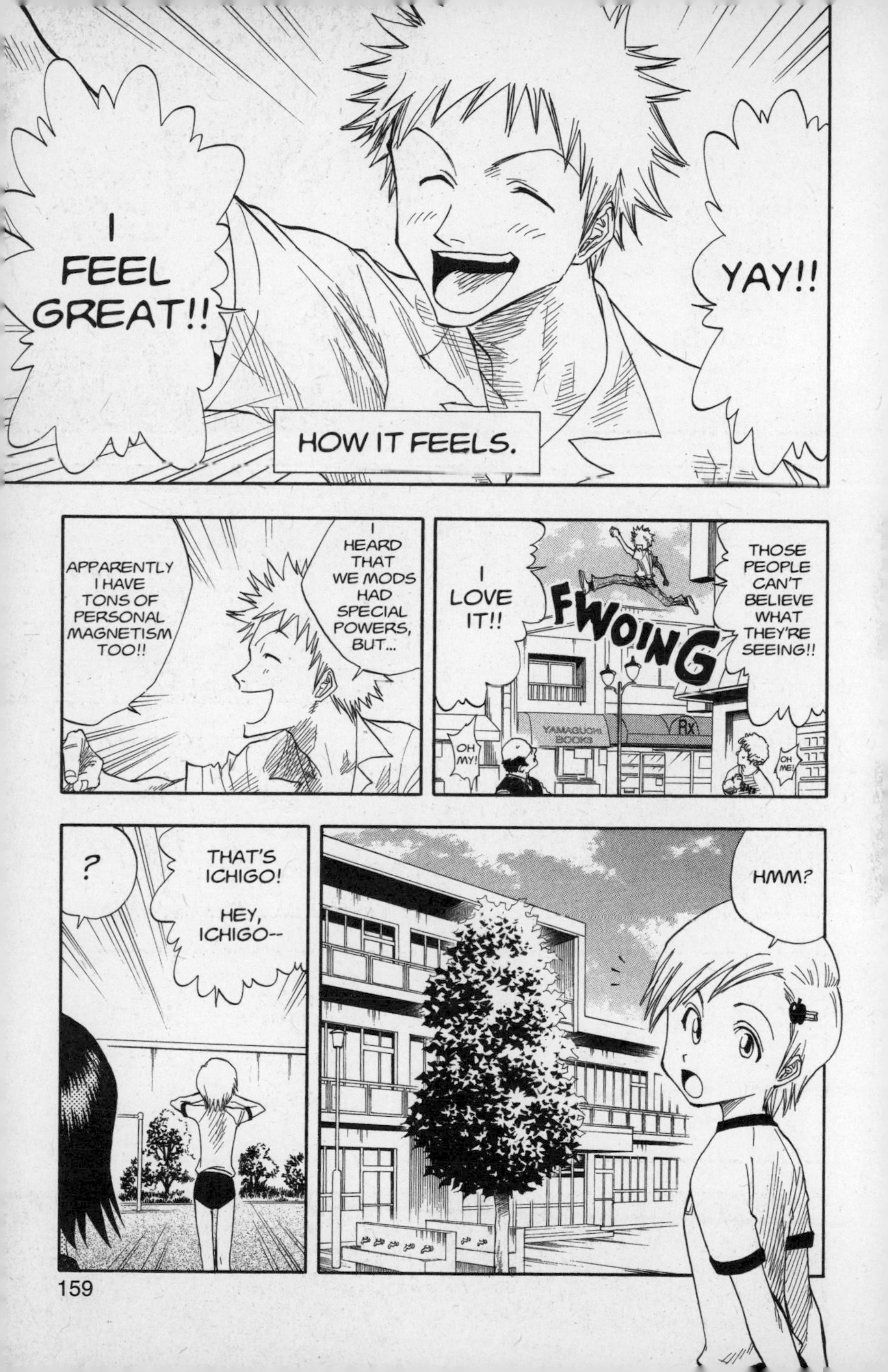
YAY!!
I FEEL GREAT!!
HOW IT FEELS.
THOSE PEOPLE CAN'T BELIEVE WHAT THEY'RE SEEING!!
FWOING
I LOVE IT!!
OH ME!
YAMAGUCHI BOOKS
OH MY!
I HEARD THAT WE MODS HAD SPECIAL POWERS, BUT...
APPARENTLY I HAVE TONS OF PERSONAL MAGNETISM TOO!!
HMM?
THAT'S ICHIGO!
HEY, ICHIGO--
?

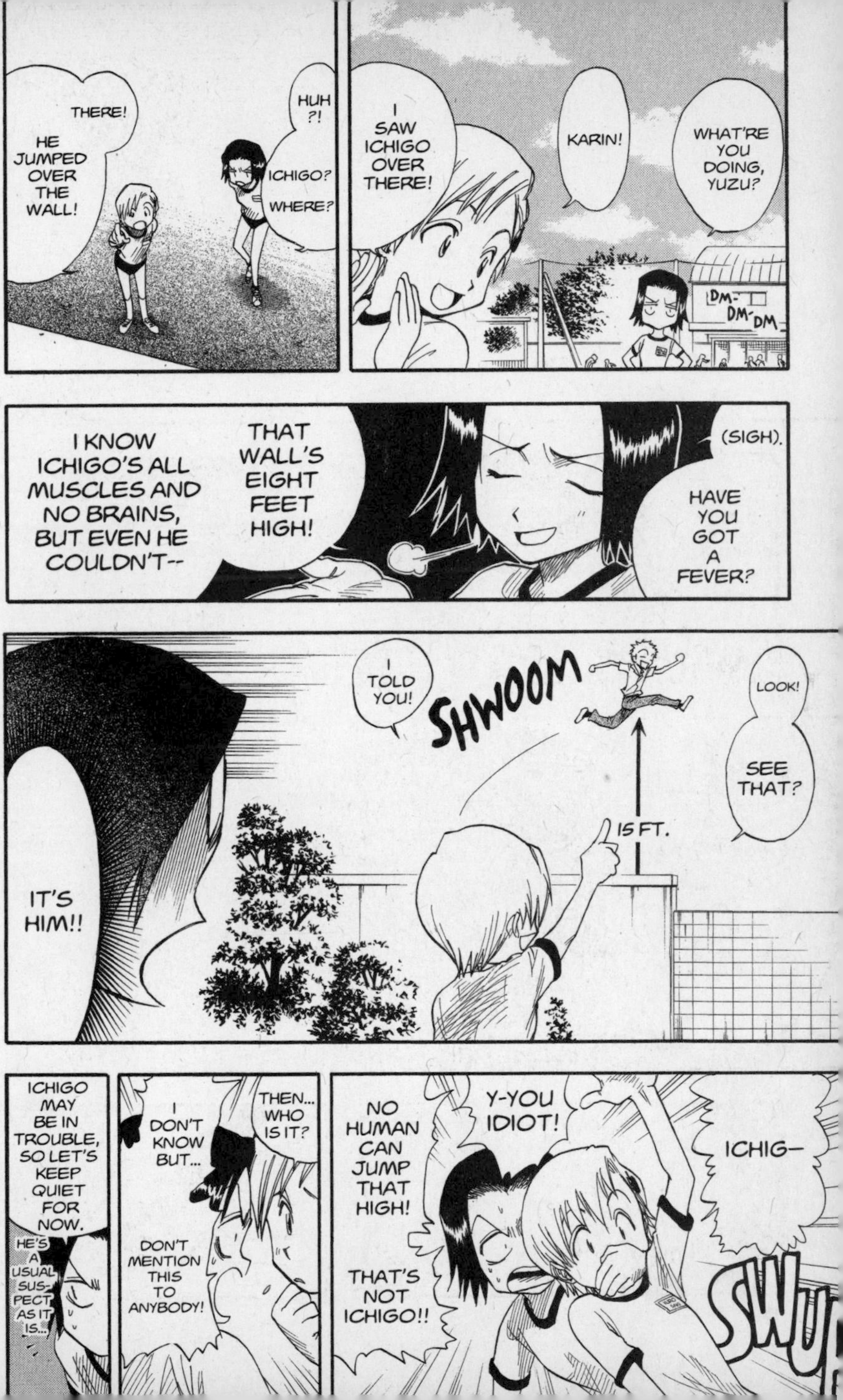
WHAT'RE YOU DOING, YUZU?
KARIN!
I SAW ICHIGO OVER THERE!
DM-DM-DM
HUH?!
ICHIGO? WHERE?
THERE!
HE JUMPED OVER THE WALL!
(SIGH).
HAVE YOU GOT A FEVER?
THAT WALL'S EIGHT FEET HIGH!
I KNOW ICHIGO'S ALL MUSCLES AND NO BRAINS, BUT EVEN HE COULDN'T--
LOOK!
SEE THAT?
15 FT.
SHWOOM
I TOLD YOU!
IT'S HIM!!
ICHIG—
SWU
Y-YOU IDIOT!
NO HUMAN CAN JUMP THAT HIGH!
THAT'S NOT ICHIGO!!
THEN... WHO IS IT?
I DON'T KNOW BUT...
DON'T MENTION THIS TO ANYBODY!
ICHIGO MAY BE IN TROUBLE, SO LET'S KEEP QUIET FOR NOW.
HE'S A USUAL SUSPECT AS IT IS...

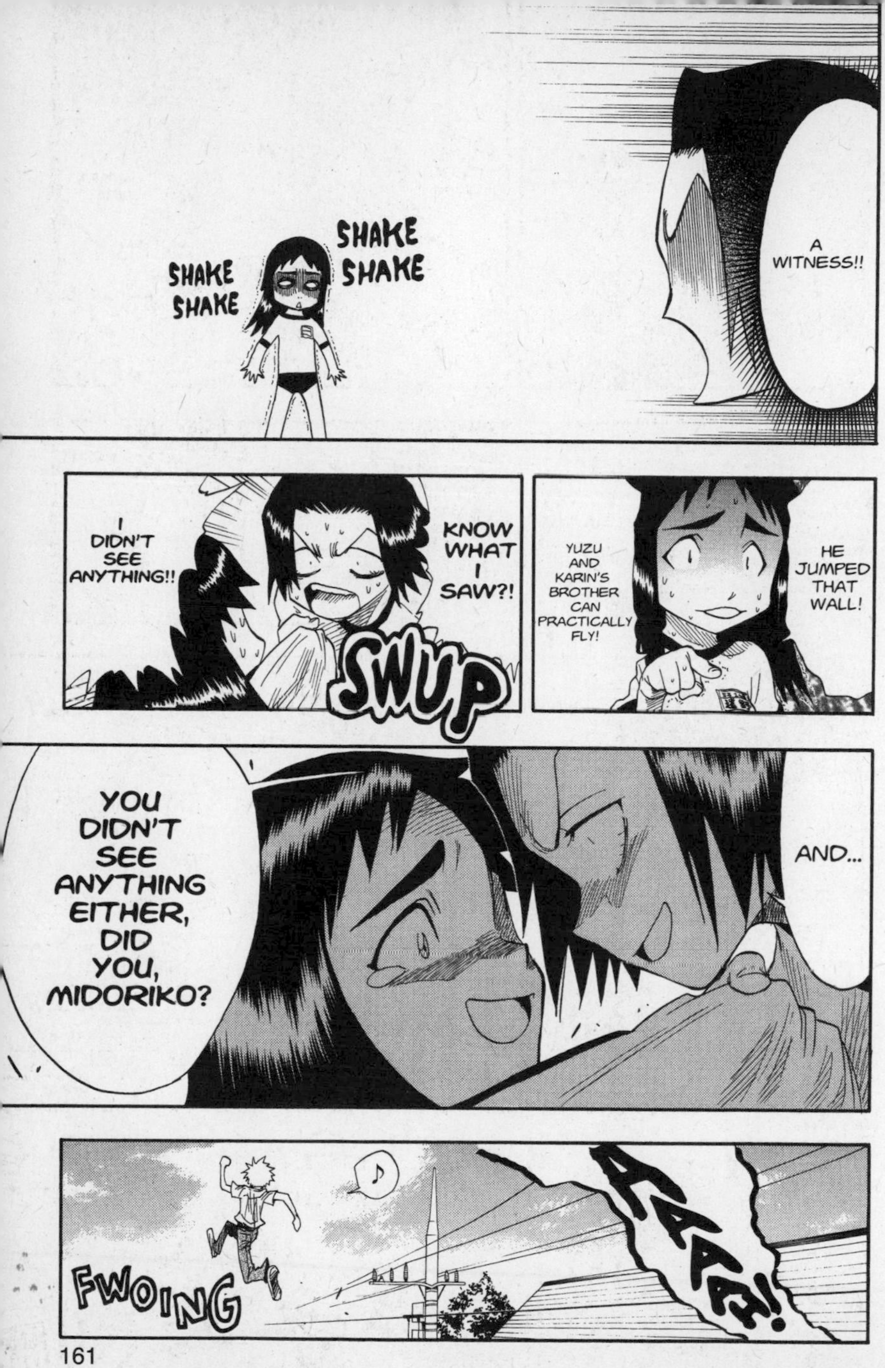
A WITNESS!!
SHAKE SHAKE
SHAKE SHAKE
HE JUMPED THAT WALL!
YUZU AND KARIN'S BROTHER CAN PRACTICALLY FLY!
KNOW WHAT I SAW?!
I DIDN'T SEE ANYTHING!!
SWUP
AND...
YOU DIDN'T SEE ANYTHING EITHER, DID YOU, MIDORIKO?
AAAAH!
♪
FWOING

READ THIS WAY

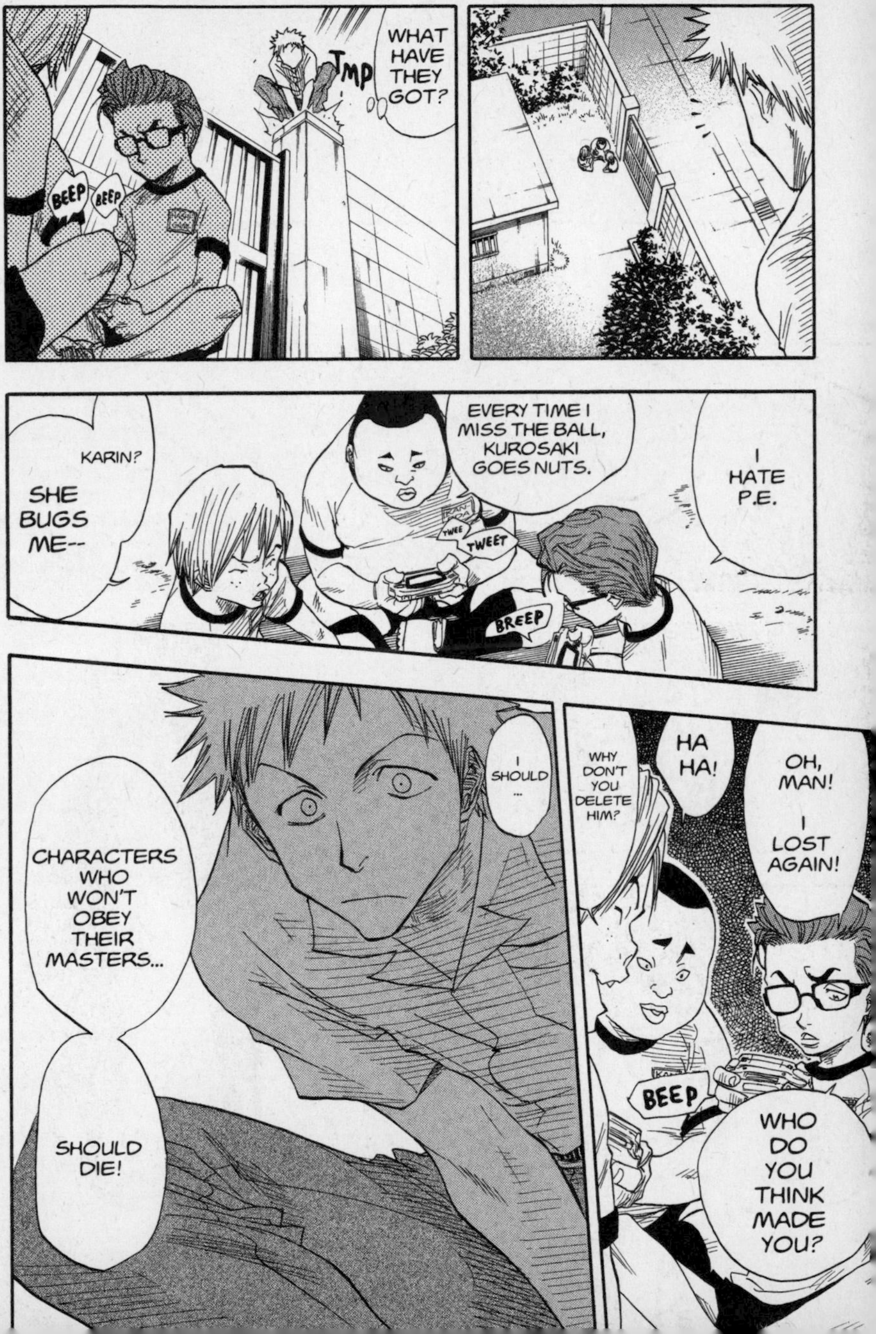
WHAT HAVE THEY GOT?
TMP
BEEP
BEEP
I HATE P.E.
EVERY TIME I MISS THE BALL, KUROSAKI GOES NUTS.
TWEE
TWEET
BREEP
KARIN?
SHE BUGS ME--
OH, MAN!
I LOST AGAIN!
HA HA!
WHY DON'T YOU DELETE HIM?
BEEP
WHO DO YOU THINK MADE YOU?
I SHOULD ...
CHARACTERS WHO WON'T OBEY THEIR MASTERS...
SHOULD DIE!

BAM!!
HE TOTALLY DELETED HIM!
IT'S OKAY! I'LL JUST MAKE A BETTER ONE!
HA HA HA!
TOMP
ALL RIGHT, THEN...
THAT'S ABOUT IT.
UM ... MR. KISUKE?
YEAH?
UM...
I'M SORRY ...
ARE YOU MAD AT ME?
YOU ARE, AREN'T YOU?
IT WAS MY FAULT.
URAHARA SHOTEN

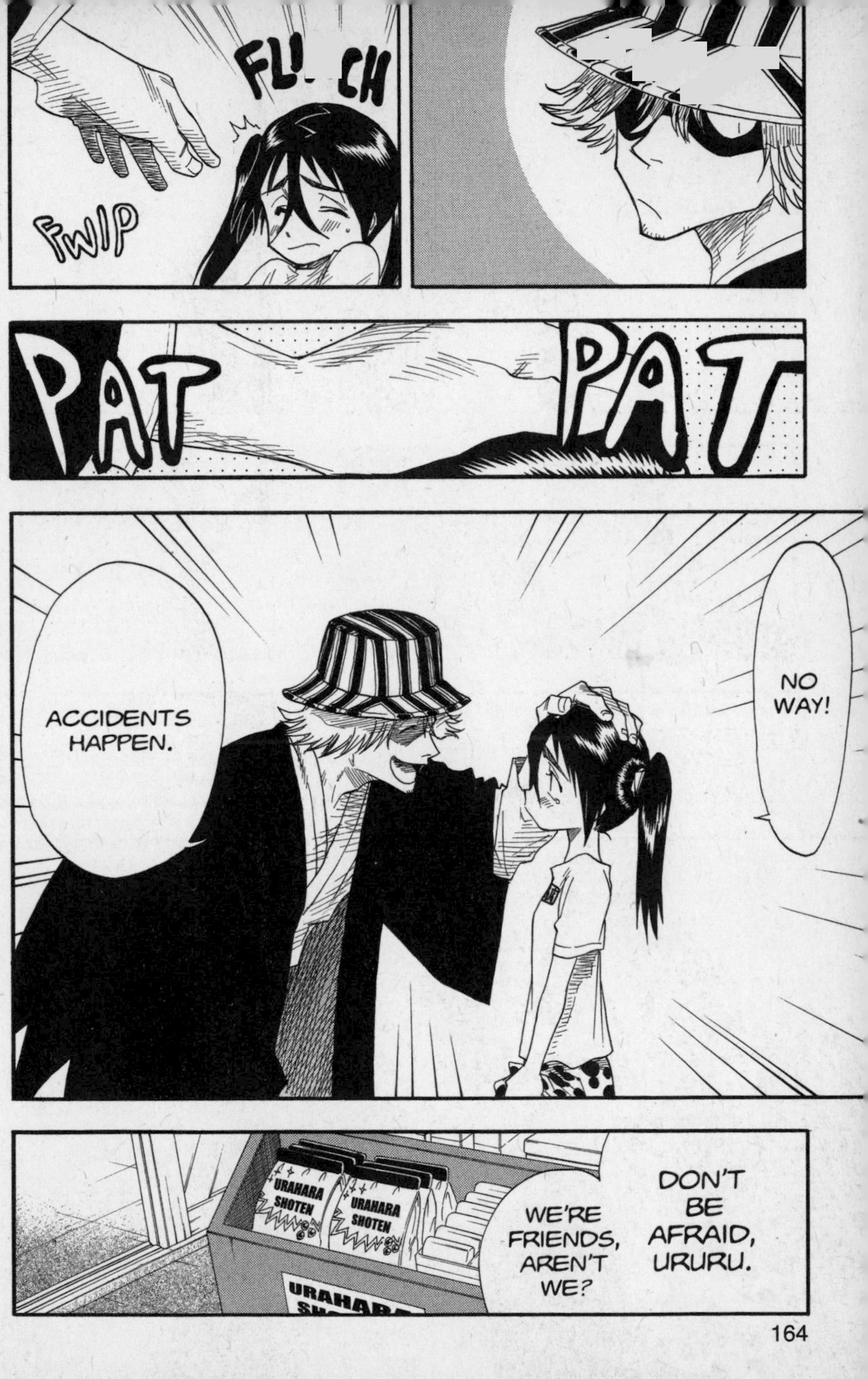
FLI CH
FWIP
PAT
PAT
NO WAY!
ACCIDENTS HAPPEN.
DON'T BE AFRAID, URURU.
WE'RE FRIENDS, AREN'T WE?
URAHARA SHOTEN
URAHARA SHOTEN

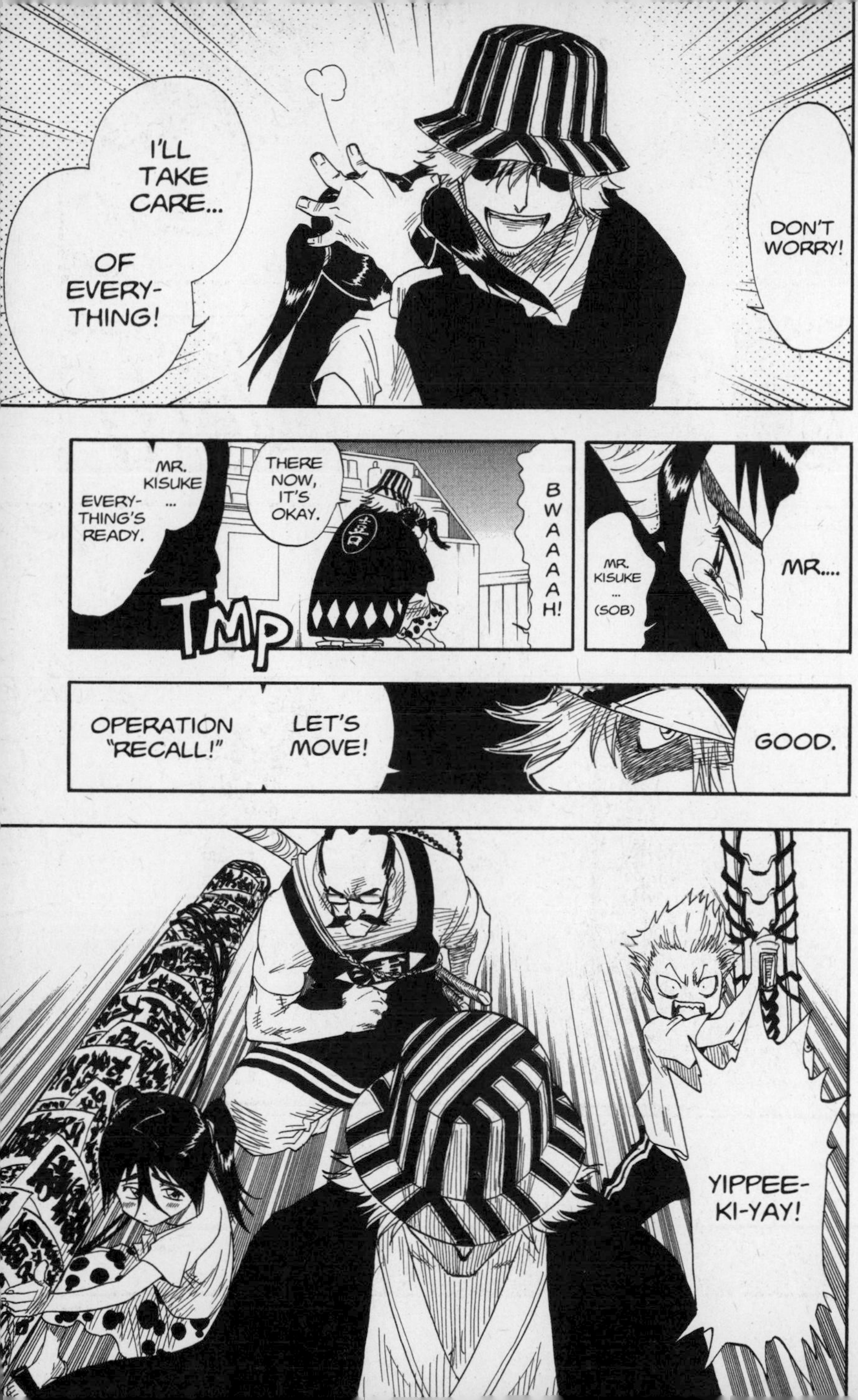
DON'T WORRY!
I'LL TAKE CARE... OF EVERYTHING!
MR....
MR. KISUKE ... (SOB)
BWAAAAAH!
THERE NOW, IT'S OKAY.
MR. KISUKE ... EVERYTHING'S READY.
TMP
GOOD.
LET'S MOVE!
OPERATION "RECALL!"
YIPPEE-KI-YAY!

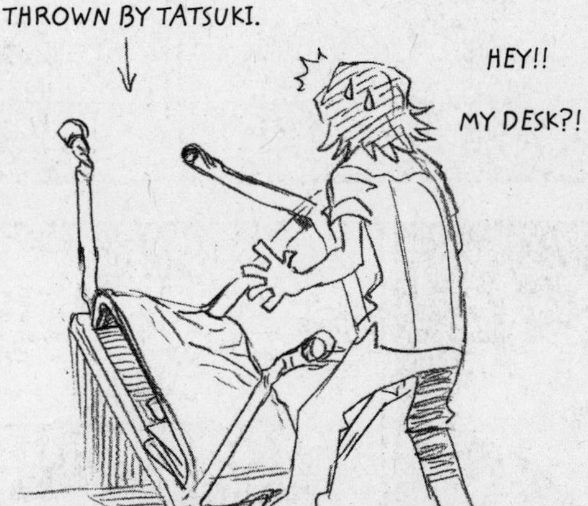
THROWN BY TATSUKI.
HEY!!
MY DESK?!

16. Wasted but Wanted

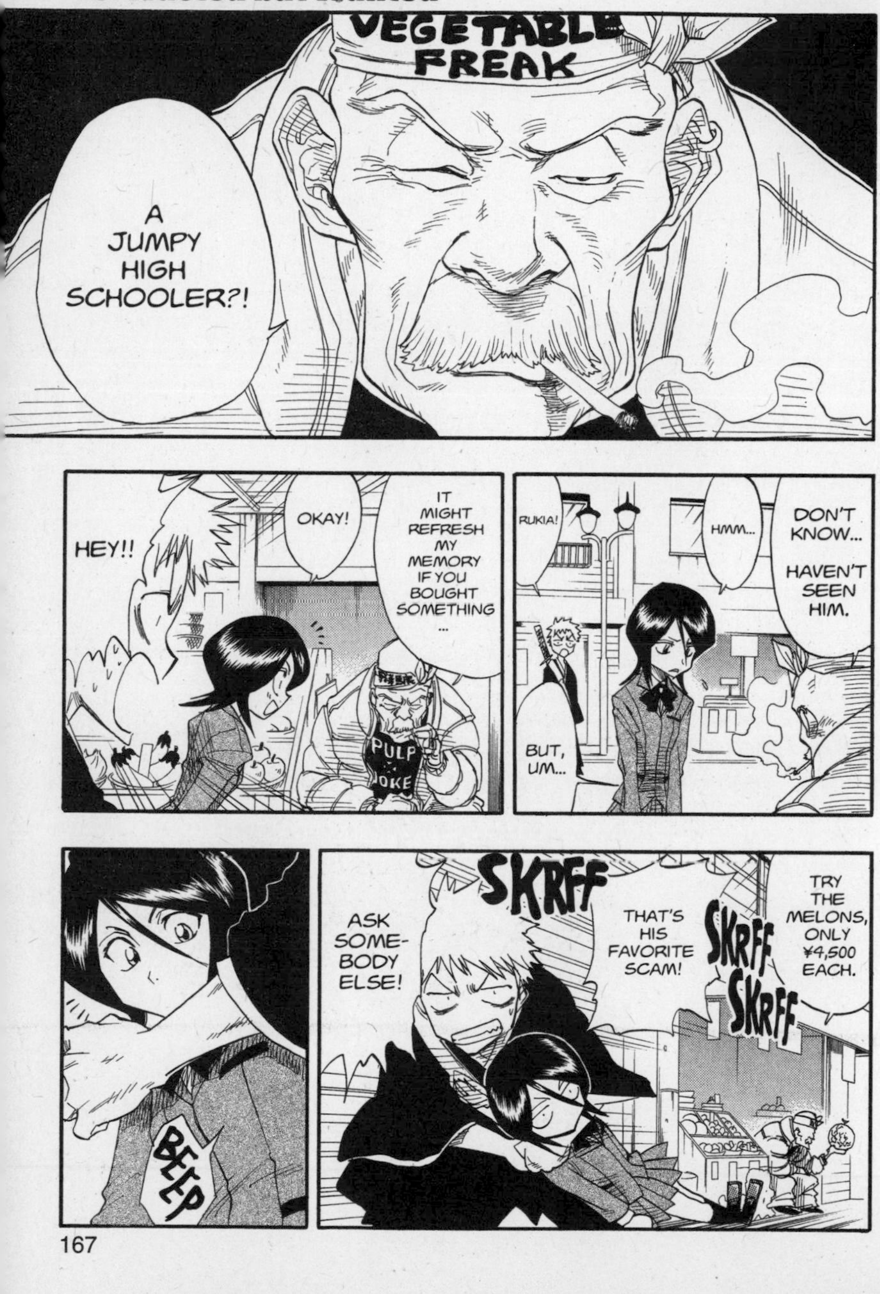

VEGETABLE FREAK
A JUMPY HIGH SCHOOLER?!
DON'T KNOW... HAVEN'T SEEN HIM.
HMM...
RUKIA!
BUT, UM...
IT MIGHT REFRESH MY MEMORY IF YOU BOUGHT SOMETHING...
OKAY!
HEY!!
PULP JOKE
TRY THE MELONS, ONLY ¥4,500 EACH.
SKRFF SKRFF
THAT'S HIS FAVORITE SCAM!
SKRFF
ASK SOME-BODY ELSE!
BEEP

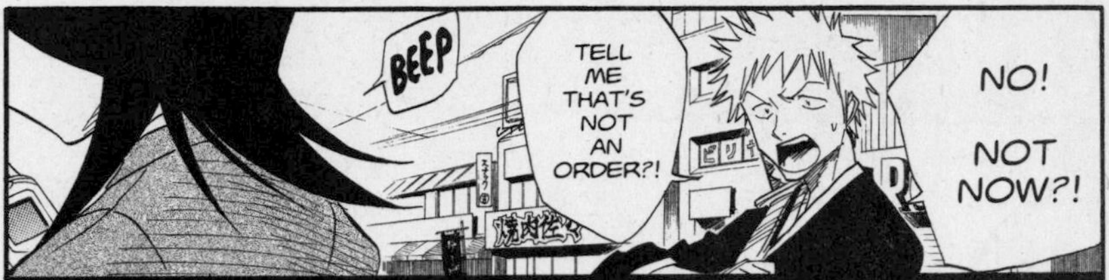
NO!
NOT NOW?!
TELL ME THAT'S NOT AN ORDER?!
BEEP

16. Wasted but Wanted

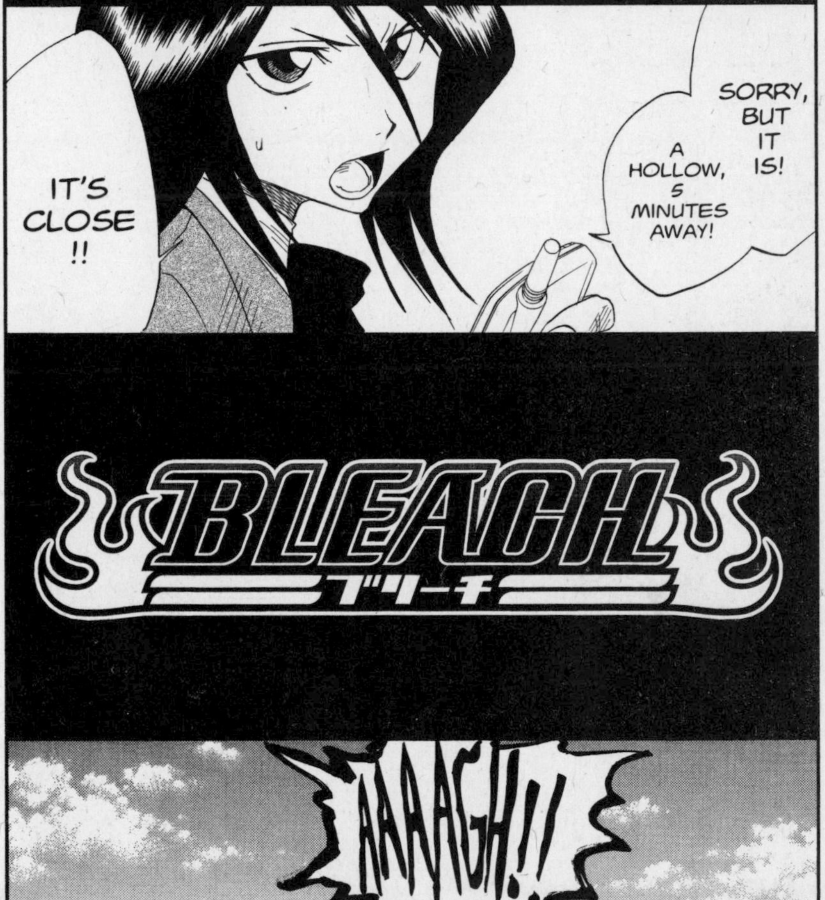
SORRY, BUT IT IS!
A HOLLOW, 5 MINUTES AWAY!
IT'S CLOSE !!
BLEACH
ブリーチ
AAAAGH!!

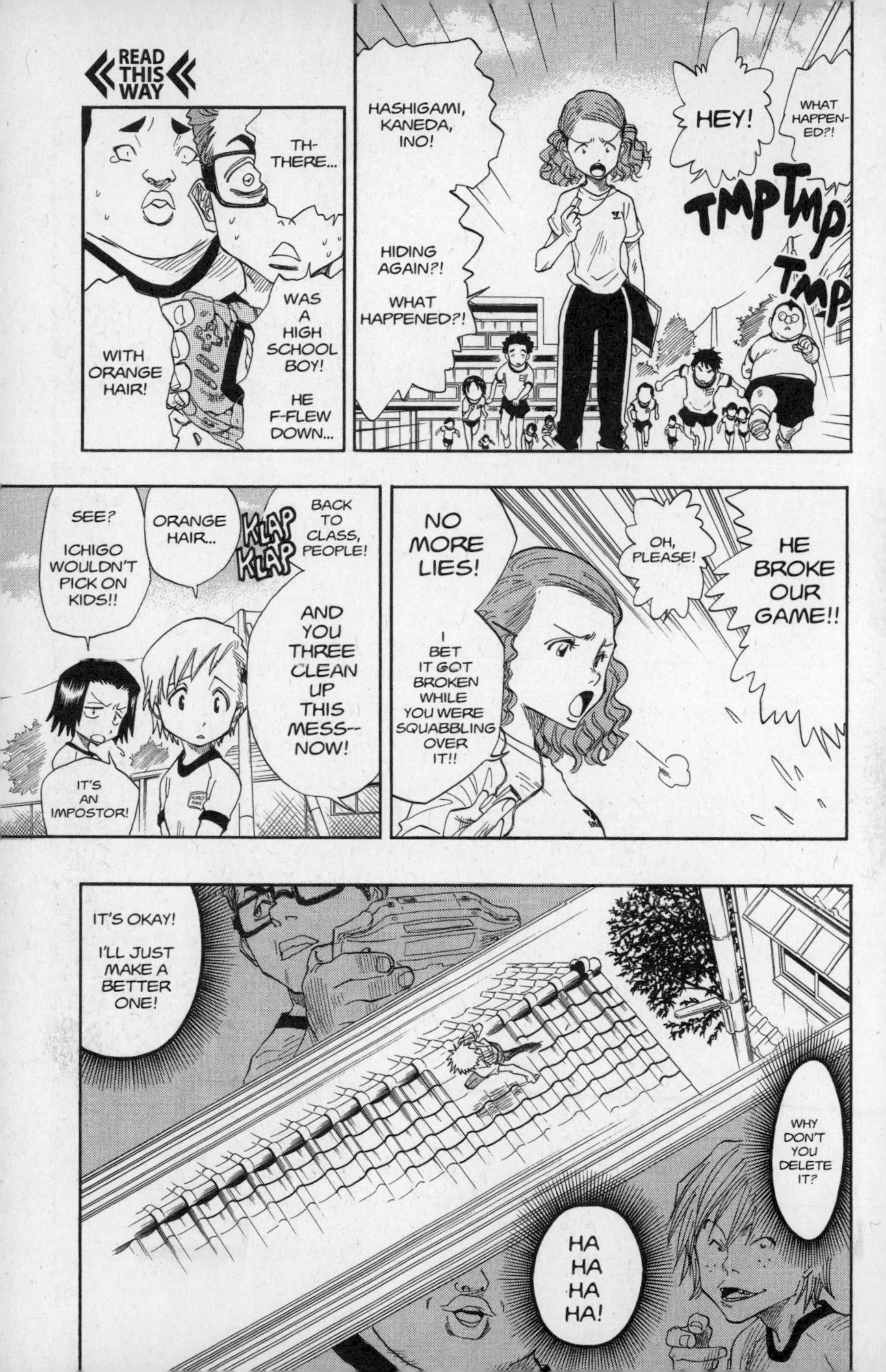
READ THIS WAY
HEY!
WHAT HAPPEN-ED?!
TMP TMP
TMP
HASHIGAMI, KANEDA, INO!
HIDING AGAIN?!
WHAT HAPPENED?!
TH-THERE...
WAS A HIGH SCHOOL BOY!
HE F-FLEW DOWN...
WITH ORANGE HAIR!
HE BROKE OUR GAME!!
OH, PLEASE!
NO MORE LIES!
I BET IT GOT BROKEN WHILE YOU WERE SQUABBLING OVER IT!!
BACK TO CLASS, PEOPLE!
KLAP KLAP
AND YOU THREE CLEAN UP THIS MESS--NOW!
ORANGE HAIR...
SEE?
ICHIGO WOULDN'T PICK ON KIDS!!
IT'S AN IMPOSTOR!
WHY DON'T YOU DELETE IT?
HA HA HA HA!
IT'S OKAY!
I'LL JUST MAKE A BETTER ONE!

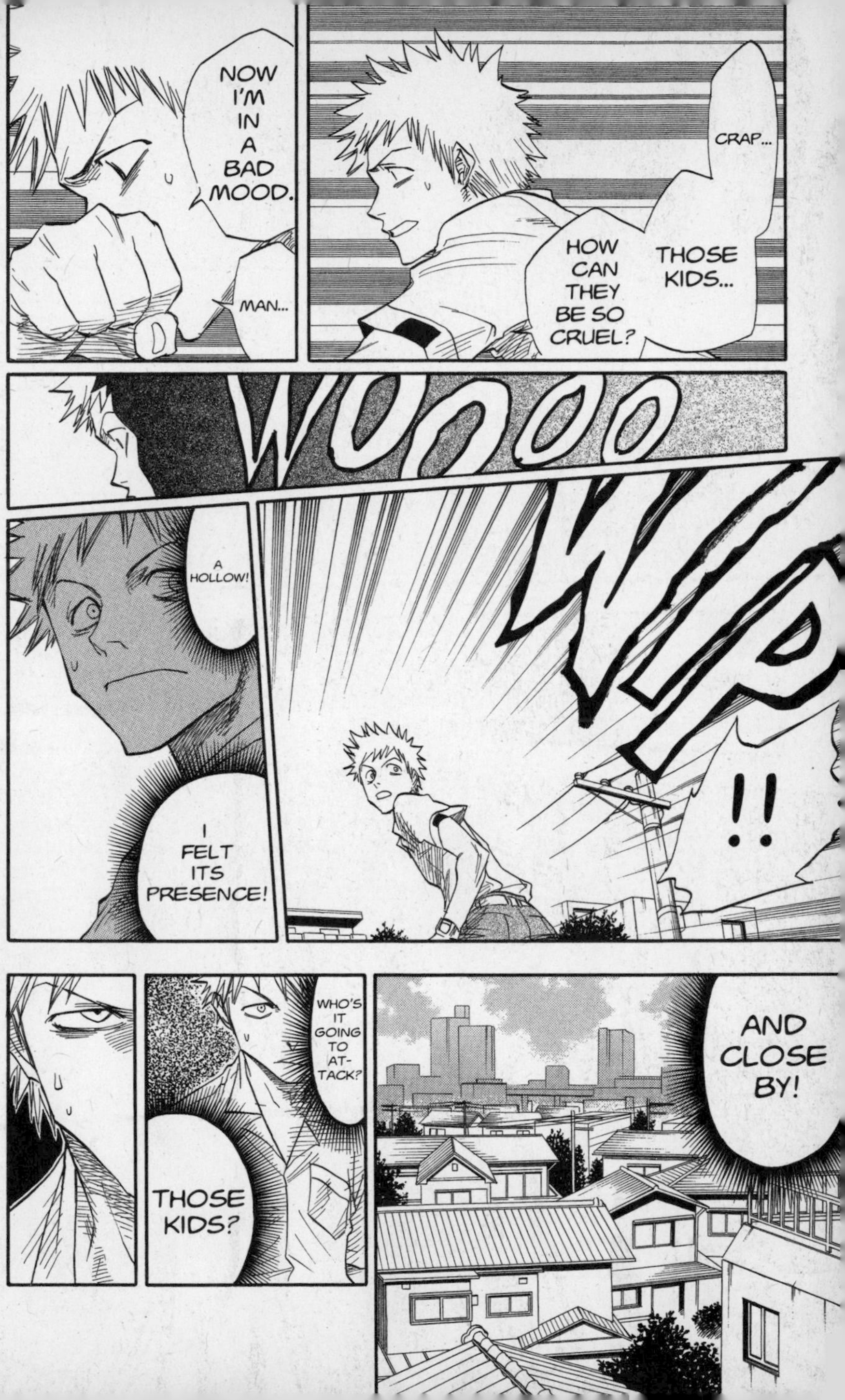
CRAP...
THOSE KIDS...
HOW CAN THEY BE SO CRUEL?
NOW I'M IN A BAD MOOD.
MAN...
WOOOO
WIP
!!
A HOLLOW!
I FELT ITS PRESENCE!
AND CLOSE BY!
WHO'S IT GOING TO AT-TACK?
THOSE KIDS?

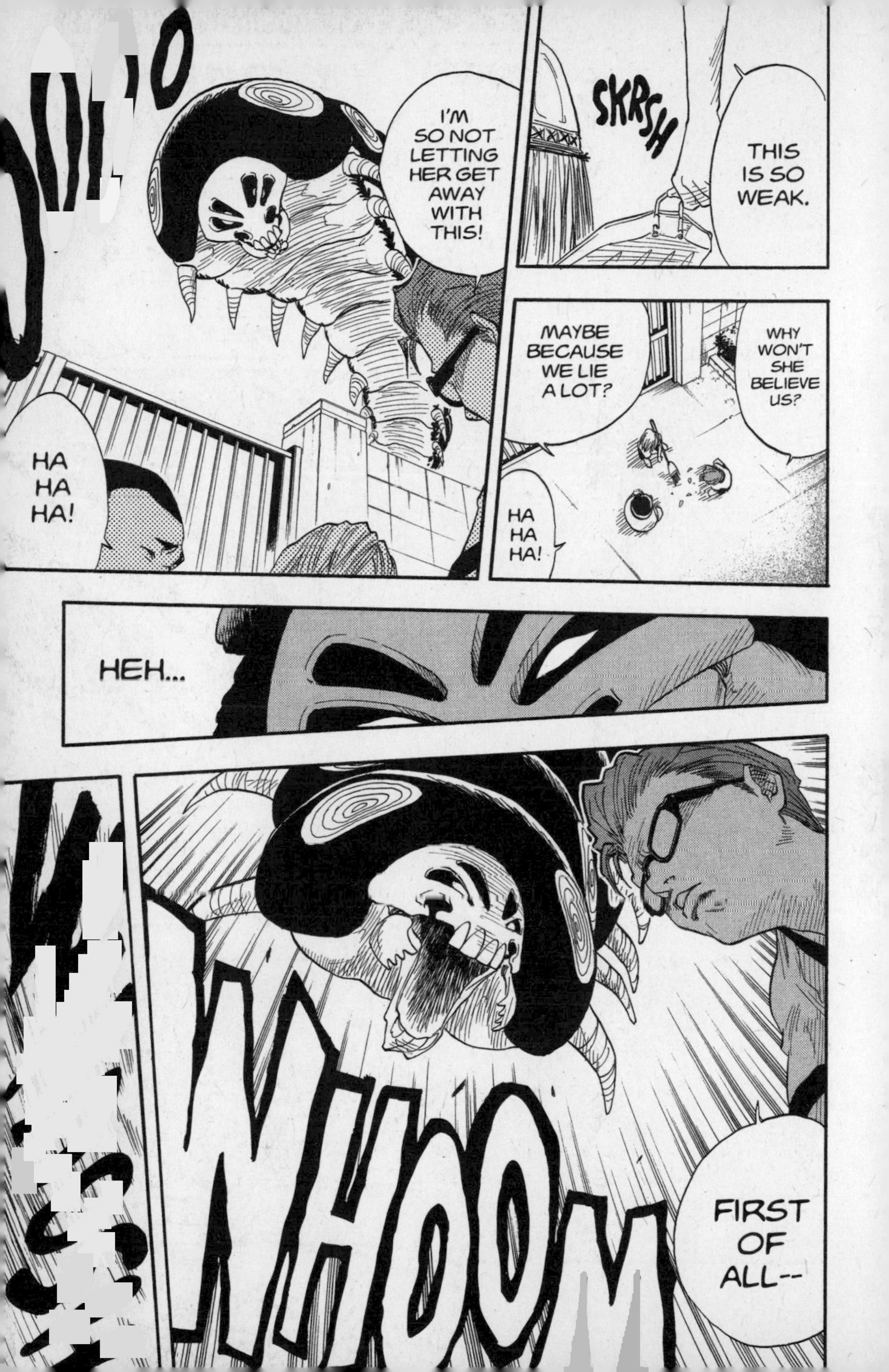
SKRSH
THIS IS SO WEAK.
WHY WON'T SHE BELIEVE US?
MAYBE BECAUSE WE LIE A LOT?
HA HA HA!
I'M SO NOT LETTING HER GET AWAY WITH THIS!
HA HA HA!
HEH...
FIRST OF ALL--
WHOOM

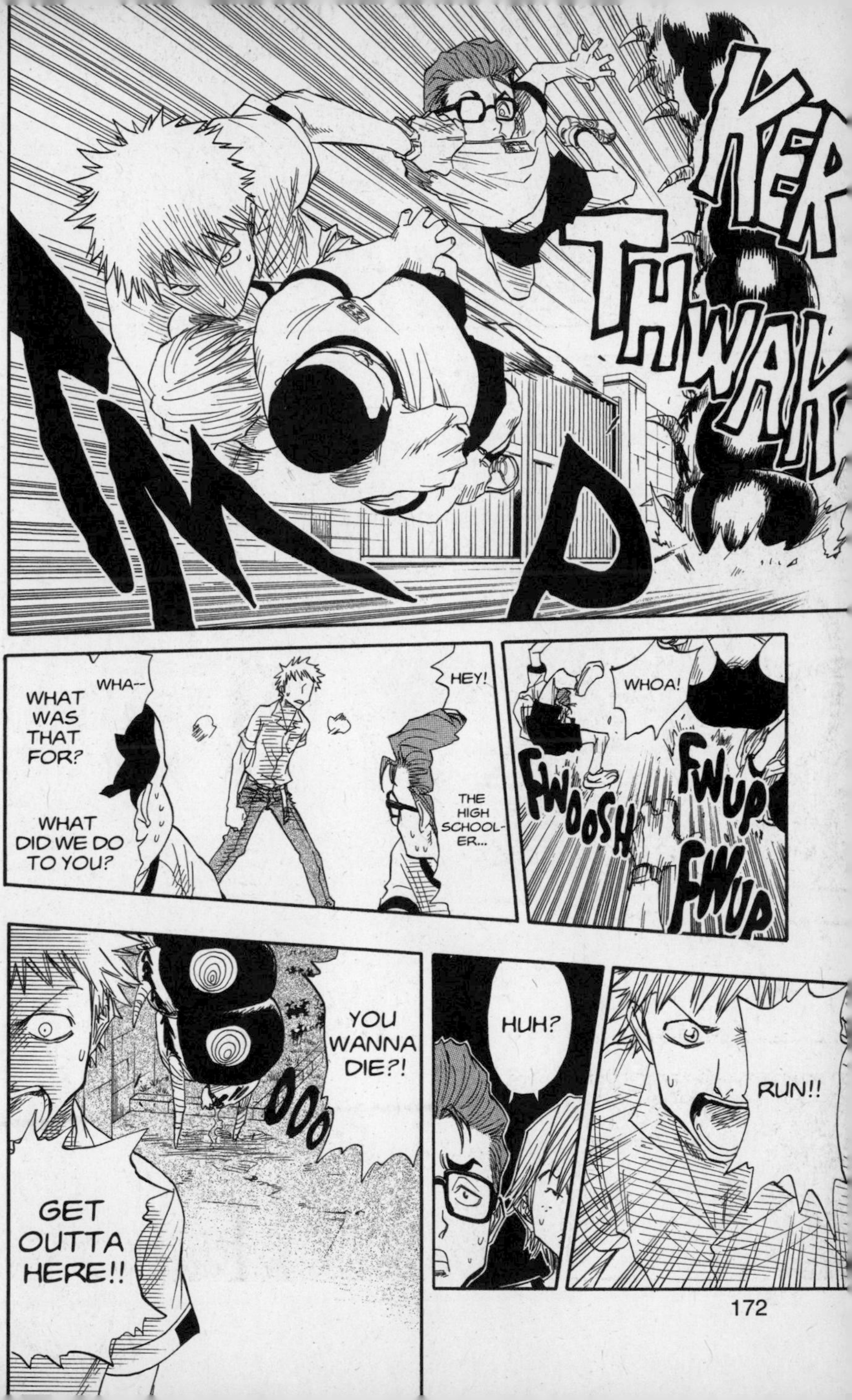
KER-THWAK
THMP
WHOA!
FWUP FWUP
FWOOSH
HEY!
THE HIGH SCHOOL-ER...
WHA--
WHAT WAS THAT FOR?
WHAT DID WE DO TO YOU?
RUN!!
HUH?
YOU WANNA DIE?!
OOO
GET OUTTA HERE!!

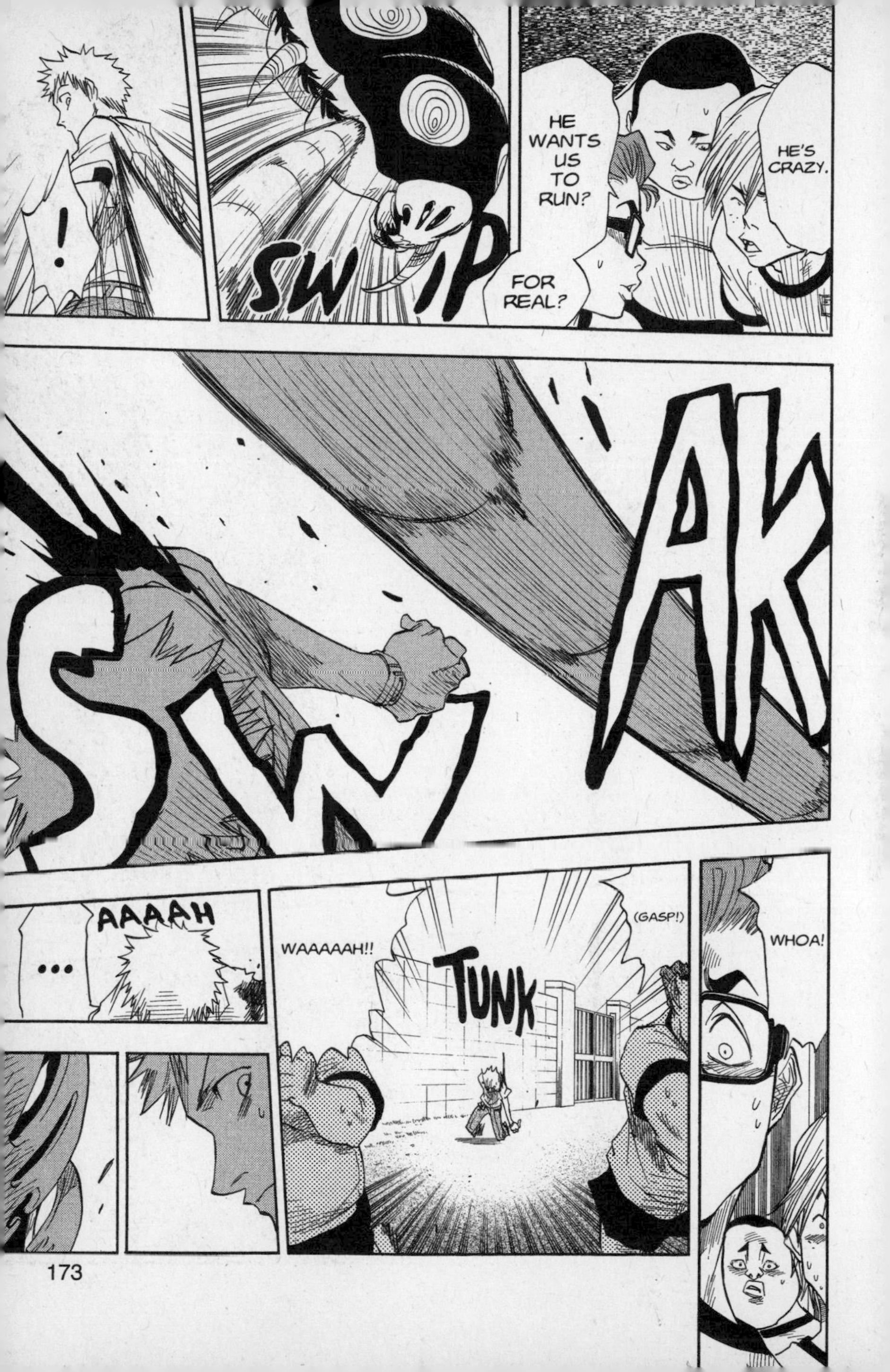
HE'S CRAZY.
HE WANTS US TO RUN?
FOR REAL?
SWIP
!
SWAK
WHOA!
(GASP!)
TUNK
WAAAAAH!!
AAAAH
...

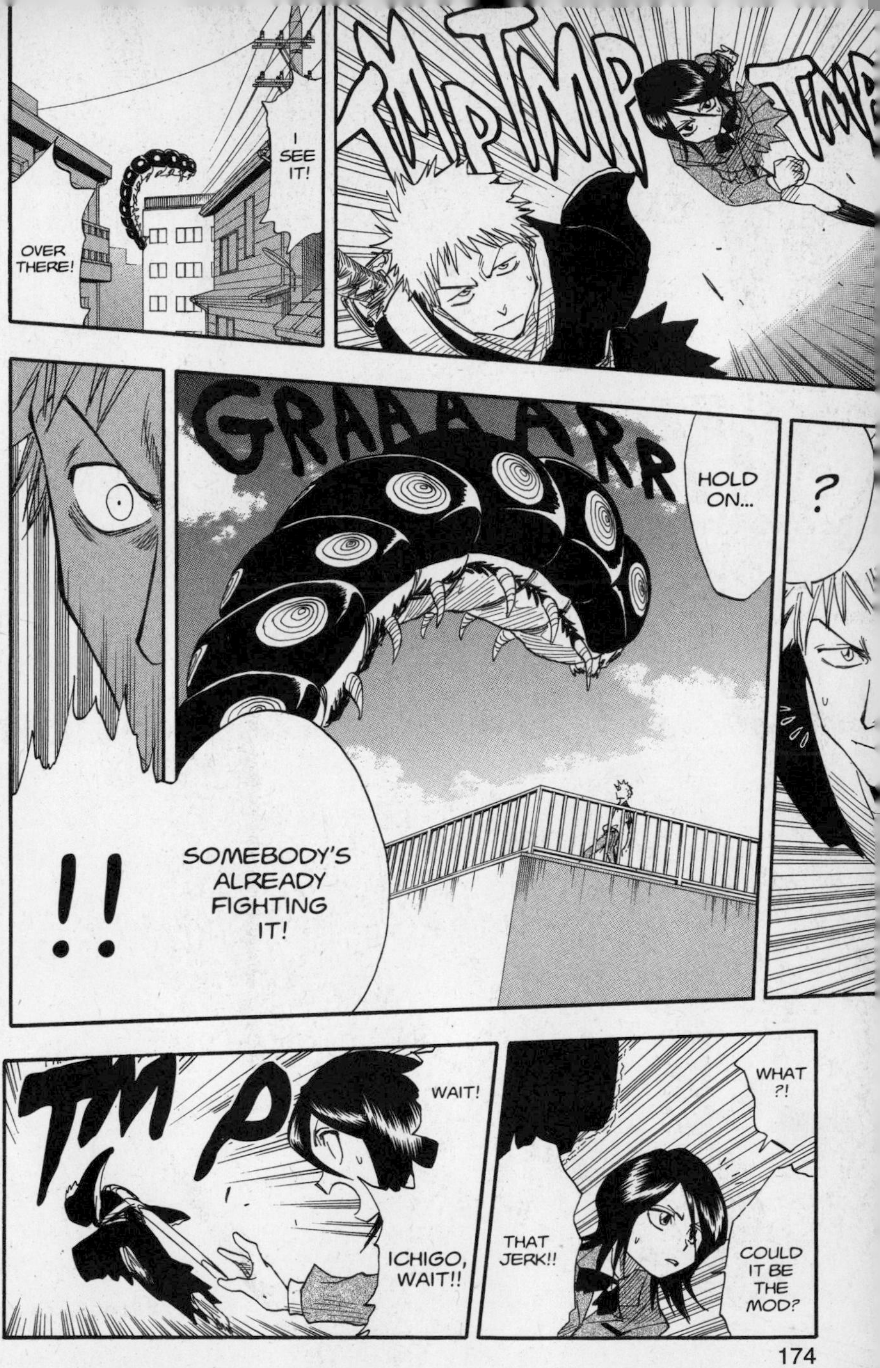
TMP TMP
I SEE IT!
OVER THERE!
?
HOLD ON...
GRAAAARR
SOMEBODY'S ALREADY FIGHTING IT!
!!
WHAT?!
COULD IT BE THE MOD?
THAT JERK!!
WAIT!
ICHIGO, WAIT!!
TMP

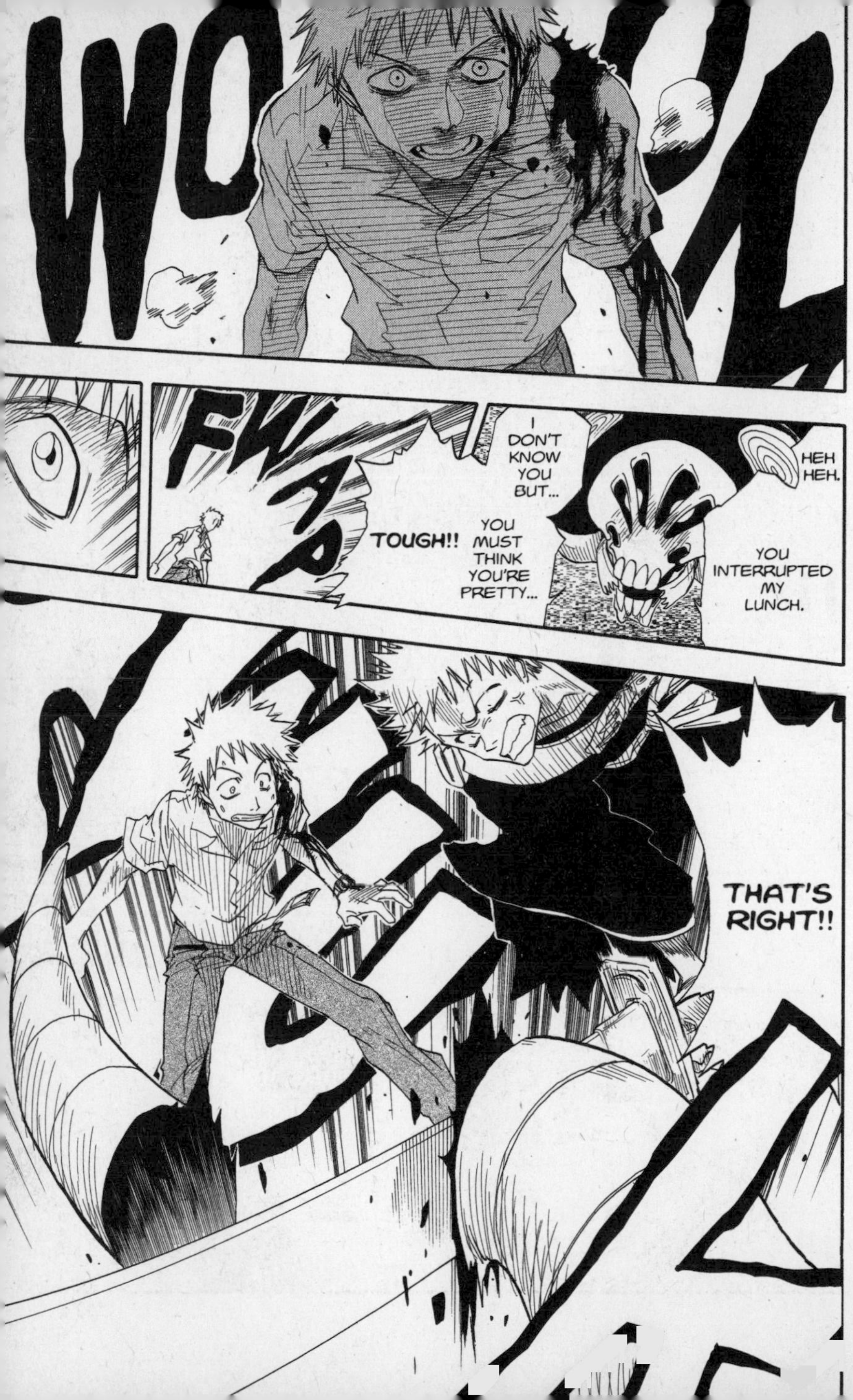
HEH HEH.
YOU INTERRUPTED MY LUNCH.
I DON'T KNOW YOU BUT...
YOU MUST THINK YOU'RE PRETTY...
TOUGH!!
FWAP
THAT'S RIGHT!!

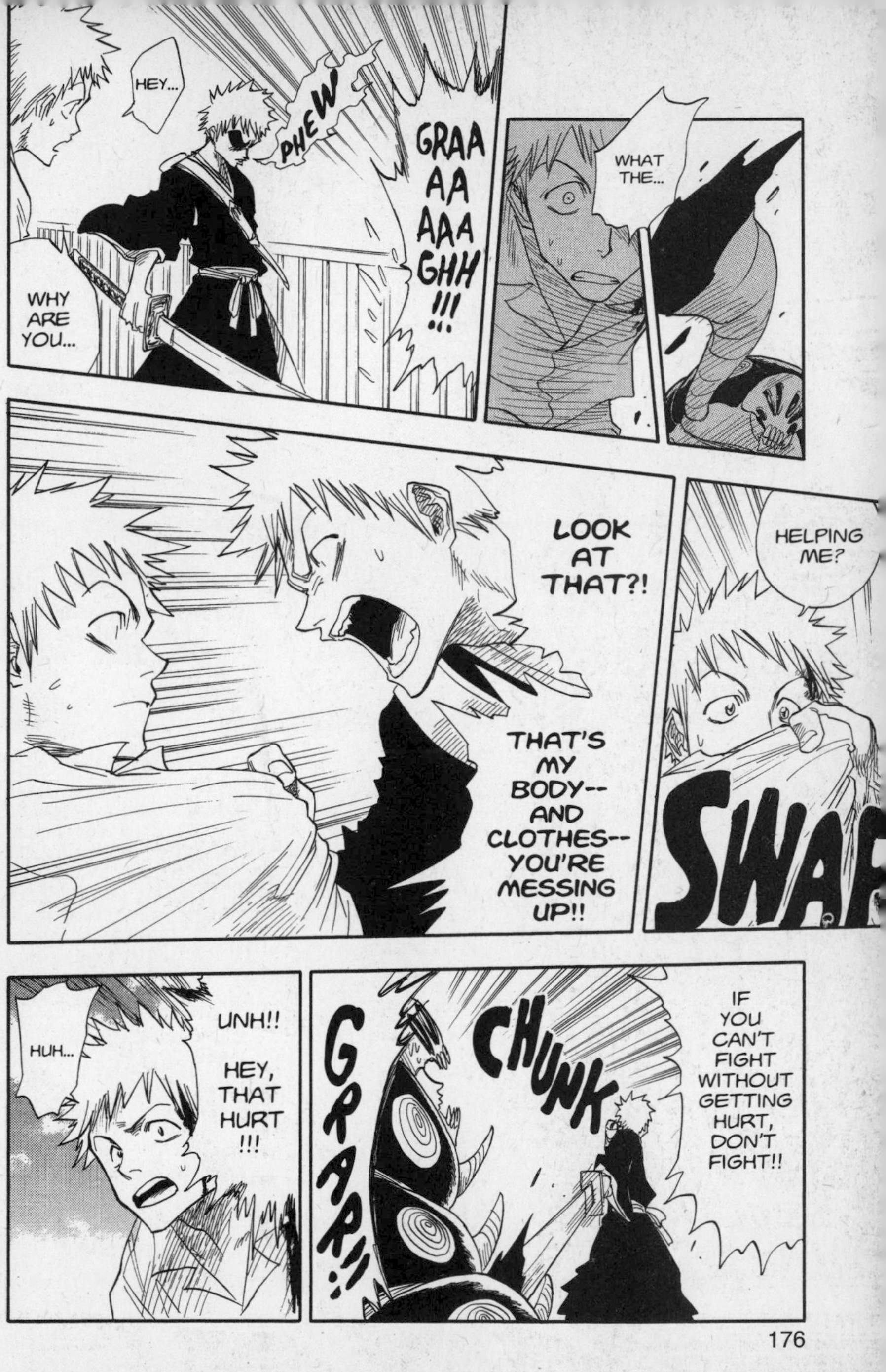
WHAT THE...
GRAAAAAAAGHH!!!
PHEW
HEY...
WHY ARE YOU...
HELPING ME?
SWA
LOOK AT THAT?!
THAT'S MY BODY-- AND CLOTHES-- YOU'RE MESSING UP!!
IF YOU CAN'T FIGHT WITHOUT GETTING HURT, DON'T FIGHT!!
CHUNK
GRAR!!
UNH!!
HEY, THAT HURT!!!
HUH...

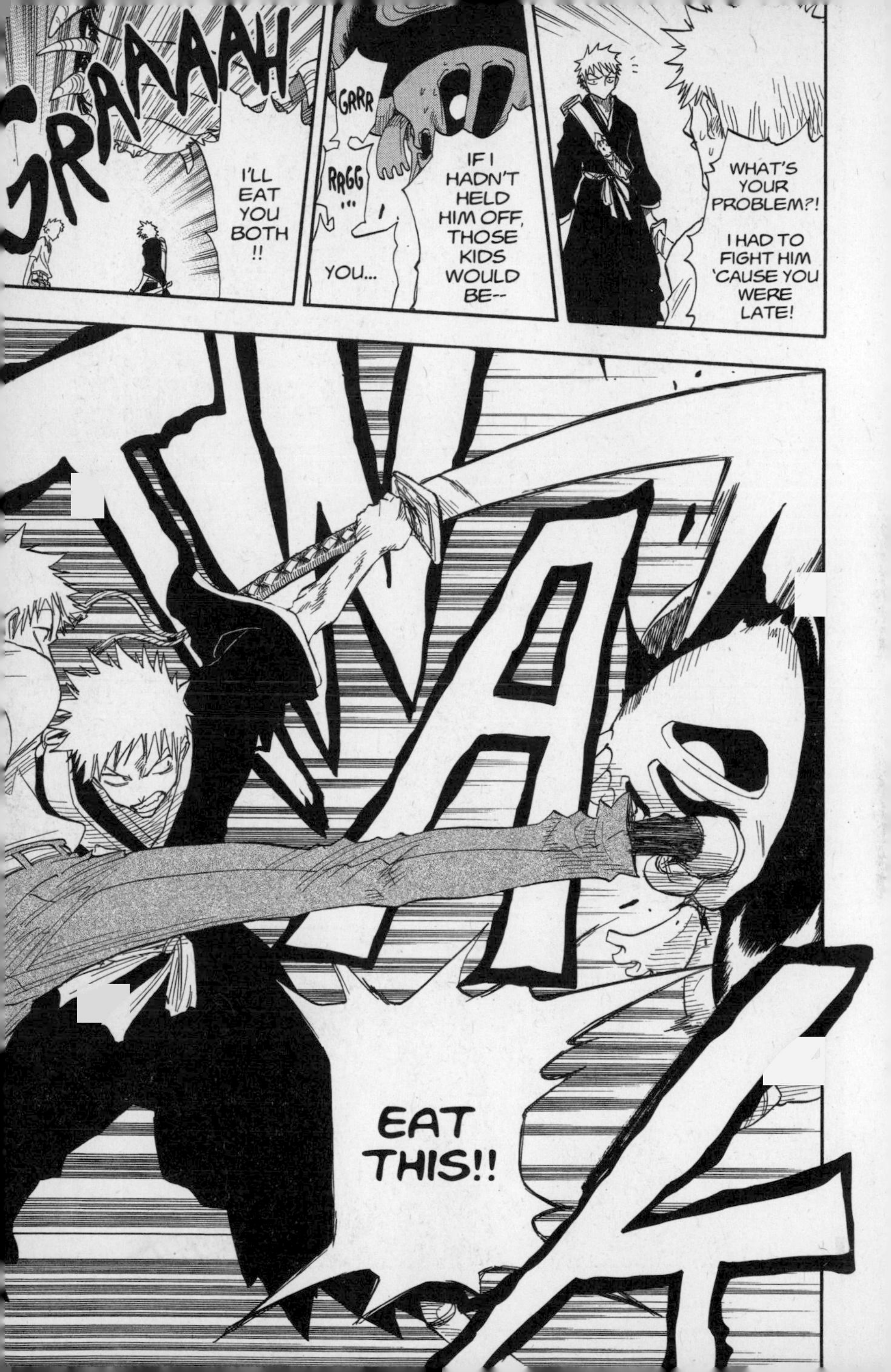

WHAT'S YOUR PROBLEM?!
I HAD TO FIGHT HIM 'CAUSE YOU WERE LATE!
GRRR
IF I HADN'T HELD HIM OFF, THOSE KIDS WOULD BE--
RRGG...
YOU...
GRAAAAH
I'LL EAT YOU BOTH!!
EAT THIS!!

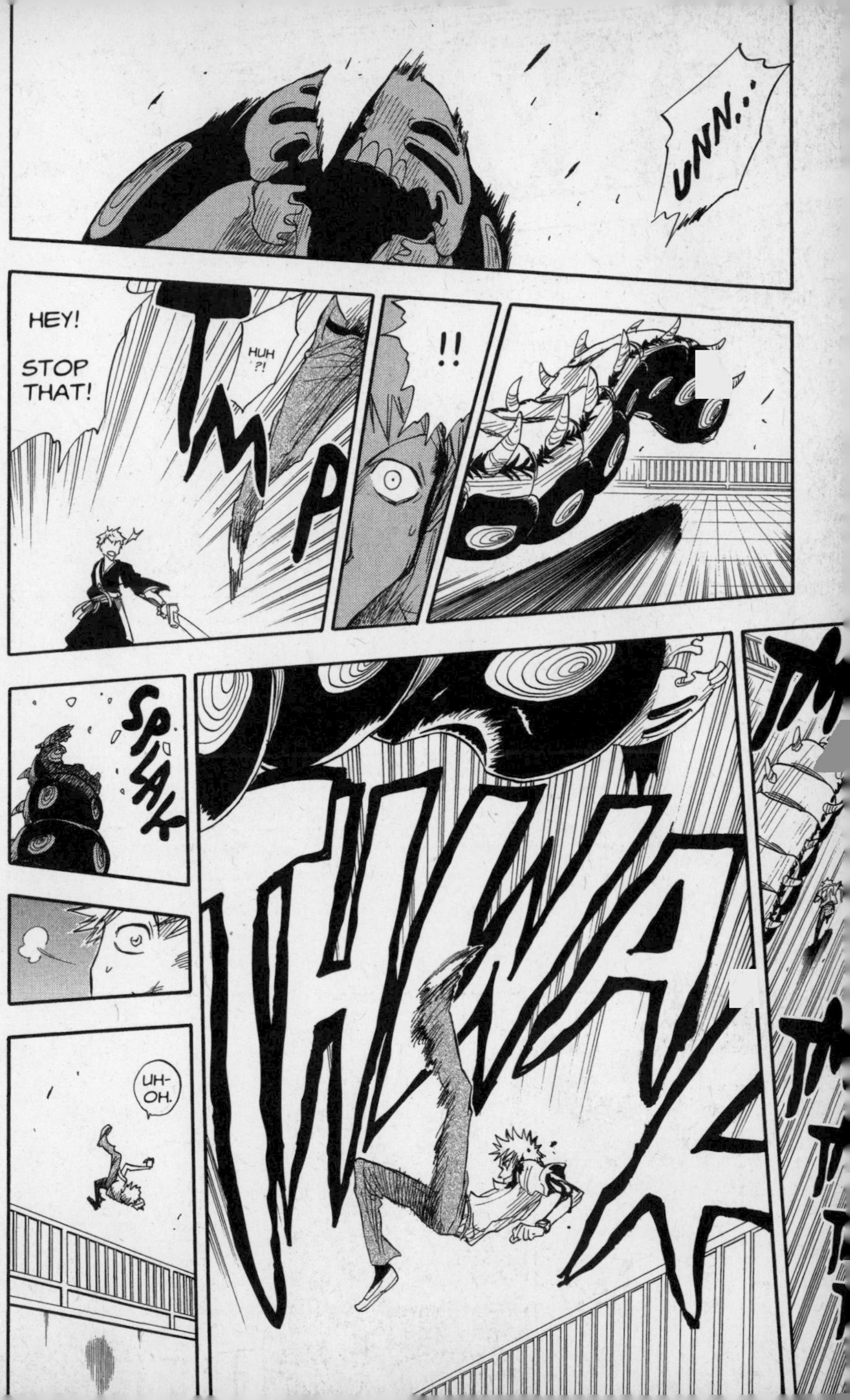
UNN...
!!
HUH ?!
HEY!
STOP THAT!
TMP
SPLAK
UH-OH.

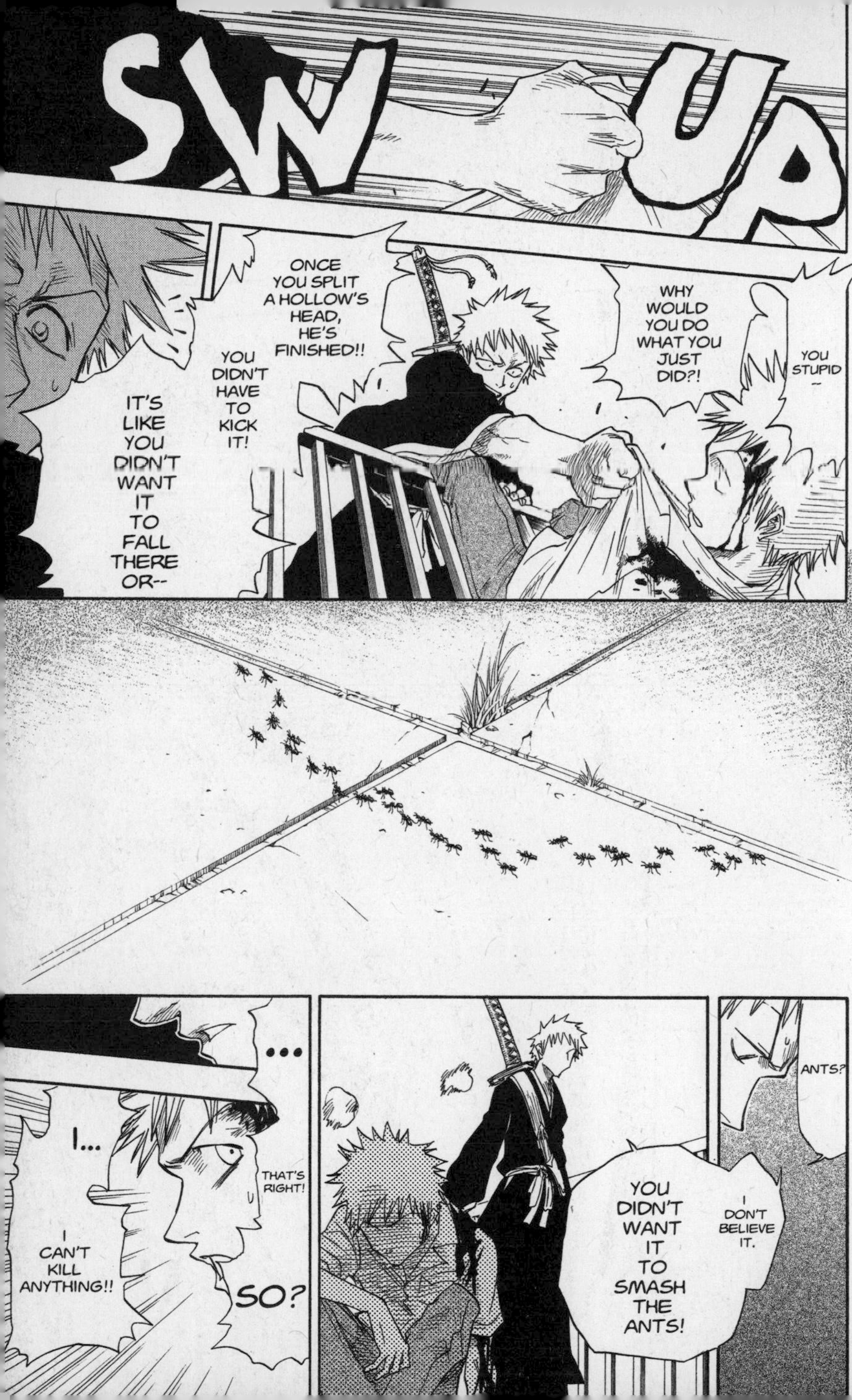
SW UP
YOU STUPID --
WHY WOULD YOU DO WHAT YOU JUST DID?!
ONCE YOU SPLIT A HOLLOW'S HEAD, HE'S FINISHED!!
YOU DIDN'T HAVE TO KICK IT!
IT'S LIKE YOU DIDN'T WANT IT TO FALL THERE OR--
ANTS?
I DON'T BELIEVE IT.
YOU DIDN'T WANT IT TO SMASH THE ANTS!
...
I...
THAT'S RIGHT!
I CAN'T KILL ANYTHING!!
SO?

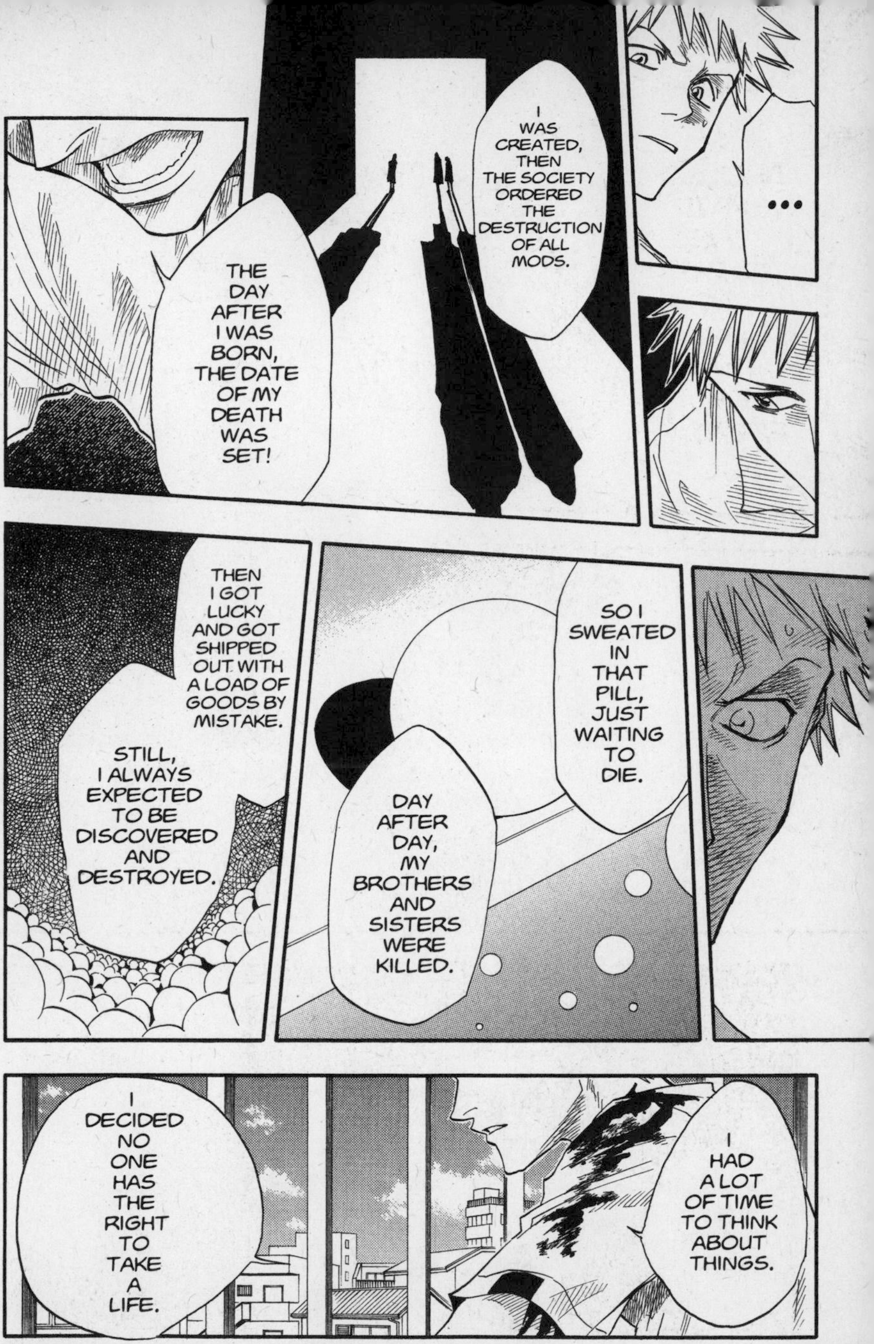
...
I WAS CREATED, THEN THE SOCIETY ORDERED THE DESTRUCTION OF ALL MODS.
THE DAY AFTER I WAS BORN, THE DATE OF MY DEATH WAS SET!
SO I SWEATED IN THAT PILL, JUST WAITING TO DIE.
DAY AFTER DAY, MY BROTHERS AND SISTERS WERE KILLED.
THEN I GOT LUCKY AND GOT SHIPPED OUT WITH A LOAD OF GOODS BY MISTAKE.
STILL, I ALWAYS EXPECTED TO BE DISCOVERED AND DESTROYED.
I HAD A LOT OF TIME TO THINK ABOUT THINGS.
I DECIDED NO ONE HAS THE RIGHT TO TAKE A LIFE.

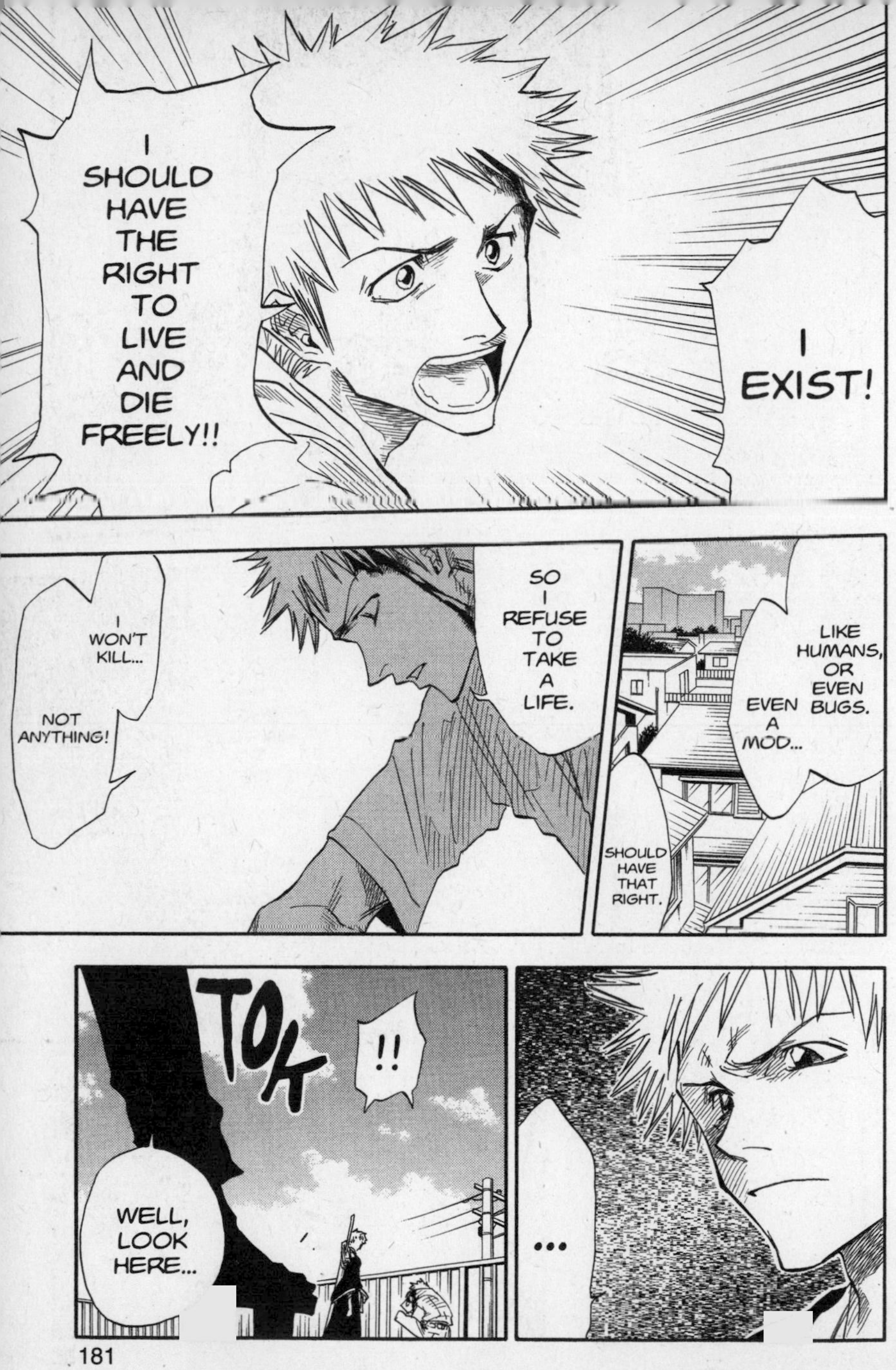
I EXIST!
I SHOULD HAVE THE RIGHT TO LIVE AND DIE FREELY!!
LIKE HUMANS, OR EVEN BUGS.
EVEN A MOD...
SHOULD HAVE THAT RIGHT.
SO I REFUSE TO TAKE A LIFE.
I WON'T KILL...
NOT ANYTHING!
...
TOK
!!
WELL, LOOK HERE...

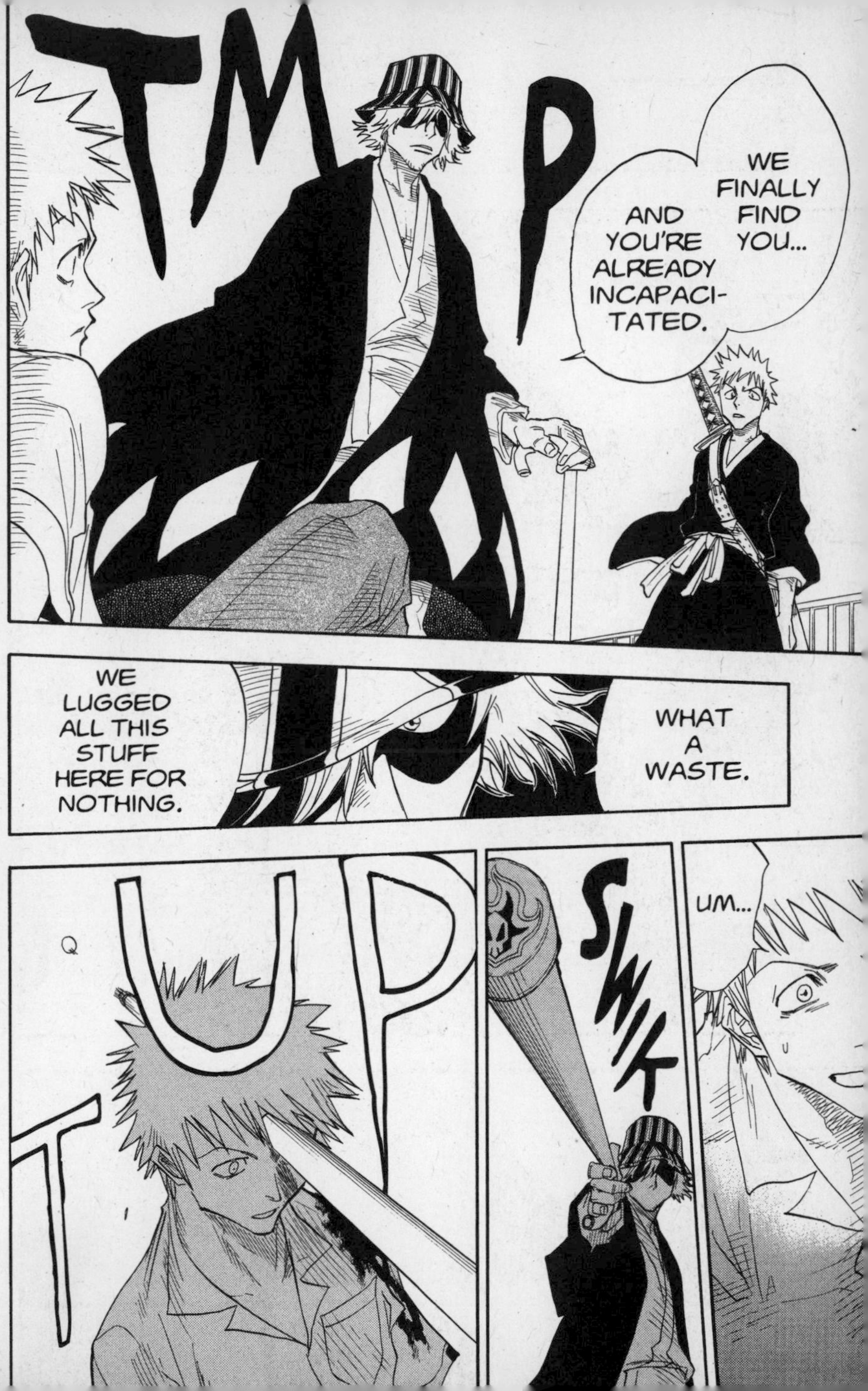
TMP
WE FINALLY FIND YOU... AND YOU'RE ALREADY INCAPACITATED.
WHAT A WASTE.
WE LUGGED ALL THIS STUFF HERE FOR NOTHING.
UM...
SWIK
TUP

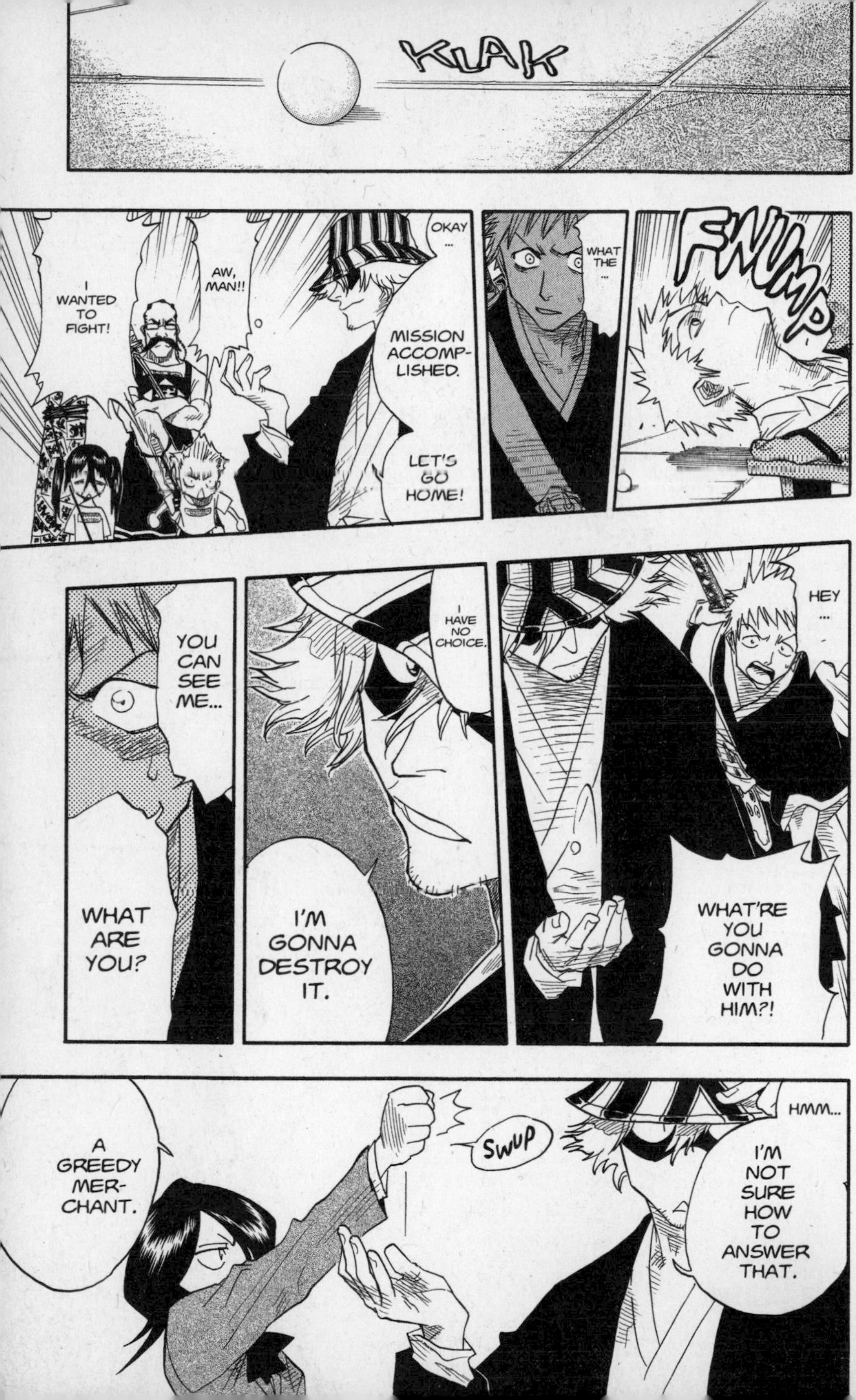
KLAK
FNUMP
WHAT THE ...
OKAY ...
MISSION ACCOMPLISHED.
LET'S GO HOME!
AW, MAN!!
I WANTED TO FIGHT!
HEY ...
WHAT'RE YOU GONNA DO WITH HIM?!
I HAVE NO CHOICE.
I'M GONNA DESTROY IT.
YOU CAN SEE ME...
WHAT ARE YOU?
HMM...
I'M NOT SURE HOW TO ANSWER THAT.
SWUP
A GREEDY MERCHANT.

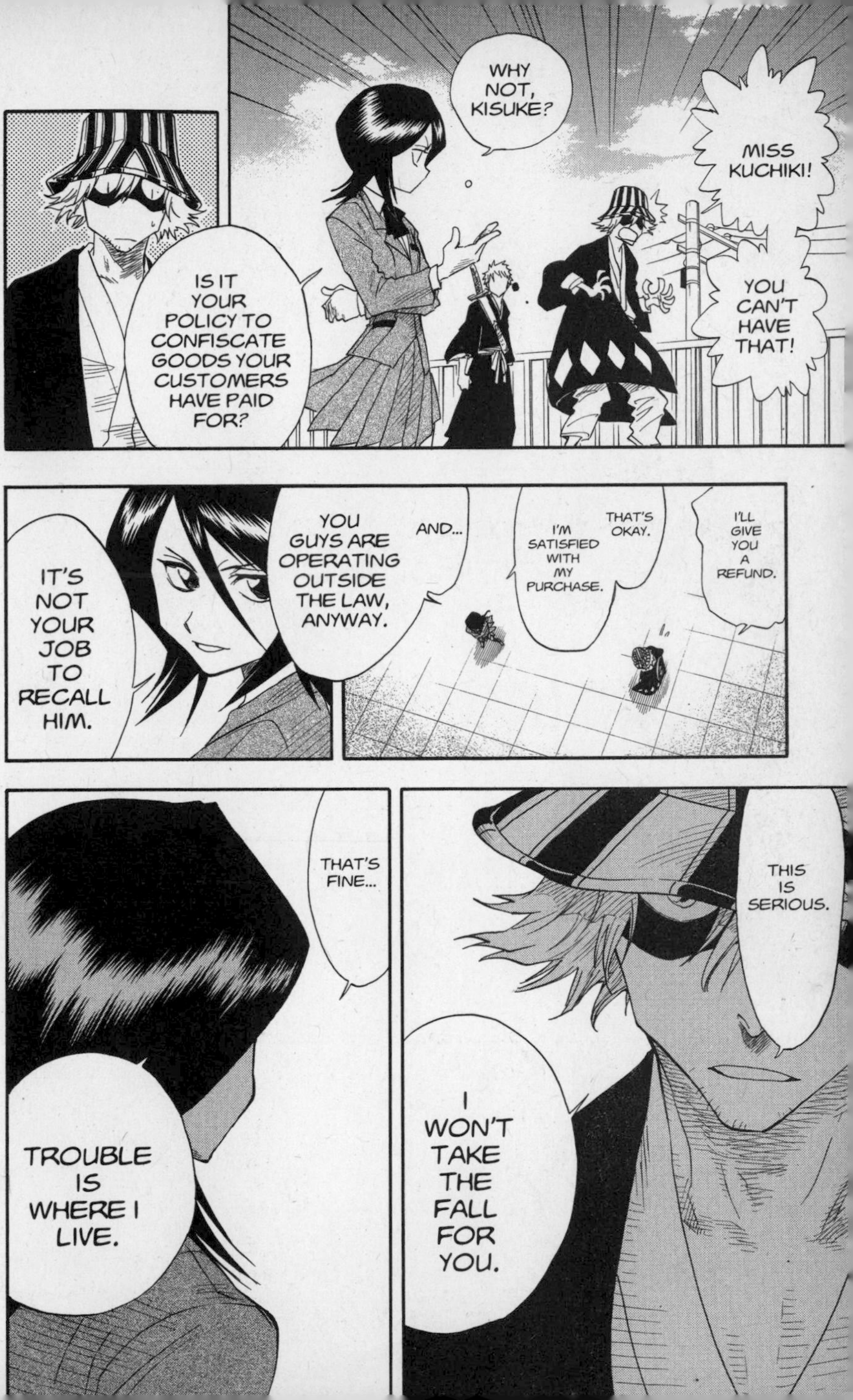
MISS KUCHIKI!
YOU CAN'T HAVE THAT!
WHY NOT, KISUKE?
IS IT YOUR POLICY TO CONFISCATE GOODS YOUR CUSTOMERS HAVE PAID FOR?
I'LL GIVE YOU A REFUND.
THAT'S OKAY.
I'M SATISFIED WITH MY PURCHASE.
AND...
YOU GUYS ARE OPERATING OUTSIDE THE LAW, ANYWAY.
IT'S NOT YOUR JOB TO RECALL HIM.
THIS IS SERIOUS.
I WON'T TAKE THE FALL FOR YOU.
THAT'S FINE...
TROUBLE IS WHERE I LIVE.

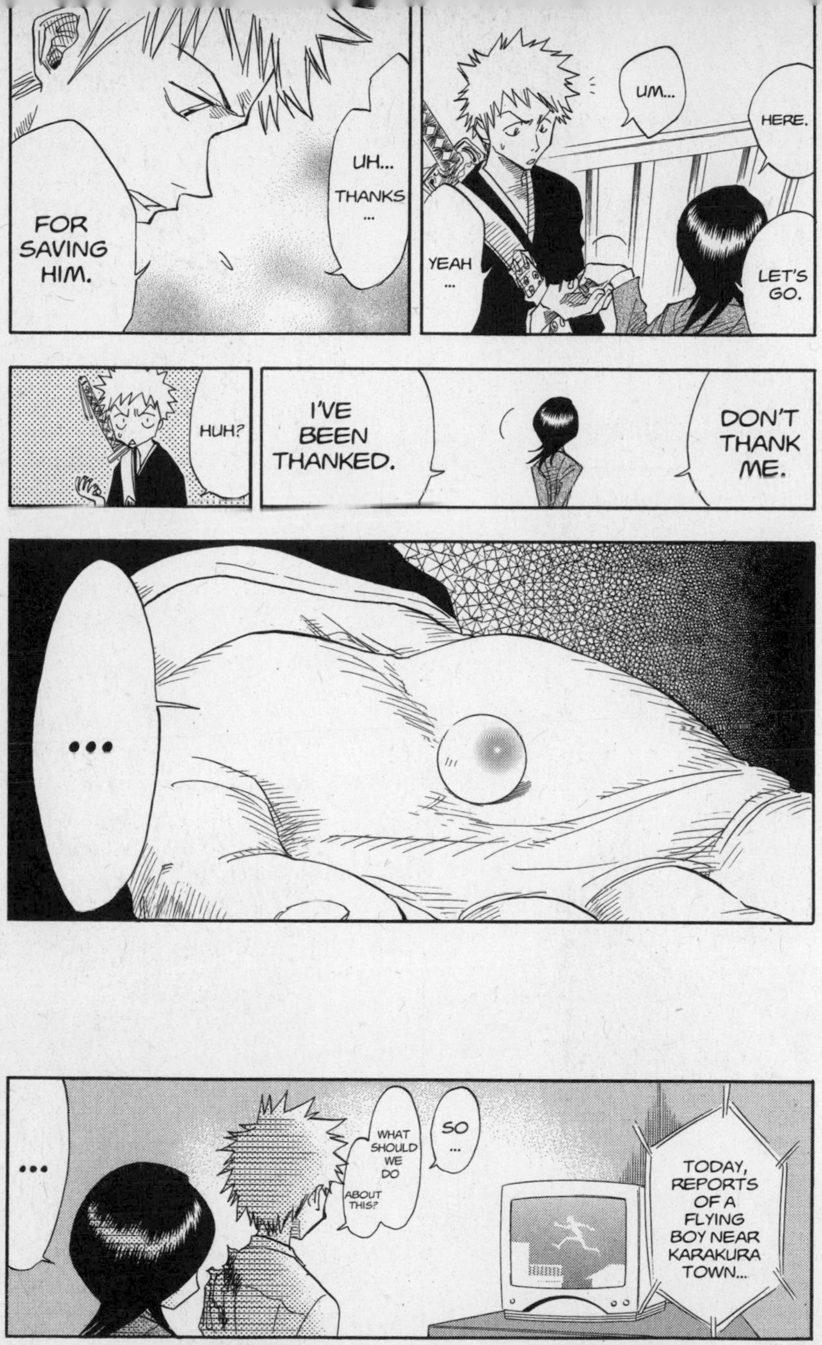
HERE.
UM...
LET'S GO.
YEAH ...
UH... THANKS ...
FOR SAVING HIM.
DON'T THANK ME.
I'VE BEEN THANKED.
HUH?
...
TODAY, REPORTS OF A FLYING BOY NEAR KARAKURA TOWN...
SO ...
WHAT SHOULD WE DO ABOUT THIS?
...

TO BE CONTINUED IN VOL. 3!

THINGS ARE GONNA GET DICEY.

EXTRA.

SOUL CANDY PACKAGE CATALOGUE

OTHER CHARACTERS

ALFRED

DIANA

CLAUDIA

GINOSUKE

GRINGO

BLUES

KANESHIRO

SCHTEINER

MOST POPULAR
"CHAPPY"

2ND MOST
POPULAR
"YUKI"

3RD MOST
POPULAR
"PUPPLES"

OVERALL ATTENDANCE	**5**	**ORIHIME**	イノウエ・オリヒメ
FEMALE STUDENT	**2**	**INOUE**	

157 CM
45 KG
BLOOD TYPE: BO
D.O.B. SEPTEMBER 3

∘ LIKES ASIAN AND FLOWER PRINTS

∘ LIKES COMEDY

∘ DAYDREAMS A LOT

∘ MOUTH OPEN WHEN DAYDREAMING

∘ LIKES CHEESE AND BUTTER

∘ PUTS BUTTER ON BAKED SWEET POTATOES

∘ IS A STUDENT HEALTH ADVISOR

∘ LOST BROTHER 3 YEARS AGO.
STATUS OF PARENTS UNKNOWN.
SUPPORTED BY RELATIVES

THEME SONG
ELSA
"T'EN VA PAS"
RECORDED IN
"L'ESSENTIAL ELSA"
1986-1993

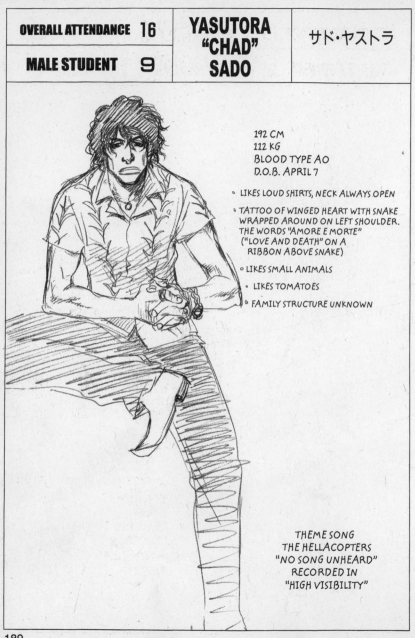

| OVERALL ATTENDANCE 16 | YASUTORA "CHAD" SADO | サド・ヤストラ |
| MALE STUDENT 9 | | |

192 CM
112 KG
BLOOD TYPE AO
D.O.B. APRIL 7

- LIKES LOUD SHIRTS, NECK ALWAYS OPEN

- TATTOO OF WINGED HEART WITH SNAKE
  WRAPPED AROUND ON LEFT SHOULDER.
  THE WORDS "AMORE E MORTE"
  ("LOVE AND DEATH" ON A
  RIBBON ABOVE SNAKE)

- LIKES SMALL ANIMALS

- LIKES TOMATOES

- FAMILY STRUCTURE UNKNOWN

THEME SONG
THE HELLACOPTERS
"NO SONG UNHEARD"
RECORDED IN
"HIGH VISIBILITY"

Next Volume Preview

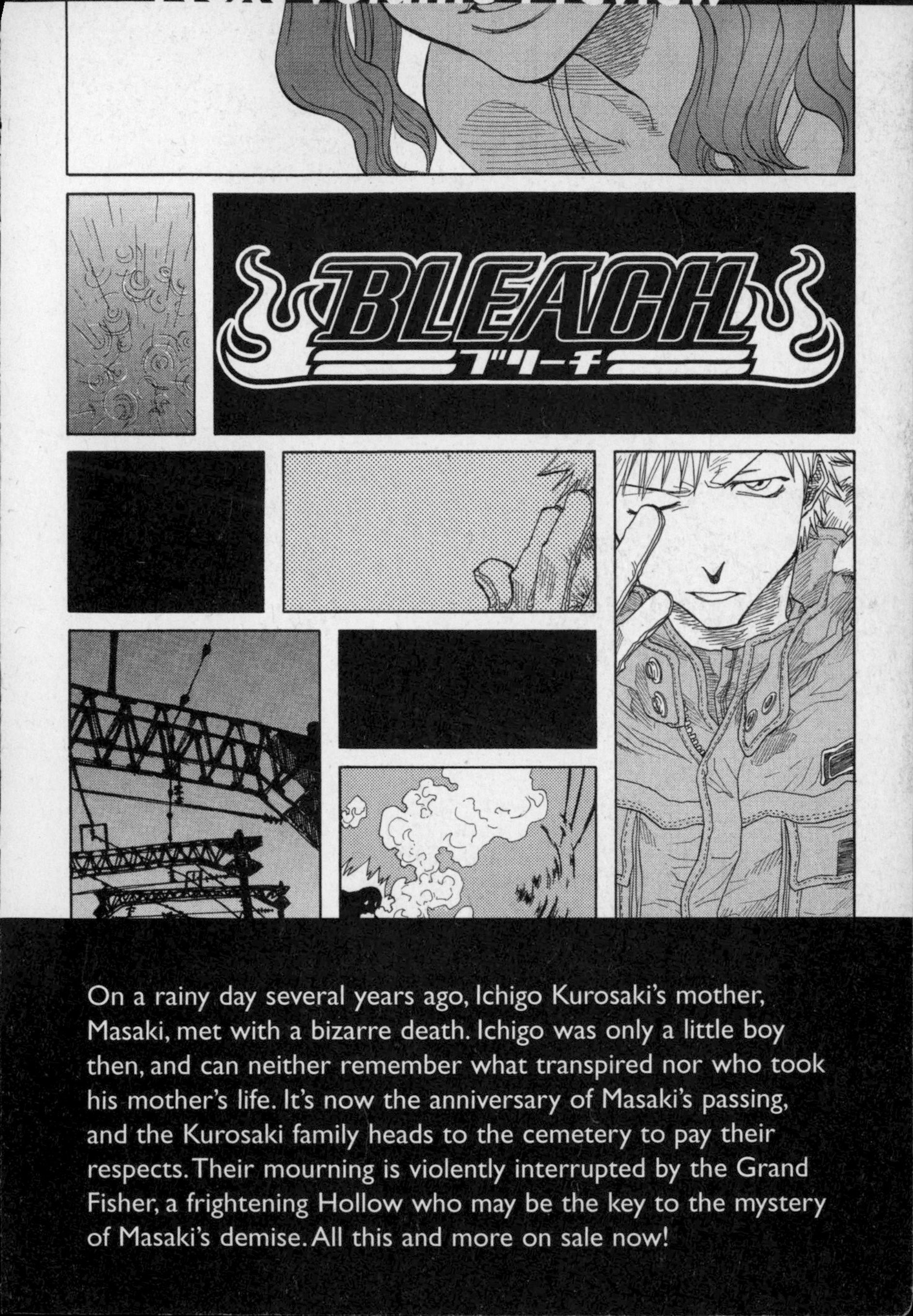
BLEACH
ブリーチ

On a rainy day several years ago, Ichigo Kurosaki's mother, Masaki, met with a bizarre death. Ichigo was only a little boy then, and can neither remember what transpired nor who took his mother's life. It's now the anniversary of Masaki's passing, and the Kurosaki family heads to the cemetery to pay their respects. Their mourning is violently interrupted by the Grand Fisher, a frightening Hollow who may be the key to the mystery of Masaki's demise. All this and more on sale now!

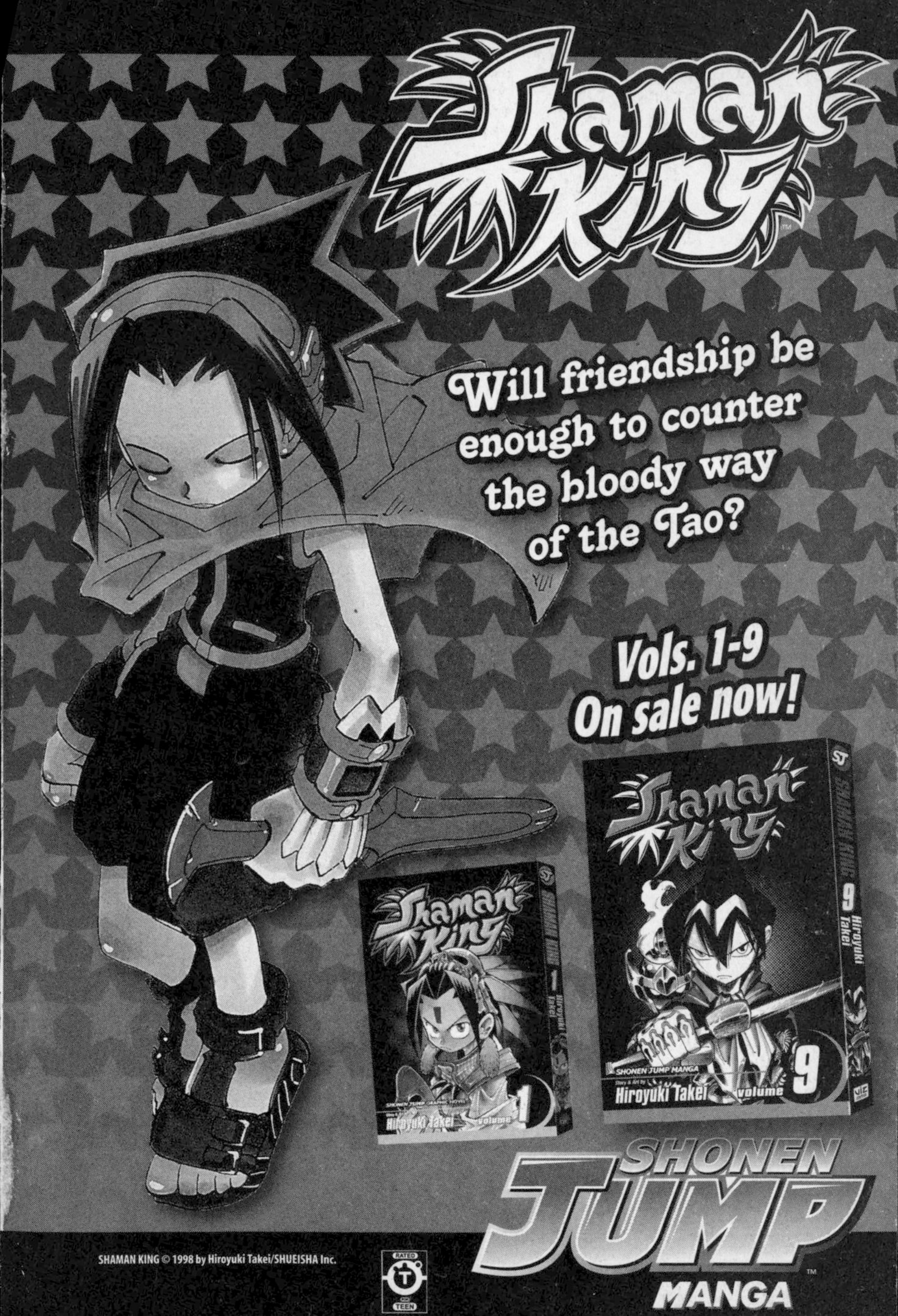
Shaman King
Will friendship be enough to counter the bloody way of the Tao?
Vols. 1-9
On sale now!
Shaman King
Hiroyuki Takei volume 1
Shaman King
9 Hiroyuki Takei
SHONEN JUMP MANGA
Story & Art by
Hiroyuki Takei volume 9
SHONEN JUMP MANGA
SHAMAN KING © 1998 by Hiroyuki Takei/SHUEISHA Inc.
RATED T FOR TEEN

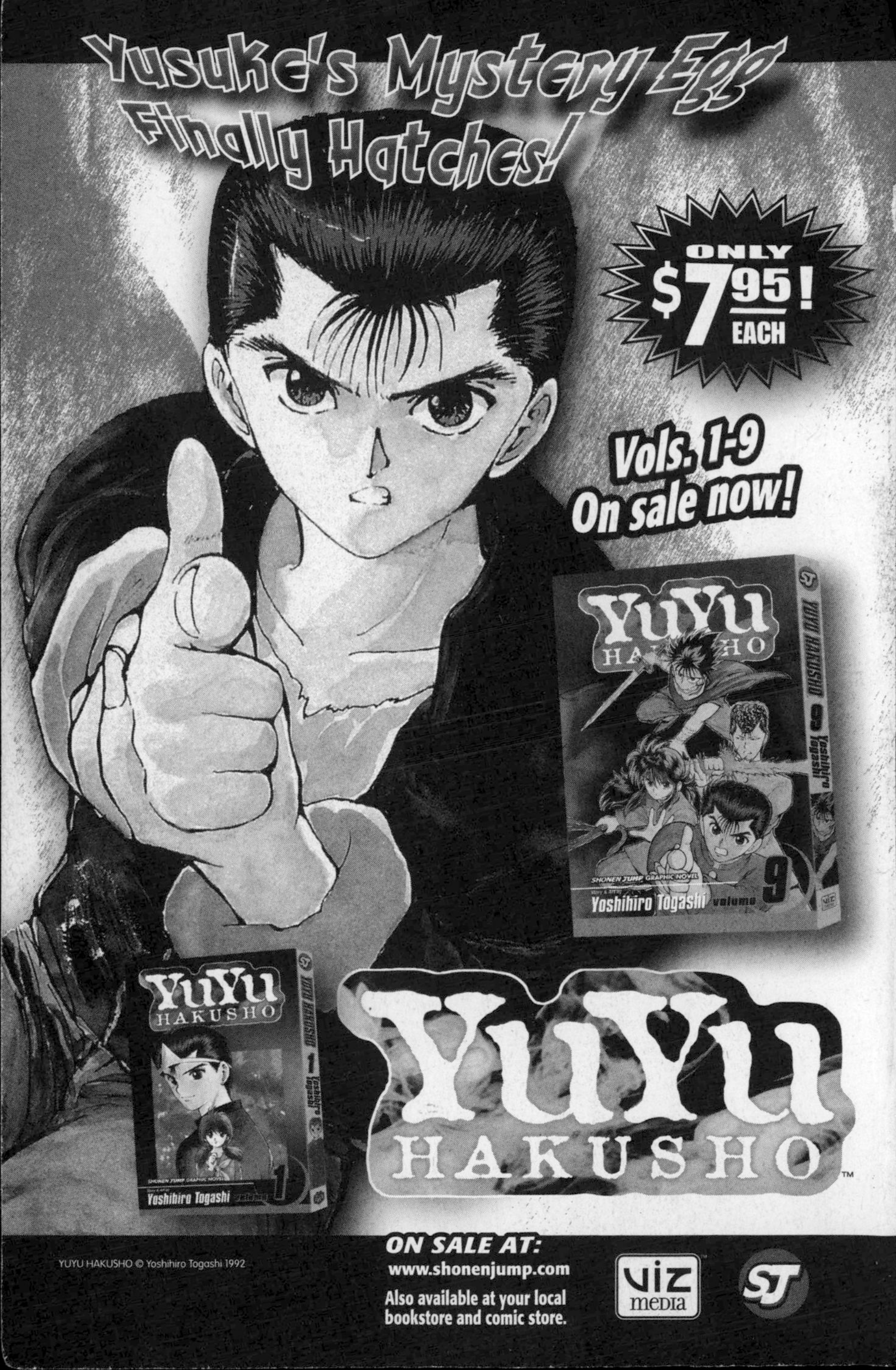
Yusuke's Mystery Egg Finally Hatches!
ONLY $7.95 EACH!
Vols. 1-9 On sale now!
YuYu HAKUSHO
SHONEN JUMP GRAPHIC NOVEL
Yoshihiro Togashi volume 9
YuYu HAKUSHO
Yoshihiro Togashi volume 1
YuYu HAKUSHO™
ON SALE AT:
www.shonenjump.com
Also available at your local bookstore and comic store.
YUYU HAKUSHO © Yoshihiro Togashi 1992
viz media
SJ

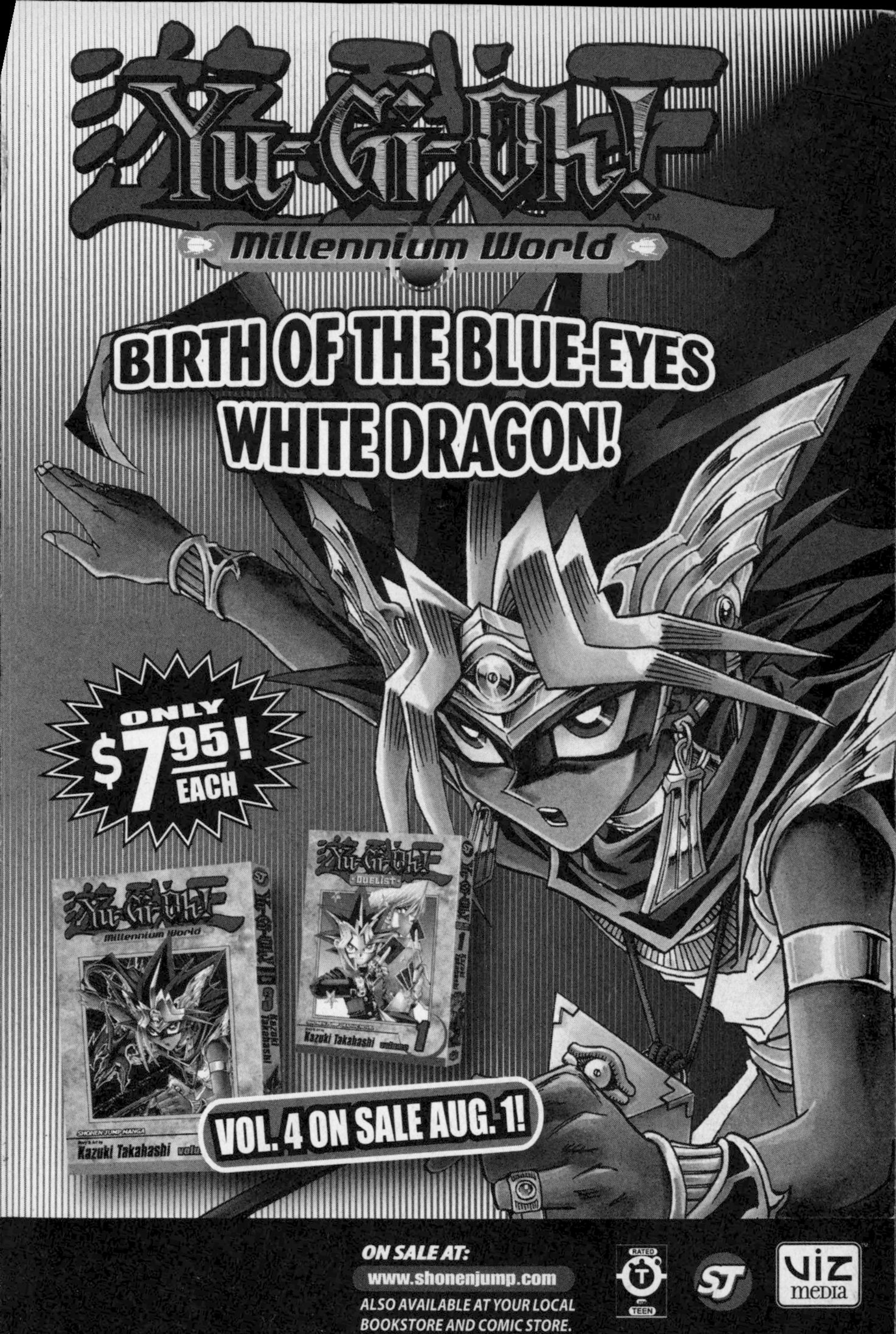
Yu-Gi-Oh!
Millennium World
BIRTH OF THE BLUE-EYES WHITE DRAGON!
ONLY $7.95! EACH
VOL. 4 ON SALE AUG. 1!
ON SALE AT:
www.shonenjump.com
ALSO AVAILABLE AT YOUR LOCAL BOOKSTORE AND COMIC STORE.
RATED T TEEN
SJ
VIZ media

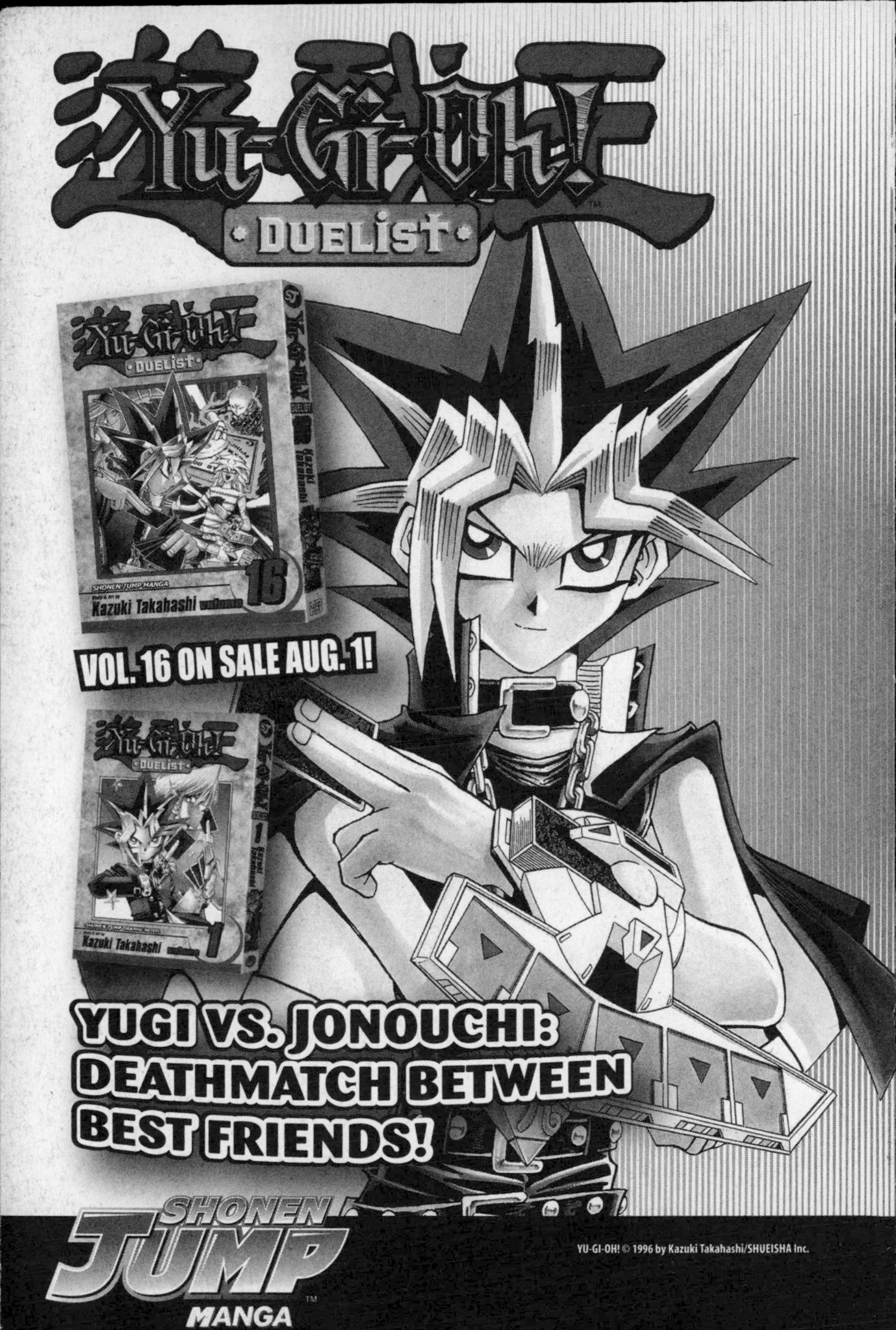
YU-GI-OH!
DUELIST
SHONEN JUMP MANGA
Kazuki Takahashi
16
VOL. 16 ON SALE AUG. 1!
Kazuki Takahashi
1
YUGI VS. JONOUCHI:
DEATHMATCH BETWEEN
BEST FRIENDS!
SHONEN
JUMP
MANGA
YU-GI-OH! © 1996 by Kazuki Takahashi/SHUEISHA Inc.

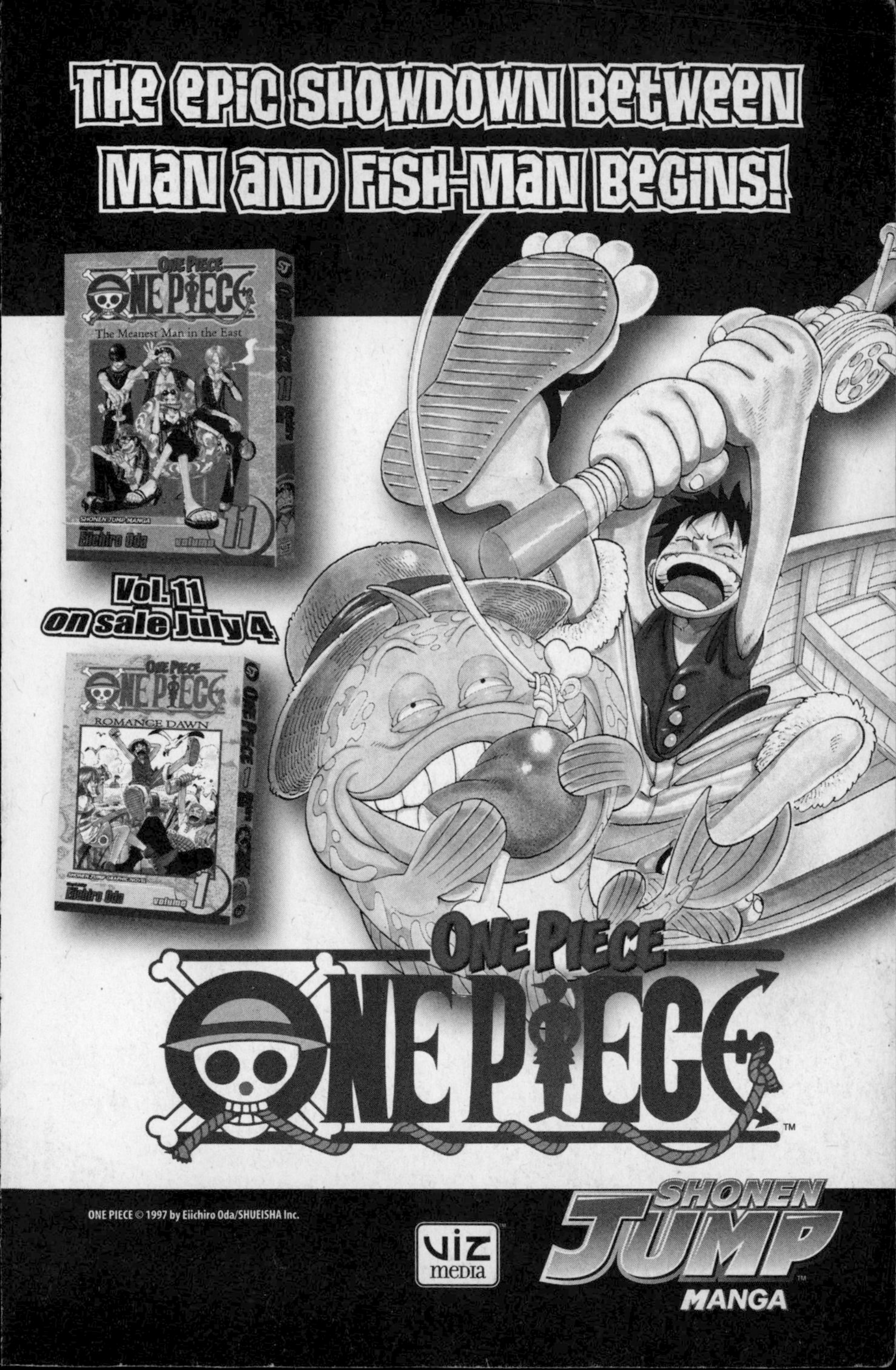
THE EPIC SHOWDOWN BETWEEN MAN AND FISH-MAN BEGINS!
ONE PIECE
The Meanest Man in the East
SHONEN JUMP MANGA
Eiichiro Oda
volume 11
Vol. 11 on sale July 4.
ONE PIECE
ROMANCE DAWN
Eiichiro Oda
volume 1
ONE PIECE
ONE PIECE™
ONE PIECE © 1997 by Eiichiro Oda/SHUEISHA Inc.
VIZ media
SHONEN JUMP MANGA

Tell us what you think about SHONEN JUMP manga!

Our survey is now available online.
Go to: **www.SHONENJUMP.com/mangasurvey**

Help us make our product offering better!

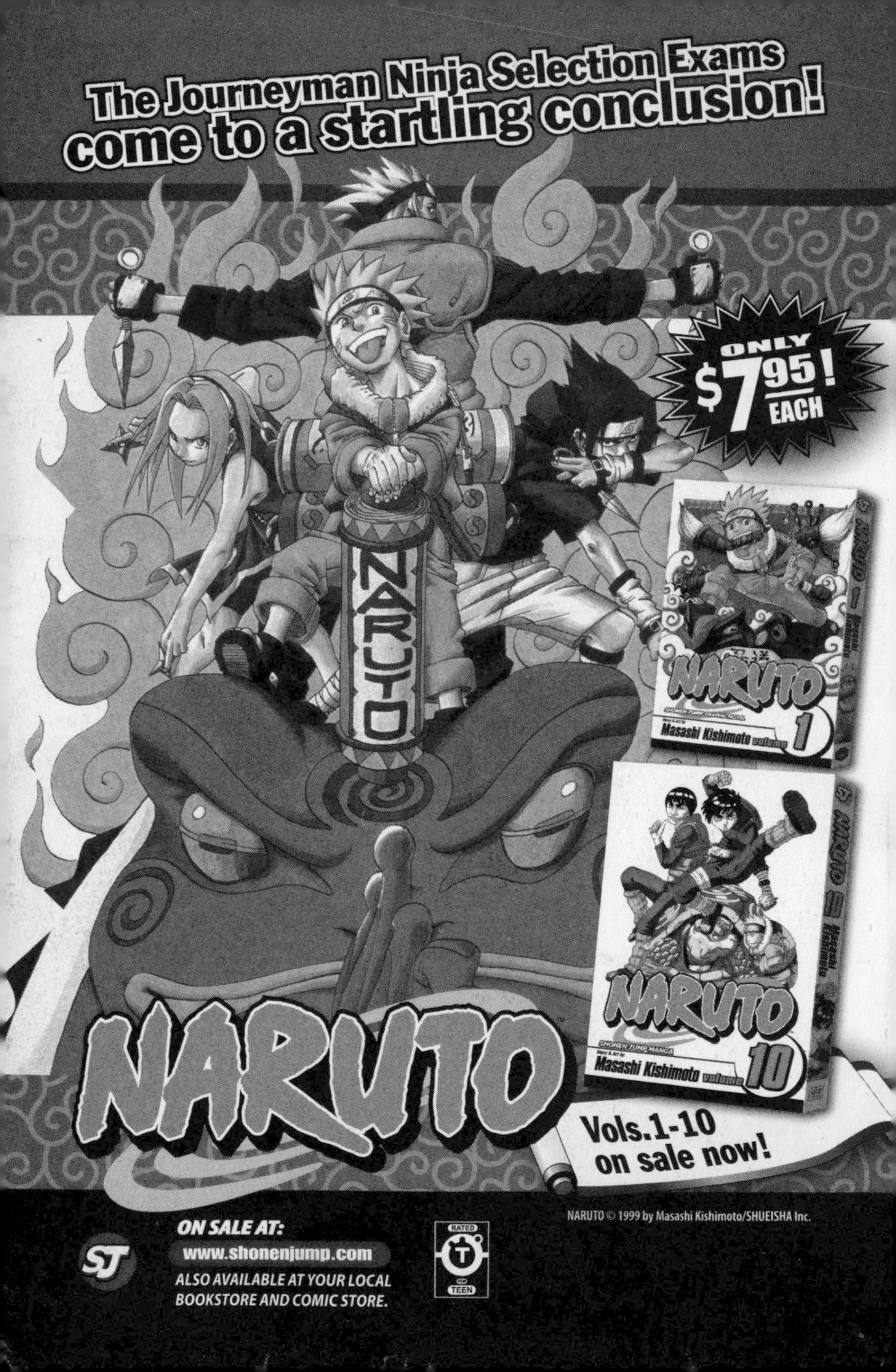
The Journeyman Ninja Selection Exams
come to a startling conclusion!
ONLY $7.95 EACH!
NARUTO
NARUTO
Masashi Kishimoto volume 1
NARUTO
SHONEN JUMP MANGA
Story & Art by
Masashi Kishimoto volume 10
NARUTO
Vols.1-10
on sale now!
NARUTO © 1999 by Masashi Kishimoto/SHUEISHA Inc.
ON SALE AT:
SJ
www.shonenjump.com
ALSO AVAILABLE AT YOUR LOCAL
BOOKSTORE AND COMIC STORE.
RATED T FOR TEEN